THE
AUTOMATED
STATE

. . .

THE
AUTOMATED
STATE

. . .

*Computer Systems as a New Force
in Society*

. . .

ROBERT MACBRIDE

CHILTON BOOK COMPANY

Philadelphia   New York   London

To Laidily, my wife

Contents

Acknowledgments

PERMISSION to quote from the following is gratefully acknowledged:

The Affluent Society by John Kenneth Galbraith. Boston: Houghton Mifflin Company, 1958.

"The Boundless Age of the Computer." *Fortune* (March, 1964). Courtesy of *Fortune* Magazine.

"Can We Manage Prosperity?" by Edwin Dale. *The New York Times Magazine* (March 6, 1966), © 1966 by The New York Times Company. Reprinted by permission.

"Computers and Changing Employment Patterns." Symposium held at Fall Joint Computer Conference of American Federation of Information Processing Societies, Las Vegas, November 13, 1963.

The Corporate Revolution in America by G. C. Means. New York: The Macmillan Company, 1962. © 1962 by the Crowell-Collier Press.

"Cybernation: The Silent Conquest," by Donald N. Michael. Center for the Study of Democratic Institutions, 1962.

Cybernetics by Norbert Wiener. Cambridge: Massachusetts Institute of Technology Press, 1961.

Democracy in America by Alexis de Tocqueville. Translated by Phillips Bradley. New York: Alfred A. Knopf, Inc., 1944.

Free Men and Free Markets by Robert Theobald. © 1963 by Robert Theobald. Used by permission of Crown Publishers, Inc.

Human Rights in a Cybernated Age. Quoted by permission of Maxwell H. Goldberg, Director, CCLE-IBM Humanities Project on Technological Change, College of the Liberal Arts, the Pennsylvania State University.

"The Information Revolution." Supplement to *The New York Times,* (May 23, 1965). Reprinted by permission of the American Federation of Information Processing Societies.

THE AUTHOR also wishes to thank the following persons for their assistance in the preparation of this book:

CAPTAIN ADAM ALESSANDRO of the New York Police Department Planning Bureau

MR. ROBERT D. ARMSTRONG of the American Bankers Association

MR. H. C. ASMUS of the American Federation of Information Processing Societies

MR. SANFORD ACKERMAN of Touche Ross Bailey and Smart

MR. WALTER CLARK of The Bunker-Ramo Corporation

CONGRESSMAN JOHN G. DOW

DR. EDGAR S. DUNN of Resources for the Future, Inc.

DR. ROBERT FANO of the Massachusetts Institute of Technology

MISS BARBARA GREY of the National Commission of Automation and Employment

CONGRESSMAN CORNELIUS GALLAGHER

MISS HELEN M. HARRIS of United Neighborhood Houses of New York

SENATOR EDWARD M. KENNEDY

SENATOR EDMUND S. MUSKIE

DR. THOMAS C. ROWEN of the System Development Corporation

DR. RICHARD RUGGLES of Yale University

MR. JOHN H. RUBEL of Lytton Industries

MR. ANTHONY J. SALTALAMACCHIA of Massachusetts Institute of Technology

The public relations staffs of:
    The Center for the Study of Democratic Institutions
    The International Business Machines Corporation
    Burroughs Corporation
    The Hudson Institute

And many others.

*One method of delivery alone remains
to us; which is simply this: we must
lead men to the particulars, and their
series and order; while men on their
side must force themselves for awhile
to lay their notions by and begin to
familiarize themselves with facts.*

●

FRANCIS BACON

Introduction

This book is about a new and powerful force in human affairs. That force is *not* the digital computer itself, for it is neither new nor especially forceful. Like the steam engine, it is interesting and potentially useful and a tribute to human ingenuity, but it becomes a force to reckon with only when an integral part of a larger entity: an organization directed by men to a specific goal or purpose. For example, the steam engine became part of the steamship or locomotive or factory, which in turn became parts of a larger transportation or industrial system. Only as this stage was approached did the steam engine become an economic and social force—a source of power for some men and an agent for the destruction of the power of other men.

The computer that parallels these earlier forms of power is the computer *system*. Like the engine, as the computer became linked to other specialized machines it became comparable to a locomotive or steamship (or to an automobile or airplane), and then, through specialization, became comparable to a railroad line or a bomber squadron. Now, as its specialized functions and capacities are related to wider goals and objectives, the computer system is becoming comparable to a transportation system or a military machine. And, like its predecessors, the computer system includes men as essential components at every stage.

Our concern with these systems begins at the stage that is comparable to railroads or steamship lines, the stage at which they begin to be a social and economic force or factor. We are not, therefore, concerned with how computers work as machines, except insofar as this relates to the way in which computer systems function. Moreover, we are as much concerned with the system's human components and partners in their roles as—to return to the railroad analogy—engineers, firemen, and freight agents, and as passengers and stockholders as well. Within this frame of reference—the large computer system as an assemblage of machines and human beings—we are concerned first with its appearance as a force disruptive to the established economic and social order, and then with its possibilities as a constructive force in bringing about a new kind of economic and social order. This separation is actually a literary device only, for the two forces operate more or less simultaneously, and, as we shall see, are inextricably linked.

Thus the viewpoint is that of someone outside the system—not merely outside a particular computer system, but all computer systems and the larger and more loosely organized system of social and economic research and development of which all computer systems are a part. The approach to the whole subject is, therefore, journalistic rather than scientific. Its sources are in the main those available to the layman, augmented in my case by more-than-casual exposure for 15 years or more to government-sponsored research and development in the areas of defense and aerospace systems and, of course, to computer systems themselves. The principal effect on me has been the acquisition of no special technical competence but rather of a vivid appreciation of the extent to which this special world is closed to outsiders, and of how within it, any compartment is almost equally closed to persons working in another. This situation is not the result of a devious plan or conspiracy, but is nonetheless real. As a result, normal procedure calls for the making of decisions of incalculable consequence without serious public discussion or comprehension. In no area is this more evident than in computer-system development. As we shall see, a great deal of lively controversy is associated with this development, but almost without exception, its participants are "professionals"—computer scientists, economists, and social scientists.

Little of this discussion reaches the public. Regardless of their particular positions or bias, the participants are united in that they are seriously interested in communicating only with other professionals. There are good reasons for this. Most professionals, in addition to being highly intelligent, are the products of long, arduous schooling, and, further, are either formally or informally members of cadres that impose definite standards of professional behavior. One standard is: don't talk about what you don't know. Thus, for a psychologist to involve himself in economics, or for an economist to involve himself in psychology, is to risk the disapprobation of not only specialists in both disciplines but also the entire professional community. To include the layman in such an involvement would compound the offense. Individual professionals often chafe at this, and on occasion even accept the risk, but in the main they tend to accept the conditions that this standard imposes.

Another important restriction has been imposed upon professionals by the larger "lay" society. It is a commonplace that the history of science is the history of scientists being misused by society. For generations scientists have been vilified and exploited by society, from its highest to its lowest levels. An appreciation of this is virtually built into the professional disciplines. Thus professionals regard with considerable reserve the curiosity of legislators and journalists in particular.

Finally, there is the restriction that laymen tend to impose upon themselves. With, perhaps, their own appreciation of the rather dismal history of science in society, they increasingly tend to accept without question the judgment of professionals. After all, few of us doubt the complexity of the world, and we need all the help we can get. One sure way to cut ourselves off from a great deal of help is to badger those who know much more than we do.

But however valid these conclusions are, and however appropriate they may be to such areas as national defense and space exploration, something about the development of computer systems and the issues they raise transcends them. Although someone might argue that nuclear weapons and spaceships are special cases that need not be of universal concern, this cannot be said about computer systems. What is done with them will affect everybody on virtually every level of existence. In view of this, computer systems must become the subjects of public discussion and controversy, with all the risks involved.

This necessity places a burden on the professionals—those who design and develop the machines and those who develop and use computer systems to cope with the sombre array of economic and social problems. A greater burden, however, is placed on laymen. They themselves, as individuals and as organizations of individuals, must learn what computer systems are all about—something that, as a whole, they have not done, particularly with regard to the implications of nuclear power, or race prejudice, or various forms of social and economic waste that beset our civilization.

PART I

The Matter of Automation

I
.

A Brief Examination of Computer Systems

In the late nineteen fifties the aggregations of switches and relays and push-buttons that most of us had come to know as *computers* began to be transformed into *computer systems*. As a result, they began to play a significant role in the lives of all of us—to influence in an increasing number of ways our actions and ideas about ourselves and our society. The process is still going on, and we cannot foresee its conclusion.

The essential difference between a computer and a computer system is subtle. One way of describing it is this: a computer is no more than an electromechanical device which can perform a number of set functions; a computer system is an *organization* designed to complete certain predetermined tasks, to accomplish clearly specified goals or objectives. A computer is a *means;* a computer system is a means to an *end*—one that employs a certain number of computers in specific ways to accomplish its tasks.

The computer was incorporated into the popular culture soon after its invention. The first ones received distinctive names rather like those of ocean liners, and their reputed "personalities" and attributes became the subject of innumerable cartoons. Some computers even became briefly the stars of television shows. In this role they were somewhat awesome, but all-in-all not too unfamiliar; they were, after all, objects —a familiar enough class—with rather obvious functions. They seemed to be a kind of oracle—again a not unfamiliar class. One approached them from the outside; one posed questions to them after a fashion; they answered the questions—after a fashion. This personification of computers has continued to flourish. The cartoons with faintly ominous overtones still appear, and they invariably present the same reassuring image of the computer as some kind of big box with a mouth, something that a human being approaches and speaks to.

But a computer *system* is nothing like this. It is doubtful that it could become the subject of any cartoon. What, then, is it exactly, and why is it so important?

First of all it is an organization. The system begins not with equipment or even with people; it begins with the definition of a goal to be attained—a task to be accomplished. When this has been done in a sufficiently precise way, the steps necessary to attain and accomplish it are determined. The equipment and persons involved in these steps are allocated and brought together—organized.

All along the way something else is produced: an intangible body of knowledge that is peculiar to the system. It includes policies, strategies, procedures, routines, and programs. Some are precise and defined; some are implicit. Some are alterable; some not. Computer experts call this illusive collection "software." It means simply the part of the system that is not "hardware"—and not people. In computer circles, software is considered more important than hardware. It is another way of saying "it's not what you have but how you use it that counts."

Actually, it is a question of all three components of the system—hardware, software, and people. The system's goals are specified by people and ultimately *for* people. Equipment capabilities and limitations have a great bearing on the nature of these goals. The system's software has a great bearing on the equipment's capabilities. And both people and equipment determine the nature of the software. This three-way interplay, in fact, makes the system what it is: an organism which, after its own fashion, functions and takes care of itself and those who depend on it. This interplay also makes computer systems extremely difficult to describe, understand, and, above all, anticipate. They tend to be diffused in both space and time. They operate on many different levels, and the interrelationships between these levels are not always readily defined. They frequently reach out across the boundaries of formal organizations. Much of what is known about them is expressible only in the mysterious language of higher mathematics.

However, all computer systems react actively to their environment. They do not wait for people to approach them with specific requests; they reach out to the environment, seeking information and delivering it transformed where it is needed. In so doing they tend to alter that environment in many significant ways.

Our consideration is also handicapped by the speed and intensity with which computers and computer systems have been evolving. While the socioeconomic controversy rages, the machines continue to be developed with a rapidity which has been widely noted. Dr. Thomas Rowan, a vice-president of the System Development Corporation, described this phenomenon in a paper presented to a congress of

4

the American Orthopsychiatric Association in 1965. He noted that in 1954 a computer was first used commercially. A year later 700 were in use, not counting military computers. By 1964, 22,000 were in operation and 10,000 were on order. "A very conservative estimate for 1970," he said, "is that there will be some 70,000 computers in operation." And then he added something that should make even the most jaded reader of computer-age predictions sit up and take notice. "The *number* of computers," he said, . . . "hardly expresses the potential impact of this new device. A more meaningful projection to make is that of the capacity that is possible with a computer. Expressed in units that are functions of size and speed, the capacity curve is a rapidly rising, almost an exponential one. In 1954 the state-of-the-art allowed a computer to have 200 units of this capacity measure. In 1958 the number was 340. Two years later, 1960, it jumped to 2,200. In another two years, it stood at 8,000, and in 1964 it was 21,000. In a ten-year period, capacity has thus increased by a factor of 100, and, I might add, the price per unit of capacity has dramatically dropped." Rowan stated that this increase in power undoubtedly would continue.

Aside from knowing a few historical facts, most of us are generally aware that computers solve complex problems of mathematics and engineering far more efficiently than men. Almost any daily newspaper can provide examples of this. News accounts tell how computers predict the future courses of rivers and decipher the Dead Sea Scrolls. They organize satellite data and calculate stresses and loads for architects and builders. According to *Inside News* (a publication devoted largely to interesting forms of homicide and the high jinks of celebrities), a computer has even been used to "take" a Las Vegas casino for $5,000 at the blackjack table.

Reading these kinds of articles, one gets the impression that computers "think" to some extent. They do not. The use (in reference to computers) of terms that have been employed traditionally to describe human mental processes is only a literary device, although sometimes indispensable. In any event, computers do not "think" any more than cameras "see" or telephones "hear." Whether they will "think" someday is speculative, but in regard to the relationship of computers to people, it is much more to the point to ask, "Do people think?"

This question has a direct bearing on one of the commuter's principal capabilities—i.e., processing extensive quantities of more or less routine data quickly and accurately. We do not read so much about this in the newspapers, but in every fair-sized city are elegantly appointed computer service centers where, through large show windows, one can see the machines engaged in this kind of work. Unlike the problem-solving computers, these machines perform data-processing functions that were formerly performed by humans, and in many cases not unintelligent ones.

Along with the increase in capacity has been an equal improvement in the diversity of computers. This is more difficult to sum up, since it involves not only diversity of equipment configuration, but also mode of operation and application.

The first generation of computers, which "matured" about 1956, consists of rather cumbersome installations of custom-built equipment that require an impressive amount of electrical power and specially trained operating personnel. Though performing fantastic feats of calculation, they can handle only a limited range of problems, and those only one at a time, using in the process only a small part of their capacity at any given moment. They are, in effect, much in the same class as cyclotrons, astronomical observatories, wind tunnels and the like—useful, certainly, but in themselves hardly likely to lead to any kind of socioeconomic millennium.

The second-generation computers, which matured about 1962, are different. As Rowan has noted, they have a much greater speed and capacity, the direct result of breakthroughs in physics. They are also more practical in a thousand ways. Here is an example: all computers require detailed lists of operating instructions, or "programs," to enable them to carry out their functions. These programs must be prepared by humans, who, following a rigorous and detailed analysis of the problem to be solved, take pencil and paper and laboriously list, in the proper order, every step of the task to be performed.

In the case of a first-generation computer, all these lists of instructions have to be translated into so-called "machine language"—numerical codes that refer to the location of various bits of information stored in the computer's "memory." In a highly abbreviated form, these codes tell the computer to "do what is stored in such and such a location to what is stored in such and such another location; then store the result in still another location," and so on, through thousands of steps. Aside from being tedious and time-consuming and, therefore, expensive, this form is based largely on the structure of the particular computer to be used, and on the programmer's choice of locations. His program consequently cannot be used on another computer of different manufacture and frequently not even on another model of the same manufacturer. Moreover, it cannot be read or checked for accuracy by someone else.

This situation was improved somewhat by the creation of so-called "assembly languages." These are intermediate codes containing more or less standardized designations for the steps and operations to be listed, which a computer could translate into its specific machine language. For example, a code like "SQT (5.37)" would mean "take square root of absolute value of expression within parentheses." Even with the use of such a language, however, the programmer was obliged to invent many codes peculiar to the problem he was concerned with. Another programmer would have a great deal of difficulty understanding the program. Another computer would find it impossible to translate.

The development of second-generation computers led to the creation of a number of *standard assembly languages,* and the computers' increased storage capacity made it feasible to replace the codes with English words. A statement that would have been expressed in machine language as, "L3836 S237C L7435 M6873 E287C," or in assembly language as "LD DLMS ST OTPT, 3LD LIST SB DISC SE OTPT 3," could be expressed in one of these new standard languages (COBOL) as, "subtract discount from list giving net." Furthermore, it could be expressed this way on any number of different makes of computers.

The development of these languages opened new areas of computer application, and expanded many existing ones, by reducing the cost of programming. Also, management now has more control over computer operation. Even if a manager cannot write a program himself, he can, without special training, read one. Thus management is now much less skeptical and suspicious of computers, and "management-by-computer" has been increasingly accepted, a trend which, among other things, is one of the factors contributing to that frequently noted obsolescence of "middle managers."

Second-generation computer "input-output devices" have been equally improved. Instructions and information, as noted, must be fed into the computer. At its most basic level this is done by activating various computer switches and circuits. In the earliest computers this was actually done by hand, but even first-generation computers were soon adapted to use more efficient means—punched cards, perforated tapes and, later, magnetic recording tape. However, first-generation computers retained a rather limited format of output. Second-generation machines were much more flexible. They could, for example, print statements (in English, of course) directly on printed forms, bills, orders, and the like.

While many of the innovations of second-generation computers were applicable to the computer's role as a solver of difficult problems, their principal effect has been to augment the computer's second role as a routine data processor. In this role computers have become a factor in the automation-employment controversy. Data processing, which has been described as "the conversion of data into a more useful form," includes the linking of computers to automatic machinery. This role continues to grow, of course, and to some as yet undetermined extent it will continue to affect the employment picture, insofar as it leads the computer to take over jobs. Modifying this effect, however, will be the computer in still another role: that of a control or steering device for the whole economy or perhaps the whole society. This role, while it has its roots in the capabilities of first- and second-generation computers, is really embodied in the incipient third-generation computer systems.

The third-generation computer was developed in response to an important limitation of the second-generation systems that has been most commonly described as "batch processing." In effect, information and instructions for the second-generation computer must be accumulated in advance of the machine's operation. These are then fed into the computer and "processed," whereupon the computer yields another quantity of information. To be of use, that information must be further distributed. The accumulation, processing, and distribution periods may be quite short—a matter of minutes or even seconds—or the accumulation and distribution period, at least, may run into months. In either case, this mode of operation limits the computer's applicability as a control mechanism.

Consideration of these limitations has led computer designers to a new concept: "real-time." Real-time may be defined as the time in which information must be received to be immediately useful. When, for example, a public-spirited broadcasting station employs a helicopter to survey and report on traffic conditions and then broadcasts that information immediately, the drivers receive the information in *real-time*—in time to act on it by moving to avoid traffic jams. This gives the information an entirely different quality than it would have if it were merely published in the next day's paper. In the latter case, it might be of some interest to the motorist to know why he had been delayed, but it would be of scant *use* to him, no matter how complete.

Computers of the third generation, then, are oriented toward providing information in real-time—not merely information but solutions to problems. (They still make use of batch processing as well, but it is subsidiary.) The computer is equipped with input devices that enable it to collect information at the source as soon as it is generated. Since, in all probability, information is generated at many different sources, a number of remotely located input devices must be employed—all feeding into the computer.* The information must also be relayed to the ultimate users in time to be used, so the computer, to save time,

* Another term in current use describes such a system—"on line." This means that the input and/or output devices are controlled directly by the central computer. This is not the same as "real-time," but the two terms overlap considerably. A system could be on line with operation in real-time, and to a much more limited extent the reverse could be true. Usually, however, it is hardly worthwhile to have one capability without the other.

also takes over the distribution phase of the operation. It is thus directly linked to remotely located output devices that provide the ultimate users with timely data wherever they are.

The result is a computer-centered communications network, in which the computer, in addition to solving problems and processing routine data, directs and controls the message traffic throughout the network.

A number of real-time computer systems are now in operation. They are only prototypes, and like most prototypes they are relatively small and simple. They do give some idea of what can be expected, however, and for this reason they merit at least a superficial examination.

Some of the more simple ones (although they are getting more complex all the time) are the stock market data systems. The first to go into operation (May, 1964) was the American Stock Exchange's computerized quotation service (Amquote), which is operated by the Teleregister Corporation. This system provides accurate, up-to-the-minute information, i.e., the latest offer, bid, sale price, volume, net change from the previous close, and high and low prices of the 1,100 stocks listed on the American Exchange.

Subscribers to the service obtain this information by telephone. Each stock has been assigned a specific code number. When a number is dialed, a recorded voice, using a prerecorded vocabulary of 60 words and numbers, relays the data on the particular stock. The system handles up to 1,200 inquiries a minute (the average call takes about 25 seconds), or 72,000 calls per hour. The previous human-operated quotation system handled 60,000 calls per day.

The heart of this new system is a large computer into which information about each stock transaction is fed as it occurs. The computer validates each transaction in accordance with previously determined criteria, and rejects any figures that do not fit the pattern defined by its instructions.

Although this computer constantly revises its files as it is furnished with new information, it does not destroy outdated information, but transfers it to various storage files, thus maintaining a complete record of all stock transactions for as long as is deemed necessary. The cost of maintaining these files is relatively low, and it appears that the officials of the American Stock Exchange are not certain what use will eventually be made of them. According to an article in the *New York Herald Tribune* in May, 1964, the president of the Exchange, Edwin F. Etherington, felt that they would be particularly useful in the Exchange's program of market surveillance and in any future surveillance programs that the Securities and Exchange Commission might wish to initiate.

This illustrates an important property of information as a commodity: no matter how many times it is used, it doesn't get used up. This fact has not been lost on the company that designed, built, and operates the Amquote System. From the same computer center, and in some cases using the same computer that handles the data for Amquote, the Teleregister Corporation operates a nationwide system of electronic stock quotation boards for brokers' offices. These supply market information from not only the American Stock Exchange but also all other stock and commodity exchanges. Along with this, the Corporation provides Telequote III—another electronic quotation service that gives brokers up-to-date stock information via small "video desk units," in response to specific queries. Also, Telequote III will soon supply a series of grouped market averages and other "market barometer" information, such as the 10 most active stocks and the Dow-Jones averages.

Teleregister offers still another service—"Telelist," which provides brokers with lists of closing prices on punched cards, or magnetic tape, for account evaluations.

The New York Stock Exchange has in operation a system similar to that of the American Exchange. Designed and built by the International Business Machines Corporation, it went into operation on March 8, 1965. It provides subscribers with virtually instantaneous trading data on more than 1,600 listed stocks—last sale, open, high, low, and volume—when they dial four-digit stock code numbers on special telephones. The system handles up to 300 calls at once, and up to 400,000 per day. In addition, it handles the printing of sales on 3,750 stock tickers and other visual display devices, stores in time sequence all trading information, and constantly furnishes up-to-date data to the Exchange's "Stock Watch" operation.*

Neither system has any great capability for two-way communications. The subscribing broker dials a code number and the system replies by supplying him with some useful information, and that's the end of it. The broker cannot then make additional requests pertaining to that stock; he cannot buy the stock through the system, nor can he say to the computer, "88⅛? Let me know when it hits 85." Such a capability is planned, however.

Somewhat larger than the stock exchange systems and, from an information-handling capacity, even more impressive, are some of the automated airline reservation systems presently operated by many of the major airlines. The first of these was the American Airlines'

* The Stock Watch operation is described as a program to carry on a continuous check on the price movements of all listed stock issues, with the objective of spotting any unusual price variations. Such variations are earmarked for more detailed studies. Stock Watch helps the Exchange to pinpoint the causes of unusual market developments and to take corrective action when appropriate.

10

SABRE system. SABRE consists of a huge central computer to which are linked nearly 1,000 two-way communicating devices located at airline ticket counters throughout the country. When a prospective passenger steps up to a ticket counter and requests a reservation, the request is at once communicated to the computer by the ticket agent. The computer then checks instantly through its data storage, which contains up-to-the-second information about available space on every flight, to see if there is an empty seat meeting the customer's requirements. If such a seat is available the computer instantly notifies the ticket agent, and at the same time makes a note of the reservation and subtracts the seat from the inventory of available space. If a seat is not available, the computer informs the agent of the fact and tells him what alternate flights are available. Once a reservation is made, the agent gives the computer the passenger's name, home and business telephone numbers, ticketing arrangements, and other pertinent information. This is stored by the computer as long as it is useful.

The computer is also connected to the airline's traffic control center, and receives a constant stream of information about the status of flights. For example, if a flight is delayed, the computer is notified, and it immediately searches out the list of passengers for that flight and informs the ticket agents. The agents then contact the passengers by phone, the computer having informed them of the passenger's name and phone number along with the notification of flight delay.

Controlling seat inventory and keeping passenger records is the system's main function, but it also maintains and processes wait-lists, requests space from other airlines by teletype, and answers similar requests from other airlines.

SABRE has the same kind of provision as the Amquote system for reusing its information. It makes available to the airline's management detailed information about daily load factors (the ratio of paying passengers to seats available) for every flight, monthly production figures which break down sales by station, activity, sales account and sales agent, marketing facts such as the reservation-making habits of customers, sources of business (percentage of business coming from other airlines, conventions, etc.), and even passenger-preferences for certain types of meals.

Impressive as it is, the SABRE system is only a prototype. An example of the newer line is the as yet unnamed computer system of United Airlines, which is being designed and built by the UNIVAC Division of Sperry Rand Corporation. This system will be in operation early in 1968, at an estimated cost of $56 million. Like SABRE, the United Airlines' system will handle all passenger reservations—communicating directly with more than 1,000 agents in 116 cities—and some 15 other basic categories of information, including the

11

scheduling of aircraft and crews, flight planning, weather conditions, and all of the line's air freight scheduling and cargo information. It will also automatically schedule planes for maintenance and major overhaul, and maintain spare parts inventories in all the maintenance facilities.

These reservation systems are particularly interesting in that they cope with many of the same problems as are encountered in computerized employment systems. In both cases, persons must be "fitted" into a group of "positions." The positions have certain fixed characteristics, as do the people. The two must be matched optimally.

Virtually all major airlines have installed real-time reservation systems, and some are planning improved replacements for their systems.

After the airlines, the banking industry has shown the most interest in real-time systems. A real-time system for banking is operated in the Boston area by Bankers Data Processing, Inc. According to *Mid-Continent Banker* magazine, this system can handle almost a million individual accounts, as well as provide such accounting functions as preparing trial balances and calculating dividends and the usual data for management and reports to the government.

The *American Banker* in January, 1964, reported a similar operation planned by a group of seven commercial banks and 23 savings and loan associations in the St. Louis area. Initially this system will process 250,000 savings accounts and 50,000 mortgage loan accounts from about 60 sources. According to officials of the Bank of St. Louis, which will operate the computer, the system can be expanded to handle a million accounts, via more than a thousand sources.

In fact, it is not too much to say that bankers as a group have grasped the possibilities of computer systems better than anyone else outside the computer industry itself. It is from a banker (John J. Clarke, Vice-President and General Counsel of the Federal Reserve Bank of New York) that we first hear of NATCOM—the proposed name for a national computer utility similar to COMSAT (the joint publicly and privately owned Communications Satellite Corporation).

Through the American Bankers Association, and particularly its Special Committee on Automation, bankers have moved into the large-scale planning of computer systems with speed and thoroughness that belie their traditional image of cool conservatism. The Association's National Automation Conference, held in San Francisco in March, 1965, was devoted entirely to a practical examination of the application of computers to banking, with the emphasis on increasing profits and eliminating waste effort and risk. There was little or no long-range speculation, aside from an inspirational keynote speech by Thomas J. Watson, Jr. During the conference much time and at-

12

tention were devoted to extensions of batch-processing applications, but participants had plenty to say about real-time. In describing his company's Overnight Statewide Customers Accounting Reporting (OSCAR) System, William Butler of the United California Bank said:

"The [real-time computer] central information file, when established, will provide instantaneous responses to inquiries from the various users of the data center.

"Massive printouts and manual scanning of reports for key information will be a thing of the past. The information response time gap will be eliminated, management can quickly review a total credit position, account profitability, and make decisions while the details of the situation are fresh and vivid. . . .

"Bond acquisitions may be entered on a real-time basis with sales confirmed minutes later. . . . Conceivably every typewriter and every adding machine can become an on-line terminal for entering and retrieving information."

The stock exchange systems and the airline reservation systems are nationwide in scope. The banking systems are just beginning to be. They are spreading geographically because the long-distance telephone network can link the central computers and the terminals. The American Telephone and Telegraph Company's Bell System has long provided such service for teletypewriters (TWX), of course, and it now supplies a wide assortment of data channels that transmit data up to 200 times faster than ordinary voice channels, an essential requirement for computer systems. The Bell System is expanding this high-speed service constantly. Its availability is an important element in making large-scale real-time systems feasible.

Aside from the use of leased communications channels, these systems have other features to be considered in determining the probable course of their future development. One of the most important is "multiple access." They can send communications back and forth with a number of terminals simultaneously. A large part of the computer functions like a telephone exchange, switching and routing messages.

Another feature is quite unlike a telephone exchange: the computer monitors the *content* of each message and, in addition to switching it to its immediate destination, sends it to other predetermined destinations where the message will be of interest. It is as if post office clerks open and read every piece of incoming mail and then act in response to it. For example, let us say that a clerk, upon opening a birth announcement, checks an authorized distribution list and then, in addition to sending the letter to the addressee, sends

13

copies to the state bureau of vital statistics, the local school board, the Internal Revenue Service, and perhaps a local diaper service, and makes a file copy as well!

From a practical standpoint, these two features tend to limit one another somewhat. To increase the number of terminals handled simultaneously, one must simplify the content and disposition of the messages. If, on the other hand, more complex messages are to be handled, one must reduce the volume of message traffic.

Multiple access apparently has the most immediate possibilities, and so all the real-time systems described, and virtually all those in operation, tend to favor it; that is, they are designed to handle relatively simple messages from many sources in a relatively simple way. Real-time system designers almost always choose to work toward a capability to handle more messages rather than more *complex* messages. (Devising new ways to simplify computer messages has become almost an art in itself. Some banks, for example, use only the first five letters to encode a customer's last name. Analysis has shown that this is generally sufficient.)

Extensive efforts are being made to develop the other feature, however—to increase the computer's capacity to examine, store, and analyze the content of messages—so that more complex messages can be handled, at the expense, if need be, of handling an increased quantity of messages. Instead of handling 1,000 routine exchanges, all concerned, for instance, with seats on airplanes, the goal of this kind of system is to handle 100 conversations concerning 100 completely different and highly sophisticated subjects in real-time.

The most advanced work in this direction is by a group at the Massachusetts Institute of Technology—Project MAC. "MAC" stands for "machine-aided cognition." It has also come to mean "multiple-access computer." Like most other significant prototype computer systems, its development is sponsored by the Department of Defense.*

The MAC system sounds rather simple. A large computer is connected with 100 or more remote terminals, most of which are on the M.I.T. campus. All but one of these terminals are electric typewriters that have been adapted, somewhat in the manner of teletype machines, to provide two-way communication with the computer. (The operator types his requests and instructions in lower case letters; the machine responds with capitals.) One remote terminal only is a multiple display system, which features a pair of picture tubes similar to those used in television sets upon which information is displayed visually. The user, by means of a special electronic "pen," can also

* Specifically, the Department of Defense's Advanced Research Projects Agency finances Project MAC and the Navy Department's Office of Naval Research manages it.

communicate visual data to the computer by actually "sketching" on the faces of the tubes.

The operators at these remote terminals are mostly faculty members and graduate students of M.I.T., representing a whole range of academic disciplines. These persons use the computer to solve problems in their particular fields, whether physics or linguistics. They all have access to the computer 24 hours a day. In the course of problem-solving, they all pour instructions and information into the computer constantly, and, certainly, according to no prearranged plan or design. They use many different formats, or languages, to describe their problems. By and large the users are not particularly interested in computers and in problems relating to computers—they are specialists using the computer as a tool.

The computer itself is given a basic set of "supervisory programs" for sorting out and handling all incoming data. It also has a set of programs relating to the special requirements of each user. These programs enable the computer to, in effect, "recognize" each user, and quickly plug into his special file of instructions and data, and then do its best to help him out. It can service only one user at a time, but so rapidly that it can shift back and forth among many users in the course of each second—recognizing them, doing something for them, and then moving on. Each user is thus under the "illusion" that he is receiving exclusive attention. In addition to accommodating each user as he comes on the line, the computer performs a number of more routine processing operations. These are batch-processing operations such as long-term filing, sorting, and arithmetical operations, the results of which are not needed immediately.

This system is considerably more sophisticated than the commercial real-time systems we have examined. To use a crude analogy, the commercial real-time systems can be likened to a busy hot-dog stand where hard-working vendors hand out cokes and two or three kinds of sandwiches to many not too particular, and more or less anonymous, passersby. The MAC system, on the other hand, acts more like a competent short order cook who has regular customers and knows their personal likes and dislikes.

In one respect, however, the MAC system is less sophisticated. There is no intercommunication between users. Their instructions, files, etc., are kept entirely separate from one another. The computer cannot search physicist A's files in response to a query from physicist B on another terminal. In fact, elaborate precautions are taken to avoid this.

However, the MAC system does contain a "public file" of programs and data that is available to all users. Included in this file is a service called "TIP" (Technical Information Program), which is actually a

15

computerized citation index. TIP stores in the computer's memory, data on some 35,000 articles (authors, article titles, bibliographies, journal titles, volumes, and pages) from 23 leading physics journals, and supplies them to users on command. TIP also supplies an "automatic order filling service." Users inform the computer of their areas of special interest. Then, when articles on these subjects appear in the literature, the users are notified automatically.

Providing more intercommunication between users, and the means by which they can pool information and make joint use of programs and instructions, is an objective of the system's designers, however. The MAC Project Director, Professor Robert Fano, sees a trend toward a "memory centered system," in which the combined experience of the many users would be shared to a much greater degree than is now possible. "When the system is seen from this point of view," wrote Professor Fano, "it assumes the appearance more of a message store-and-forward communication system than of a traditional computer system."

While the scientists of Project MAC are still refining and studying this prototype system, others are putting time-sharing systems into commercial operation. In late 1965, the first of these was inaugurated by the KeyData Corporation, a Cambridge neighbor of M.I.T. and Project MAC. The KeyData system, designed primarily to handle the requirements of small businesses, began its operations with about 20 customers located in the Boston area and with the capacity to handle more than 200 more in any part of the country. Close on KeyData's heels in time-sharing were such communications giants as Western Union, the International Telephone and Telegraph Company, and a number of the major computer manufacturers who are already operating second-generation computer service bureaus.

The outcome of Project MAC may well be the prototype for the "fourth-generation" computer systems which will be distinguished from the third-generation real-time computer systems in several ways. First, they will have a greater variety of terminals. Whereas the third-generation system tends to have large numbers of identical terminals, and to work toward simple, general purpose units of modest cost, the fourth generation will stress, in addition to these, a wide selection of highly sophisticated equipment tailored to specific purposes. Users will supply to and receive from the computer, information in many different physical forms, such as printed material, pictures, and even audio forms.

Also the fourth-generation system's overall handling of data will be considerably more flexible. A much greater part of its capacity will be devoted to extremely complex switching operations and techniques. A fourth-generation system will thus appear to meet almost any kind

16

of demand, to solve almost any kind of problem, or to provide almost any kind of data. Actually, it will not so much have this capability itself as it will "plug in" the user quickly to a particular subsystem which can satisfy his needs.

The fourth-generation system, it appears, will be the "agent extraordinary," advising its users that, "If I can't do it myself, I can certainly get it done for you." Its memory will be full of instructions enabling it to cut into any number of first-, second-, and third-generation subsystems, each processing certain kinds of data, and to use them to answer the requirements of many users with diverse needs. This capability is easier described than appreciated. To function satisfactorily, the fourth-generation system must perform extraordinary feats of timing and control, plugging into hundreds of subsystems with thousands upon thousands of separate requests each second. The subsystems themselves may be located thousands of miles apart, may be in full-time local use and subject to the demands of any number of other fourth-generation systems as well. In spite of this, it undoubtedly will not be long before the fourth generation of computers appears. They seem to present none of the technical problems of, let us say, the achievement of "artificial intelligence," or computers that think like humans.

All this, then, is the computer systems' "scene" or environment in the late sixties. The general trend of computer development is flourishing. One technical problem after another, which at some time implied a practical limit to the widespread or more sophisticated development of computer systems, has been overcome. For example, in the mid-fifties the relative bulk of the basic electronic components of computers, by imposing physical limits to their proximity, made that ubiquitous factor c, the velocity of light, as much of a limiting factor in computer operations as it is in interplanetary communications. In other words, it appeared that large, complex computers would not be practical, because it would take electricity too long to flow around in them. Also, to sustain them would require enormous amounts of electrical power. But before this could become much more than a theoretical possibility, breakthroughs in the study of solid-state physics and of the interactions of weak electrical currents led to such a dramatic reduction in the size of the computer's basic components, and to a new compactness in their assembly, that c was no longer a real problem. This development was not especially planned or foreseen. Similar breakthroughs have occurred with such regularity that the incidence of new ones in the future is taken for granted by even the most hardened scientists.

The socioeconomic implications of all this technical progress are a different matter, however. Three generations of computers in 15 years have dazed the social and economic experts. If, by some magic, a modern army division had appeared on the field of Waterloo or Fontenoy, it could hardly have caused more consternation than has been caused here and now by these machines and their masters. It is to this state of affairs that we now turn our attention.

2
·
The Optimistic and Pessimistic Views of Automation

The New York Times of October 15, 1964, contains the kind of report that gives the layman the uneasy intimation that the computer revolution has some negative implications involving him personally. This article reports a speech by a person the *Times* called a "distaff banker," Mary G. Roebling, Chairman of the Board of the Trenton (New Jersey) Trust Company, to a convention of the National Consumers Finance Association.

Mrs. Roebling points out that 70 per cent of the nation's working women are engaged in clerical jobs—precisely the kind of jobs, she says, that will most surely be taken over by computers and associated automatic data processing equipment in the future. She predicts that this will destroy most job opportunities for women within 20 years, thereby producing economic disaster, unless something is done. She compares this situation to Frankenstein's monster, and concludes by calling for action by the Chamber of Commerce, trade associations, and research groups (but not, apparently, by the government) to prevent "what now appears to be a potential disaster."

The subject of this blast is certainly the chief concern of critics of the computer industry. Referring to a similar criticism by Marion Harper, a prominent advertising executive, *Computers and Data Processing* magazine strikes back irritably: "This department has its own opinion as to what is needed, and that is—an end to all the moaning and groaning over how computers are going to destroy the world, and a little more cool calculation about how to employ a useful tool as an adjunct to man's mental prowess, and not as its replacement."

Time magazine, in a more cheery vein, sums up the situation this way: ". . . a lot of people are bound to suffer for awhile. But by gradually raising educational levels, retraining those displaced by automation, and seeing to it that displaced workers retain their buying power, society will somehow support the change."

Although this is the tone of the computer industry's public response to its critics, the possibility that workers will be replaced is being anxiously discussed by industry, business circles, and the socioeconomic pundits of the Government and the foundations. Conferences and symposiums on the problem are held almost weekly, and no meeting or convention of the computer people is complete without at least one earnest round-table discussion of the subject.

One such symposium was presented at the 1963 Fall Joint Computer Conference, organized by the American Federation of Information Processing Societies and held in Las Vegas, Nevada. At this meeting were two opposing teams of experts. One drawn from the computer industry was made up of Fletcher Jones of Computer Sciences Corporation (which is engaged in providing various computer services to government and industry), Walter Finke of Honeywell, Inc. (a computer manufacturer), Dr. Richard Hamming of Bell Telephone Research Laboratories, Walter Ramshaw of United Aircraft Corporation (a user of computers and automated machinery), and Wesley Bagby of the Pacific Mutual Life Insurance Company (a heavy user of office data processing equipment).

The other team represented, in varying degrees, the "public sector." Leading off was Dr. W. H. Ferry of the Center for the Study of Democratic Institutions, an agency of the Ford Foundation. Ferry might well be considered the leading pessimist on the implications of automation and the computer in the United States today. He was supported by two labor union leaders, Ted Bates of AFL-CIO Headquarters and Donald Camp of the Office Employees International of Southern California, and, somewhat less enthusiastically, by Arthur Carstens of the University of California and Dr. Samuel Ganz of the U.S. Department of Labor.

The discussion is in no way epoch-making but is fairly typical. It rather accurately represents the opinions prevailing at that time (November, 1963) concerning the technological unemployment controversy. Moreover, it is couched in terms a layman can understand. This session is consequently worth reviewing in some detail.

Jones begins by fairly stating the computer industry's general position. He says that there has not been a significant amount of technological unemployment that could be shown to be traceable to the use of computers, and that there would not be any for at least 10 years. He shows some of the same irritation that the editors of *Computers and Data Processing* magazine had displayed when answering Marion Harper in saying, "I strongly, but only intuitively, feel that even the general problem of worker displacement due to automation is beginning to be overworked by what I am confident is, at least, the field's fair share of the harbingers of doom."

Finke and Bagby enlarge on this. Both cite examples of how the computer actually increases manpower requirements. "We've created new jobs and then have had to build people up with the necessary skills to fill those jobs," says Finke. Bagby adds, "We've been a user of computers since 1955 and we still need more clerical workers." After conceding that his company is nevertheless using far fewer employees than it would be if it had *not* changed over to computers, he cites Department of Labor statistics on projected manpower needs in the banking industry. These show that the need for clerical workers would increase more rapidly than the available labor force. "Now, I can't match these figures with any other industry," he says, "but it is clear to me that the demand for clerical workers in all these industries is greater than the rate of increase in the labor force."

Bagby's intuitive statement is confirmed by events. Any long-range projections are, of course, fallible in either direction, but the fact remains that the demand for skilled workers has not decreased after almost 10 years of extensive automation. Bagby goes on: "What creates the problem is that the jobs that need filling now require higher skills. They need people with more judgment and higher I.Q.s. The people who used to do the ditchdigging office jobs are the ones who are creating the unemployment problems for you."

At this point Ramshaw, of United Aircraft, dissents, and offers an example from his company: "A computer is being used here to produce control information which is [then] fed into factory machinery. Prior to this, the factory machinery was run by the highest level skilled blue collar workers that you could get and they were always in short supply. . . . In this area you certainly have displaced some highly skilled blue collar people, you have a smaller number of people in the factory and the people who are there are going to be paid less. What they do is trivially easy compared to the skills of the men who were there before them. . . . I don't think that they can find comparable jobs; in most cases they go looking for a less progressive company that has not yet changed, but inevitably they will be pushed out the bottom."

Finke protests that the situation Ramshaw describes could not be blamed solely on computers. ". . . it's a system of instrumentation *and* computers," he says.

Jones takes a different tack, maintaining that individual initiative, with a minimum of Government assistance, would take care of the problem. He speaks of the necessity of "stimulating individuals to do what conforms to . . . a natural law—the law of survival, or the law *requiring* the upgrading of one's capabilities—the framework within which man has developed and progressed since earliest times."

These remarks in no way refute Ramshaw's point, of course, and as the discussion progresses a rough consensus concerning it is achieved. In the opinion of all the panel members, it is inevitable that the society, or the economy, will be faced before long with large numbers of idle persons. The panel members differ about the cause of this, but, in general, the industry team feels that the soon-to-be-displaced workers are either not intelligent enough or not sufficiently motivated to be of much use in the sophisticated society that the computer revolution is calling into being. As Hamming of Bell Laboratories puts it, "Where the job is *specific-task* oriented . . . we look for machines to do it. It is not obvious to me that the type of person thus displaced can be changed [retrained]. It [will] take a highly motivated man who is willing to work long hours (and thinking hard all the time) to compete with a machine. It's not only the blue collar worker . . . it involves also people at my level. . . .

"I'm not sure how much can be accomplished by retraining. When we talk about how much retraining should be done I want to get out of the discussion—I have no simple answers."

Hamming's doubts are explicated by the equally doubtful Ramshaw: "Right now the situation is that the kind of job openings which are being made require a high ability to handle things in a general way. It used to be that a man had a specific job to do. It might be a very complicated task and it might have taken a long time to train him to do it, but he had a particular task to perform and he performed it. . . . The need for that kind of work orientation is going down very rapidly. The kind of people you need now are those who can take a more general and abstract view. . . ."

These bleak comments are made by industry representatives, not by their erstwhile critics from the public sector. Furthermore, as the discussion progresses, the industry representatives almost unanimously admit that they have no suggestions for coping with this impending situation, other than the sort of conventional appeals to individual enterprise and to man's instinct for survival made by Jones.

Ferry finally comments on this situation. "[It] is a very curious thing. I notice that in the meetings I go to of this kind I find myself among some of the very brightest people in the world—some of them self-confessed—who stand for the development of the most sophisticated machinery. . . . And now we find ourselves urged, with this phenomenal display of ingenuity all about us, not to be politically ingenious or politically imaginative. . . .

"It seems to me that the real crux of the situation is the increasing insignificance of the human being. We have to realize that these wonderful machines, which we keep all shined up and running properly, are really a wild jackass which we are riding without much idea of where it is taking us. We pay a lot of attention to the needs of these machines and only occasionally, such as at meetings like this, to the needs of the human beings."

Ferry's Center for the Study of Democratic Institutions is also a center for analyses of the computer revolution that are as sombre as any expressed by representatives of business and industry. One paper on this subject published by the Center bears the rather ominous title, *Cybernation:* *The Silent Conquest*. It was written in 1962 by a sociologist, Donald N. Michael, who presented a bleak view of the coming computer era. This paper subsequently inspired a rash of alarmed articles in the liberal press—some predictably intemperate. At the same time, the paper was virtually ignored by the journals of the computer industry and of business generally, although it was evidently widely read.

Michael describes the plight of the blue collar worker in substantially the same terms that Ramshaw was to use, and then turns his attention to the service industries, which are optimistically seen as the ultimate hope for solutions to blue collar and clerical unemployment. He writes: "It is all very well to speak of the coming growth in the service industries and the vast opportunities for well-paid jobs and job upgrading that these activities will provide as blue-collar jobs diminish. But is the future as bright as this speculation implies? In the first place, service activities will also tend to displace workers by becoming self-service, by becoming cybernated, and by being eliminated. Consider the following data: the U.S. Census Bureau was able to use fifty statisticians in 1960 to do the tabulations that required 4100 statisticians in 1950. Even where people are not being fired, service industries can now carry on a vastly greater amount of business without hiring additional personnel; for example, a 50 percent increase in the Bell System's volume of calls in the last ten years with only a 10 percent increase in personnel. . . .

"If people [continue to] cost more than machines—either in money or because of the managerial effort involved—there will be growing incentives to replace them in one way or another in most service activities where they perform routine predefined tasks."

The two examples Michael offers to support this conclusion are, to say the least, somewhat fragmentary. Anyone who seriously attempts to ascertain future trends in the technological displacement of human workers obviously must come up with far more precise data than this. It is not an easy task. No valid statistics exist, although the U.S. Department of Labor's Bureau of Labor Statistics has made

---

* A term invented by Michael, combining the terms "cybernetics" and "automation."

23

limited statistical studies of office automation in specific locations. The *present* number of jobs lost to automation throughout the country, as estimated by informed observers, varies from 4,000 to 40,000 per week. Numerical estimates of the future simply are not made by prudent persons.

It is possible, however, to get at least a glimpse of the future, and a more detailed one than Michael offers, from the press of the computer industry.

By and large, the computer trade magazines are not concerned either with defending the industry from its critics or convincing its readers that computers are a great boon to humanity. Their concern is with reporting accurately the common run of developments in the industry, the technical innovations, and the other factors that are significant to computer people now or that could be in the future.

A casual inspection of these publications indicates an intense and continuing interest within the computer industry in labor-saving devices of all kinds, and that a great deal of brilliant research and development is being devoted to perfecting such replacements for people. Specific examples of this are the efforts to eliminate human punch-card, or key-punch, operators.

The ubiquitous punch card has become a virtual symbol of the computer to many people, and, indeed, their most immediate contact with it. It is today the principal means for converting such source data as time cards, sales slips, bills, and deposit slips into magnetic tape records and other forms that are comprehensible to the computer.

The necessity to punch these cards has created literally hundreds of thousands of new jobs in the past 10 years or so, not only in computer installations but also in all kinds of businesses and other organizations as well. Unlike many jobs associated with computer technology, keypunching requires little training and modest skills. Typists, file clerks, and even completely unskilled teenagers with average manual dexterity easily learn to operate manual keypunching equipment. (Inmates in a midwestern prison have been trained as keypunchers.) The ease with which people can be trained, coupled with the obvious need to do the work, has made the change to computers in many service industries much less difficult than it might otherwise have been.

Nevertheless, compared to the high-speed operations of the computer itself, keypunching is still slow and expensive. Computer systems designers and users are aware of this, and of how profitable it would be to transfer original source data directly to magnetic tape. Here are some developments in this direction, as reported by the computer industry press during *one month* (May, 1965).

24

Datamation magazine reported the impending installation of a PHILCO GENERAL PURPOSE PRINT READER, which "reads" typewritten copy and transfers it to machine-readable magnetic tape, and of a similar device manufactured by Recognition Equipment, Inc., at the facility of a Los Angeles programming service company. These readers, or "scanners," would be matched against human key-punch operators in a microfilm conversion project. This should "test the validity of one man's claim that a scanner can equal the output of 170 keypunchers in an eight hour day." *Data Processing Magazine* also mentioned the newly developed PHILCO GENERAL PURPOSE PRINT READER, describing its leasing to a New York concern, aptly named New Era Data Systems, Inc. The Philco machine was described here as being capable of scanning up to 2,000 type characters per second in most type faces, and of converting these directly to magnetic tape.

Datamation also carried an advertisement for another system that promised to "virtually eliminate key punching and verifying. . . ." This was UGC Instruments' SOURCE ORIENTED DATA ACQUISITION SYSTEM, or SODA. SODA was described as a system using a manual recorder with which any worker could record digital information directly on magnetic tape. Photos showed this handhold recorder being used by factory and warehouse workers, meter readers, surveyors, etc. Desk models are available for more sedentary users.

Data Processing Magazine provided an account of a similar machine developed by the Mohawk Data Sciences Corporation, the MDS 1101 KEYED DATA RECORDER. Mohawk's claims were modest; they estimated that six of their machines would do the work of seven human keypunchers and three human verifiers, thus dispensing with only four human operators.

Data Processing Magazine described still another machine, the Control Data Corporation's 915 PAGE READER which "directly converts typewritten information into a form suitable for processing by computer, thus eliminating or greatly reducing [the] need of keypunching information onto punched cards."

Computers and Automation magazine contained a full-page advertisement for another machine, this one developed by Information International, Inc., of Cambridge, Massachusetts. According to the ad, the fully automatic PROGRAMMABLE FILM READER can read engincering data in virtually any format, including graphs, lines, points, and type characters, and can, of course, convert it directly into a form the computer could use.

A feature article in *Computer Design Magazine* described the International Business Machines Corporation's new "Scanistor," a *dime-*

25

sized optical scanning device used experimentally to read and convert typed copy into electric signals. In the judgment of IBM engineers, the Scanistor can be used to read printed texts and other optical patterns and to enter the data directly into the computer, apparently bypassing even magnetic tape in the process.

Obviously, these devices were not all developed in one month. Moreover, the reports ignored the economics involved in replacing keypunchers with this new equipment. It does not take a detailed statistical study, however, to conclude that many human keypunchers have a rather limited future.

The workers were not the only object of Michael's scrutiny; their bosses' future was assessed as well. He quotes from an article in the *Harvard Business Review:* ". . . [Computers] should move the boundary between planning and performance upward. Just as planning was taken from the hourly worker and given to the industrial engineer, we now expect it to be taken from a number of middle managers and given to as yet largely nonexistent specialists: 'operation researchers,' perhaps, or 'organizational analysts.' Jobs at today's middle management level will become highly structured. Much more of the work will be programmed, i.e., covered by sets of operating rules governing the day-to-day decisions that are made."

As one might infer from the source of this quotation, the fate of middle management in the computer age is of considerable interest in business circles, and in the computer industry itself. The question is intimately related to the larger question of the trend toward the *re*centralization of American business. After 40 years of decentralization, brought on by the utter inadequacy of traditional data processing techniques to handle the operations of large corporations, the computer has come to the rescue. Computers, and the automatic equipment they direct, can, according to Michael:

". . . perform with a precision and a rapidity unmatched by humans. They also perform in ways that would be impractical or impossible for human [managers] to duplicate. They can be built to detect and correct errors in their own performance. . . . They can make judgments on the basis of instructions programmed into them. They can remember and search their memories for appropriate data, which has either been programmed into them along with their instructions or has been acquired in the process of manipulating new data. Thus they can learn on the basis of past experience with their environment. They can receive information in more codes and sensory modes than men can. They are beginning to perceive and recognize."

Computers neither pack up and go off to work for the competition at inopportune moments nor ask for more money! The prospect of eliminating much of this sort of thing and replacing it with the marvelous computer systems is attractive in some business circles, although many management experts still doubt that economic considerations will permit this replacement to come to pass, no matter how feasible it may be from a purely technical standpoint. To a certain extent this doubt is founded on a different conception of what constitutes the function of middle management. Michael and his source (Leavitt and Whistler in the *Harvard Business Review*) see middle managers as being engaged in essentially routine policy decisions. Such original "nonprogrammed" decision-making and thinking as is performed by this group is more likely to be devoted to putting down their rivals and similar extracurricular activities. The alternate opinion of the function of middle management is that it is concerned principally with nonroutine, "hunch" type policy decisions, or what Professor Melvin Anshen of Carnegie Tech calls "agenda problems" and "goal choice problems." These Michael would consider to be part of top management.

Michael is moved to speculate on what will then become of those hapless field grade bureaucrats. Where, he asks, can they go?

"To firms that are not yet assigning routine liaison analysis and minor executive tasks to machines? This may take care of some of the best of the displaced managers and junior executives, but if these firms are to have a future, the chances are that they will have to computerize eventually in order to compete. To the government? Again some could join it, but the style and format of government operations may require readjustments that many junior executives would be unable to make. And, in any case, government too is turning to computers, and it is entirely possible that much of the work of *its* middle management will also be absorbed by computers. Up to top management? A few, of course, but necessarily only a few. . . .

"Middle management is the group in the society with the most intensive emotional drive for success and status. Their family and social life is molded by these needs, as the endless literature on life in suburbia and exurbia demonstrates. They stand to be deeply disturbed by the threat and fact of their replacement by machines. One wonders what the threat will do to the ambitions of those who will still be students and who, as followers of one of the pervasive American dreams, will have aspired to the role of middle manager on the way up?" He then comments on some of the more optimistic forecasts which suggest that redundant middle managers may find suitable employment in the ranks of the "professionals."

"There are service jobs, of course, that require judgments about people by people. The shortage of people with these talents is evidenced by the 60-hour and more work weeks of many professionals. But these people are the products of special education, special mo-

27

tives, and special attitudes. . . . Increasing the proportion of citizens with this sort of professional competence would require systematic changes in attitudes, motives, and levels of education, not to mention more teachers, a professional service already in short supply. Alterations of this magnitude cannot be carried out overnight or by casual advertising campaigns or minor government appropriations. It is doubtful indeed, in our present operating context, that they can be done fast enough to make a significant difference in the employment picture for professional services in the next decade or two. Values become imbedded early in life. They are subject to change to be sure, but we are not, as a democratic society, adept at or inclined to change them deliberately and systematically. . . .

"Once the computers are in operation the need for additional professional people may be only moderate, and those who are needed will have to be of very high calibre indeed. *Probably only a small percentage of the population will have the natural endowments to meet such high requirements.*"

This last statement agrees in substance with the view expressed by Hamming, and is the most pessimistic element not only in Michael's and Hamming's thinking, but also in the predictions of most other observers. We appear, in the opinion of these people, to be on the verge of creating a social order in which most of us simply will not be bright enough to get by. The vaunted "tool to increase man's mental prowess" will be available only to the happy few.

In March of 1964, *Fortune* magazine took notice of the kind of pessimism that Michael's paper exemplifies (although he is not mentioned by name) in the course of a series of articles by Gilbert Burck, one of its senior editors. Entitled "The Boundless Age of the Computer," the series begins by attending to the skeptics who are "taking potshots at abuses of the computer, real and imaginary, and at the 'dire threat' it presents to employment and the social order.

"Although the [computer] is the bête noire of critics who fear it will accelerate unemployment and compound the worst problems of modern society, it seems destined to shine as a powerful instrument for making business more creative and efficient and hence for raising the nation's real income per person, for eliminating a vast amount of drudgery, and for increasing leisure. In short, for measurably expanding free man's range of choice."

Burck also considers the same Las Vegas symposium quoted earlier in this chapter. Before doing so, however, he emphasizes the positive side of the computer story:

"The benefits that the computer has conferred on government and science are tolerably familiar. . . . For government the machine has done something that has never been done before, at least on a big

28

scale: it has vastly improved the efficiency of the bureaucracy. . . .

"To science and technology the computer has of course been a colossal and unprecedented boom. Chemistry, weather forecasts, physics, education, missile design and operation—these are only a few fields in which the machine is responsible for totally new techniques and achievements.

". . . The vast bulk of American computers operate in the plants and offices of several thousand companies. Almost invariably the companies that made the machines pay off put computer operations in the hands of senior managers. These men did not look on the machine as a gift package that needed only to be plugged in, but subjected themselves to its rigorous discipline. They analysed their businesses and kept looking for new ways to use the computer even when they were employing the machines profitably on routine jobs. They were also willing to reorient their operating routines and their company organizations, if necessary, to exploit the computer. They are the kinds of managers, many are convinced, who will be running U.S. businesses tomorrow. 'The time when executives could fool around with the machine is gone,' says one computer-company officer. 'Either they make the computer an indispensable part of their business, or they become a dispensable part of the business.' "

This leads Burck to consider the fate of middle management: "Computer men predict [that] jobs at middle management level will become more specialized, specific, and highly programmed; they will also become fewer. On the other hand, managers at top levels, freed of the need for analyzing details, will more than ever require the faculties of innovation, creativeness and vision. The computer, precisely because it will make all relevant information instantly available to top management, will mean more centralization. . . . At the middle management level . . . much time is now taken up with pacesetting, work pushing, and expediting. As decision making becomes automated and rationalized, these functions are likely to become less important. The manager will deal with well-structured problems, and won't have to spend so much time persuading, prodding, rewarding and cajoling 'unpredictable and sometimes recalcitrant people.' "

Having thus arrived at pretty much the same point as Michael had reached concerning middle management, Burck then turns to the Las Vegas symposium: "The realization that the computer may be able to do a lot a man can do has accelerated the uproar about unemployment, in certain quarters, to panic proportions. Fevered by vague premonitions about the long-range consequences of the computer, many social pundits are discharging pneumatic predictions about how the machine will plow up the whole order. The consensus of a high level symposium at last November's convention of the American Federation of Information Processing Societies seemed to be that the computer would be a large factor in making relatively full employment hard to achieve.

"Most pessimistic of the lot was W. H. Ferry . . . a man given to looking into the future farther than the eye can see."

After summarizing Ferry's views, he comments: "This kind of thinking, like King Lear's threats to do such things as 'What they are, yet I know not, but they shall be the terrors of the earth,' gets considerably ahead of the facts in the short run, and woefully distorts the possibilities over the long run."

Essentially, Burck's rebuttal is based on the same statistically demonstrable fact that no significant amount of unemployment has yet been traced to the advent of computers and automation.

He writes: "In 1963 alone, when rising productivity in effect subtracted about two million jobs from the economy, non-farm wage and salary employment increased by more than 1,500,000. In other words, the economy in effect created a total of more than 3,500,000 jobs, and practically all were created by private enterprise."

After pointing out that "the doomsday prophets ignore this," he goes on, rather charitably, it would seem, and summarizes their arguments: the jobs created by the changeover to computers and automated processes are essentially temporary; the rate of new candidates entering the job market will double in the next decade; and finally, the increase in productivity which computers will bring about has not yet begun to make itself felt.

These points, he maintains, are only one side of the argument. The computer will continue to generate jobs directly and, as a clincher, the huge profits resulting from the increased efficiency and productivity will generate "a colossal boom in capital spending," which will create still more new jobs, presumably in the service industries.

The computer then, he concludes: ". . . will doubtless go down in history not as the scourge that blew unemployment through the roof, but as the technological triumph that enabled the American economy to maintain and gradually increase the spectacular growth rate on which its greatness depends."

He does not mention the problem that was bedeviling the members of that symposium—the fact that the people who are going to be displaced are not fitted for the kinds of jobs that the machine presumably will create. All of his solutions are economic and technological.

A year after the *Fortune* series appeared, the parent body of the American Federation of Information Processing Societies, the International Federation of Information Processing Societies, sponsored a handsome supplement in *The New York Times* devoted to extolling the "boundless age" just around the corner. The authors are, with one exception, American, and, with two exceptions, employed by either computer manufacturers, computer service companies, or users of computers. In other words, they constitute a panel as reputable and distinguished as the members of the Las Vegas symposium, even to being members of the same American Federation of Information Processing Societies.

Although the tone of the articles in the supplement is somewhat more restrained than that of Burck's "Boundless Age," it is equally positive and optimistic. The authors are generally in complete agreement with the premise held by Burck, Michael, and the Las Vegas symposium that computers will take over a lot of the present tasks of humans. Isaac Auerbach, President of the International Federation of Information Processing Societies, writes:

"The computer-based information revolution now directly affects almost every aspect of life: manufacturing, banking, insurance, accounting, transportation, communications, economics, government, traffic control, weather forecasting, physical and behavioral scientific inquiry, space exploration, medicine, education."

Dr. Simon Ramo, Vice-Chairman of the Board of the Thompson Ramo Woolridge Corporation and President of the Bunker-Ramo Corporation, is more specific:

"The mass extension of man's intellect by machine and the partnership of man and machine in the handling of information may well be the technological advance dominating the century. . . . Industry, government, education, and all of the professions will be greatly altered, and so, thus, will be society." After conceding that it is not yet possible to describe all the intellectual processes of decision-making in a manner suitable to a computer, he has this to say about the more routine, task-oriented intellectual functions:

". . . It is generally possible to design machines that will handle some or all of the intellectual-informational tasks in a superior fashion to that of an unaided human. The electronic computer is better suited than the human brain for handling huge quantities of mundane information. It does this more economically, faster, and with less error. . . .

"One basic concept, then, that guides today's application in our man-machine partnership is that the more mundane, but high capacity, information handling tasks are assigned to the machine, while the more contemplative decision-making intellectual tasks remain for the human mind. Even here, however, the mind can be aided by the machine. And the machine stands ready to sort, categorize, display, search for, and retrieve information, as a willing, tireless, high capacity partner."

The man-machine relationship of the future is also discussed by Dr. J. O. R. Licklider, Manager of Information Sciences, Systems, and Applications at the Thomas J. Watson Research Center of the International Business Machines Corporation:

"It looks as though the next decade will see the development of close partnerships between men and computers, of team work in which the special capabilities of men and the special capabilities of computers blend together in a new kind of interaction. Men and computers will work together as men now work together at the blackboard or over blueprints."

Other articles in the supplement provide detailed examples of how this man-machine combination will function and of the benefits that would accrue from it in hospitals, in traffic control and planning, and in education, where:

"A computer network, properly applied . . . can remember the progress of millions of students, comparing their tested learning with anticipated results, measuring and reporting deviations in progress from what was expected. Yet, remarkably, that same electronic system can be designed to immediately recognize an individual student, examine his record automatically and provide him an accelerated or other special presentation or test, again as a result of rules that have been set into the system by the wiser human educator."

And what of that bleak question raised by their confreres at the Las Vegas symposium? Dr. Edwin Harder, Chairman of the Board of Governors of the American Federation of Information Processing Societies, and Manager of the Westinghouse Electric Corporation's Analytical Department, actually raises it:

"But *is* the computer really beyond the understanding of the average person? Does one have to be a trained electronic specialist or an engineer or mathematician in order to have some insight into what one magazine recently called the most beneficial invention in history?"

Harder attempts to answer this by describing some tentative education programs for teenagers: a six-weeks course in basic computer programming in Santa Monica, California; a series of 15 weekly lectures at a Washington, D.C., high school; a series of three lectures at a Chicago high school by a professor from the Illinois Institute of Technology. Harder writes:

"True, most of [the students] were fairly bright youngsters, and only a few of them delved very deeply into the electronic circuitry of the machines. But what they came out with was a clear understanding of how computers worked and how humans used these fantastic computer industry new tools. . . ."

Auerbach is the only computer industry spokesman who directly faces the question:

"The advent of the computer has upset, inconvenienced, or actually hurt some people. So did the advent of the engine, but the comparison provides little solace to the man who is thrown out of work; a more energetic program to put him back on his feet is desperately needed. I believe that accommodations to the human problems raised by the computer will come; it is just a matter of time."

These buoyant views are a fair sample of what the leading spokesmen of the computer industry are offering the public by way of an introduction to the computer. The mountain of publicity material generated by them will certainly yield many more fascinating examples of the computer's potential to solve difficult problems, and will present equally inspiring, but fragmented, vistas of a profitable future. It will not, however, yield much information about how this future will come about, and what it will mean to the masses of "laymen," the day laborers who are neither brilliant scientists nor owners or managers of larger organizations, but who nevertheless will pay for this future and live with its consequences. The nearest that these spokesmen come to considering these questions is by drawing analogies to the industrial revolution of the nineteenth century and its initial dislocations, which, in the normal course of events, were put right.

Now, it should not be necessary to belabor this view, but it has been repeated with such intensity and conviction by business leaders, not only of the computer industry but also of the entire business community, that apparently some people still take it seriously. The industrial revolution analogy is a bad one for businessmen to employ, for it assumes that the dislocations caused by that revolution happened only during some finite period of time, and rather a long time ago. In fact, those dislocations are very much with us today. We have hardly begun to cope with them—such problems as the "plight of our cities," modern war, Appalachia, auto graveyards, polluted rivers or farm surpluses. Hardly a problem or irritation in modern life is not directly traceable to the industrial revolution, and to the lack of foresight and direction that characterized it then and now.

But, of course, computer industry leaders are aware of this. When talking among themselves rather than to the general public, they admit that some of the dire predictions of the pessimists are likely to be correct. Being supreme optimists themselves, however, they do not consider that such problems are insoluble. The reason: they have learned what intelligent, realistic planning and control can accomplish, and by and large they are ready and willing—even eager—to participate in efforts to plan and control the computer revolution.

One of the most specific expressions of this willingness was made by Isaac Auerbach in his testimony to the Senate Subcommittee on Employment and Manpower in October, 1963:

"It is incumbent on us to foresee the future, to predict its occupational and social attitudes, to direct the pattern of both automation and the information revolution, and to determine the specifications that technology and society demand. We must have criteria for coordinating education and technology so that most people can be educated for meaningful participation in what we can no longer regard as the world of the future.

"It remains . . . for the Federal Government to take the leadership in forming the coalition that will direct the coordinated approach to the problem of equating the technical progress to human progress.

". . . Educators must find some means of closing the gap between the highly educated and the poorly educated, with the goal of raising the overall education level. Most children in school today will probably have to be retrained three or four times for as many occupations during the course of their lives.

"There is no question as to the need for a well ordered plan for the collection, integration and dissemination of information on the educational implications of automation and the information revolution—and on the social, economic, and political implications as well.

"The need for this sort of clearinghouse is best met by the combined and cooperative forces of Government, business and labor—with Government acting as the initiator, coordinator, and, quite honestly, principal financial backer."

3
.

Automation as a Socioeconomic Controversy

After the hearings of the Senate Subcommittee on Employment and Manpower to which Auerbach addressed himself, the possibility of widespread unemployment due to automation began to receive serious attention. It was generally recognized that much more data on the subject was needed. The Subcommittee itself, in its final report, goes on record as being "particularly impressed with the need for more information concerning the nature, pace, and present and prospective impact of technological change." The report notes:

"No aspect of the manpower situation has been the subject of more discussion in recent years, but the absence of factual data had made most of the discussion inconclusive. Overall information on output per man and per man-hour is reasonably adequate for manufacturing as a whole, and probably for agriculture. Productivity data for public employment is non-existent (and perhaps non-producible), the little data available for construction appears misleading and the data for the service sectors of the economy needs improvement. . . .

"From a policy point of view the future impact of technological change is even more important than the present. The spectacular nature of some speculations concerning the future of automation and cybernation and the sanguine nature of other forecasts have been noted. Actually, there appears to be little dependable information concerning the pervasiveness and rate of introduction and potential applications of various technological developments."

So, in its ponderous way, the Subcommittee expresses the opinion that neither the optimists nor the pessimists even come near to proving their cases. It takes an eminently reasonable position, and one that is taken by many other authorities. However, this does not impress the partisans of the optimist and pessimist factions (any more than similar observations would impress the interested parties in the civil rights or the Viet Nam situations), but it does indicate the Government's seri-

35

ous interest and that it is presumably open to a certain amount of persuasion.

If this does not result immediately in systematic efforts to collect the elusive data, it does lead to a kind of closing of ranks and to serious attempts to move from the stage of individually held opinions to that of statements of position by organized groups, statements that were presumed to be based on some evidence, and certainly on some judicious samplings of the computer revolution in action backed up by some powerful intellectual convictions. Some of these samplings are noted in the preceding chapter.

These convictions will serve as the basis for evaluating the "factual data" (the data on you and me) which the Subcommittee considered so vital. They will be woven into all the pronouncements and plans made with us in mind. They are worth examining.

To begin with, these convictions differ not only in content for the two factions (which we will continue to designate as the optimists and pessimists even though at this stage the labels are no longer entirely accurate), but also in form. The convictions of the optimists are cast in a mold of economic theory, and those of the pessimists, while they contain important elements of economics, are based more on considerations of sociological and even psychological truths. In this respect, they resemble the convictions held by civil rights advocates, who are considerably less impressed with legal and even constitutional niceties than are their opponents. The optimists are mostly professional economists and businessmen, whereas most of the pessimists are lawyers, sociologists, and various "humanists" (and, to be sure, some economists).

At the risk of oversimplification, one may say that the optimists' position is based on the assumption that production efficiency leads to profits, profits lead to increased demand for goods and services, and increased demand creates more jobs. They assume that the potential demand for goods and services is limitless. No matter how much production may increase, demand will soon catch up to it. Such dislocations as sometimes occur in the workings of the economy are explained as local, and essentially temporary, imbalances.

This basic doctrine is most forcefully stated in a recent report to the President of the United States by the Government's Council of Economic Advisers, as august an assembly of economists as it is possible to find on this planet:

"If the Nation's ability and eagerness to buy output can and does keep pace with its ability to produce, a speeded-up pace of technological advance means that standards of living and economic security can rise more rapidly than ever. In this case, faster progress of productivity is to be sought and welcomed. Only if demand cannot keep pace (or if the required adjustments cannot be readily accommodated) is there a basis for fearing more rapid technological change.

"Historically, there is surely no evidence of any inability of demand to rise along with productive capacity, or of any permanent inadequacy of total job opportunities. . . ." Demand, in fact, does not merely keep pace with production, continues this report, but can lead and stimulate production.

". . . Since 1929, output per worker has almost doubled . . . demand . . . is almost three times as high. . . . Clearly, the increase in total demand for our potential output is the factor that has reconciled advancing technology with rising employment. . . .

"There is surely no reason to believe that any plausible rate of technical progress could lead to consumer satiation within the lifetimes of persons now on earth." The remainder of this passage is a complete and succinct statement of invincible optimism:

"Technological change permits any given level of output to be produced with less labor and, in that sense, destroys jobs. But it also provides a significant spur to investment and consumption and thus creates jobs. Technological change makes existing capital equipment obsolete. New processes and products increase the profitability of investment and stimulate business demand for new machines, new equipment, and new buildings. Technological change both generates high levels of investment and gives consumers new purchasing incentives. Historically, periods of rapid technological change have generally been periods of high and rising employment.

"There is, of course, no automatic mechanism which guarantees that actual demand will grow each year at exactly the same rate as potential full employment output. An economy characterized by technological change and growth always faces the challenge of maintaining a growth in demand sufficient for full employment, but not so high as to lead to inflation. Fortunately, growing sophistication in the uses of economic policy, particularly fiscal and monetary policy, make this goal more nearly attainable than ever before.*

* A year's experience with somewhat greater inflation than had been seen in the 1960 to 1965 period obliged the Chairman of the Council of Economic Advisers to "eat" these words. On October 26, 1966, Gardner Ackley, in delivering the Vanderveer Memorial Lecture at Southern Illinois University, admitted that although it is still theoretically possible to reduce unemployment by furthering policies favoring an increase in total demand, "it would now be at a substantial cost in terms of inflationary pressures. When there is an inadequate supply of workers," he continues, "with particular skills and in particular places, both employers and workers can and do adjust. . . .

"But such adjustments become increasingly costly the further they are pushed. Rather than make the most costly of these adjustments employers will raise what they are willing to pay for a worker who already meets their preferred specifications." This, Ackley admits, would inevitably lead to other wage and price increases, and to more inflation. He might have added, incidentally, that the "worker who already meets their preferred specifications" need not be a human worker.

37

"These tools of economic policy are capable of righting the balance whenever the job-destroying effects of technological progress outweigh its job-creating effects."

Some optimists, particularly those in the Department of Labor, are skeptical of the position taken by the Council of Economic Advisers. They are the proponents of the "active manpower policy," i.e., a policy of government-supported measures to make workers more "employable," which was called for by the passage of the Employment Act of 1946 and subsequently implemented in such measures as the Area Redevelopment Act of 1961, the Manpower Development and Training Act of 1962, the Vocational Education Act of 1963, and the Economic Opportunity Act of 1964, as well as in a host of other anti-poverty plans. Louis Levine, of the United States Employment Service, sums up the position of these skeptics in the course of a research conference sponsored by the National Bureau of Economic Research in 1966:

"In the resurgent periods that followed the four postwar recessions, unemployment not only continued at high levels but there was also a higher residual of unemployed after each recession. It became apparent that increase in aggregate demand alone was an inadequate response to current needs. The impact of unemployment was not distributed equally throughout the labor force. Mass unemployment of the thirties had given way to class unemployment of the sixties." At first glance this reads almost like a pessimist text, but actually the disparity of this view with reference to that of the Council of Economic Advisers is not so great. The increases with which both factions are concerned—the increases in demand and unemployment—are a matter of only a few percentage points of the national totals. Levine's conception of an inadequate increase in aggregate demand would fail to satisfy the employment needs of perhaps 1 or 2 per cent of the labor force. He is confident that demand can be held that close, and that the active manpower policy can handle residual unemployment resulting from discrepancies of this magnitude. And, as a prudent man, he should be confident; for, as notes one impartial observer (Edwin Dale of *The New York Times*), "If past form is any example, it is a losing proposition to bet against the Council of Economic Advisers.

"The Council in the past few years has diagnosed the economy's trouble as insufficient demand and it acted to boost demand, as we have seen. Even within the Government there were fears that such methods would not do the trick. But the record is clear.

"The Council said expansion of demand would easily offset the problem of automation and sharply boost employment and it did. Jobs grew by 2.5 million last year [1965] alone.

"The Council said the bulk of the unemployment was not struc-

38

tural—a mismatch of the employed labor and the available jobs because of insufficient skills—and it wasn't, as the drop in unemployment shows.

"The Council said that demand could be expanded in the then existing conditions, without producing inflation, and it was right."*

In attempting to examine the pessimists' basic convictions and beliefs, one could not cite such a clearcut and definite statement as the Council of Economic Advisers provided for the optimists. This is due to a number of factors. Whereas virtually all the optimists are found in the councils of the Government and in the big corporations (and, in some cases, in their affiliated university research groups), the pessimists are either on their own or at best linked to small and usually highly specialized groups whose main purpose is to advance a particular cause or viewpoint. In short, they are not part of a well organized defense system devoted to maintaining the established order, but are a widely dispersed "guerrilla force" devoted to attacking it. Their positions are thus extremely varied, and often serve as no more than advanced staging areas for specific assaults. They also pride themselves on being intellectuals—original thinkers and observers—who can evolve their own views without recourse to the revealed wisdom of others. When one attributes a statement of theirs to the influence of another authority, it is at one's own risk.

Bear this in mind as we examine some of the more notable expressions of the pessimists' views. These are all examples of widely held views, and their logic has been generally acknowledged but they are still no more than personal convictions.

One of the main lines of the pessimists' attack is directed toward the conventional economic concept of demand which was so ably defined in the report of the Council of Economic Advisers. The most determined assault, and certainly one of the most lucid and sardonic analyses of conventional economics, is made by John Kenneth Galbraith in his *The Affluent Society*. He states:

"Assume that demand stems from needs or wants. Some needs or wants are obviously more urgent than others. These wants will be the first to stimulate production to satisfy them. As production is stimulated to greater efficiency these wants will tend to be filled. As they are filled other, less urgent, wants will come to the fore, further stimulating production. These wants in turn will be filled, to be replaced by still less urgent ones, and, as production efficiency continues to increase the urgency of wants will continue, in the normal course of events, to decrease." This does not happen in practice however. Why? Because, argues Galbraith, in order to grow and to in-

* See footnote, p. 37.

crease its efficiency, the production apparatus itself begins to create demand, and to endow it with an urgency that it really does not of itself possess.

"If the individual's wants are to be urgent, they must be original with himself. They cannot be urgent if they must be contrived for him. And above all they must not be contrived by the process of production by which they are satisfied. For this means that the whole case for the urgency of production, based on the urgency of wants, falls to the ground. One cannot defend production as satisfying wants if that production creates the wants."

Galbraith then questions the stability of such a system. It appears to him that the greater efficiency resulting from technological advances would force a progressively greater effort to create the necessary demand for the product of that efficiency. Any faltering of these efforts would tend to undermine the economy as even the Council of Economic Advisers indirectly admits.

Galbraith's point appears at first to be excessively moralistic. If demand requires stimulation, what of it? The wants thus created certainly *seem* urgent enough to consumers, so much so that they are eager and even desperate to acquire the products that promise to fulfill them, and that keep the system functioning. But there is more to it than this. The conventional theory, as we have seen, in holding that demand is created naturally and inevitably, relies on its fiscal and monetary policies solely to make rather minute adjustments in the balance of demand and production—a few percentage points one way or another as the case may be. Moreover, these controls are designed to do nothing more than to speed up or slow down a current of demand that is held to be flowing of its own accord. But, Galbraith says, in effect, this is simply not the case at all. In reality, in this situation demand must be created just as surely and carefully as the things to satisfy it must be produced. We are thus in the position of a driver who is coasting down a rather bumpy hill using only the brake and the clutch, and all the while imagines that he is driving the car on level ground. And, to continue the analogy, the hill is leveling out rapidly—just as production increases and wants become progressively less urgent—and the driver had better start looking around for the gas pedal—if he has one.

Galbraith's solution to the problem is the now famous one of increasing consumption in the "public sector" of the economy, a proposal that was received with great favor by the Kennedy Administration, and which has been adopted by the Johnson Administration as well.

"The final problem of the productive society is what it produces.

40

[He had chided his fellow economists for not demonstrating much interest in this.] This manifests itself in an implacable tendency to provide an opulent supply of some things and a niggardly yield of others. This disparity carries to the point where it is a cause of social discomfort and social unhealth. The line which divides our area of wealth from our area of poverty is roughly that which divides privately produced and marketed goods and services from publically rendered services. Our wealth in the first is not only in startling contrast with the meagerness of the latter, but our wealth in privately produced goods is, to a marked degree, the cause of crisis in the supply of public service. For we have failed to see the importance, indeed, the urgent need, of maintaining a balance between the two."

Galbraith amplifies this explicitly and in detail, touching on the limitations of fiscal and monetary control devices and of conventional investment policies, in some of the most brilliant analyses that the so-called dismal science of economics has ever been subjected to. Then, commenting on the dangers inherent in these limitations, he concludes reasonably that, "However great or small these dangers, they will be lessened if our consumption is widely distributed—if productive energies serve uniformly the whole span of man's wants. Since public wants are not contrived, they are not subject to a failure of contrivance. Since they are not sold on the installment plan, they are not subject to curtailment by any of the factors which may make people unwilling or unable to incur debt. Thus the better the social balance [the balance between spending and consumption in the public sector of the economy and the private sector], the more immune the economy to fluctuations in private demand."

Included in these "public wants," along with better schools and cleaner air, is a more equitable or, at any rate, a more humane system of unemployment compensation and relief, which he calls Cyclically Graduated Compensation. Briefly, this would be designed to fluctuate with the economic cycle. When business is brisk and employment high it would provide rather small payments to the unemployed—just enough to tide a man over to the next job. When business is slow and unemployment high, the payments would be higher, rising to as much as half the worker's normal wages, thereby stimulating the economy by providing more purchasing power, and stimulating demand. Galbraith is enthusiastic about this proposal: ". . . it is hard to think of a single measure of economic reform that would have a more satisfactory effect. Apart from breaking the connection between output and economic security . . . it would largely eliminate the hazard of depression unemployment for the worker. By stabilizing demand it would go far to mitigate the threat of depression." By

41

offering the nation's economic managers a powerful new tool for regulating production and demand, Galbraith's proposal tends to place him in the camp of the champions of the existing order.

Many pessimists believe that this is at best a partial solution to the automation-employment problem, one that underestimates its magnitude. It takes no more notice of the particular nature of automation and computers in relation to the job-producing effects of any kind of increased production than had the assumptions of the optimists. Even so, his diagnosis of the failings of the present economic system is pleasant reading for pessimists. We shall see it incorporated into pessimistic manifestos as the basis of far more revolutionary schemes.

A view of the development of the modern industrial corporation and its relationship to the Government and the economy is the inspiration for a second line of attack on the optimists' position. The definitive expression of this view is probably *The Modern Corporation and Private Property* by Adolf Berle and Gardiner Means, published in 1933. It has been progressively updated by both these economists, and further embellished by the work of such sociologists as David Riesman and William H. Whyte, Jr.

The essentials of this view are: the modern large corporation, far from having declined in power and prestige from the bad old days of the late nineteenth century, has become more ubiquitous and influential than ever. It has survived the crash of 1929, the Great Depression and the New Deal, and, by enormously increasing its size and the diversity of its activities, has come to rival the Government itself as a force directing and controlling the course of people's lives.

Along the way it has evolved from the "owner operated" institution of Rockefeller and Ford to one in which ownership is spread among thousands and tens of thousands of faceless stockholders, and in which effective control of operations is in the hands of a small, self-perpetuating group of professional managers.

Largely owing to this growth of corporate power, the "free market" upon which so much of conventional economic theory is based, has in reality ceased to exist. Consumer prices, which, conventional theory maintains, are free-market expressions of the fluctuations of supply and demand, are actually determined administratively by the directorates of the large corporations in response to corporate needs and objectives. This is possible because each major industry has come to be dominated by a few corporate giants—usually no more than three to five. Antitrust laws notwithstanding, their common structures and goals, and the common economic environment in which they operate, have generally led them to adopt price structures so similar that their suppliers and their customers have little choice but to go along with them. Competition has become primarily a question of quality of product, not of price.

Naturally this state of affairs raises a number of questions which are being studied by a whole generation of economic thinkers. Gardiner Means, in a lecture given at the College of William and Mary in 1957, provides a sample:

"Traditional [economic] theory suggests that with only four producers [to each industry] and no price wars, the rate of return on capital would tend to be abnormally high in relation, say, to interest rates or to the current costs of capital. Is this in fact true? What would place a roof on excessive earnings? Would strong labor unions prevent too high earnings? Would labor and capital gang up on the consumer? And if this happened equally for *all* industries would it make any difference, since the high money prices would be met out of high money incomes? Would competitive advertising and promotion so increase costs as to absorb excessive profits, keeping costs and prices in line not by reducing prices but by increasing costs? Would the threat of new entrants into a given market keep profits in bounds? And if profits were not kept in line, who would benefit from high rates of earnings—stockholders who do not control the enterprise or management that does? Also, would it be possible to maintain full employment in such an economy and avoid inflation?"

Means attempted to answer the questions he had raised, but, generally speaking, pessimists have not shown any great interest in his answers. Many, however, have applied his concepts of corporate irresponsibility to the automation controversy, raising the question of whether these organizations should be trusted with the additional power that automation and computers confer.

A third line of attack is based on the ideas of a scientist who disclaimed any economic expertise, but who nevertheless had some profound thoughts about the implications of automation and employment. This was Norbert Wiener, a mathematician, and one of the first and foremost computer theoreticians. Wiener was in on the development of computers and automated devices from the beginning, and in the preface to his *Cybernetics* (1947) he goes right to the point:

"The automatic factory, the assembly line without human agents, is only so far ahead of us as is limited by our willingness to put such a degree of effort into their engineering as was spent, for example, in the development of the technique of radar in the second world war . . . this gives the human race a new and most effective collection of mechanical slaves to perform its labor. Such mechanical labor has most of the economic properties of slave labor, although unlike slave labor, it does not involve the direct demoralizing effects of

43

human cruelty. However, any labor that accepts the conditions of competition with slave labor, accepts the conditions of slave labor and essentially is slave labor. The key word in this statement is *competition*. It may very well be a good thing for humanity to have the machine remove from it the need of menial and disagreeable tasks; or it may not. I do not know. It cannot be good for these new potentialities to be assessed in terms of the market, or the money they save. . . .

". . . Perhaps I may clarify the background of the present situation if I say that the first industrial revolution, the revolution of the 'dark satanic mills,' was the devaluation of the human arm by the competition of machinery. There is no rate of pay at which a United States pick-and-shovel laborer can live which is low enough to compete with the work of a steam shovel as an excavator. The modern industrial revolution is similarly bound to devalue the human brain at least in its simpler and more routine decisions. . . . taking the second industrial revolution as accomplished, the average human being of mediocre attainments or less has nothing to sell that is worth anyone's money to buy.

"The answer, of course, is to have a society based on human values other than buying and selling."

In *The Human Use of Human Beings,* published in 1954, Wiener returns to this subject:

"It is perfectly clear that this will produce an unemployment situation, in comparison with which the present recession and even the depression of the thirties will seem like a pleasant joke."

The uncertain relationship of demand to production in conventional economic theory, the self-serving character of the modern corporation, and the revolutionary character of computers themselves appear to be the basis for the main points of the pessimists' argument. To these may be added some minor ones—compassion for the poor perhaps—a mistrust of an increasingly more powerful and all pervasive government, and a concern for the psyches of individuals made to feel more and more dominated by machines. What do they add up to?

Robert Theobald is a socio-economist who, since 1957, has devoted himself to studying the more ominous implications of automation and the computer revolution, and has become, along with W. H. Ferry and Donald Michael, one of the most widely quoted pessimists. In a paper presented at a conference at the Pennsylvania State University in December, 1963, he ably sums up the pessimist position:

"Our existing socio-economic system was founded in the nineteenth century: its major institutions reflect the aims of this period with superb fidelity. The drives of the nineteenth century were to achieve

44

the maximum rate of growth in production and the availability of knowledge; and increasingly as the century progressed, to advance understanding of how the universe is structured. Both of these goals were built into our pattern of institutions and they have both been largely achieved.

". . . The viability of our present socio-economic system is based on a very simple relationship: it is assumed that it is possible for the overwhelming proportion of those seeking jobs to find them and that the incomes received from these jobs will provide adequate funds to allow the job-holder to live with dignity.

"In turn, provision for the required number of jobs depends on there being enough people who are willing and able to absorb a sufficient volume of goods and services to ensure effectively full employment.

". . . Year by year we are less successful in balancing the number of jobs with the number of job-seekers. The number of people seeking jobs has risen steadily during the post-World War II days. . . . In coming years, the number of people requiring jobs will grow still faster because of the enormous influx of young workers."

He goes on to cite expert predictions that this pace will increase astronomically, middle management will be hard hit, and ultimately the goods and services of the whole society will be produced by perhaps 2 per cent of the population. While he disclaims responsibility for the accuracy of these predictions, he concludes that the economy has already failed to bring the rate of unemployment down to acceptable levels, and that "a large proportion of those born in the fifties and sixties have no realistic prospect of ever holding a market-supported job."

Nevertheless, the fear of unemployment is so general and pervasive that it is difficult to imagine that, as long as any coherent leadership exists in this country, mass unemployment will be permitted to occur. Whatever the causes, it would not happen overnight. It seems reasonable to assume that, as the rate of unemployment rises, efforts to do *something* about it will increase in intensity with each additional percentage point. No organized body of opinion, or political influence, or economic power can ignore it.

What conditions, then, can be substituted for unemployment? To answer this question it is necessary to go beyond the analytical stage and consider first what we might call organized proposals for specific action.

4
·
Two Proposals for Coping with Automation

It is a measure of the widespread disarray in the face of the computer revolution that almost 15 years after the machines had appeared on the national scene the first public statement concerning their impact on society came from a group of noncomputer experts who frankly described their association as being "ad hoc."

During the 15 years in question, the firms that designed and built computers became affluent and powerful, and the use of their product became widespread. The computer industry and its major users had come to support a vigorous trade press, from whose pages issued a steady cascade of high-grade thinking about problems of computer application and development. This effort was supplemented extensively by an equally high-grade research effort in the nation's universities, much of it directly supported by the Federal Government. In spite of all this, and of all the automation symposiums, discussions, and dialogues, the first direct approach to the issue comes from outside, from a most heterogeneous collection of individuals speaking as private citizens. All of them could be called intellectuals and all could be classified as liberals, but beyond this they can hardly be characterized as a group. Their number includes several business executives, several trade union leaders, authors, editors, economists, civil rights leaders, and a number of academicians. Some are fairly well known to the public, notably Norman Thomas and Linus Pauling, and perhaps Michael Harrington, the young author of the best seller on poverty, *The Other America*. A number of others have at least a limited following either as civil rights leaders, pacifists, etc., or writers or scholars. Owing perhaps to this varied background, they call themselves the Ad Hoc Committee on the Triple Revolution.*

Two of the guiding spirits of the Ad Hoc Committee are W. H.

* For the memorandum and a complete list of the Committee's members, see Appendix 1.

Ferry of the Center for the Study of Democratic Institutions, who, as discussed, grappled with the computer experts at their symposium in Las Vegas (Chap. 3), and Robert Theobald, whom we encountered in Chapter 4. These two, together with Ralph L. Helstein, President of the United Packinghouse, Food and Allied Workers (a union with no little experience with the job-eliminating effects of automation), are the principal movers behind the Ad Hoc Committee's ultimate purpose for existence: a lengthy memorandum addressed to President Johnson, and entitled "The Triple Revolution—An Appraisal of the Major U.S. Crises and Proposals for Action" (otherwise known as the Ad Hoc Committee Memorandum). It was received by the President (and the public) on March 22, 1964. It stands as the major statement of what we might call the nonofficial (i.e., not sponsored by the Government) approach to the problems posed by automation and the computer revolution.

The Ad Hoc Committee Memorandum begins by defining its "Triple Revolution."

"At this time three separate and mutually reinforcing revolutions are taking place:

"*The Cybernation Revolution:* . . . brought about by the combination of the computer and the automated self-regulating machine. This results in a system of almost unlimited productive capacity which requires progressively less human labor. . . .

"*The Weaponry Revolution:* . . . We are recognizing only now that the great weapons have eliminated war as a method for resolving international conflicts. . . .

"*The Human Rights Revolution:* A universal demand for full human rights is now clearly evident. It continues to be demonstrated in the civil rights movement within the United States. . . ."

The authors state at once that they are interested primarily in the first revolution. The subsequent text bears this out so clearly that the other two appear to have been included only to broaden the Memorandum's appeal by enlisting the support of pacifist and civil rights groups.

The main body of the text itself is divided into three parts: a critique of conventional economic theories and a statement of the economic convictions of the Committee, a description of the current state of the economy as seen by the Committee, and a list of recommended policies for coping with the situation.

"Up to this time," the critique begins, "economic resources have been distributed on the basis of contributions to production, with machines and men competing for employment on somewhat equal terms." In other words, an investor might choose to use his capital

47

either to buy machines or to hire human labor, depending on which was more profitable.

"In the developing cybernated system, potentially unlimited output can be achieved by systems of machines which will require little co-operation from human beings. As machines take over production from men, they absorb an increasing proportion of resources while the men who are displaced become dependent on minimal and unrelated government measures—unemployment insurance, social security, welfare payments. . . ."

The Memorandum then explains that, according to conventional economic theory the Government could remedy this situation by pumping more money into the economy (tax cuts, easier credit, increased Government spending, etc.). This would increase demand for goods and services, which would in turn create more jobs. Implicit in this theory is the assumption that "all of the available labor force and industrial capacity is required to meet the needs of consumers and industry and to provide adequate public services."

But with the advent of automation, according to the Ad Hoc Committee's view, this does not follow. Machines alone can meet the increased demand, or at any rate such a large portion of it as to leave a considerable fraction of the labor force without jobs. Each time more money is introduced into the economy it creates a demand for more machines, not more jobs.

"The [present] industrial system was designed to produce an ever-increasing quantity of goods as efficiently as possible, and it was assumed that the distribution of the power to purchase these goods would occur almost automatically. The continuance of the income-through-jobs link as the only major mechanism for distributing effective demand—for granting the right to consume—now acts as the main brake on the almost unlimited capacity of a cybernated productive system. . . .

"An adequate distribution of the potential abundance of goods and services will be achieved only when it is understood that the major economic problem is not how to increase production, but how to distribute the abundance that is the great potential of cybernation. There is an urgent need for a fundamental change in the mechanisms employed to insure consumer rights." The Memorandum then cites the following statistics in support of these statements:

". . . The increased efficiency of machine systems is shown in the more rapid increase in productivity per man-hour since 1960, a year that marks the first visible upsurge of the cybernation revolution. In 1961, 1962 and 1963, productivity per man-hour rose at an average pace above 3.5%—a rate well above both the historical average and the postwar rate. . . .

"A $30 billion annual increase in gross national product is now required to prevent unemployment rates from rising. . . . *

". . . Job creation in the private sector has now almost entirely ceased except in services; of the 4,300,000 jobs created in this period [1957–1962], only about 200,000 were provided by private industry through its own efforts. . . .

". . . The Department of Labor estimates, however, that on the basis of present trends, as many as 30% of all students will be high school drop-outs in this decade [1960's].

". . . A permanently depressed class is developing in the U.S. Some 38,000,000 Americans, almost one-fifth of the nation, still live in poverty. The percentage of total income received by the poorest 20% of the population was 4.9% in 1944 and 4.7% in 1963."

The Memorandum then turns to its policy recommendations:

". . . We assert that the only way to turn technological change to the benefit of the individual and the service of the general welfare is to accept the process and to utilize it rationally and humanely. The new science of political economy will be built on the encouragement and planned expansion of cybernation. The issues raised by cybernation are particularly amenable to intelligent policy-making: Cybernation itself provides the resources and tools that are needed to ensure minimum hardship during the transition process.

"But major changes must be made in our attitudes and institutions. . . . Gaining control of our future requires the conscious formation of the society we wish to have. Cybernation at last forces us to answer the historic questions: What is man's role when he is not dependent upon his own activities for the material basis of his life? What should be the basis for distributing individual access to national resources? Are there other proper claims on goods and services besides a job?" These two questions are answered by this proposal:

". . . We urge . . . that society, through its appropriate legal and governmental institutions, undertake an unqualified commitment to provide every individual and every family with an adequate income as a matter of right."

This proposal, not surprisingly, received more publicity and comment than anything else in the Memorandum. An editorial in *Life* magazine calls it "instant socialism," but concedes that "some degree of severance between work and income may be closer to real politics than you think." The day after the Memorandum was released, Secretary of Labor Willard Wirtz criticized it in the course of a speech to a convention of the United Auto Workers. "I don't believe that the

* According to the Bureau of Labor Statistics, the annual increase required is on the order of $15 billion. A $30 billion annual increase would be required to keep unemployment below 3 per cent, however.

world owes me a living," he said, "and I don't believe it owes any-body else a living." Editorial opinion elsewhere generally follows ideological lines closely.

But the income proposal itself hardly warrants all this attention. The Memorandum presents no details on the guaranteed income, be-yond stating that the economy of abundance could well afford to sus-tain all of its citizens, and that this was "the only policy by which the quarter of the nation now dispossessed and soon to be dispossessed by lack of employment can be brought within the abundant society."

Then, after admitting that the Committee does not pretend to be able "to visualize the consequences of this 'change in our values,'" the Memorandum proposes a whole series of rather conventional pub-lic works programs, which, in effect, would have the same purpose as the guaranteed income. These programs are described as transi-tional—designed to lead to "those changes in political and social in-stitutions which are essential to the age of technology," but the empha-sis is largely on job creation, including:

". . . A massive program to build up our educational system. . . . Federal programs looking to the training of an additional 100,000 teachers annually. . . .

". . . public works to construct dams, reservoirs, ports, water and air pollution facilities [!], community recreation facilities . . . 150,000 to 200,000 jobs would be created. . . .

". . . low-cost housing . . . aimed at a rate of 700,000–1,000,000 units a year.

". . . rapid transit systems, urban and interurban. . . ." In addi-tion, a greater amount of Government intervention in the economy is proposed, including:

". . . A major revision of our tax structure aimed at redistributing income as well as apportioning the costs of the transition equitably . . . an expansion of the use of excess profits tax . . . Subsidies and tax credit plans. . . .

". . . The use of the licensing power of government to regulate the speed and direction of cybernation . . . the use of minimum wage power as well as taxing power to provide the incentives for moving as rapidly as possible toward the goals indicated by this paper."

Robert Theobald notes that these transitional programs contradicted the guaranteed income proposal. In a footnote to the Memorandum, he stated his refusal to be associated with them. He holds that these programs would preserve the existing economy rather than aid in moving toward a new one. In the transition period, he maintains, men should concentrate on using machines to do the work, while devising new forms of "work" and "leisure."

Theobald's position is consistent with the one he defined in more detail a year or so previously in *Free Men and Free Markets*, in which the principles of the guaranteed income were proposed for the first time. In this book, Theobald describes these principles as: ". . . specifically designed to break the link between jobs and income. Implementation of these principles must necessarily be carried out by the Government as the sole body concerned with every member of society and with the adequate functioning of the total socioeconomic system. . . .

"In order to ensure that Government concern with the total socioeconomic system would not outweigh its responsibility to every member of society, a due-income from Government should be given as an *absolute constitutional right,* for unless this is guaranteed, the Government would have the possibility of developing the most extreme form of tyranny imaginable.

"During the process of implementation of the due-income principles, the number of people obtaining the totality of their living expenses from the Government would increase rapidly; if the right to these incomes could be withdrawn under *any* circumstances, Government would have the power to deprive the individual not only of the pursuit of happiness but also of liberty and even, in effect, of life itself. This *absolute* right to a due-income would be essentially a new principle of jurisprudence. Most present constitutional rights can be curtailed when the overall good of society is held to require them; however, the right of an individual to a due-income could not, in itself, endanger the state. . . .

"The principle of an *economic floor* under each individual should be established. This principle would apply equally to every member of society and carry with it no connotation of personal inadequacy or implication that an undeserved income was being received from an overgenerous government." Theobald calls this principle "Basic Economic Security." He estimates that while ". . . the full economic implications of any particular level of BES entitlements would probably have to be worked through on computers . . . it might be expected that a level of $1,000 a year for every adult and $600 a year for every child would be feasible levels to use as a starting point for calculations. It . . . seems reasonable to estimate that *twenty* millions of Americans, or one person in nine, would immediately be covered."

He did not feel that the level of payments should be higher than this at the beginning of the program, ". . . for it is essential that the operation of the scheme be efficient, and this goal might not be achieved if the initial number of beneficiaries was too high." Theobald then turns his attention to those perennial candidates for obsolescence—the "middle managers":

51

". . . It can also be expected that many of those now engaged in middle management and similar occupations will lose their present jobs and be felt by prospective employers to have insufficient intellectual flexibility to take on new types of work. The drastic and abrupt drop in income which will follow will mean that members of this group will suddenly find themselves unable to meet the expenditure commitments already undertaken as part of their way of life. . . . In contemplating the possibility of hardship for the individuals of this group, we should not forget that their personal difficulties will have far wider implications for society as a whole. . . .

"A second principle should therefore be introduced, embodying the concept of the need to protect the existing middle-income group against abrupt major declines in their standard of living; this principle could be called *Committed Spending*.

"The payments to those receiving Committed Spending from the Government would be related to their [previous] incomes. . . . However . . . no payment . . . would exceed a given multiple of the amount available to a family of the same size under Basic Security. This multiple might possibly be three; thus, if a family receiving Basic Economic Security would be entitled to $3,200, a family of comparable size would have an income ceiling of $9,600 from Committed Spending.

"An Economic Security Plan of the type proposed is essentially designed to promote freedom for the individual. But would it also meet the goal of minimizing Government intervention in the market?" To answer this he describes, rather caustically, how: ". . . the Government has been forced to intervene [in the economy] in its attempt to provide minimum incomes for all and to try to ensure that the number of available jobs keeps up with the number of people seeking work. However, even the totality of present Government measures is not effective in ensuring minimum incomes for all. An Economic Security Plan would take the place of the present mosaic of measures: Social Security, unemployment compensation and welfare, subsidies to housing, 'stamp plans' and all the smaller measures designed to provide for 'hardship' cases. . . .

"Measures to provide minimum incomes, however, are only one part of the present pattern of Government intervention in the market mechanism. The Government is also increasingly involved in the necessity to change interest rates, tax rates, tariff rates, etc. in its efforts to keep the number of available jobs growing as fast as the number of people seeking work. The introduction of an Economic Security Plan would provide the Government with a comprehensive mechanism which could be used to keep the number of *available* jobs in balance with the number of *desired* jobs. . . .

". . . Acceptance of the principle of Basic Economic Security would also have favorable effects on easing the shortage of funds at the local and state level. If the Federal Government provided a minimum income for all, many present local and state budget items would be reduced and eliminated, and this would allow a larger proportion of local and state funds to be made available to meet other urgent community requirements."

In short, Theobald's plan aims at reducing the amount of Government intervention in the economy by offering a radically new means for the Government to meet the obligations imposed on it by the Employment Act of 1946 and the "mosaic" of welfare measures which began with the passage of the Social Security Act in 1935. The Ad Hoc Committee, on the contrary, proposes to do just the opposite.

Returning now to the Memorandum, we find that its final section is equally committed to centralized planning:

"The historic discovery of the post-World War II years is that the economic destiny of the nation can be managed. Since the debate over the Employment Act of 1946, it has been increasingly understood that the Federal Government bears primary responsibility for the economic and social well being of the country. The essence of management is planning. The democratic requirement is planning by public bodies for the general welfare. Planning by private bodies such as corporations for their own welfare does not automatically result in additions to the general welfare, as the impact of cybernation on jobs has already made clear.

"Planning agencies should constitute the network through which pass the stated needs of the people at every level of society, gradually building into a national inventory of human requirements, arrived at by democratic debate of elected representatives." The description of the role of these planning agencies is a computer man's dream: Their tasks, states the Memorandum, should be:

"To collect the data necessary to appraise the effects, social and economic, of cybernation at different rates of innovation.

"To recommend ways, by public and private initiative, of encouraging and stimulating cybernation.

"To work toward optimum allocations of human and natural resources in meeting the requirements of society." And, with a nod to Theobald:

"To develop ways to smooth the transition from a society in which the norm is full employment within an economy based on scarcity to one in which the norm will be either non-employment, in the traditional sense of productive work, or employment on the great variety of socially valuable but "nonproductive" tasks made possible by the economy of abundance.

"The aim throughout will be the conscious and rational direction of economic life by planning institutions under democratic control.

"In this changed framework the new planning institutions will operate at every level of Government—local, regional and Federal—and will be organized to elicit democratic participation in all their proceedings. These bodies will be the means for giving direction and content to the growing demand for improvement in all departments of public life."

Two weeks after the Ad Hoc Committee Memorandum was dispatched to President Johnson, the Committee received a perfunctory letter of acknowledgment from the White House, promising to consider thoughtfully its recommendations. The letter also mentioned that "The President has also asked the Congress to establish a Presidential commission to study the impact of technological change on the economy and to recommend measures for assuring the full benefits of technology while minimizing any adverse effects."

Five months later, on August 19, 1964, President Johnson signed a bill establishing the National Commission on Technology, Automation,* and Economic Progress. This body was charged with investigating "the impact of technological and economic change on production and employment" over the next 10 years and, further, with recommending administrative and legislative action to be taken to cope with the problems presumably created by that impact. In the words of the bill, this action meant:

". . . specific administrative and legislative steps which it [the Commission] believes should be taken by the Federal, State and local governments in meeting their responsibilities (1) to support and promote technological change in the interest of continued economic growth and improved well-being of our people, (2) to continue and adopt measures which will facilitate occupational adjustment and geographical mobility, and (3) to share the costs and help prevent and alleviate the adverse impact of change on displaced workers."

The Automation Commission was headed by Dr. Howard R. Bowen, President of the University of Iowa. It included Walter P. Reuther, President of the United Automobile Workers, and an impressive selection of business leaders: Thomas J. Watson, Jr., Chairman of the Board of the International Business Machines Corporation (who rather

---

* Soon after the Commission was established the word "automation" came into disrepute as a term to describe the replacing of human workers with machines. In the opinion of Government and industry leaders it had become a "scare word." Consequently, although retained in the title of the Commission, it was used in the report only in one or two limited cases where it applied to automating a mechanical or production process. The more general term "technological change" is now in vogue.

delicately disassociated himself from any specific recommendations involving the use of computers); Patrick E. Haggerty, President of Texas Instruments; Edwin H. Land, President of the Polaroid Corporation; and Philip Sporn, formerly President of the American Electric Power Company. Its Interagency Advisory Committee included the Secretaries of Defense, Commerce, Agriculture, Labor, Health, Education and Welfare, as well as Donald F. Hornig, one of President Johnson's Special Assistants and Director of the Office of Science and Technology, and Gardner Ackley, Chairman of the Council of Economic Advisers. It was a blue ribbon panel.

Throughout 1965, the Automation Commission held hearings and pursued its studies of the situation in the manner of Government fact-finding commissions. When it issued its Report,* in January, 1966, there was some newspaper comment to the effect that some of the Commission's members felt that the Report was too tame and lacked urgency. Moreover, its timing was bad. During the Commission's investigations, the unemployment rate had dropped from more than 5 per cent of the labor force to 4.1 per cent, the lowest point in almost nine years. If anything, a shortage of skilled manpower was looming. "This situation," commented the *Wall Street Journal*, "will rob the Report of some of the sense of urgency needed for any broad attack on the problems raised by automation."

In its opening pages the Report is indeed optimistic about the situation. It categorically rejects the basic premise of the Ad Hoc Committee Memorandum:

". . . According to one extreme view, the world—or at least the United States—is on the verge of a glut of productivity sufficient to make our economic institutions and the notion of gainful employment obsolete. We dissent from this view. We believe that the evidence does not support it, and that it diverts attention from the real problems of our country and the world. . . .

"Our study of the evidence has impressed us with the inadequacy of the basis for any sweeping pronouncements about the speed of technological progress. . . .

"There appears to be no direct method of measuring the rate of technological change through the number of significant innovations or their economic effects. Therefore, indirect measures must do. The most useful appear to be indexes of productivity and productivity growth, particularly output per man-hour. . . ."

After conceding that output per man-hour has its limitations, the Report cites the trend rate of the rise in output per man-hour: from 1910 to 1945 it increased at the average rate of 2 per cent per year.

* See Appendix 2.

55

Since 1945, the average rate has been 2.5 per cent a year—hardly indicative of a millennium.*

This happy analysis is challenged immediately in a dissenting footnote by five of the Commission's members, led by Walter Reuther: ". . . in our opinion, the report lacks the tone of urgency which we believe its subject matter requires and which its recommendations reflect." The footnote goes on to point to "the more than 50 per cent increase in the trend rate of productivity advance in the post-World War II period compared to the prewar period . . . ," and mentioned the prospective increase in the rate of growth in the labor force which the wartime "baby-boom" would effect.

There is certainly some validity in this view. The Report stands as an earnest but almost complacent defense of the tried-and-true. While cheerfully confessing its inability to evaluate meaningfully the future effects of technological change, it does not hesitate to maintain that the change can be managed by existing agencies and policies and their extensions. Moreover, the Automation Commission does not even consider the basic question that automation poses: if automation is so profitable, will there not be a tendency to invest in more automation rather than in job-creating, "human-powered" activities?

The nearest that the Report comes to considering this is probably in the course of a capsule account of the economic verities that the Automation Commission holds to be valid for the near future.

"As productivity rises, less labor is required per dollar of national product, or more goods and services can be produced with the same number of man-hours. If [total] output does not [then] grow, employment will certainly fall." Then the Report makes its crucial point. "If production [or output] increases more rapidly than productivity . . . , employment must rise." (Now here the question of automation might have been introduced. It could have been described in a number of forms, and whatever the form, it would of necessity have discarded the traditional concepts of "labor" and "employment" as entirely human activities.)

"It is the continuous obligation of economic policy to match increases in productive potential with increases in purchasing power and demand. Otherwise, the potential created by technical progress runs to waste in idle capacity, unemployment, and deprivation.

"We believe that the general level of employment must be distinguished from the displacement of particular workers at particular times and places if the relationship between technological change and

---

* For an interesting example of "statisticsmanship," compare this statement, based on a 20-year average, with the Ad Hoc Committee Memorandum's statistic on productivity per man-hour on page 196, which is based on the experience of the past *five* years.

unemployment is to be clearly understood . . . the basic fact is that technology eliminates jobs, not work."

The argument, in this case, again appears to be based on the concept of "work" and "employment" as human and only human control functions. One gets a picture of a group of men operating an assortment of machines. Let us say that one man operates a "cutting machine" and another operates a "driller." Together they turn out 100 parts an hour. A new machine is installed that cuts and drills in one operation, turning out 150 parts an hour. One man has to be trained to operate it. And the other? Well, perhaps he can be transferred to the sales department, or perhaps it would be feasible to purchase *two* of the new machines. But nothing is said of the possibility that a machine be devised to cut and drill with no operator at all.

Having delivered itself of this confident analysis of the recent past, the Report turns to projections of the future. Here it is less sanguine: ". . . the output of the economy—and the aggregate demand to buy it—must grow in excess of 4 percent a year just to prevent the unemployment rate from rising, and even faster if the employment rate is to fall further, as we believe it should. Yet our economy has seldom, if ever, grown at a rate faster than 3.5 percent for any extended length of time." And after considering the available statistics on the rate of job displacement, it comes to this conclusion:

"If all occupations have the same composition by age in 1975 as in 1964, opportunities for younger workers . . . will be substantially fewer than the number in this age group seeking work. The unsatisfactory current relation of youth unemployment to total unemployment will worsen unless utilization patterns change." Now come the recommendations:

"Constant displacement [of workers] is the price of a dynamic economy," says the Commission. "History suggests that it is a price worth paying. . . .

"Our analysis of the economic impact of technological change suggests the following organization of our recommendations for facilitating adjustment to change.

"1. For those with reasonably attractive skills and no other serious competitive handicaps, ample job opportunities and adequate incomes can be assured by management of the total demand for goods and services.

"2. For those less able to compete in the labor market, productive employment opportunities adapted to their abilities should be publicly provided.

"3. Under the best of circumstances, there will be some who cannot or should not participate in the job economy. For them, we believe there should be an adequate system of income maintenance, guaranteeing a floor of income at an acceptable level."

In considering the first recommendation in detail—the management of total demand—the tone of the Report is cautious, and even vague, even though the consensus of the Automation Commission is that this is the most important recommendation of the three. There appears to be the usual difficulty in reconciling the goals of full production and employment with the desire to avoid inflation. All that could be said is that to tolerate unnecessary unemployment is a costly way to police inflation. The Commission then comes out in favor of some form of tax reduction to stimulate private spending, and increased expenditures in the public sector for what have become the conventional worthy causes: education, health, transportation, pollution control and development of natural resources. The real purpose of programs in these areas is to fulfill the goals of the second recommendation—i.e., to provide employment for the dullards and incompetents which a computerized private economy can no longer accommodate. If this conclusion seems harsh, compare it with the words of the Report itself:

". . . New Deal public works programs provided sorely needed employment and created valuable facilities during a period of mass unemployment. The new [proposed] programs are different; they are aimed specifically at those left behind in an otherwise prosperous economy. They recognize the anomaly of excessive unemployment in a society confronted with a huge backlog of public service needs in its parks, its streets, its slums, its countryside, its schools and colleges, its libraries, its hospitals, its rest homes, its public buildings, and throughout the public and nonprofit sectors of the economy. They recognize that employing the unemployed is, in an important sense, almost costless. The unemployed consume; they do not produce. To provide them meaningful jobs increases not only their income but that of society. Much of the work that needs doing calls only for limited skills and minor amounts of training. Some of it is manual in character; some of it is subprofessional."

The Commission's recommendation for the third group, the "unemployables," received more publicity than anything else in the Report. It describes a system of federally supported relief payments to all those with incomes below a minimum for adequate subsistence. It would attempt to soften the ego-destroying effects generally associated with doles, partly through payments sufficient to a consumption level that would allow the recipients to blend into the general population, superficially at least, and partly through semantic devices that our society finds so useful and satisfying. In this case the device would consist of calling the relief program a "negative income tax" program. The Report explains: ". . . A minimum income allowance would

58

complete the symmetry of our tax system, under which tax payments are related to income, family size, medical, and other costs, by acknowledging the continuity beyond zero tax rates. It seems anomalous to us that a family of five now pays the same tax—zero—whether its total income is $500 or $3,500."

The resemblance of the Automation Commission's income maintenance plan to that of the Ad Hoc Committee is somewhat disconcerting. The resemblance of its second recommendation, for a public works program to provide employment, is equally remarkable. From two sets of assumptions almost diametrically opposed, and two different sets of selected statistics, the two parties arrive at pretty much the same conclusions. Considering the ideological spread of the two groups, one finds this remarkable, and all the more so since, in addition to agreeing on solutions for the problem, they agree almost equally that present knowledge about the problem itself is inadequate.

The Ad Hoc Committee, for example, confesses that it is "not able to predict the long-run patterns of human activity and commitment in a nation when fewer and fewer people are involved in production of goods and services." This candor is matched, perhaps more obliquely, by the Automation Commission Report. The Report begins with the assumptions that "technological change will not be a significant factor in determining the total number of jobs available," and that "if unemployment does creep up in the future it will be the fault of public policy, not of technological change."

The basis for the latter statement, according to the Report, is a Bureau of Labor Statistics projection of manpower requirements for 1975, supplemented by projections of likely progress in some of the new technologies by experts in those areas. But the Report also noted that there "appears to be no direct method of measuring the economic effects of this progress, although output per man-hour could serve as a reliable measure."

The Bureau of Labor Statistics itself is less confident on this point. In a statement in *The New York Times* on January 30, 1966, Arthur Ross, the Bureau's head, is candid about the inadequacy of present data on employment: "We have good national data," he says, "but our sample is just too small to tell us much about regions, even in a city as big as New York." This consciousness of inadequate data is widespread. Thomas J. Watson, speaking to the Special Committee on Automation of the American Bankers Association in March, 1965, calls attention to it:

"Every one of you, I am certain, has confronted the wide—and in some instances, appalling—divergence in expert opinion on the man-machine relationship. One group of experts numbers the jobs destroyed by machines in the millions. Another pooh-poohs this conclusion, arguing that many of the industries which have the most have expanded their employment the most. One group reports that hundreds of thousands of manufacturing jobs are lost every year because of the improvements in productivity, implying that machines are to blame. Another group says that productivity has increased all right, but because of such things as reorganization and better planning . . . machines [have not increased] . . .

"I believe that [these differences of opinion] demonstrate that we need a far more searching and rigorous analysis of the facts and the problems than we yet have." Watson goes on to allude hopefully to the then forthcoming Automation Commission Report as a possible agent of this needed analysis.

Louis Davis, Professor of Industrial Engineering, of the University of California's Human Factors in Technology Research Group, describes in more detail the whole problem of measuring the effect of technological change on employment patterns. At the North American Joint Conference on the Requirements of Automated Jobs, a convocation organized by the Organization for Economic Cooperation and Development (the civilian counterpart of NATO), in December, 1964, Davis has some harsh words for labor statistics, and labor statisticians:

"I find it rather late in the day, given the manpower problems related to automation confronting our society, to engage in and perpetuate general studies of historical data. This may be a narrow view but it is being taken very deliberately.

"In the company of the well known historians* [for this is how we must view labor statisticians] who have presented papers in this session, an analyst finds himself in an uneasy position with respect to the presentations. . . . Perhaps this uneasiness is imbedded in the essential difference between historians and analysts, the former interested in forecasting from trends representing the past and the latter interested in developing predictive instruments which can be tested and updated. . . .

"It is most important to emphasize that there is very little information available that is unequivocal. There is also no analytic base upon which public policy can be based which is addressed to the future rather than the past."

Davis then lists some of the objectives of a study of how automation affects employment. As we might expect, the prime objective is

---

* These included, among others, Leon Greenberg, Asst. Commissioner for Productivity and Technological Developments, Bureau of Labor Statistics, U.S. Dept. of Labor; Dr. Seymour J. Wolfbein, Director, Office of Manpower, Automation and Training, U.S. Dept. of Labor; and Dr. Ewan Clagne, Commissioner of Labor Statistics, U.S. Dept. of Labor.

to identify the extent and the rate of the application of automation to jobs in various areas of the economy. (The remainder deals with costs, efficiency, manpower needs, and educational needs, all dependent on the success of the first objective.) Lewis emphatically states that little or nothing has been done toward attaining these objectives.

What, indeed, are we to make of all this? We began by sampling two sets of what amounted to individual opinions of the implications of automation and the computer revolution, each containing more than a suspicion of individual prejudice and self-interest. Then we explored some of the intellectual and statistical foundations of these sets of opinions, and found them largely wanting, except in their opposition to each other. And now, the conclusions derived from them appear to be identical, in a practical sense at least.

It might be argued that they appear only at first glance to be identical—that the resemblance is superficial. The Ad Hoc Committee's program may be based on the assumption that unemployment will reach unheard of levels, as high as 90 per cent perhaps, whereas the Automation Commission is thinking in terms of a maximum level of 8 per cent or possibly 10 per cent.

A closer examination of their programs does not indicate any such variance, however. The Ad Hoc Committee's recommendations are too general to examine at length, but as far as they go they call for the creation, by government policies, of about 500,000 jobs a year—not exactly a millennial figure. As for the Commission Report, in its proposal for a program of public service employment, the same figure is mentioned, although it is not clear whether this rate of job formation would be maintained indefinitely. The Report also describes an estimated 5,300,000 new public service jobs that could be created to fill existing needs, but again it is not clear whether this is a yearly estimate.

Quite beyond this, and beyond the three recommendations that we have examined, the Report describes a vast program of somewhat longer range measures—policies to increase the efficiency of the economy and to reduce the burden of frictional unemployment and displacement. In view of the Commission's economic position, which the Report summed up once more as "fiscal policy calculated to provide at all times brisk demand for labor," these addenda might be considered as mere verbal expedients—concessions, perhaps, to the more liberal members of the group—or even as trial balloons to encourage public discussion. If so, it is to be noted that they were extraordinarily detailed and well thought out.

On the contrary, they might be considered entirely serious. If so, their scope alone tends to cast some doubts on the Report's optimistic prognoses for the economy, for they envision some enormous changes in the whole socioeconomic structure. They range every bit as far as anything the Ad Hoc Committee contemplated, and they have the added authority of the Commission's access to the citadels of political and economic power. These are the deliberations of princes, not philosophers.

This part of the Report first considers policies of education and training:

"High quality compensatory education should be [made] available to every child whose life opportunities would be improved by it. . . . The Economic Opportunity Act and the Elementary and Secondary Education Acts are a beginning.

". . . High school graduation should become universal. . . . To accomplish this, both the problems of motivation and family income must be faced realistically. . . . The task is neither easy nor cheap. . . .

". . . For most secondary school pupils, vocational training should be deferred until after high school. . . . A nationwide system of free public education through two years beyond high school (grade 14) should be established . . . [to] provide training in trade, technical, and business occupations at the skilled worker level . . .

". . . All qualified students should have realistic access to university education . . . support for both tuition and maintenance . . . should be available through scholarships, loans, and work.

". . . Education, training, and retraining should be available to individuals throughout their lives."

The Report gives considerable attention to this last point. It notes, for example, that in some States unemployed workers cannot receive job training while drawing unemployment compensation. It recommends that such laws be changed, and that such workers receive not only full unemployment compensation, but also incentive payments over and above it.

In discussing on-the-job training (by private industry) the Report notes that: "Great Britain recently passed the Industrial Training Act which imposes a training tax on all employers that is rebated to those who establish approved training programs. Small employers may pool their training efforts in order to obtain the rebate. . . ." And finally, the Report has something to say regarding one of the favorite dreams of computer people:

". . . It has been far too common in the tradition of mass free education to ascribe inadequacies to the individual student rather than to adapt educational techniques to meet the needs or to overcome the limitations of individuals. . . . The task of expanding educational opportunity must also focus on adjusting the system to meet the needs of those who cannot make effective use of existing educational methods. A considerable amount of experimentation and research in applying computer and information technologies to educational problems is under way. . . . The new technologies can also relieve teachers of mechanical and administrative chores . . . [and] are also being applied to keeping curriculums up to date in a wide variety of subject matter areas." The problem of matching men and jobs is then considered:

"The first requirement for an orderly labor market and satisfactory adjustment to change is adequate information. . . . [but] The job seeker, whether unemployed or seeking better employment, has little information available concerning alternative job openings.

". . . those who want to improve their standing in the labor market can make reasonably appropriate decisions only if they have information, not only about present opportunities but about the future outlook for alternative occupations. . . . But there is simply no place in any local labor market, let alone on a regional or national basis, where individual job seekers or employers can discover the full range of possible jobs or employees available. . . .

". . . To give job seekers and employers access to specific job openings and specific employees, the Commission recommends that a *computerized* nationwide service for matching men to jobs be established." Visionary? Not in the least. The Report spells it out.

"The technical feasibility of such a system has been established in studies sponsored by the Commission. With local centers feeding into regional centers information relevant at that level, and these in turn feeding into a nationwide job and manpower bank, the service could provide detailed information on the manpower requirements of job vacancies and the personal characteristics of job seekers. The technological knowledge is available for the development of the equipment and the costs are within reason. Problems relating to the most effective methods of coding and similar problems remain to be worked out, but these can be solved if the commitment is made to develop the system."

The Report discusses this scheme in considerable detail. It tends to favor the creation of a nonprofit corporation with joint public and private ownership to handle the system. In a footnote, some members of the Commission urge that, by Executive order, "all Government procurement contracts would require the contractors to list with the public employment service all job openings. . . . Other measures to encourage comprehensive job listings suggest: legislation to deny to recalcitrant employers experience-rating tax benefits under the unemployment insurance laws, and "a new Federal standard . . . for State unemployment insurance laws which would prevent the states from requiring claimants to make an independent search for work in addition to registering. . . ."

Aside from this footnote, however, voluntary compliance is emphasized:

"Every employer could, if he wished, have in his own establishment

63

a terminal* giving access to information concerning the detailed characteristics of all job seekers. Employers could themselves choose whom to interview. . . . The job seeker would participate in the system either directly or through his own chosen representative—the public employment service, a private employment agency, . . . a labor union, or some other agency which, through its own terminal, would have access to the requirements of prospective employers. Either employer or employee could place any desired restriction upon use of the information supplied, and appropriate safeguards could be established to guard against invasion of privacy. . . ."

The recommendations that follow the description of a computerized employment system are somewhat less spectacular, but equally far-reaching. One calls for the establishment of "focal points" in each community ". . . where national trends and information from local businessmen, public officials, universities, and other sources can be translated into 1 to 10 year forecasts of likely local and regional manpower and employment developments. Not only employees and employers but those concerned with counseling and guidance, educational and urban planning, and economic development would be assisted by such guides to future prospects." Though not mentioned in this recommendation, the computer is implicit. Computer expert Isaac Auerbach, in his testimony to the Senate Subcommittee on Employment and Manpower (1963),† describes the role of the computer in just such an information system as this recommendation describes. He calls it an "early-warning employment-prediction system":

"It is possible to build a mathematical model of a situation and manipulate this model inside a large data-processing system to see the effect caused by changing various factors affecting the situation. This is called "gaming" or "simulation" and it is used to make predictions about highly complex situations. The military uses gaming to test and develop strategies. In fact, gaming techniques are the basis of Project OMEGA, a computer model used by the Air Force to make strategic, tactical, and procurement decisions. This technique is also being used in meteorology and in industry to solve complex engineering problems.

"It is my belief that it is possible to develop an early-warning employment-prediction system based on 'gaming' techniques. Such a system would be invaluable for identifying specific needs for education and retraining. The prediction model must include geographic and skill details to enable the Government to predict accurately the areas in which trouble is developing and the action that would be

* A direct link to the central computer system.
† See Chapter 3.

most appropriate for the particular situation. Much of the data required to structure such a model is already available within the Department of Commerce.

"As an initial test of an employment-prediction game, it is possible to structure a model of a small geographic area, preferably one that is geographically self-contained. The model would have in it representations of: the total number of people in the area; the total number of employable people; the kinds of skills that the employable people possess and the level of the capabilities; any peripheral skills that the individuals may have or are being trained in; the distribution of the employed people among the various companies, government agencies, and educational institutions; the backlog of work forecast by business classification; and—rather than bore you with the details—all of the data pertaining to the total economic employment situation within the area being modeled. Using this model, it would be possible to conduct 'games' to predict the effects upon employment of various business and government actions, and to test various strategies, e.g., introducing new industries into the area, initiating special training programs, etc., formulated to increase employment in the area.

"I assure you, this type of employment-prediction system is feasible, if it is approached in the proper manner and developed in small stages that permit us to solve the technical problems that will be involved before trying to do it on a large scale. There is no denying the fact that it is much easier to rectify a declining employment situation early in its decline than it is to resolve the problem once it has reached the disaster stage. An early-warning employment-prediction system that could enable us to react long before the disaster stage would be an invaluable economic tool."

The Senate Subcommittee itself, in its final Report, also considers the implications of this kind of system:

". . . the possibilities for applying computer technology to manpower research and policy making should be examined. Testimony extolling the versatility, speed, and capacity of modern data processing equipment and computers was impressive. Is the 'information revolution' being applied to manpower research? Can the very devices which are playing an important role in present changes in manpower requirements contribute to the solution of manpower problems by adding to the accessibility and analysis of manpower data?" Such a system need not, and would not, be limited to considerations of employment and manpower allocation, of course. Similar modeling techniques are already in general use in industry for resources and financial planning over 10, and in some cases, even 20 year periods.

One of the Automation Commission Report's subsequent recommendations, relating to regional planning and development, also implies a computerized planning system. In outlining the advantages of a program to stimulate regional economies via the Federal Reserve System, the Report proposes that:

". . . Each Federal Reserve bank should establish a regular program of regional economic analysis as a means of continually evaluating the problems and opportunities facing the region, . . . [and should] establish an "advisory council for economic growth" composed of leaders from business, labor, government, the universities and other interested groups. . . . The council's activities should include the identification and interpretation of *all factors* [author's italics] affecting or likely to affect the *economic well-being* [author's italics] of the district. On the basis of this analysis the council should prepare comprehensive program and policy recommendations directed at both public and private institutions within the district. . . ." It then describes a proposal to establish capital banks in each district which would "provide venture capital and long-term financing for new and existing companies," a program that the celebrated Rockefeller Panel Report also recommended in 1958.

". . . Regional technical institutes should be established within each region to keep abreast of new technological developments . . . [and to] assist new and existing firms to take maximum advantage of the opportunities offered by technological advance[s]." Finally, the Report wraps up the whole package with this proposal:

". . . A high-level Federal executive . . . within each region to coordinate the efforts of various existing Federal programs at the regional level . . . [who] could also serve as a focal point for Federal contacts with State and local programs."

There is a lot more to this Report. Sections deal extensively with the special problems of minority groups and the aged. There is considerable discussion of the role that private organizations, prodded and policed directly and indirectly by the Federal Government, should play in making the great adjustment, and of a variety of specific recommendations, if rather limited and small-scale, to define and implement that role. These recommendations, however, only supplement and round out the broader recommendations described here.

Beyond this, the Report launches into a long and high-flying consideration of the long-range aspirations of humanity. Perhaps the Automation Commission feels that it is entitled to this essentially spiritual exercise after so much diligent spadework in the here and now. This is not to denigrate their visions, which are nothing less than inspired. But they are not accompanied by any detailed plans and in any case their relevance depends largely on the operation of the plans that we have already examined.

The last section of the Report (exclusive of the Summary) returns to the real world, although on a somewhat theoretical level. It begins on a marvelously plaintive note, which, given the membership of the Commission, ought to make the angels weep:

"Given our technological capability and our relatively abundant resources, why have we not been more successful in meeting our human and community needs?" This is a big question.

In attempting to answer it the Commission again pays tribute to the principles of both the free market and public spending.

"We do not question the validity of these economic and political mechanisms in allowing for the greatest variety of free choice for the consumer and the democratic participation by the voters. We feel, however, that in the 'accounting systems' which guide such choices there are various inadequacies, that local governmental units are not drawn along the functional lines necessary to meet modern needs, and that decisions are made piecemeal, often without regard to context or to the effect on other decisions. This is why, so often, there are unintended consequences of social actions." And to remedy this? The Commission proposes that "the Government explore the creation of a 'system of social accounts' which would indicate the social benefits and social costs of investment and services and thus reflect the true costs of a product."

The discussion that follows is essentially concerned with that perennial preoccupation of the computer age: information—data, the need for collecting it, processing it, and using it creatively.

". . . we do not have, as yet, a continuous charting of social changes, and we have been ill-prepared (in such matters as housing, education, or the status of the Negro) to determine our needs, establish goals, and measure our performance. Lacking any systematic assessment, we have few criteria which allow us to test the effectiveness of present policies or to weigh alternatives regarding future programs."

Then, referring to the development of national economic accounting systems and to the collection of data on national income, it points out that "in effect, the Government's decision about the type of data to be collected shaped in considerable measure the subsequent direction of economic theory and practice."

But economic data tell only part of the story, and in particular are insufficient for "effective policy" decisions in response to the new "social problems."

". . . The need for this kind of [social] data is urgent. And just as the development of economic accounts influenced a new body of theory, the collection of new social data could influence decisively the development of social science for the next generation."

After conceding the difficulty of defining social relationships in the kind of measurable terms necessary for accounting, the Report outlines the objectives of such a system. The first is the "measurement of social costs and net returns of economic innovations." In reference to this, it is pointed out that the present system of "national economic accounting does not directly assign the costs generated by one group which are borne by others." It cited, as an example, the costs to the community of strip mining, and the air and water pollution which derives from industrial operations. "The problem is not only one of social costs unfairly generated and widely borne, but the broader cost matrix which would allow us to balance gains against costs." The same points are made in reference to the second objective, "the measurement of social ills" that affect the economy, such as crime, illness, juvenile delinquency, and family disruption.

Then the Report dips into the starry future again and describes the third objective, the "creation of 'performance budgets' in areas of defined social needs" such as housing and education.

"The American commitment is not only to raise the standard of living, but to improve the quality of life. But we have too few 'yardsticks' to tell us how we are doing. A system of social accounts would seek to set up 'performance budgets' in various areas to serve as such yardsticks. A series of community health indexes would tell us how well we are meeting the needs of our people in regard to adequate medical care. A national 'housing budget' would reflect our standing in regard to the goal of a 'decent home for every American family.' It would also enable us to locate by city and region the areas of greatest needs and so provide the basis for effective public policy."

The last requirement was for "indicators of economic opportunity and social mobility," which are described as:

". . . Data on social mobility [which] can measure the extension of equality of opportunity and identify the barriers (e.g., inadequate school opportunities) to that equality. Economists have a term, 'opportunity costs' which allows us to calculate not only direct costs, but the gains foregone from the use of those resources if they had been employed elsewhere. 'Social opportunity costs' may allow us to reckon the possible gains in the utilization of unused human resources, and to weigh, in terms of social costs and social benefits, alternative social policies."

The Automation Commission's Report marks the end of one phase of the computer revolution and the beginning of another. From this time on it could no longer be maintained that the Federal Government at its highest levels was either unaware of the implications of the computer revolution or inclined to take a neutral position in the controversies that the revolution had engendered.

But beyond this, what does the Report itself add up to? As noted, it seems to consist of two distinct and conflicting statements: first, it insists that automation is nothing to get excited about, and, second, it calls for some solutions, which, in regard to the first statement, seem drastic. This, and the marked resemblance of these solutions to those outlined by the admittedly more radical Ad Hoc Committee, are certainly something to ponder. Its real import is foretold in John Kenneth Galbraith's *The Affluent Society*:

"It still seems more satisfactory to say that we need [production] than to stress the real point which is that social well-being and contentment require that we have enough production to provide income to the willing labor force. But if anyone has any doubts as to where the real priorities lie, let him apply a simple test. Let him assume that a President, or other candidate for re-election to major public office, has the opportunity of defending a large increase in man-hour productivity which has been divided equally between greatly increased total output and greatly increased unemployment. And let it be assumed that as an alternative he might choose unchanged productivity which has left everyone employed. That full employment is more desirable than increased production combined with unemployment would be clear alike to the most sophisticated and the most primitive politician."

Although written in 1958, this is perhaps the real message of the Automation Commission Report, and the one sure indication of what may be expected in the future. The national goal is continued full employment, and, one is tempted to say, little more. Whatever social and economic policies are put into effect in the near future will be measured against that goal.

And so the question is not, "Will automation lead to widespread unemployment?" but, "How extensive will be the social and economic measures to prevent widespread unemployment?" This question, far from dismissing computers and computer systems from the picture, leads us directly back to them, although by a different route. Another message in both the Ad Hoc Committee Memorandum and the Automation Commission Report, another point on which the two documents are in full agreement, is what we can charitably call their lack of data about the causes and effects of the situation with which they are concerned. This ignorance has also been conceded, as noted, by industry spokesmen, the Senate Subcommittee on Employment and Manpower, and, on occasion, even by spokesmen of the Administration. It is usually expressed as a lack of reliable and *detailed* statistics concerning the actual, as opposed to the assumed, performance of the economy.

Statistics, either as a lack, or a need, have never fired the imagination or stirred the spirit. They are, at best, usually seen as embroideries or embellishments to more substantial creations of the fancy or the intellect. Computers, however, appear to see them somewhat differently. At any rate, computers, both as agents of socioeconomic change, and as instruments for responding to these changes, seem to have endowed statistics with an unwonted importance. They have also made the whole process of collecting information take on an aura—or a sanctity—that is presently almost beyond comprehension.

The computer people come closest to understanding this. Others, to be sure, allude to the general state of ignorance regarding the drift of events. But it is hard to ignore the air of complacency about most of these allusions. When such men as Thomas J. Watson or Isaac Auerbach take note of the same phenomenon, one detects a more urgent conviction. They are less interested in noting the non-existence of such and such a category of economic or social data than in insisting that, before any momentous conclusions are drawn in the absence of such data, extensive steps be taken to acquire it. This is a harsh fact for social and economic thinkers to face. It goes against a tradition, which for all its scientific pretensions, has always accorded the palm of intellectual accomplishment to the fellow who could draw the grandest conclusions from the most meager sources of information. It is difficult, therefore, to believe that the computer has once and for all made this tradition obsolete.

The future, however, will soon prove this. All of us—optimists and pessimists, radicals and conservatives alike—are about to learn that there is more to the story. The computer is not just the disrupter of an established order or the complacent handmaiden of a nicer one. It is also a prophet come to reveal us to ourselves. The revelation itself will be our response to our problems. Before taking the steps outlined by distinguished panels, we must launch a mammoth effort to acquire self-knowledge. Computers will play a significant part in this effort.

What is not sure, however, is how this effort will affect us. We see our Promised Land from across a wide river; how we will cross it, and what condition we will be in when we do, is perhaps a more interesting question than what is on the other side.

PART II

After Automation

5
.

The Further Development of Computer Systems as Socioeconomic Control Devices

Large and highly sophisticated computer systems are now a technical and financial reality. Business systems, examples of which we encountered in Chapter 2, are widespread and well developed enough to indicate a success greater than that expected. The operations of these systems have convinced both optimists and pessimists that as they become the major vehicle of communication and control in an explosively developing society, they can bring about fundamental changes in the structure, content, and distribution of jobs, and possibly in the nature of employment itself.

This patent statement was neither demonstrated nor considered seriously 10 years ago. The inevitable condition described has since become so manifest as to prompt the attention of serious tycoons and orthodox-minded public servants. In spite of their obvious attachment to the best of all possible worlds, these persons have reassessed some of their most cherished principles and beliefs. Board chairmen and bureaucrats alike have been moved to advocate measures of social and economic novelty that rival, if not surpass, the pronouncements of the most doctrinaire liberal theorists. Their conclusions, moreover, have been ratified by most practicing politicians of both parties. In a decade of exposure to one set of implications of the computer revolution, the shrill accents of the lunatic fringe have become the mellow tones of reason.

But this change in attitude is in reference to only one sector of the economy—production and employment. Even here the consensus is only on what to do about the new situation, not on what brought it about.

In view of this, some of us may still be content to rely on the theory of the "computer as merely a tool" to maintain that the massive realignment of social and economic forces now being forecast is a product of many factors, among which computer systems are only one—only the latest expression of the by now traditional force of technological change, itself only one expression of the age-old unfolding of the human spirit, etc. This is the attitude particularly of professional humanists who are reluctant to concede that any mere machine can play such a decisive role in human affairs.

But this only begs the question. Computers are not, of course, alone in the world. What can be accomplished with them *does* depend greatly on how we use them. (If, let us say, the computer revolution had occurred in Nazi Germany in the thirties, the use of computer systems would have differed from that in the United States of the sixties.)

Many similar statements can be made in an effort to move the discussion back to familiar surroundings. But the familiar leads nowhere. The unfamiliar world of the computer is as disconcerting as ever, like that of nuclear power.

One can also follow the lead of some of the more cloistered computer scientists and go too far in the other direction, reasoning that because such and such a computer technique is technically feasible, it must inevitably impose itself on our socioeconomic scene. An example of this is the repeatedly offered vision of a great computer utility to consumers. We are asked to imagine an enormous library of facts and problem-solving routines run by a vast computer system to which we will all be linked via remote terminals. To "help the kids with their homework," "figure out our income taxes," and even "plan the most economical and tasty meals," we will, so the visions go, have only to contact the computer and request the services of the machine, paying only a small monthly service charge in return. These and similar prophecies so ignore the basic economic realities of our present society that it is with difficulty that we can concede the otherwise obvious good faith in which they are offered. At best they recall the visions of the early aviation enthusiasts who foresaw, instead of the present air transport system, the day when the airplane would replace the automobile as a means of personal transportation for every man.

The truth must lie between these views, the one maintaining that the computer will merely improve a familiar world, and the other that it is an unlimited resource for recasting the world nearer to our heart's desire. Computers will not only further the prevailing socioeconomic trends, but will also modulate them to a far greater degree than most of us now believe possible. This truth still needs to be demonstrated. To do so, we must make several assumptions, based on observations of the computer's impact on this single area of our lives—jobs and employment.

74

The first assumption goes something like this: Computers must be seen as more than just another technological innovation. Since they have played a major role in changing the environment of unemployment, computer systems must be unique and revolutionary beyond their obvious technical characteristics (e.g., their speed and reliability). Otherwise, it would be difficult to account for the fact that in the mid-fifties, when full employment was of great concern, the computer's effect on employment was not anticipated with any great assurance. In fact, even after almost 10 years of experience with automation, the experts still wrangle and the public still remains bemused.

The second assumption is that even at the level of its technical operations, the computer can invalidate many of the traditional and habitual human responses to the environment. The manner in which the introduction of computer systems forces changes in the structure and procedures of the human organizations that they are designed to serve has been so widely noted as to be a commonplace. Their presence puts hitherto unattainable goals within casual reach—and even sometimes makes them no longer worth the candle. It goes on, in many cases, to replace these goals with new ones, many of which were not even foreseen when the systems themselves were installed. This is not only true at the operational level. In a larger frame of reference computer systems appear to have had the same effect. In ten years of desultory computer system operations, for example, the guaranteed annual income has somehow changed from a utopian dream to a possibility worthy of the serious consideration of reasonable men. And this has occurred without that concept being seriously advocated or supported by any appreciable segment of the population, by any significant political efforts, or by any help from the mass media.

The third assumption, less spectacular than the first two, may be the most useful. Judging from the experience of the automation-employment problem, computers tend strongly to take a hand in their own further development and extension. Computer-caused problems are met with computer-based solutions. These solutions then lead either to new computer-based problems, or to further opportunities for the employment of still more computers.

One of the most striking examples of this phenomenon is the "early-warning employment-prediction system" proposed to the Senate Subcommittee on Employment and Manpower by Isaac Auerbach, which was described in Chapter 4. This computer-based solution was proposed in response to the problem of job dislocations caused by automation. It amounted to a program of regional economic analysis directed toward pinpointing impending automation requirements in time to prepare for the unemployment they would cause. This was its primary purpose.

Once undertaken, however, this kind of analysis would be useful for many other purposes. It would create a new range of opportunities for other kinds of economic planning. These opportunities, it is safe to assume, would lead to still more computer applications. Thus a chain reaction begins.

As we have seen from the Automation Commission Report itself, this tendency of computers to lead to the use of more computers is widespread—a specific example being the Report's proposal for an automated job-skill bank as a solution to automation-caused unemployment. Another example—not as concrete—is to use computers to teach people the new skills that the computer revolution demands. Another is for management computer systems to cope with the increased complexity and speed of production and service operations brought about by computers and automation. Still another example is to use computers to exploit the information by-products of routine computer operations, a subject that is examined in more detail later.

At first glance all this may seem fortuitous. The introduction of computer and automation creates in its turn certain problems (or opportunities) to which a response must be made. Happily, a further application of the agent that created the situation offers a solution to it. This seems to be the conventional viewpoint of the situation. Computers are thus conceded to have made an impact on a socioeconomic structure. Whereas this was initially shocking, the structure has enough "give" built into it to absorb it, and will remain essentially the same as before, or at any rate the alterations will be imperceptible and possibly compensated for by entirely different shocks and pressures.

This view may be considered to be consistent with history and tradition, permitting the fond supposition that although the external circumstances of our lives do change, underneath the ancient verities remain.

But there is another way to look at this phenomenon. Suppose that instead of a socioeconomic *structure*, we are dealing with a process, a system, or a kind of fermentation. If we then see our socioeconomic system as the manifestation of a flow of intelligence—of transfers of information—a complexity of varying quantities and rates forming various channels, then the computer's alteration of even some of these ultimately changes everything. Established channels are overloaded, bypassed. New channels are formed. Each new application of computers leads to a stage of more extensive ones. Equilibrium never occurs. And the socioeconomic pattern itself is entirely and unintentionally transformed.

The course of our lives will depend on which view—the static or the dynamic—is closer to the truth. If the first view is, then all the more esoteric attributes of the computer are of only limited interest to us. It will take over some functions that it does demonstrably better than humans, becoming a sort of intellectual steam shovel or power loom, and we will find something better to do, preserving in the process our preferred modes of existence. Computer systems will become part of the landscape, like the telephone and automobile.

If the second view is the more accurate, then we are not faced merely with an automation-employment problem, or (anticipating a little) an invasion of privacy problem, but with an interlocking set of rapidly evolving situations in which computer systems will exert an unforeseen effect. The form of every social and economic development will be more than subtly determined by the manner in which computer systems are woven into them. It is not too much to say that the whole manner of our lives, the limits of the possible for each of us, will be subject to the continuous effects of the evolution of these machines.

Which view shall we accept? To answer this let us examine some expressions of the direction being taken by computer systems planners.

In several other broad areas apart from employment the introduction of computers has had a significant effect, and can elucidate the lines of computer development. Aside from the more specialized areas of national defense and space exploration, banking is the most extensively computerized area. For this reason alone it is a good place to start. Another reason is that bankers as a rule are exceptionally realistic and tough-minded. They are somewhat conservative in pursuing the new and untried—disinclined to tamper with the status quo for sentimental reasons alone. If the application of computers to banking is radically changing the banking environment, rather than simply improving it, then the second and dynamic view in question is to some extent confirmed, although not necessarily proved.

Computers first appeared in the banking industry as simple production tools. They replaced a number of clerks and speeded up routine operations—processing checks and the like. Also, banks had to hire new—and often highly paid—categories of people. The clerks were replaced by technicians as tellers and cashiers gave way to systems analysts and programmers, the names of customers gave way to account numbers. This first stage was essentially a reaction to changes brought about by a set of conditions antedating the computer.

The use of computers and automated data processing soon enabled banks to go beyond their own internal needs and offer novel computerized banking services to their customers, beginning with demand deposit accounting to correspondent banks and then proceeding to installment loan and savings accounting. This brought in more money in two ways—as fees for the services themselves, and in more bank deposits as demand for the computer service led more banks to become correspondents. Along with this, the automated banks drifted into payroll accounting—at first processing their own payrolls, then those of their correspondent banks, and, through these banks, those of the individual companies who were *their* customers. All this led to the creation of banking computer service departments engaged in selling computer processing to outside customers both within and without the banking industry itself.

This second stage also increased activity at the first stage of internal computer processing as it brought more and more depositors to the banks. When a company was signed up for payroll processing services, great efforts were also made to acquire that company's employees as depositors.

So the first stage of computerized banking was the mere automation of some housekeeping operations—a development not unlike the earlier changeover to, say, typewriters. As in such earlier developments, the process should have stabilized itself there. For example, in the nineties, a law firm that changed over from handwritten briefs to typewritten ones improved its operations somewhat. It needed fewer employees and produced more paper in less time, but did not find it expedient, therefore, to branch out into public stenography or publishing. But, in effect, the banks in the sixties did just this; internal efficiency improved to such a point as to become a commodity to be marketed—or, more properly, a service to be sold. And the process did not stop there—the customers for the computerized bank's new services also became depositors, which stimulated greater internal efficiency, which in turn allowed for the sale of still more services.

William J. Kenney, Jr., of the Bank of New York, explains the process:

"Generally, payroll accounting is offered on a fee basis with the charge based on the number of employees and the frequency of the payroll period. If, in addition to the estimated profit produced by the fee structure, the bank is able to add to its total account by opening checking accounts for each employee, the bank's earnings are enhanced by the float on balances maintained in these accounts. Moreover, it is able to expand sharply the total number of individuals with whom it maintains a regular contact, and should be able to utilize this broadened market area to solicit other business, such as consumer loans, savings accounts, or mortgage loans."

This happy circumstance surprised banking leaders. With the same equipment and personnel engaged in handling their banking operations, banks turned to processing their own payrolls as a minor side-

78

line—somewhat in the manner of a typist who types her personal correspondence on her lunch hour. This was so easy that they began to market it, with the profitable results described by Kenney.

Moreover, the rewards and opportunities of computer operations are further qualified by an important factor: increased speed. More money comes into the bank, but the bank's automated systems process it much more rapidly. In addition, other computer operations, although not directly linked to banking, speed up the flow of its customers' money. One of these is automated stock and inventory control in industry. While computers constantly check on inventories, there is a trend toward smaller and perhaps more frequent purchases of parts and materials, toward what is called a "short-order" economy. Money, consequently, circulates more rapidly. The bank has less time to "play" with it. This, of course, is both a problem and an opportunity for the bank's management. The response to it has been computer-based: an automated management information system—the second stage, or level, of computer operations.

At the 1965 National Automation Conference of the American Bankers Association, computer-based management systems were one of the principal areas of interest. This development was discussed in detail by Richard Le Kachman, an assistant vice-president of the National City Bank of New York. His immediate concern is "improved liquidity forecasting," i.e., forecasting the amount of cash at the bank's disposal. His significant remarks go far beyond his immediate subject. They illuminate one of the basic principles of computer systems, one that has a great bearing on how they develop and expand into new areas. We can call this second stage computer operations—the uses of *information about information*, as contrasted to information about things (or persons or events) which is the characteristic concern of primary level computer operations. Le Kachman says:

"Assume that deposit and loan accounting functions are either already, or soon will be, automated. The capture of relevant data for liquidity forecasting purposes can be achieved through the use of little more than additional computer output tapes and sorting routines, providing that master records for both deposit and loan data are properly designed. If the master records are properly designed to facilitate computer production of the by-product data, the accumulation of the desired information, comprehensive as it may be, will take but a fraction of the time currently devoted to performance of the routine accounting functions."

He says simply that as long as the major costs of gathering and processing information are covered by the system's primary level output, by-product data can be had at virtually no extra cost. As it stands, this is interesting but hardly of epochal significance. However,

79

it becomes so when you consider that the amount of by-product information that can be obtained in this way is virtually unlimited.

The appreciation of *this* is what the computer revolution is all about. Traditionally, most knowledge has been limited to information relating to *things*, to dealing with gods, or apples, or battles, or gravity. Only certain classes of scholars, logicians, literary critics and the like have been in a position to exploit the further possibilities of information itself. Lately in the scheme of things, they have been joined by more practical men, of whom the most representative are probably speculators in the stock market—and, of course, bankers. Like the logicians, they tend to deal not so much in facts for their own sake, but in the commodity that can be extracted from them.

Operating as they have been on the very frontiers of knowledge, it is not surprising that as a whole these people have had only indifferent success. Those who confine their attention to primary level information become saints and heroes; those who grapple with the secondary level are classed as pedants and visionaries. In a terse paragraph, Le Kachman, explains why. Although he is concerned only with his own profession, his remarks seem to apply to all branches of pure and applied intellectual efforts:

"Many analytical approaches considered in the past may well have been abandoned because problems associated with data collection, classification, computation, and analysis appeared to be too forbidding to be practically undertaken by manual means." Having summed up the past, he goes on with equal elegance to define the future of us all:

"With the advent of modern data processing systems that record, store, classify, calculate, compare and print at lightning speed in accordance with specific instructions prepared by human beings, former limitations on the use of data for analytical purposes have disappeared." This statement is twofold. It explains why the dynamic view of computer development is to be taken most seriously—suggesting that computer systems will of necessity grow and expand into every part of our society, affecting far more than just employment; and it describes how this will happen—by the removal of those limitations that have made planning on anything but the most limited scale an exercise for dreamers, and that have made intuition (sometimes called good judgment) the mark of the practical man.

Le Kachman illustrates this by sketching a whole range of possibilities for computer analyses of his clients' deposit and loan seeking behavior—all founded on the same basic data acquired in the course of the bank's primary level computer operations. He spoke of liquidity analyses by time series, by industry, by phases of the business cycle— all eminently profitable. Only a working banker can fully appreciate these, but in sum they provided the bank's management with a set of reliable indications of the future, indications that rather insist on specific courses of action. He states: "For instance, a projection revealing a sharp increase in the availability of funds for investment might lead to the consideration of the bank's investment in FHA or VA mortgages, or alternately, in substantially increasing the portfolio holding of municipal securities. Should the investment outlook not be encouraging, perhaps consideration might be given to a reduction in the rate offered on negotiable certificates of deposit, leading to a run-off of some of these funds."

Le Kachman does not speculate on the next stage. We can easily imagine it, however. Other banks would begin to employ the same kind of analyses; and, indeed, several similar ones were presented at the same conference. Each tended to begin with the same assumptions as Le Kachman's, i.e., a single bank analyzing raw data on the deposit and loan seeking behavior of its clients—certainly a reasonable course for employees of particular banks to pursue. It seems likely, however, that once a significant number of competing banks operate such analysis systems, and, consequently, begin to base policy decisions on them, the very pattern they are all analyzing would itself be altered. Random elements in deposit and loan seeking behavior would not be as random anymore. This would become evident to the managers of the various banks, to their customers, and, of course, to the Government as well. The FHA, for example, would be obliged to take an interest in the processes by which banks arrived at their policies regarding FHA mortgages once those policies were found to be based on the kind of analyses Le Kachman describes. To do this, the FHA, or some other Government economic planning agency, would make its own analyses—by computer—using data supplied by the private banking system. From here the trail would lead to the Federal Reserve Banks, to the Council of Economic Advisers, or to some economic research and planning body as yet unborn.

Thus we see a line of development from a computer solution for a specific problem—automated deposit and loan accounting—to a whole range of new banking opportunities. It appears to be a dynamic process, and banking will never be the same again.

Such developments as described here have led American bankers to talk of a nationwide banking computer system that would integrate all the expanding individual banking systems. This prospect has attracted the attention of such responsible banking leaders as John J. Clarke, Vice-President and General Counsel of the Federal Reserve Bank of New York. In a paper presented at the 1965 National Automation Conference of the American Bankers Association, Clarke cited some of the system's objectives: the storage of credit information and its dissemination to extenders of credit, and the instantaneous transfer of credit between banks in any part of the country. He examined the legal aspects of such a system, and concluded that it did not present any insurmountable legal problems.

Most of the attention, as one can judge from Clarke's remarks, was devoted to the system's primary level—it was seen as a massive computer-directed communication system along the lines of the well-known "bank wire." Unlike the bank wire, however, it has the same potential for analyzing data as Le Kachman's system—on a larger scale, of course. It would analyze banking behavior on a nationwide scale, which would alter the entire economy.

Does this superficial look at the applications of computer systems to banking prove anything? Obviously, it does not. But every computer-system application in banking seems to be only the embryo of a series of larger and more extensive systems. The proposed national banking computer system can also be expected to form links with the developing nationwide stock exchange system and to encounter some sort of computer system based on the Federal Reserve System, perhaps of the kind outlined in the Automation Commission Report. If there is some stage ahead where further system development and expansion in this area is not feasible or not practical we cannot glimpse it.

Similarly, it appears that the various airline reservation systems that were examined in Chapter 1 must of necessity link up into a nationwide system encompassing all air travel. This, in turn, will be a logical component of a "people and product moving system" whose outlines are now only vaguely perceived, but which is perhaps foreshadowed in the newly founded Federal Transportation Department.

Computer systems devoted to aspects of our lives other than banking and air travel will probably follow the same line of development, because it is axiomatic that any activity performed by many persons on a regular, or continuous, basis will be monitored by the managers of our socioeconomic system. The activity need not have any other significance than this. If enough people are doing it, it will become either a source of profit to some group or a problem to another.

This being the case, a computer system devoted to processing the data relating to that activity will be developed. Put another way, activity produces information, and information produces a computer system. But the computer system itself, as it records, processes, and stores all this source data, becomes a source of information. In many respects, it is a far richer source than the activity itself, since the data are already in machine-readable form. So it is also axiomatic that if an activity is of sufficient interest to warrant the use of a primary computer system, it will become at least equally profitable to develop a second-level system capability.

This is exactly what has happened to all third-generation computer systems (those that process data in real-time). Now each purely operational system can summarize and analyze the mass of operational data that it processes. This capability was added to the primary systems in many of the earlier systems, but as its value comes to be appreciated, a second-level capability tends to be built in from the beginning.

The most obvious use of the second-level capability is for management information. By having totals and rates of activity available, for instance, the managers of the system can obtain valuable insights into either the activity itself or their system's handling of certain features of it. We saw, as an example of this, how the American Airline's SABRE system informed its management about daily load factors (the ratio of paying passengers to seats available). This information has obvious value for the airline; when summarized, it indicates which routes are profitable and which are not, even though this is of scant concern to the system's primary users—the passengers and reservation clerks—who are interested only in placing a particular individual in a particular airplane at a particular time with the least possible fuss and bother.

The range of information of interest to any system's management is considerable—far greater than it would be for the individual primary users—but it is still limited. This interest alone would hardly lead to an unlimited expansion of the system. However, another potential level might be defined as the interests of those outside the system itself. As an example, in an airline reservation system, the potential users of the information that this third level of operation could supply might be the Civil Aeronautics Board, the Air Force, the Federal Aviation Agency, and perhaps the airline's sources of capital and equipment. These users would not, in general, require much primary information, but they would certainly be interested not only in the summaries and analyses that the airline's management would make for its own purposes, but also in additional summaries to their own specifications. And their interest would extend to all airlines.

To avail themselves of this information, these third-level users would have to "plug into the system." They must acquire their own hardware and software in order to make efficient use of the data routinely produced by the hitherto independent airlines reservation systems. One can imagine how this would be accomplished. The Federal agencies in question would impose certain software requirements on all reservation systems. All these systems would have to structure certain information in certain forms to make it accessible to retrieval by these agencies. In time, their specifications might even reach the system's primary level; for example, they might require that original reservation requests include information that is not essential to either the airline reservation clerks or the airline management, but that is of value to the third-level users.

Once these agencies regularly use the system's information, they would, in effect, be part of the system itself. Their needs, as well as those of the primary users and the system's managers, would have to be taken into account in any additions or alterations to the system. At the third level, the system's development is open-ended.

Given the prevailing socioeconomic climate, in which the Federal Government takes active responsibility for the optimum functioning of all phases of the economy, if not of the society itself, third-level computer systems should develop wherever primary systems of a certain capacity are in operation. Along with this, and greatly owing to it, many computer systems would develop horizontally at their primary and secondary levels, as third-level requirements oblige otherwise independent systems to standardize many of their programming procedures.

In addition to the certainty that there will be many more computer systems is the certainty of various implications. Their effect depends on who you are, or, perhaps more accurately, who you are not. Leaving aside the question of employment, if you are not in the upper echelon of the leadership of this country—among those who study, anticipate, and in some manner direct the destinies of the rest of us— then whatever benefits you derive from the development of computer systems will stem principally from their primary level of operations. Some of these benefits will be in the form of greater convenience or lower costs. The checks you write and receive will clear the bank more rapidly, your tax refund will arrive more promptly, your purchases at department stores will be made with more efficiency as it becomes feasible to stock greater varieties of merchandise. Service charges for these conveniences will also be lower—at least relatively. More appreciable savings to you will undoubtedly result from the increased application of primary-level computer operations to manufacturing and distribution activities.

In regard to second-level computer operations, you will derive considerable benefits indirectly, insofar as they contribute to the maintenance of efficient primary-level computer operations and to efficient management. Again, these benefits are relative. Costs will rise, but not as much as they would have if computers had not entered the picture. It is thus comforting that many routine services and conveniences are not deteriorating due to the congestion brought on by population increases and rising expectations. In, say, 1975, when twice as many automobiles may be on the highways as are now, one could still drive into town in about the same time as at present, and perhaps even find a place to park, thanks to a computerized traffic control and parking space allocation system.

Developments like these require detailed study and design, and much more long-range planning than has until now been possible. Thus, you will also benefit from the third-level computer operations which promise to provide the means to this end.

At each level, however, it will become increasingly difficult for you to relate the benefits to the costs. Certainly, this is not a new problem. We all experience it in one form or another even in the first grade of school, if not sooner. Our success in life is determined largely by how well we deal with it. Computer systems just make this more difficult. With each level, the terms of the problem are more complex and subtle, more completely stated in a language that can be appreciated only with the aid of a large, efficient computer system, and more intricately interwoven with the costs and benefits to other people and to the system itself.

At the primary level, we may assume that the problem is not insurmountable. If the immediate benefit of, say, the machine-readable number on your bank account deposit slip or the pattern of holes on your magazine subscription renewal form, is not apparent, the costs of putting them there are no more so.

At the second level, the problem is more difficult. As the system examines and assesses its own operations, it improves its own performance by altering somewhat the pattern of its relations with you. It, therefore, qualifies its primary level operations. It may, for example, only summarize your transactions rather than state them in detail, with the provision that, if you require more information, you must request it. It may begin to employ a language that is more convenient to it, with the obligation that you learn the new language, too. You may have to furnish more information than is strictly necessary for your purposes, but which is necessary to its own. There are many such possibilities. These will all be to the system's advantage, and they *may* be to yours—and it will be up to you to decide if this is the case. Thus, to the convenience of having your payroll processed by a bank must be matched the possible disadvantages of having the bank acquire your employees as depositors. There may be no disadvantages, certainly, but you must ascertain this.

At the third level, however, the problem of deciding who pays and who benefits is most acute. Just as the principal beneficiaries of second-level computer operations are the system's managers, and you only insofar as your interests coincide with theirs, the principal beneficiaries of third-level operations are inevitably the "authorities." Large-scale computer systems are as advantageous to them as aerial reconnaissance and radio and telephone communications are to mili-

85

tary leaders and staffs. No longer are leaders obliged either to march at the head of their troops, and suffer the consequences of such exposure, or to limit their direction of affairs to what can be seen from the highest hill. Instead, they can employ all of the amenities of a secure and extensive command center and a smoothly functioning intelligence and communications network to gain a real appreciation of the big picture and then can do something about it.

In effect, with the availability of efficient and reliable methods of monitoring most of the day-to-day activities of millions of individuals, and with the capability of rapidly summarizing and analyzing the effects of these activities, we must expect to see the rough-and-ready workings of many of our institutions increasingly refined. The broad social and economic classifications and categories with which we deal and the often whimsical results of rule-by-exception will be replaced by more detailed and intricate indexes, and more consistent applications of policy.

The principal agency for this use of computer systems will be the Government. This is so for two reasons. First, as things stand, only the Government is responsible for "maintaining the general welfare"— the standard by which the effectiveness and appropriateness of our institutions and ways of doing things must be judged. This, of course, does not relate to computer systems as such, but to which of their capacities are worth developing and which are not.

The second reason has a great deal to do with computer systems. As noted, the higher the level of computer system operation, the more useful the range of information produced. At the third level, this range is so great that only the Government, with its broad mandate, can take advantage of it. However much the users of commercial computer systems collect and routinely process information, in the end they can concern themselves only with its applications to their own limited situation, i.e., for management at the second level, and for a narrow range of interests at the third—for marketing possibilities perhaps, and for a small amount of long-range resource and facilities planning. Beyond that, the Government must enter the picture, as an information broker if nothing else.

The development of Government computer systems, then, will foretell the direction of our future. Purely commercial systems in themselves will never, as far as we are concerned, be more than a convenience or an irritation. Government systems will be the decisive factors in our lives.

6

·

The Evolution of Local Government Computer Systems

When historians begin to delve into the origins and early develop-ments of computer systems they will undoubtedly be struck by the unevenness of Government participation in the computer revolution. Certain Government agencies are avant-garde, blazing a trail, as it were, for others to follow; others with a seemingly equal stake ig-nore or misunderstand for an unconscionably long time the most ele-mentary possibilities. This is all the more remarkable because the benefits of computer systems, unlike those of earlier technological developments such as steampower, aircraft, and even atomic energy, apply equally to all Government activities.

This unevenness is perhaps an index of the very condition that computer systems promise most to repair—a condition in which the Government's "left hand seems not to know what the right hand is doing." In any case, the main division of interest and application has been between the right hand of the Defense Department and, with some notable exceptions, the left hand of the rest of the Executive Branch, along with all of the Legislative and Judicial Branches—and, equally, among all State and local governments.

The military appreciated the computer before the digital version of the machine itself was invented. From the beginning of World War II at least, the armed services directed and financed the research and development of a variety of automatic bomb sights and devices for aiming anti-aircraft guns which were to evolve, during the war, into authentic computers, although of the simple analog variety. While authorities differ as to exactly which was the first digital computer, one of the first was the U.S. Army Ordnance Depart-ment's ENIAC, designed and built at the University of Pennsyl-vania's Moore School of Electrical Engineering. ENIAC's principal purpose was to solve complex ballistics problems, and to prepare bomb-ing and range tables for aircraft and artillery.

ENIAC marked the beginning of a program of computer development that may be said to have culminated with the development of at least an interim solution to a more extensive ballistics problem: the Air Force's SAGE system, which went into partial operation in 1958. SAGE aimed at no less than directing the entire air defense of North America by means of a vast network of radar stations linked to a system of 16 computer centers. As such, it was unquestionably the most sophisticated computer system in existence and will remain so for some time. Its development spanned the entire three generations of computer development—in fact, it initiated the third generation, and to a great extent was the model for all other third generation (real-time) systems.

Along with their obvious interest in locating and destroying hostile objects, the armed services during World War II became less spectacularly but as intensely interested in keeping track of military goods as they moved from the raw material stage to their ultimate expenditure. By the end of the war, the services were the acknowledged masters of the new planning and management techniques that have come to be so intimately associated with the computer revolution—operations research, systems design and management, and so on, a primacy that they have maintained to this day. This has been in marked contrast with earlier conditions. Formerly, we saw the military as pupils of the civilians, sometimes apt and attentive pupils, as in the Civil War (with regard to the possibilities of railroads and ironclad ships), and sometimes not; since World War II these roles have been reversed in more and more areas.

However, the military has not monopolized the development of Government computer systems. Among notable supplements to their efforts are the U.S. Census Bureau's computer systems, beginning with UNIVAC in 1951, those of the Social Security Administration, and of the Internal Revenue Service, whose facilities include its National Data Center at Martinsburg, West Virginia, seven regional computer centers in various parts of the country, and its Data Center in Detroit, Michigan. These are certainly among the most extensive second-generation computer systems, although not necessarily the most sophisticated.

Apart from these three giants, there are a vast number of smaller and more specialized computer installations scattered throughout the Federal complex, and the development of new ones has gathered force yearly.

The general lines of this development, however, have been chaotic up to now. First, there has been a separate development at the local, regional, and national levels. At all three levels, lack of overall planning is conspicuous. Some systems spill across administrative boundaries, others are too narrowly confined by obsolete departmental structures. Obvious links to other systems are often ignored, particularly links to existing commercial systems. Much of this is due to "growing pains." The trend everywhere is to greater organization and more efficient operations. As more computer experts are brought into contact with governments, either as employees or as consultants, traditional inefficiencies are brought under more searching scrutiny and subject to more determined and disinterested criticism.

Compared with that of military and commercial systems though, the sophistication of government systems has been increasingly modest as one moves from Federal to State, and then to local levels. Their potential, nevertheless, is not at all modest. Their development in the near future should be far more extensive and spectacular than that of either commercial or military systems. The imperatives of social and economic development demand it, as evidence so far demonstrates. Moreover, they can take advantage of much of the previous commercial and military development—much of the equipment, trained personnel, and procedures that have been accumulated in the past 15 years. This includes the services of computer consultants of all kinds, and of the far-flung service departments of the major computer manufacturers, and, as we shall see, the assistance of some of the large commercial computer users as well. Unlike commercial users, at least, the designers and planners of public systems are not restricted by considerations of immediate profit. The initial cost of virtually any computer system application to government operations can be readily justified by comparing it to the existing costs of not using it. In fact, in view of the condition of routine record-keeping in most State and local governments, considerable ingenuity would be required to justify *not* installing automated systems to handle these functions.

With this in mind, it is more to the point to look at the present state of Government computer system development rather than its past accomplishments (such as the Internal Revenue Service system), for it is likely that most previous developments, although extensive enough in their technical aspects, were essentially routine. The obvious advantages of computer processing were first applied to well-defined and well-established information-handling situations. Their introduction did not especially call for dramatic redefinitions of organization or mission on the part of the agencies that adopted them.

This was the prevailing climate of computer development throughout the fifties and the early sixties. But from then on, change has been dominant. Computers are no longer seen as merely the means for improving existing functions. As they appear throughout the country, they are the harbingers of entirely new functions—formidable weapons in the arsenal of the War on Poverty and essential stepping stones to the Great Society.

But even now, Government computer systems generally begin with the installation of rather modest accounting and filing systems, since in this area even with simple equipment and limited programming, cost and service can be improved impressively almost immediately. This phase, of limited importance in itself, demonstrates the practicality of computers to the keepers of the public purse, and establishes the base for further development. Data processing staffs and departments are thus formally organized, contacts are established with suppliers and consultants, and advanced systems planning projects are set in motion.

Typical of these preliminary systems is that of the Rockland County (New York) Board of Cooperative Educational Services. Its experience in setting up a county-wide educational data processing system illustrates the smoothness with which a system of extensive potential can now be brought into being.

Hitherto "underdeveloped" Rockland County, directly across the Hudson River from populous Westchester County and within commuting distance of New York City, was, by the mid-sixties, bracing itself for a boom. Important industries were moving in, along with large branch department stores. An impressive residential building spree was in progress, and the County was currently leading the State of New York in rate of population growth. Demographic projections indicated that the County's population would double by 1975, and that educational demands would increase accordingly.

In view of this prospect, an efficient electronic data processing system for the County's schools was desirable. Some school districts were already utilizing primitive, or, at any rate, simple, electronic equipment—key punchers, card sorters and the like. These were being operated on a piecemeal basis by individual school districts with inevitable duplication of cost and effort. As each district expanded its data processing capability, the prospect of further inefficiencies arose as the scope of duplication increased.

The only countywide educational organization in existence at the time was the Board of Cooperative Educational Services, which operated a vocational school for all of the school districts in the County. It was the logical choice to administer a countywide data processing system. Consequently, in May, 1964, the Superintendent of the Board, together with the Superintendents of the eight school districts of the County, met with representatives of the New York State Education Department, and formally decided to explore the feasibility of providing the school districts of the county with a centralized electronic data processing capability, to be operated under the Board's authority, and jointly supported by the eight school districts. Soon after this, a questionnaire study was made by the two parties, and the results,* not unexpectedly, indicated that the project was indeed feasible and desirable.

Immediately after the publication of the study report, a three-month data processing requirements study of the school districts was undertaken. For this phase, the Division of Educational Management Services called upon the talents of an outside contractor, the System Development Corporation, a subsidiary of the renowned Rand Corporation, experienced in designing information systems for the Government. In essence the System Development Corporation study reviewed and evaluated the "questionnaire" study. It confirmed that study's conclusions, finding them in agreement with the experience of other pioneering school systems around the country.

On no more basis than this, the Board's countywide educational Data Processing Center began operations in the summer of 1965. A data processing consultant who had assisted the Board in its questionnaire study was hired to direct the center, and it was initially equipped and staffed by incorporating the facilities of the various school districts. This was not done all at once, and the initial period of the Center's operations was confused and difficult, since it was obliged to maintain without interruption the data processing services that the participating school districts relied on, and at the same time had to standardize and improve the more or less home-made procedures which they had individually evolved. Progress was slow and predictably hectic, but by the Spring of 1966, three of the five school districts that had been operating electronic data processing equipment independently had been integrated, and the cost of equipment rentals had been reduced by almost a third. No school district was using all of the Center's 13 services, but all were using some of them. A central computer and full-time systems analyst would not be had for six months to a year. Also, the Center's new quarters were under construction.

This is how a local government system gets started. Without the stimulus and discipline of profit, its preliminary planning is often casual and apparently chaotic. Long-range planning and any attempt to assess the impact of the system on its parent organizations and on the public at large are nonexistent, and well nigh impossible. Future planning in the Rockland County system is limited to the next stage of operations and no more. An IBM 1401 computer is expected

* Published by the Division of Educational Management Services of the New York State Education Department in February, 1965.

91

to be installed and in operation in the Spring of 1967. The Data Processing Center's personnel will be trained to make the transition from the cumbersome punch cards to magnetic tape. The computer will be used for primary level operations; the only second-level (analytical) operations presently anticipated are analyses for the planning of new school construction. However, the system will continue to expand and develop, leading to no one knows where.

Rockland County's system is of a class that is essentially "inner directed." Primarily, it monitors and services the activities of the large organizations that support it and of which it is a part. It has, or will have, a certain surveillance and control capability, but this is directed toward the students of the County's schools, who may be seen as either components of the system or its lawful prey. In either case, one's sympathies tend to be with the system.

Surveillance, and what we might call "social monitoring" by computer, however, is of great interest to many persons, second only to the prospect of unemployment in the catalogue of computer-based public anxieties. It is normally a poor second—there's not much you can say about it without sounding somewhat paranoid, but every so often it produces a virulent outburst of public jitters. A classic example of this phenomenon occurred during two weeks of July, 1966, when it was announced in New York City that traffic scofflaws were about to be tracked down by computers. No details were given. Newspaper accounts merely reported that a computer routine would shortly be put into effect to track down every scofflaw in the metropolitan area within 45 days of the date of his offense, and that records of traffic violations committed during an unspecified period in the past would also be searched. Those who had ignored tickets and summonses, it was implied, would be swiftly brought to justice. The effect of this news on the populace was absolutely electric. During the two-week "amnesty" before the new procedure was to be put into effect, more than 156,000 traffic delinquents rushed to pay more than $3,500,000 in overdue fines, choking the Traffic Court and the mails with payments on traffic tickets issued as far back as 10 years.

While no sympathy is due these scofflaws, the nature of the pressure brought to bear on them and their lively reaction to it have certain ominous overtones which even the most exemplary citizen must contemplate with at least momentary uneasiness. This uneasiness usually takes the form of concern with the privacy of the individual, even though, as in this case, there was no such invasion or infringement. Since this subject is likely to become the focus of much public controversy in the future, it is worth taking a closer look at some of the possibilities of government surveillance and control computer systems.

They can be conceived and put into operation in much the same almost casual manner as was the Rockland County educational system; that is to say, there need be no broad examination of their potential range and implications, no public discussion of the pros and cons of endowing public officials with the capabilities they represent. They can start up in some obscure corner of the bureaucracy and flourish, subject to all the same imperatives of development as systems of more innocent scope. They begin at a primary level, and develop second- and ultimately third-level operations just as any other system.

A striking example of the development cycle is an early attempt by the New York Police Department in computer system design—actually an exercise in resourcefulness and ingenuity that rivals the Department's efforts in solving crimes: a system bluntly named "CORRAL."

Plagued with mounting problems of manpower allocation, the New York Police Department in 1964 began to look for a solution in the capabilities of computer systems. In that year, the Department received more than 43,000 alarms for stolen cars, and over 200,000 traffic warrants and license suspension and revocation notices, each of which required action, i.e., a number of hours of police time. The results were less than adequate. Whereas 80 to 85 per cent of stolen cars were eventually recovered, most were found after they had been abandoned; the thieves were not apprehended. Thirty per cent of the traffic warrants issued were eventually returned to the courts unserved—the people named in them could not be located. The percentage of undelivered suspension and revocation notices was even higher. The prospects for the immediate future were even worse, of course.

To cope with this depressing situation, the Research and Development Group of the Police Department's Planning Bureau began to develop a computer surveillance and detection system. The group decided against tracking offenders to their "lairs," preferring to spot them on the streets. This called for a real-time system approach; one in which police could rapidly survey many vehicles and sort out the thieves and scofflaws. The idea was not wholly original, of course—police have long employed roadblocks and checkpoints to detect lawbreakers—but such tactics were always too time-consuming, as well as unduly annoying to the innocent, to be used on a large scale.

The technique that was evolved was more sophisticated than a road-

93

block. Basically, it worked like this: Two police teams were stationed about a mile apart on a busy highway, and both were linked to a computer stocked with the license numbers of all the reported stolen cars and traffic violators. The first team observed the license numbers of all oncoming cars and transmitted them by radio to the computer. The computer checked each number against its file of the license numbers of "wanted" vehicles. If no "match" was made, i.e., if the number in question was not in the file, no further action was taken. If, however, a match was made, the number in question was then radioed to the second police team further up the line, which then stopped the vehicle as it approached. Of course, all this activity had to take place in the few minutes during which the cars were between the two teams.

Sound as the scheme appeared, there was one immediate difficulty in putting it into effect. The New York Police Department had no computer with a real-time capability and no funds available to acquire one, to say nothing of funds for planning and programming. Undaunted, the Research and Development Group tested the idea manually, using telephones and a card file search. Four weekend tests at the Brooklyn-Battery Tunnel in New York City were made, and the results indicated that the idea was sound and feasible.

The problem of the lack of a real-time computer was then dramatically solved when the UNIVAC Division of Sperry-Rand Corporation donated the use of an up-to-date real-time computer, a UNIVAC 490 located at the New York World's Fair. This machine was in use at the United States Pavilion at the Fair, part of the American Library Association's demonstration of the computerized library of the future. It is worth noting, as another example of the computer's capacity for extending itself into unforeseen areas, that the police not only used this computer without disturbing the library operation, but also used much of its programming. The library operation involved matching visitors queries on the exhibits at the United States Pavilion with reference data on the same exhibits stored in the computer's files. The requirements of the CORRAL system, were, to the computer, quite similar.

With some additional programming, mostly devoted to the coding and storing of license numbers, and with the installation of a police teletype link (conveniently located in the nearby New York City Pavilion) with the computer, CORRAL went into operation in May, 1965. It utilized three two-man teams—two teams on the highway and one at the computer center.

From a technical point of view, the operation was a huge success. It took no more than seven seconds, from the moment an officer began radioing the license number, to get a negative response from the computer, and only 10 seconds to get a positive one, i.e., that the vehicle in question was "wanted."

CORRAL was conceived and carried out only as an extended field test. During the eight months of its existence, however, it impressively demonstrated the expectations of computer surveillance systems. Using only the three two-man teams, the police checked 183,950 vehicles in a five-month period, with the teams working only one eight-hour tour a day, seven days a week. During the first month's operations, when data on only auto thefts were stored in the computer, the ratio of "hits" to inquiries was 1:62. When, in June, 1965, data on traffic warrants, and shortly after, on license revocations and suspensions, were added, the ratio dropped to 1:47. These hits did not all result in arrests, because it was impossible for the police to have arrest warrants for all offenders accessible and in their possession. Before CORRAL can become truly practical some way must be found to provide the warrants in time to be executed. This, obviously, is another problem for the computer to solve.

Of equal interest are some of the projections and concepts that CORRAL generated for the future. Captain Adam D'Alessandro of the New York City Police Department's Planning Board, offered some of these in the course of a conference on large scale government computer systems held in New York City in April, 1962.*

If CORRAL were to be made a permanent operation, said D'Alessandro, "Three units [6-man teams] working three tours per day could check—at least in total numbers—every vehicle in New York City, including transients, more than twice a year. . . .

"The file which is used for CORRAL can also serve as the basis for other tactics," he continued. "In pursuit of this, we also tested the feasibility of having [other] members of the [police] force on patrol call the control center with the plate numbers of [those] vehicles that had been stopped on current violations. If a "hit" for a warrant was made, an arrest was effected for the current violation instead of serving a summons."

D'Alessandro then turned his attention to CORRAL's second-stage implications.

"The primary objective of Operation CORRAL was twofold," he said, "[first] to demonstrate how a computer could be utilized by law enforcement agencies as an operational tool; and secondly to serve as a starting point for an expanded data processing system for the New York City Police Department. We think we have accom-

---

* A New York University Conference on: The Large-Scale Public E.D.P. System: Its Problems and Prospects. (Sponsored by the Graduate School of Public Administration of New York University and held on April 1–2, 1966.)

plished the first objective. We are in the process of fulfilling the second."

He went on to describe Police Department plans for a "total system," one that would integrate the functions of surveillance, routine record keeping, and, in fact, all of the Department's information-handling procedures. Planning for this system was still mostly at the requirements survey stage, but he revealed the outlines of some of the total system's first stage features:

"One application that is being developed . . . is a Location Index which is intended to provide a field commander with information, by size of city block, of all police incidents occurring within the territory under his jurisdiction."

Then he went on to the second stage: "In addition," he said, "the reports he will receive will relate crime to type of premises to permit him to spot any trends that may be developing. Some of the types of data which will be included in this index are the following:

    a. Premises susceptible to emergency conditions (arsenals, banks, jewelry stores, communications, etc.).

    b. Premises useful for criminal intelligence purposes.

    c. Location data on relevant persons."

With this last statement the New York Police Department's proposed computer system attains to the third level of operation.

The correlation of which D'Alessandro speaks cannot be made by the Police Department—it requires, first of all, access to information that the Department does not have. While theoretically the Department could obtain it by some kind of unilateral arrangements with other sources, the prospect is most unlikely. Any agency that supplies information to the police is more than likely to expect something in return. Unofficial arrangements such as this are the bane of government. It is more probable that once the police begin to accumulate the kind of information that permits such correlations, a third-level system and organization will be devised to handle it—along with information on housing, income, population, etc., supplied by other municipal agencies that will have been just as busy with computers, and perhaps just as resourceful as the police. The stage will thus be set for the development of a kind of super-system catalogued to know everything about everybody. The prototypes of such super-systems are even now appearing. Let us look at two of them, the City of Detroit's Social Data Bank and the Santa Clara (California) County LOGIC system.

In 1964, the City of Detroit moved to concentrate its urban redevelopment planning efforts by formally establishing an advanced planning agency called the Community Renewal Program (CRP).

The leaders of the CRP realized in the initial planning studies that reliable source data on the city's social problems were greatly needed. These data were not in usable form. Various statistics were already being compiled by public and private agencies—the Police Department, the Department of Public Welfare, the Legal Aid Bureau, and so forth—but this information was subject to the same failings that have been so evident in other cities. Each agency collected data according to its own requirements and particularly within its own geographic area. A police precinct in no way conformed to a health district, or a health district to a school district. Thus, the data required could not be correlated meaningfully except on a city-wide basis.

In response to this problem the planning authorities called in a team of professional management consultants who set about designing a computer-centered, information-collecting system that could store the statistics being gathered by all the various city agencies. It was not precisely a real-time system, although in view of the time scale of the renewal program, it could almost be considered one. In many other respects the system was a routine, even a primitive, management system of the kind that has been widely adopted by industry.

The city was first divided into "planning districts" of about 100 acres. These were adopted to provide the common geographic basis which was so necessary for statistical comparisons. After extensive interviews with the various participating agencies, in the course of which the types of data processed by each agency were analyzed and evaluated in terms of volume, legal requirements, confidentiality, etc., a common reporting form and a common set of reporting procedures were adopted. This was followed by the design of a set of computer programs, to which was added the necessary background data—population figures from the latest census, etc. All-in-all it was a thoroughly professional but in no way revolutionary systems design approach.

The result was something that Detroit had never had before, and that few other cities have even now, a master file containing the latest information on:

Police Department Offense Complaints
Police Department Arrests
Police Youth Bureau Histories—Contacts
Police Women's Division Law Enforcement
City Welfare Relief Openings and Closings
City Welfare Food Stamp Openings and Closings
Registration Bureau Service Inquiries

Visiting Nurses Service Requests
Social Hygiene Clinic Venereal Disease Cases
Tuberculosis Clinic Tuberculosis Cases
Sanitary Engineering Complaints and Violations
Health Department Births
Health Department Deaths
Health Department Stillbirths
State Welfare Aid to Dependent Children Openings and Closings
State Welfare Aid to Dependent Children of the Unemployed
    Openings and Closings
State Welfare Old-Age Assistance, Aid to the Disabled, Aid to
    the Blind Openings and Closings
Legal Aid Bureau Requests for Aid
Board of Education Truancy
Board of Education Dropouts

Using this file, the computer could prepare a monthly report on each planning area for the various planning authorities and other interested parties. The report provided current-month statistics ranging from crimes committed through 23 other categories to school dropouts, and included such categories as city and state welfare cases, venereal disease cases, and arrests of minors. For comparison, monthly figures for the preceding 12 months were also included, and a 12 month running average in each category as well.

The computer was also programmed to provide special sets of statistics on request. A planner, for example, could receive a listing comparing the number of high school dropouts to the number of juvenile offenses for a period of months, or by district, or in whatever frame of reference suited his purpose.

A summary report on the Social Data Bank stressed that as an essential feature of its design and operation, "detailed source data should be retained in a manner that would not limit the future use of the data." Some idea of the range of these future uses may be gathered from examining some data that were *not* included in the Data Bank, and particularly the reasons for not including them at that time.

Mental illness cases, for example, were excluded because the volume reported was too small (on the order of only 30 cases per month) and from only two sources. Data on alcoholics were excluded for the same reason. Employment statistics, in the form of applications for unemployment assistance, were ruled to be confidential by the Michigan Employment Security Commission, and were not made available. In view of prevailing trends in this area, a suspicion exists that this decision was due to administrative or bureaucratic considerations. Data on the number of dependents, rents, etc., from the records of the Detroit Housing Commission were also considered for inclusion in the data bank. They were found to pertain only to specific housing projects, however, and thus, in the opinion of the planners, were of only narrow significance. Finally, an extremely important source of data was considered—the city personal income tax returns. The systems planners noted that this information would be included whenever the appropriate summary and search computer programs could be written.

These data sources were all considered in the course of the preliminary planning for the Social Data Bank itself and, although they were excluded at that time, their inclusion in the Data Bank may be considered to be an eventual goal. A summary of the entire Community Renewal Program, of which the Data Bank was only a part, indicated some further areas of interest for which the Data Bank would eventually be expected to supply information. These included real property values, sources of capital funds, land use, and additional statistics on social problems related to the renewal process itself.

Many of the potentials of the Detroit Social Data Bank have actually been realized in the Local Government Information Control System (LOGIC) set up in California's Santa Clara County early this year. Included in LOGIC's data storage was the so-called "people component," or alphabetic persons index record—a list of all persons who have been involved with the County's Welfare Department or law enforcement agencies. Associated with each individual's name was his: alias, social security number, address, record of birth, driver's license data, including his vehicle registration number, as well as his voter registration and property holdings.

All of this information was, of course, more or less available from existing files in various departments of the County government. What was novel, and to some persons rather frightening, was the assembling of all of these facts in one readily accessible file. This raised the specter of a luckless individual's "record" being used against him, a record of a juvenile misdemeanor, for example, being used to bar him from employment. And further, if there were technical advantages to storing information in this form, there was no reason why the "people component" could not be expanded to include every individual in the county. Officials in charge of LOGIC were reassuring on this point, of course, some of them with a kind of cheerful brutality. Karl Sheel of the County's data processing division was quoted as saying that there was nothing to fear on this point "if you have no arrests, no outstanding warrants against you, or if you are not on welfare or if you've stayed out of the clutches of adult probation."

Unfortunately, hardly any aspect of government computer operations is not a threat to the privacy of some individuals. As we shall see, it need only be glimpsed as a future contingency, for some people to become concerned. Computer experts and public officials are powerless to give assurances that such and such an application or development can never develop into some version of "Big Brother." For this reason alone, the question of individual privacy ought to be approached with great caution by apologists and critics of the computer revolution alike. Something is "too easy" about it, both as an untidy peripheral consideration to be brushed aside by experts in favor of such neater aspects as costs and measures of efficiency, and as a means to blanket condemnations of something that really requires hard thinking and study to be fully comprehended. Ignoring considerations of privacy is like ignoring sex; opposing intrusions upon it is like opposing sin.

In any case, as far as the privacy issue is concerned, much depends on who will ultimately control the systems we see evolving. We see the line of development running from local agency to municipality to county. The next logical stage is statewide computer systems. Given the uneven pace of county computer development, however, this stage still seems to be some years away.

Not unexpectedly, California appears to be foremost in statewide systems planning. In 1964, its Department of General Services was assigned overall responsibility for all of the government's existing data processing operations and for future computer systems planning. A financial policy office was also set up at the same time in the Finance Department to provide assistance in long-range planning, and finally, an Automatic Data Processing Committee reporting directly to the governor was organized. Altogether, it is a thoroughly rational approach—differing only in scale from that followed in Rockland County's school system.

In November, 1964, Governor Edmund Brown announced his widely publicized program to enlist the aid of California's aerospace industry in solving the State's urbanization problems. The basis for many of these solutions, Brown made clear, was an improved data processing capability. The aerospace companies, he noted, "have developed vast memory systems to help solve the mysteries of space. Can they design research and fact-gathering systems to take some of the guesswork out of the future planning industry and government must do?" The Governor felt that the answer was "yes," and he went on to award a number of contracts to the said companies for study in four general problem areas: crime and delinquency, transportation, waste management, and, most significantly, computer systems.

100

Somewhat behind California is New York State, which has a number of computer systems planning studies well under way (one in education and law enforcement, for example), but has as yet no total systems approach comparable to California's. Other states follow New York, or lag behind. In general, the level of a state's overall economic development is a good index of its progress in computer systems planning. No state completely ignores the prospect of establishing statewide systems, but no state has done much toward implementing them.

The nature of local development of government computer systems up to now permits us to envision at least two alternate futures. In one, these systems will continue to be conceived almost casually as resourceful and enterprising local officials take advantage of the knowledge and facilities made readily available by the widespread development of commercial and, to a somewhat lesser degree, nonprofit private systems such as are being installed at universities. As we have seen, this is not difficult. Even now, almost any public official of even moderate rank and stature, often by simply making a few phone calls, can assemble an advisory group of expert systems planners. With hardly more resourcefulness he can avail himself of the use of a fairly sophisticated computer, at least on a temporary basis.

From this modest beginning, the official can rapidly push on to a prototype primary-level system which can pay for itself in a relatively short time. Once at this point, the system can be counted on to develop internal pressures sufficient to guarantee its own further expansion. As it matures, and as its operations begin to interlace with those of other systems of equally casual origin, a number of knotty problems of communication are likely to result: jurisdictions are threatened, missions may be compromised, requirements may conflict, and so on. But by this time a sizable public investment is at stake and the tendency is to resolve the situation by a great deal of cutting and patching. This tendency is also reenforced as the responsibility for resolving the problem is passed on to senior officials—governors and the like, who cannot penetrate its technical complexities. They will apply their political acumen instead.

As this sort of thing develops in all 50 states and in most of the myriad local jurisdictions, much of the potential effectiveness of computer systems will be lost forever. The computer's acknowledged superiority as an instrument of large-scale social and economic planning will be theoretical, while the tangle of local systems will function adequately only at the primary level, with a marked decrease in efficiency with each successive level.

This, then, is one possibility. It must be conceded that it is very much in the American tradition. It finds its parallels in the development of our educational system, our police forces, our roads, our disastrous experiments with local militias, and so on. In the past, we simply made the best of this approach; we had no alternatives.

Now, however, there is an alternative. Instead of a hodgepodge of autonomous systems, all growing like Topsy, we can have one well organized super-system, in which all the local systems can take their assigned places and perform their allotted functions. Obviously, it must be designed and directed by the Federal Government. Local systems might continue to be operated and paid for on a local basis, but the design, specifications, and, most of all, the scope of their operations will be in accordance with standards set up by Federal authorities. Since the Federal Government has become increasingly involved with resource development, urban problems, etc., as well as concerned with national economic planning and regulation, much of the basis for these standards must be the information require-ments of the Federal Government. That is to say, the third-level capabilities of local systems must be as good as those of their pri-mary and secondary levels.

This possible future does not have the weight of tradition behind it, but it has just about everything else. It is no longer merely in-sulting to say that the Federal Government has more money than brains. Federal officials themselves from the President on down are increasingly willing to admit this, although perhaps not in quite these terms. As they grapple with the details and the initial feedbacks of their relatively modest experiments in social and economic planning, and begin to contemplate much larger ones, they become almost plaintively vocal on the subject of lack of information as well as lack of sufficient means for monitoring the progress and results of what they have accomplished. These needs can be met in part by intelligently planned and directed local information systems.

Also, more and more Federal agencies have, in the subsidy and the grant-in-aid, admirable mechanisms for effecting a consensus on the kind and amount of local information that is due the Federal Government. Even the implied promise of Federal aid is an incentive for local authorities to accept Washington's guidelines and sugges-tions for organizing local information systems. The effectiveness of such persuasion is precedented by the Defense Department's in-fluence over its contractors, the contracts serving as subsidies and grants-in-aid.

In sum, the future utilization of a vast centralized computer sys-tem encompassing in some respects virtually all of the ferment of the local government systems, and, to a lesser extent, most big com-mercial systems, is as probable as the use of its decentralized alter-native. Such a computerized future is, in fact, about as probable as the future that holds a reasonably satisfactory end to the Viet Nam War and a continuation of the War on Poverty and of the attempts to create the Great Society. The two futures are so closely linked as to be one and the same.

It is safe to assume that a national computer system would affect us much more than would any aggregation of lesser systems. A future in which it appears is worth exploring more fully.

7

Toward a National Computer System

What, exactly, do we mean by a national computer system? To answer this we might begin by taking a leaf from the systems designer's book itself and define the system in terms of what it must be able to do. A national computer system, then, will be able to:

- process source information relating to national affairs, i.e., nationwide economic and social activities
- manage these (primary level) activities
- act as a research instrument for national planning and policymaking
- manage specific projects and programs of national scope
- monitor the actual functioning of these projects and programs as they are translated into reality.

To perform these functions the system will have:

- a set of "sensors," or remote terminals, located wherever information from local sources is fed into the system
- a central "exchange," where information from local sources is assembled, sorted, and stored and dispatched to those who need to use it
- a central "control unit" which generates programs and specifications for the use of information
- a set of "outlets"—again, remote terminals—located throughout the country and particularly throughout Government departments, to which orders, instructions, and commands are dispatched.

As thus outlined, the system resembles in many respects an air defense system such as the U.S. Air Force's SAGE System. SAGE has two distinct functions: it gathers information and it controls and directs actions. The information is in two categories—one relates to the environment (the airspace around the United States) and includes data on all happenings within it; the other relates to the larger system of which SAGE is a part (the Continental Air Defense System), and includes data on all happenings within it. Data from these two categories are continuously analyzed and compared in SAGE's central computers, and as a result, the actions of the Continental Air Defense System are controlled and directed.

Lest this comparison give rise to visions of vast control complexes and mechanized surveillance equipment on every hilltop and street corner, let us examine how the system will not resemble SAGE.

SAGE was designed and built from the ground up by an organization with great resources in response to a specific situation or problem. Our system will be in large part assembled not from the ground up but out of bits and pieces of existing systems and in response to a much more complex situation. It will resemble, perhaps, the sort of system that a small and not too wealthy nation—Portugal, let us say— might assemble to handle not only its air defense but also its sea and land frontier defenses (and possibly its defense against smugglers and illegal fishermen as well). In reacting to these requirements, Portugal would probably integrate all existing facilities, from the air traffic control system at Lisbon airport to the lighthouse keepers and frontier police, into a network that would interfere with the normal functions of these units as little as possible. They would then top this off with a central information exchange and control center whose functions would largely consist of making policy, enforcing reporting procedures, and of issuing operational orders in response to reports received.

A less fanciful analogy than this is the Bell Telephone System. As most of us know, Bell has many subsidiaries throughout the country. Although wholly owned by the American Telephone and Telegraph Company, these local telephone companies operate with considerable autonomy in certain areas—mainly in the setting of rates—in accordance with local conditions. A.T.&T., however, continues to manage the technical aspects of all these subsystems. For example, all local companies must use the same telephone codes. The numbers "555–1212" mean "information" to all of them. Through its research and manufacturing subsidiaries, A.T.&T. also sees to it that all equipment and procedures continue to be compatible throughout the system. Its subsidiaries, in effect, supply it with information and carry out its general instructions.

Even if we assume that a national computer system will be set up along the lines of these examples, the prospect of Federal management is at first glance hardly more than a rosy—or dismal—vision of the remote future. Its development will be a stupendous undertaking, not only with regard to technical problems but also from a political and administrative standpoint, for the number of State and local agencies presently involved in administering various Federal programs has been estimated as 90,000. The number of these Federal programs, and of the Federal departments and agencies that administer them, is also impressive. On the order of 170 aid programs are now being handled by 21 Federal departments and agencies. This number will no doubt increase drastically. Added to these are the "regular" activities of all of these agencies and departments—internal administration, regulatory functions, and statistical data-gathering functions. A nationwide computer system must handle virtually all the data processing needs of this crowd—in real-time—and simultaneously tend to its own functioning, too. This large order is far beyond the capacity of any present system or combination of systems. Nevertheless, it is being taken seriously by reasonable men.

For the system to develop, the Federal Executive Branch must be reorganized extensively and its relationships to the various State and local agencies that administer its programs must be redefined. The lack of such a reorganization does not preclude the development of at least a prototype Federal system, but the job would be much more difficult.

Indications are that such a reorganization is coming. President Johnson, in his State of the Union message to Congress in January, 1966, called for the establishment of a commission to study the problems of Federal agency coordination at the Federal level and at the level of State and local governments. Senator Edmund Muskie of Maine, Chairman of the Senate Subcommittee on Intergovernmental Relations, has gone even further. In March, 1966, he made this issue the subject of a major speech to the Senate. While he was only one voice in a rising chorus, his remarks indicate the trend in some detail:

"Consideration should be given to designating a special assistant to the President for program coordination and intergovernmental relations. . . . This special assistant should, in turn, be aided by a top flight Bureau of the Budget official, equipped with a sufficient staff, who would make continuing investigations of intergovernmental problems and recommend policies for improving Federal-aid administration." Then Senator Muskie describes, in precise detail, one approach to the national computer system itself: "To help both the special assistant and the President, the [Bureau of the Budget] should develop—far more than it is presently planning—a computerized information clearinghouse system which could provide immediate information to the President and others concerning: (a) social, economic, and other basic characteristics of individual states and local areas; (b) efforts on the part of these jurisdictions to meet their growth problems and projected needs; (c) Federal aid programs which are now assisting specific State and local jurisdictions; and (d) those available

Federal assistance programs which have not been utilized but [which] could improve State and local programs.

"Such a clearinghouse system would be of great benefit if it were linked to regional, departmental, and the Bureau of the Budget levels, with each providing pertinent information concerning its particular jurisdiction. . . ."

Senator Muskie also emphasizes regional program organization. He particularly commends the newly organized Housing and Urban Development Department as an example of the kind of regional organization needed in the future:

"According to its new organizational scheme, [the Housing and Urban Development Department] has brought all its functions at the regional level under a regional administrator from whom it expects 'strong local-level program leadership and coordination through decentralization of operations. . . .'

". . . Federal departments with key aid programs would do well to follow its example." He then outlines the regional management system that might result from this:

"Regional offices should be set up in accordance with standard geographical boundaries. Each should be headed by a regional director who would represent the secretary or the agency chief. . . .

". . . A Federal Regional Coordinator—not connected with any department or agency [should] be established to obtain across-the-board implementation of Federal programs in accordance with State and local comprehensive plans—of course consistent with national objectives and standards. He would be the President's man in the field, concerned with effective interrelationships of programs, the efficiency of administration, the cooperation of Federal officials with their State and local counterparts. . . . He should have . . . a status which would be above all other Federal regional officials in his area. . . .

"Consideration . . . should also be given to creating Federal coordinators and services in State Capitals for the benefit of State planners and the non-metropolitan communities. There must be more emphasis on Federal planning and technical assistance to encourage areawide and regional planning as it affects the broad scope of economic and social development."* To cap this proposed regional administrative structure he adds this: "One suggestion—which I think makes a tremendous amount of sense—would be the creation of a National Intergovernmental Affairs Council—NIAC—chaired by the President and composed of those Cabinet officials and agency heads

* Some of the technical assistance was specified by Senator Muskie. It includes: ". . . up-to-date program and planning information, government publications, administrative counseling, and data-processing services."

whose activities have a major impact on domestic grant-in-aid programs and intergovernmental relationships. Its membership would include the Secretaries of Housing and Urban Development, Health Education and Welfare, Labor, Agriculture, Commerce, the Attorney General, the Director of the Office of Economic Opportunity, the Head of the Bureau of the Budget, the Chairman of the Advisory Commission on Intergovernmental Relations, and others. . . .

"Patterned somewhat after the National Security Council, this body would have an Executive Director, and a working secretariat composed of the deputy undersecretaries representing the departments and agencies, and top-level executives independently selected and responsible to the Executive Director.

"The Council would go far beyond the advisory responsibilities of the Bureau of the Budget and the Council of Economic Advisers. It would be an operating mechanism for developing the President's policies of program coordination, and overseeing their implementation. It would provide the forum for determining basic intergovernmental policies and provide the President with an immediate liaison with State and local governments.

"At the same time, it could be the President's 'ombudsman,' a watchdog for crises, a central domestic information agency and an inspector general for program effectiveness. It would be concerned with both urban and rural development as a multidepartmental responsibility involving education, housing, transportation, public facilities, law enforcement, civil rights, and other issues. It would play a strategic role in long-range planning, and assist States and local governments in regional planning." At the time of these remarks, the Senator also announced his intention to sponsor legislation to further the objectives they specified.

Senator Muskie's proposals do not in themselves comprise a comprehensive plan for reorganizing the Federal Executive Branch. His recommendations were generally limited to furthering those ambiguous functions designated by such terms as "coordination" and "policy recommendations." Any workable reorganization scheme will undoubtedly require the establishment of more precisely defined relationships between the agencies concerned. Aside from this perhaps politically inspired limitation, however, his proposals are entirely sound. They represent accurately not only the prevailing consensus* on this particular problem (witness the Automation Commission's

* The widely publicized hearings of the Senate's Subcommittee on Executive Reorganization, held in August, 1966, under the direction of Senator Abraham Ribicoff (ably seconded by Senator Robert Kennedy) and devoted to the "plight of American cities," were concerned with this same problem of "coordination."

remarks on regional planning, for example), but also the kind of problem approach that has become almost traditional in governmental affairs. Indeed, in comparing his proposed National Intergovernmental Affairs Council (NIAC) to the National Security Council, Senator Muskie was, in a sense, comparing his whole reorganization scheme to the monumental reorganization of the armed services after World War II. The comparison is apt. It does not require any great stretch of the imagination or the facts to see a parallel between the establishment of an independent Department of the Air Force and the vastly expanded Departments of the Army and Navy, followed by their subsequent integration into an even vaster Department of Defense, and the recent establishment of the Departments of Health, Education and Welfare, Housing and Urban Development, and Transportation, along with the (again) vastly expanded Departments of Commerce and Labor, to be followed by a subsequent integration into some kind of super department exactly comparable to the Department of Defense.

If we take the parallel one step further, this second exercise in monumental government reorganization will probably be attended by as much resistance on the part of the agencies concerned as was the first.

In any case, the drama is already unfolding. While the Automation Commission and men like Senator Muskie turn their attention to the higher levels of reorganization, being content with only general considerations of the computer system design, others make their way along lower paths to the same goals.

The Appalachian Regional Development Act passed in March, 1965, while it contained no specific computer system provisions, is most probably a step in this direction. Even before the Act was passed, the ubiquitous System Development Corporation had been retained by the Area Redevelopment Administration of the Department of Commerce and assigned to develop a system and a model for a "Regional Development Organization in the area of the United States known as the Appalachian Region." The System Development Corporation continues to provide this service to the newborn Appalachian Regional Commission. An article in the company's house organ, *SDC Magazine* in October, 1965, indicated what can be expected:

"The unique contribution of SDC's involvment in implementing the Appalachian redevelopment program [has been] to demonstrate the application of system and operational analysis concepts and techniques in addressing problems of the creation and evolution of organizations and institutions. Such structures cannot be blueprinted in final form, but these techniques can help systematize human action and deliberation and build in mechanisms that permit such action systems to be self correcting and accomodating of differences." Reading between these somewhat tortured lines—we get the message: a regional computer system of as yet undetermined complexity and extent is in the making for Appalachia. At a minimum it will encompass the affairs of all the Federal agencies and programs of the region. It will require for its functions a vast amount of source data in machine usable forms. Since most of this data does not exist it will be necessary to establish the primary systems required to obtain it. The details are still to be worked out, but it is likely that this network of primary systems will be implemented by making the development of at least a prototype primary level information system a prerequisite of Federal aid to a locality. That is to say, before a town or county qualifies for Federal assistance to housing, schools, or other purposes, it must agree to create and organize its data processing facilities along lines specified by the Federal grant-making authorities. Expert technical assistance will, of course, be supplied by these authorities and the resulting systems, although perhaps ostensibly under local control, will become functional components of the regional system. Since the Appalachian region is sparsely populated and has a relatively simple socioeconomic structure, and leverage will be afforded Federal planners by the relatively large amounts of Federal grants-in-aid earmarked for the region, it is a logical testing ground for a prototype system.

The effectiveness of even a single regional system requires more than a network of local subsystems and a regional computer. In spite of all the protests favoring regional autonomy, the regional development system must continue to serve as a halfway house between the sources of information and the sources of money, plans, and power— i.e., the people in Washington. Therefore, a central computer system to manage and direct the various regional systems is equally necessary.

Until recently, nothing was done even to provide the groundwork for such a Federal central computer system. Many departments within the Government were using computers and developing specialized computer systems of nationwide scope, but apart from the assigning of certain responsibilities to the Bureau of the Budget for uniform equipment specifications, there was no concerted effort directed toward this objective. In 1965, this state of affairs came to an end when the establishment of a Federal Data Center* was proposed.

In April of that year, the Director of the Bureau of the Budget received a communication from the Social Science Research Council

* There is yet no agreed upon name for this "Center." It is variously known as the Federal Data Center, National Data Center, National Data Service Center, National Data Bank, Statistical Reference Service, and Federal Statistical Data Center. Before it becomes a reality it will probably acquire a few more designations.

(a research organization of eminent social scientists and economists largely supported by the Ford Foundation) titled: *Report of the Committee on the Preservation and Use of Economic Data.** It subsequently became known as the Ruggles Report, after the chairman of the Committee, Professor Richard Ruggles of Yale University's Department of Economics. The essence of the report is contained in this opening passage:

". . . the committee urges that the Bureau of the Budget, in view of its responsibility for the Federal statistical program, immediately take steps to establish a Federal Data Center. Such a Federal Data Center should have the authority to obtain computer tapes and other machine readable data produced by all Federal agencies. It would have the function of providing data . . . and service facilities so that within the proper safeguards concerning the disclosure of information both Federal agencies and users outside of the Government would have access to basic data. The Federal Data Center would require computer facilities, and it would need to be staffed with personnel capable of understanding the data problems in the various areas. In view of the importance of the Federal Data Center, the Committee suggests that the Center be established with specific responsibilities for these functions and interagency authority to carry them out."

The Ruggles Report then describes in great detail the shortcomings of the existing decentralized information gathering facilities of the Federal Government, essentially from the point of view of the scholar or research organization outside the government—in other words, that of the ultimate third-level user.

The Ruggles Report became the subject of a searching review sponsored by the Bureau's Office of Statistical Standards, and later provided the impetus for a more detailed study by a presidential task force headed by Professor Carl Kaysen of Princeton University's Institute of Advanced Studies. Also, the redoubtable Representative Cornelius Gallagher made it the focus of a series of hearings of his subcommittee investigating the invasion of privacy.

The Office of Statistical Standards review was made by Dr. Edgar S. Dunn, Jr., a Bureau of the Budget consultant and a former Deputy Assistant Secretary of Commerce (Economic Affairs) with the assistance of representatives of the Census Bureau, the Bureau of Labor Statistics, and the National Bureau of Standards. While the document† that resulted from this review is far from a complete plan for a Federal central computer system, or even a detailed proposal for such a system, it is still of enormous scope and significance. It may come to be regarded as the watershed of the Federal Government's central

* See Appendix 3.
† See Appendix 3.

computer system planning, for it recommends, in unequivocal language, the establishment of a "National Data Center"—precisely the kind of organization required to plan, design, and manage a central computer system. Dunn prefers that the organization be set up as an independent agency, "unencumbered by existing agency jealousies." Realistically doubtful that this could be done in the face of those same jealousies and the prevailing attitude of the Congress toward new independent agencies, he indicates that he would settle for expansion of an existing independent agency to accommodate the National Data Center. In this case, he prefers the Bureau of the Census, "the most logical candidate," he writes, "by virtue of both its mission and its staff."

As he describes it, the National Data Center would first be a central storage for the computer files of the agencies that comprise the so-called "Federal Statistical System." This is, as indeed Dunn himself makes clear, a "system" in name only; more accurately, it refers to the group of agencies that collects and stores statistical information of some economic or social importance. A partial listing of these agencies includes: the Bureau of Labor Statistics, the Bureau of Employment Security, the Bureau of the Census, the Office of Business Economics, the Department of Agriculture, the Internal Revenue Service, the Federal Trade Commission, the Office of Education, the Bureau of Old Age and Survivors Insurance, the Securities and Exchange Commission, the Federal Reserve Board, and the National Center for Health Statistics.

In addition to storing the files of these agencies, the National Data Center would serve as a central referral and reference service for *all* users of the data contained in the files. In order to do this, the Center would have to develop a master index, a whole series of cross reference indexes, and, of course, the procedures for keeping its files up to date. This would lead it to devise common standards for coding and classifying information for all the participating agencies (something that cannot be done at present).

As outlined, the proposed National Data Center is still a long way from a central computer system for the Federal Government. It cannot gather information at the source, nor can it initiate communications with its users. Initially, it could not assess the importance or value of a particular piece of information in its files, nor could it, let us say, alert an agency that, owing to a new statistic supplied by another agency, the importance of such and such a program had been altered. Also, it cannot deal with regional computer systems as such. Its sponsors were content, quite prudently, it would appear, to leave the whole question of regional organization to the community of

Federal departments and agencies that would constitute the Center's sources and users.

Nevertheless, it does have the essentials for both of these activities, for the Center will have a research "capability directed to an analytical evaluation of user requirements. . . . The construction of the reference file, the definition of standards in every category and the design of software [programming] routines and other system techniques that perform the facilitating services would all be controlled by what could be learned through research and analysis about the systematic elements of user requirements." This means that it could serve as the source for all the planning and specification of regional and local system requirements.

In effect, the National Data Center's receipt, storage, and retrieval of statistical data for its users could be considered as a primary-level operation. The Center would serve as the familiar information pipeline from data source to primary data user. Once it had accumulated a backlog of data, it would begin to provide the kind of second-level analyses that would lead to its own further expansion and development and ultimately to its use in third-level operations, where it is first determined that something needs to be known and then steps are taken to obtain the desired data. When this stage is reached, the whole character of the Data Center's computer system would have changed. It could then direct the activities of information gathering systems of its client agencies. These systems would have become its receptors.

Even at this stage the National Data Center would not operate as a national computer system. It would be only a national information supply system. Dunn is specific about this. "This [research-analytic capability] does not mean developing the capability for conducting research and analysis directed towards policy and management," he states. "Such analytic functions should be centered in the Executive Office and the operating departments. Policy research and analysis should be kept separate from the supporting function of supplying and servicing information." Nevertheless, it would embody much of the hardware and software required by the complete system, and the cadres, at least, for the staff which would use it. When the kind of reorganization that Senator Muskie has heralded actually goes into effect, the National Data Center will unquestionably become the base upon which to build the management computer system necessary to complete the picture, especially since the National Data Center would almost certainly be placed under the jurisdiction of the incipient National Intergovernment Affairs Council (or whatever it comes to be called).

113

Here is how the national computer system might come into being: first the Federal Executive Branch is reorganized to strengthen its socioeconomic program planning and program managing capabilities (as opposed to its more traditional regulatory and statistic collecting activities); then a centralized data gathering computer system is developed, growing out of a National Data Center into a system of regional centers which will then tie in with a number of local systems; and, finally, the data gathering system will evolve rapidly into a full-fledged planning and program management system encompassing virtually all activities of the Federal Executive Branch (except national defense and foreign policy) down to the local level.

We cannot appreciate the full impact this development would have on our national life, but we would do well to look beyond the more obvious and formal steps to the development process and ponder the workings of what we are going to christen the "Rubel Effect."

The "Rubel Effect" is so called after John H. Rubel, a vice-president of Litton Industries, who is experienced in the business of large-scale research and development projects involving government-industry cooperation. Rubel spoke of such projects in general before a symposium sponsored by Urban America, Inc. entitled "The Troubled Environment," held in Washington in December, 1965. He notes that "the projects themselves establish a market place for the evolution of the methods and the technologies needed to get them done." This conclusion is based on his own experience with, and observations of, the development of rockets and spacecraft, and he applies it to a new approach to resolving some of the country's urban problems, a subject that concerns us here only as it applies to our national computer system:

"How can we marshall and harness our resources and our genius to attack urban problems the way we have done in space?

". . . The answer . . . is to start handling the creation of new cities or new towns the way we handle the creation of new, never-before attempted projects in space. This means: . . . creating a marketplace, a wholly new marketplace, one that does not now exist and never has, where private industry can come and sell the development, creation and administration of new cities. That is how we created the Atlas, the Titan, the Polaris [missiles] and a host of incredibly complex, wholly new, never-before-attempted missile systems. That is how we have put men and machines into space. And that is how we are going to send men on a round trip to the moon. Each new undertaking was specified, authorized, funded and administered as a 'project.' Families of projects—bombers, missiles, space—were and are given the benefits of common administration that provides a framework of scientific, developmental and administrative support. . . .

114

". . . If there is any key to the unprecedented elaboration of modern large scale technologies and the sciences with which they are allied, the creation of these special project mechanisms is that key. We must be clear, too, that these are not ordinary projects, in the sense that a dam or a bridge or a road is a project. These are projects for the creation of solutions to tasks for which the objectives, but not all the needed technologies, are known. . . . To get [these] solutions . . . markets must be created that will stimulate the evolution of the organizations that will, in turn, create the center of motivated expertise necessary to obtain the solutions which the market place rewards." Applied to the national computer system, the combination of hardheaded business logic and far-ranging idealism that this statement of the Rubel Effect contains means that as the system's objectives come to be stated, and as the Government becomes serious about developing the system and ready to spend money to this end, virtually a whole new industry will be created—one devoted to making the system a reality. Computer manufacturers, research organizations, management consultants—a whole galaxy of specialists—will come flocking for a piece of the action, for it will be a big project indeed. Large companies will be moved to create new operating divisions devoted to participating in the development of the system, and small companies will spring into being for the same purpose. In short, long before the system is a functioning reality it will have been endowed with the same kind of "half-life," if indeed that is doing it justice, enjoyed by the "man on the moon" and even "the man on Mars" projects. These may never succeed but they put bread on a great many tables nonetheless.

Moreover, unlike these fabulous projects, there will be much more "spin-off" from the research and development of the national computer system. No one, after all, has much use for satellites and missiles except the agencies that direct their design and manufacture. This is not so with many components of the national computer system. Long before Federal authorities can insist that local authorities and private organizations use Federal software, private concerns that have made it their business to know Federal specifications (and perhaps even to write them) will eagerly market "program packages compatible with the new Federal specs, at no extra cost," and as they are called in on purely local computer system development projects they will tend to recommend measures that will at least anticipate eventual linkups with the Federal system.

Along with the Rubel Effect will be another—one that has been noted with some chagrin in the course of Federal development grant programs. We might even call it the "LBJ Effect." It is simply this: there is a marked tendency to defer purely local programs—for area redevelopment, education, etc.—as soon as local officials detect the possibility of getting Federal aid. The major overhaul of a municipal sewage system, for example, normally a routine local project, becomes the wildest sort of civic imprudence and financial irresponsibility the moment there is the chance that Washington might be persuaded, in several years time, to contribute to its cost. To carry out the project now would result in the squandering of perhaps millions of local tax dollars.

Thus, as it becomes known, or even widely believed, that the Federal Government will soon underwrite part of the development of local computer systems, local officials increasingly tend to mark time and hang back in these areas in the hope of picking up some Federal money. In view of such considerations we should perhaps not take too much to heart some of the more vehement expressions of congressional disapproval of the proposed national computer system and the Bureau of the Budget's National Data Center.

As noted, the National Data Center proposal was searchingly and hostilely investigated by the House of Representatives Special Subcommittee on Invasion of Privacy of the Committee on Government Operations. Representative Cornelius Gallagher of New Jersey presided, and Representatives Benjamin Rosenthal and Frank Horton, both of New York, were present, as were Professor Richard Ruggles and Dr. Edgar Dunn, Jr., along with Dr. Raymond Bowman of the Budget Bureau's Office of Statistical Standards.

The Subcommittee's concern was, not unexpectedly, with the Data Center's potential for acquiring and storing quantities of personal and perhaps intimate details about the lives and characters of millions of defenseless individuals, and for supplying such details to interested public officials and researchers. Although the Subcommittee, on the whole, treated Ruggles, Dunn, and Bowman rather harshly (even to the extent of bringing Vance Packard of *Naked Society* fame to testify against them), the record of the hearings, together with its companion records on the uses of psychological testing in government, ought to stand as one of the great documents on this subject.

The substance of the Subcommittee's position is expressed by Gallagher, and addressed to Bowman:

"We do not want to impede progress," he said. "The computer is here to stay, and it can be a source for good. We would hope that you are not underestimating the computer. I think you are. I think in centralizing all this information in one giant computer, you have not realized the potentialities of the computer, because if you feel that you can control this kind of information you are not being realistic. You are placing tremendous power in the hands of an elite. . . ." Added Representative Frank Horton: ". . . you can find out what

116

happened to Frank Horton from the time he was born until right today just by pushing that button—everything."

Bowman could not cope with this onslaught. In vain he tried to explain that the problem of safeguarding individual privacy transcended any particular computer installation, and, for that matter, computers themselves—that it was a much more general problem which the Government had, in his opinion, handled satisfactorily in the past, and could reasonably be expected to do so in the future. This clearly did not satisfy the Subcommittee and its eminent "witness for the prosecution."

Ruggles and Dunn fared somewhat better, if only because they observed Bowman under fire before taking the stand themselves. Dunn in particular perhaps best illuminated the whole discussion of "privacy invading systems" and may have influenced the whole future development of the national computer system:

"I think it is important to recognize clearly that there are two basically different types of information systems," he said, "(1) there are statistical information systems, and (2) there are information systems that have as their purpose the generation of intelligence. . . .

". . . The distinction is basic. Intelligence systems generate data about individuals as individuals. They have as their purpose "finding out" about the individual. They are widespread and common and essential in our private and public business. They include such things as the medical records a doctor keeps to trace the changes in the well being of his patient and the educational records the teacher keeps to trace the progress of the student. They include requirements essential to public administration, such as the licensing authorities' need to know whether a driver has legal vision, or the tax authorities' need for information to administer taxes.

"Most of the intelligence information systems with which I have had any direct contact are restricted systems which have a specific administrative purpose and have not as their purpose the organization of intelligence about individuals into an integrated dossier of any kind.

"It is conceivable that an intelligence system of this kind could be developed.

"A statistical information system," he continued, "produces information which does not relate to the individual. It only identifies characteristics that relate to groups of individuals or populations. It has as its purpose answering such questions as these: What proportion of the residents of Appalachia possess incomes [of] less than $2,000? In what way does the mix of economic activities in New York City differ from Chicago? What activities seem to figure prominently in [the] recent rapid growth of the Southeast, Florida, the Gulf Coast, and the Boston-Washington corridor? What proportion of the registered voters turned out in a recent primary and how were they divided between Republican and Democrat, urban and rural, white and non-white? . . .

". . . This is sufficient to emphasize that a statistical system is busy generating aggregates, averages, percentages and so forth that describe relationships. No information about individuals need be generated." Dunn sees the proposed National Data Center as entirely a statistical information system.

The Subcommittee was not mollified by Dunn's argument, even when he described some of the more obvious ways of protecting the source data of such a statistical system. Gallagher was quick to point out that regardless of the form of the system's output, i.e., as statistics pertaining to aggregates or as individual dossiers, personal data relating to specific individuals was still the system's principal input. As long as this was the case—as long as the system stored individual personal data—someone might figure out a way to get it out, and neither Dunn nor anyone else could guarantee that this could not be accomplished.

One of the reasons for Dunn and Bowman's discomfiture on this point—for Gallagher was correct—was that no one who testified at the hearings, neither the pro-computer partisans nor the anti-computer partisans, thought to distinguish between the two kinds of privacy invasion that must be taken into account, i.e., what we might call "lawful" and "unlawful" invasion. An example of the former might be the Civil Service Commission's recourse to the Internal Revenue Service's tax records or the FBI's files, in order to obtain or verify information about job applicants, or the Peace Corps' queries to universities for information concerning an individual's psychological make-up or moral character. Such invasions may be deplorable and unjust, but they are made through the front door, or the side door at least. They require the formal consent of the organization whose sources are to be tapped. An unlawful invasion, on the other hand, is little more than a kind of burglary. It is done by covert and illegal or unethical means—wires are tapped, individuals in trusted positions are bribed, intimidated, or seduced. That government agencies are known to resort to such methods does not change their basic character.

Apart from the means by which these invasions are made, another important distinction must be considered. "Legal" invasions can affect the lives and careers of perhaps millions of people if they become routine. "Illegal" invasions, on the other hand, can affect only a relatively few. You cannot rifle a premises every night, nor can you continue to bribe and intimidate a whole agency. This, of course, does not make the illegal invasions any less heinous, but it puts them in the category of such things as automobile accidents and rapes.

Entirely different techniques are necessary to guard against these

118

two forms of privacy invasion. Strangely enough, this was not obvious to the participants in the hearings. Representative Gallagher was equally concerned with both forms, but he appeared to take the position that if one could not guarantee that no individual could ever be menaced by the system, one had no business proposing it at all. While his experience with some of the sly practices of certain government agencies may have given him some emotional justification for this, he was unreasonable. One could just as well argue against the existence of banks on the grounds that no one can guarantee that they will not be robbed and embezzled, or against nuclear weapons on the grounds that they might go off accidentally or tempt a mad missile man to bring on Armageddon.

Once the distinction between legal and illegal invasions of privacy is fully grasped, if not by Representative Gallagher, then by his associates, it is likely that earnest bureaucrats like Bowman will extricate themselves from the trap created by their proposal. They will assure that both legal and illegal invasions of privacy would be controlled strictly by combined legal and technical safeguards which even their more informed critics concede are feasible. One of Gallagher's prosecution witnesses, Paul Baran of the Rand Corporation, who is, in Gallagher's words, "one of the few persons in the United States acknowledged as an expert in the relationship of computers and the invasion of privacy," provides some suggestions along these lines:

"Provisions for minimum cryptographic-type protection of all communication lines that carry potentially embarrassing data—not super-duper unbreakable cryptography, just some minimal, reversible, logical operations upon the data stream to make the eavesdropper's job so difficult that it isn't worth his time. The future holds the promise of low-cost computer logic, so this may not be as expensive as it sounds.

"Never store file data in the complete 'clear.' Perform some simple —but key controllable—operation on the data so that a simple access to storage will not dump stored data out into the clear.

"Make random external audits of file operating programs a standard practice to insure that no programmer has intentionally or inadvertently slipped in a 'secret door' to permit a remote point [to have] access [to] information to which he is not entitled by sending in a 'password.'

"When the day comes when individual file systems are interconnected on a widespread basis, let us have studied the problem sufficiently so that we can create sensible, precise ground rules on cross-system interrogation access.

"Provide mechanisms to detect abnormal information requests. That is, if a particular file is receiving an excessive number of inquiries or there is an unusual number of cross-file inquiries coming from one source, flag the request to a human operator.

"Build in provisions to verify and record the source of requests for information interrogations.

"Audit information requests and inform authorities of suspected misuse of the system. . . .

"Clearly," Mr. Baran concluded, "here is an example of the trade-off between dollars and the type of society we want. We will face such decisions more and more often in the future."

To Baran's excellent presentation we might add that there is every reason to suppose that the Rubel Effect will operate in this area too. At present, as Baran himself notes, there is no money in privacy safeguards:

"Perhaps this may be attributed to the lack of sophistication of each individual user or perhaps no individual user can demand extra new safeguards when almost comparable systems have been built in the past without such protection. I think it time that Government speaks clearly as an advocate of the public interest in the future and initiates the improvements we desire. The first step would be to start considering some of the individual computer systems now being built from the viewpoint of larger, overall systems now under growth.

"The men guiding the computer companies, the ones who must perform the detailed work in building safer systems, in my experience are among the most public spirited and enlightened in the Nation. But I believe they will get on with the job more rapidly once their attention has been turned to the long-range implications of their babies." Assuming then that the issue of personal privacy will be resolved along these lines, at least to the satisfaction of the general public and Administration leaders, what about the timing of the national computer system? When will it be in operation?

This is obviously difficult to answer. Unofficial estimates of the time it will take to establish the proposed National Data Center vary from three to seven years from the time the project is authorized and funded, which, if Representative Gallagher has anything to say about it, is still several years away. During the interim, development will certainly continue on other government systems that, even though having no plans for this now, will eventually be integrated into the system; the FBI, for example, is pushing its computerized National Crime Information Center, and the Civil Service Commission will continue to expand its automated personnel systems, which even now include (wrote its Chairman, John W. Macy, Jr., in the Saturday Review of July 23, 1966) a "computerized file containing the names and employment data of some 25,000 persons, all considered likely prospects for [high level] Federal appointive positions."

As for the concomitant governmental reorganization, no one is estimating how long it will take, although one official close to President Johnson has been quoted as saying that "if Johnson is President until 1972 you won't recognize the Federal Government" (in that year presumably). This did not refer specifically to a computerized government, but just as the reorganization is the *sine qua non* of a national computer system, something at least approaching that system will be essential to making such a reorganization a success.

In any case, barring the unlikely possibility that the partisans of individual privacy succeed in making the system a major public issue, it is likely that the system will not be realized totally. Rather, it will develop as a series of related projects, much as the space program has been developed. In this case, it may be 20 years before the national computer system is generally perceived for what it is. And by then it will be a fact of life for most of us.

8

·

Living with a National Computer System

What we will notice most—and probably take for granted—about the environment created by the national computer system will be its uniformity, and then within this, its complexity. Throughout the country, happenings will have a common format; the same laws and public policies will be administered evenly in every State. This will be most evident in the paper forms of officialdom; a parking ticket issued in San Diego will look exactly like one issued in Boston. The same will be true of employment applications, permits, licenses, and all the rest of the paper by which the authorities make known their wishes, reproofs, and expectations. To a lesser extent this will hold for "private paper"—bank statements, bills, etc. They will continue to bear the logos of their particular sources, but the information they request and contain will follow a general pattern.

This will undoubtedly be a boon to the traveler and the increasingly mobile household. A move from one state or region will no longer necessitate learning a new complex of laws and customs. The courthouses and the school systems will be as standardized as the shopping centers and roadside restaurant chains across the country.

Along with this standardization will come, however, a vast increase in the detail of official preoccupations. Organization will be more refined. Instead of, for instance, one minimum wage standard there will be a whole scale of them for different occupations and levels of skill and experience. The present crazy quilt pattern of State and local taxes will give way to more evenly applied regional systems, within which will be more shadings and variations; for example, instead of one retail sales tax more or less uniformly applied there will be a whole range of them. A tube of toothpaste in a drug store may thus bear one tax, whereas one in a supermarket may bear another of a different amount. Or a suit of clothes may be taxed differently from a household appliance selling for the same price, and, as taxes become increasingly used as much for economic and social regulation as for producing revenue, they will increasingly tend to fluctuate in response to economic and social conditions.

This tendency for official policies to become more responsive to constant and subtle changes in the environment will be universally felt. Interest rates, like taxes, will fluctuate almost daily, and the principle of the escalation clause could be in widespread use, whereby a lender may, under certain conditions, require the borrower to pay an increase over the original rate of interest. Seekers of capital will thus be confronted with a whole spectrum of lending conditions, in which the social and economic implications of their capital requirements are an increasingly crucial factor in the sort of treatment they receive.

Those who seek employment will find much the same conditions. As employment requirements change from quarter to quarter and from region to region, job and educational entrance qualifications will vary also. The job category that requires a Bachelor's degree one day will require a Master's degree the next, as, perhaps, the beginnings of a surplus of applicants is routinely noted, or as a potential shortage of job applicants in some other area signals the advisability of diverting some of the available human resources in its direction by discouraging their movement in another.

The same applies to applicants for schooling. The schools of all levels will tend to become what critics now scornfully accuse them of being—sorting bins for future employees. The primary school grades will be devoted as much to measuring and evaluating the potentials of their little charges as to educating them. At the completion of each grade the students will be routinely assessed and dispatched to any of a number of specialized environments, some remedial, some merely custodial, some oriented toward specialized achievement. As in the employment situation, the conditions and qualifications for individual entry into these various classifications will vary with estimates of future personnel needs, the availability of various kinds of educational facilities, and educational trends and developments.

This picture does not differ substantially from the only partially computerized present. Its major elements are already well developed. The changes will be ones of scale and emphasis; the baroque character of today's socioeconomic planning will merely give way to something rococo.

For the individual person, company, or community the most pervasive characteristic of this future world is this: most of what happens in it will be almost totally incomprehensible. Wants and needs of all kinds will be given more consideration, causes will be ascer-

123

tained and effects anticipated with more certainty, rights and obligations will be defined with more precision, but the whys and wherefores of all this will be beyond anyone's understanding. Individual initiative will thus be limited to presenting oneself to what are hoped to be the proper authorities and then to awaiting the disposition of one's case.

The mystery will be made all the more acute because the traditional and familiar official facades will all be relatively intact. The Court House under the old shade trees will still be open for business, the mayor will sit in City Hall, and the friendly neighborhood bank will be around. (It has even been seriously suggested that it be put on wheels—as a traveling bank-mobile, providing full service to your door!) But this is just a facade.

Some changes will be superficial. First, the traditional seedy image of local government will be transformed. The peeling walls and battered desks of the Court House and the City Hall will give way to the disciplined suavity of institutional modern, for data processing equipment requires solid foundations and ample air conditioning, plentiful storage space, and room for expansion.

Along with improvements in plant will be an upgrading in personnel—the doddering and surly clerks will be replaced by bright young specialists—professionals to whom this place is only one step in a long and, hopefully, interesting career.

More important than these essentially cosmetic improvements, however, is the virtual lack of autonomous planning or administration by local governments. The conduct of routine, day-to-day government operations will no doubt remain in local hands—but it will be subject to a stream of directives, guidelines, and decisions from "further up the line." Community planning will be handled increasingly by teams and task forces of highly trained specialists backed by the inestimable resources of the Federal Government and the national computer system. The employment of such teams will be an absolute condition of the Federal support upon which all local governments will have come to depend.

In accordance with smoothly functioning systems design and management procedures, such teams will handle routinely the design and development of local "subsystems" of all kinds, using pretested "design packages" of proved reliability, guaranteed to meet Federal requirements. Using advanced computer techniques, they will—again routinely—thoroughly study and analyze the local situation as it relates to the problem at hand to a point at which they will understand it far better than local officials themselves. They can do this because the system to which they are linked will inform them of local happenings (data that presumably would be equally available to local

124

officials) and will permit them to compare and relate the affairs of the locality to other localities and to those of the region and the nation as well. In short, *all* the functions of local governments will be applications of a kind of social and economic engineering carried on in the same fashion, basically, as are the physical engineering projects of today such as roads, bridges, and sewage plants. Individual citizens will be the sidewalk superintendents or bond holders of the operation.

But in one area local governments will most likely remain preeminent—the collecting of source data for the system. They will be provided with superb equipment for gathering and collating social and economic information of all kinds. Making good use of these facilities will become their primary function. Much of what they gather will be forwarded to regional and national data centers as a matter of course—the raw material for a continuing program of incredibly delicate and complex adjustments in the social and economic processes of the whole country, and for research into new areas of social and economic promise.

In addition, local authorities will stand ready to handle special data-gathering efforts at the system's behest. Some of these will be incidental to local projects. The dispatch of a team to reorganize a school system or a tax structure or a program of industrial expansion will be preceded by a local effort, under proper system guidance of course, to gather considerably more information about various local conditions than is warranted in normal system operations.

Other efforts will be in response to more specific requests from "higher up." One of the most attractive features of a national computer system is that the whole country can be used as a kind of socioeconomic laboratory. To put it simply, it will be feasible, and certainly in the public interest, to test new techniques of social and economic management. The process is simple if you have access to a large and reliable computer. Let us say that you wish to field test a new program for the training of disadvantaged youths. Using the computer, you locate two similar communities—areas in which, to a given approximation, the same mix of social and economic factors are present. In one, you try out the new program and in the other you don't. Then you observe the results as they are reflected in changes in the source data and statistics of economic and social activity in the test areas.

There is literally no limit to the good results that can be obtained from this technique, as the experts in the Departments of Health, Education and Welfare, Housing and Urban Development, etc. have discovered. We can, however, pinpoint a few areas in local government where, due to many imponderables now in evidence, it is most likely to be employed.

ZONING

Zoning is traditionally an exclusive concern of local government, and consequently one of the wildest variables in national economic and social planning models. As such, it has had much to do with whether new industries can economically locate in a particular area, whether proper school facilities can be made available to minority groups, where public housing and other civic improvements can be located, and so on.

Even at the local level, zoning policies are usually mysterious and confusing. Rarely can one determine whether the zoning laws and variances of a locality reflect economic or ethnic discrimination, the need to maintain a certain kind of tax base, the inclination to favor particular power or special interest groups, or simply devotion to maintaining the status quo. With a precise and uniform accounting of the socioeconomic factors influencing zoning policies, the particular relevance of these factors can be determined with some accuracy.*

VOTING BEHAVIOR

Ever since John F. Kennedy's blitzkrieg in the 1960 Democratic primaries, interest in computer studies of individual and group voting behavior has increased. (In brief, does a Negro, Catholic businessman vote as a Negro, a Catholic, or a businessman?) To date, it has been possible only to make broad studies along these lines—to measure the probabilities of general categories of voters voting for one party or another, or, in a few instances, for one major candidate or another. Voting behavior in a given locality on a particular issue cannot be determined accurately because not enough is known about the distribution of the many factors—such as race and income status—that determine preferences.

It would be of considerable value to social and economic planners to be able to do this. Local elections, much more than national elections, tend to focus on social and economic issues rather than on personalities. These issues are likely to be presented in somewhat parochial terms, of course—the racial integration issue is thus reduced to a question of bussing students, for example. Even so, local elections can be matchless indicators of the attitudes of different classes and groups within the community. Even more could be learned by the comparison technique, i.e.,—two similar localities are isolated, and one is presented with an issue and the other is not, etc. Understandably, some local candidates might object strenuously to such a use of their

* Preliminary studies to this end are underway. The Department of Housing and Urban Development recently awarded a contract to the American Society of Planning Officials for an 18-month study designed to find "ways by which states and localities may improve and utilize [zoning] laws to obtain further growth and development."

election campaigns, but perhaps they could be compensated if the experiment was successful. Or perhaps graduate students in economics and sociology could be persuaded, in the interests of science, to run for local offices and conduct campaigns in defense of unpopular issues.

Special studies relating to voting behavior are planned or in progress. The Social Science Research Council's Annual Report for 1964–1965, for example, in its list of grants awarded for research, mentions "research on changes in patterns of voting behavior in five states, 1892–1895; research on Southern Republicanism, 1952–1964; research on the political orientations of the poor; research on components in the emergence of a local political community; research on popular democracy and judicial independence: a study of the 1964 and 1965 elections of the Justices of the Supreme Count in Wisconsin"; and, finally, a study of "computer simulation of voting behavior."

All are theoretical studies. They will be so only as long as detailed information on the factors influencing voting behavior remain relatively difficult to acquire and to assemble into meaningful patterns.

With the systematic collection of individual data on these factors, however, public officials could build and maintain elaborate profiles or models of the socioeconomic tendencies of localities. These can then be related readily to the observed voting behavior of these localities, and the results can be used to predict how the populations of these specific localities will react (as expressed by votes) to future programs and policies. The possibilities of this kind of analysis are, like so many other computer applications, virtually unlimited. The tolerances of various socioeconomic groups for various kinds of reforms can be pinpointed; voter reactions to various kinds of political campaigns can be determined. In effect every election could serve as a kind of socioeconomic experiment. A vote becomes a reaction to a stimulus rather than a stimulus to action.

Welfare

Public welfare recipients represent an important national resource insofar as they can be used to supply valuable data on social and economic factors. As the forms of public assistance become more varied, affecting more and more categories of people, the information pool they represent becomes more and more attractive as an aid to socioeconomic research. Perhaps the best way to describe these research possibilities is to quote several examples of research projects in this area sponsored by the Department of Health, Education and Welfare: *

* U.S. Department of Health, Education and Welfare: Abstracts of Research and Demonstration Projects in Social Welfare and Related Fields.

Emotional Correlates of Vocational Rehabilitation
(Project No. 1243–VRA)

Purpose:

To investigate the degree to which emotional problems are a factor in the problems of vocational rehabilitation; to determine the degree to which rehabilitation can be enhanced by the services of a psychiatric team. The project operates cooperatively with a project supported by the Cooperative Research and Demonstration Grants of the Welfare and Social Security Administrations. The sample is composed of 200 individuals selected at random from a population of 2,000 displaced by an urban renewal project in Topeka, Kans.

Methodology:

A team composed of a psychiatrist, psychologist, social worker and rehabilitation counselor evaluates the emotional and vocational adjustment of individuals in the sample. All in need of psychiatric and vocational rehabilitation services receive them. Four years later the individuals will be reevaluated by an "uncontaminated" assessment team. They will also be compared with three other groups selected from (1) the urban renewal population which received the services of a "nonprofessional" counseling program; (2) the urban renewal population which received no counseling; and (3) residents of an adjacent area with the same social class characteristics who were not directly involved in the urban renewal process.

Grantee:

The Menninger Foundation.

Socioeconomic Factors Affecting Welfare-Dependent
and Low-Income Families
(Project No. 207–WA and SSA)

Purpose:

To describe the varieties of adjustment made by low-income families to their environment; to point up the major problems associated with their adjustment and some of the major public policy issues involved; and to provide comparative data on low-income families receiving, and not receiving, public assistance. The project is located in California.

Methodology:

A sample of 1,200 families in four regions of the State are being studied. One-half receive Aid to Families with Dependent Children-

Unemployed Parents (AFDC-UP) and one-half have received no assistance for the past 2 years. Samples of intact families are matched for ethnicity and family composition. The various modes of adjustment will be compared. Information will be collected regarding job history and attitudes toward work; annual income patterns, handling of money; use and allocation of time devoted to daily routines; social relations including experience with formal organizations; social control and stability, including orientation toward work and health, and degree of commitment to values of the general society; demographic characteristics; and levels of living.

Grantee:

California Department of Social Welfare.

Demonstration of Social Group Work With Parents
(Project No. D16–CB)

Purpose:

To demonstrate and evaluate the usefulness of social group work as a method of strengthening family life in three types of families: Parents who place their children in independent boarding homes, especially lower-class working mothers who are part-time parents; foster parents who board children placed by working mother; and mothers who receive Aid to Families with Dependent Children (AFDC). The focus of this Michigan study is on prevention of emotional disturbance or delinquency in children through group treatment of natural and foster parents.

Methodology:

After a careful pretesting period, three sample groups were formed: (1) AFDC mothers whose children were having difficulties in school served as the experimental group which received weekly group counseling sessions from the project staff; (2) natural and/or foster parents who were receiving group work services from the Children's Division; and (3) about 30 AFDC mothers with comparable problems who received no services beyond those offered by the public welfare agency. Subjective evaluation, attitude and behavior questionnaires, test batteries, and structured, individual interviews have been used to secure data regarding families and children and the changes effected by the experimental variable. Attention has been focused on the training of workers, optimal group size, and number of sessions. The staff of the Michigan Department of Social Welfare will be trained in the use of group work methods so that the services can continue after termination of the grant.

Grantee:

University of Michigan School of Social Work.

Use of Selected Types of Student Aid To Encourage
School Attendance
(Project No. 017–BFS)

Purpose:

To test the effect on school attendance, school performance, and family relationships of three alternative methods of providing financial aid to youth in families receiving Aid to Families with Dependent Children (AFDC); and to enable and encourage teen-agers to remain in school through high school graduation. The project is carried out in selected counties in West Virginia by the Department of Public Welfare.

Methodology:

Three methods of providing financial aid to students are being tested: (1) payment for school-related work; (2) increase in family assistance grant; (3) scholarship without work requirement. In each instance, the payment amounts to $15 monthly. Twelve hundred youth were selected at random in the project counties, so that there would be 300 for each experimental group and 300 for a control group. School and public welfare personnel coordinate their efforts and make systematic reports. Special interviews are conducted with school dropouts to learn their reasons for discontinuing school and their future plans. Baseline measurements were secured through structured interviews conducted by public welfare workers and a review of school records.

Grantee:

West Virginia Department of Public Welfare.

Local governments, however, are concerned with only a fraction of local affairs. Even in large cities they have relatively little to do with such activities as private banking, merchandising, and manufacturing. Accurate, detailed information concerning these activities is as necessary as that generated by local government. It might be harvested in several ways. One would be to expand the data-gathering activities of the present Federal Statistical System, and the various Federal regulatory agencies, creating, in effect, a second primary system under complete Federal control, which would thus tie into the national computer system at the regional level. This would have the effect of providing, or at least seeming to provide, some of the facilities for dispersing information that the defenders of privacy consider so important. It would also strengthen Federal officials in any contest of wills with local authorities. An alternate approach would be to subcontract these data-gathering functions to local authorities. This would lead to considerable economies in personnel and equipment, and, in the long run, might permit Federal authorities to maintain tighter control over *all* local information-gathering activities by giving those authorities added reasons to impose standards and formats and by giving local authorities added incentives to live up to them.

Either way, private economic organizations will be led to supply much more information about their activities than they do at present. With all banks, retail and wholesale establishments, industrial plants, and public utilities operating their own in-plant computer systems, to supply the authorities with detailed social and economic data, on a day-to-day basis if necessary, would not work any special hardship. It is unlikely, however, that this much detail would be required. As long as private transactions of this kind were recorded to a common format, and the more detailed records kept for a reasonable length of time, the national system's requirements could probably be supplied adequately by daily totals of deposits, sales, inventories, purchases, etc., and, perhaps, with weekly totals on employment.

With all this, the management of the economy will begin to take place on a real-time basis. Instead of having to rely on economic data from three months to 10 years old, much of it based only on samples of doubtful character, Government planners will have available something approaching a complete reading of the state of the whole economy every week. Additional detail of any segment of this vast picture will be available for the asking, and at little or no additional expense.

As computer systems planners are so fond of saying, the possibilities of this are beyond imagination. The same techniques of experimentation applied to disadvantaged youths can also be applied to whole industries and markets, disadvantaged or otherwise. Questions of theoretical economics which have intrigued professional economists for generations can be put to the test, although this will probably be done only with extreme caution. More practically, taxes, tax credits, changes in interest rates, wage and hour policies, and the like will become socioeconomic management tools, or weapons, with more sophistication than they have now. It will become perfectly feasible to apply the techniques of the graduated response, so favored by military tacticians, to all sorts of economic and social situations. For instance, if the beer bottlers of Peoria are automating too abruptly and ignoring guidelines for the retraining of displaced personnel, remove a part of such and such a tax credit on beer-bottling machinery in the

131

Central Illinois sub-district. If a glove manufacturer is importing too much suede, to the detriment of the plastics industry, raise the interest rate on a certain category of capital he is using, or raise the sales tax on suede gloves a trifle, or raise the minimum wage for the suede stitchers he is using. These examples may be fanciful; the range of techniques they imply is not.

This is not to suggest that there will be an implication of caprice or vindictiveness in their applications. The purposes of this kind of economic and social regulation will be clearcut and universally agreed upon: to maintain full employment, to avoid inflation, and to provide a decent measure of social and economic progress in such areas as cleaning up the air and water and preserving natural resources. In another decade at the most a real consensus on these issues will be achieved, and any irritations felt toward the restraints imposed by the pursuit of such objectives will be comparable to those felt by the motorist faced with traffic laws. Like traffic laws, the laws determining the use of such economic restraints will be enacted by freely elected legislators. The only innovation will be that the laws themselves will be largely written and evaluated by computers on the basis of many hours of detailed analysis of past events and equally detailed simulations of future ones. Legislators, of course, will continue to evaluate them, too.

Laws developed this way will tend to contain extremely detailed statements of logic which include many variables. Fortunately, computers will also play a large part in applying and administering them.

In effect, the enactment and enforcement of laws will tend to lose some of their sacred character, and so will become merely another form of information exchange. Much of the Government's surveillance and regulation will be seen to have essentially the same character as that of the communications of the air traffic control center of a busy airport with the aircraft in the air surrounding it. In other words, information processing will continue to be a two-way street. Those who supply the system with the information can reasonably and legitimately expect to receive useful information in return. Much of this will be routine, of course, but much will also be specialized. A business firm contemplating a new course of action can doubtless approach the system and, after describing its intended course of action, receive a detailed statement indicating such things as its present and probable future legality and its consistency with various economic patterns and objectives. It is likely, too, that the Government will make available program packages for at least routine analyses of laws and policies on much the same basis as it presently offers accounts of tax court decisions and the like. Businessmen will ignore this assistance at their peril.

Let us return now to the affairs of local governments. We have seen that, while local governments can be readily equipped to collect source data, it is unlikely that they could use it for planning. The kind of approach to local planning exemplified by such local prototype systems* as CORRAL and the Detroit Social Data Bank will become antiquated and inefficient with the advent of a national computer system. Instead, the initiative for local planning will rest largely with regional development authorities, backed by the resources of the national computer system.

Day-by-day, the system will receive detailed information about the affairs of each locality which will be summarized and routinely evaluated in terms of established norms of all kinds, themselves integral parts of larger designs for regional and national harmony and progress. As long as events in the locality are in accord with plans and predictions, no unusual action on a regional level will be taken regarding them. The moment they do not, however, alarms start ringing at headquarters. As it is noted, for example, that the ratio of population increase to the increase in allocations for school construction is changing drastically, some regional specialist concerned with school construction will be apprised of the fact. This official will undoubtedly study the implications and relate it in some way (with the aid of the computer) to regional school construction programs. He will notify local authorities of his actions only when he thinks it expedient to do so.

This means that if local officials, in a burst of ambition or civic pride, or perhaps even a base desire to enrich some of their backers, seek to float a bond issue for a new school construction, they would find it hard going to act in opposition to the impartial regional computer, and, of course, to the grant-giving regional managers associated with it. If, on the other hand, the regional computer notes that the locality's development was at variance with established norms, and that, as a result, certain changes in local planning and administration were called for, the same local officials would be hard put to it to refuse to carry out these changes.

In both cases, the local officials would have to contend with the judgments of impartial experts from afar who were immune to local pressures, instead of having to deal merely with local opinion, which would be unlikely to vary much from that of the officials themselves. These experts would be in a position to point out that what the local officials were proposing was contrary to what other localities were doing under similar conditions, and that their policies, if put into

* A group of local officials independently examines the local situation, casts about for similar situations and responses in a few other localities as possible models, draws conclusions, and makes plans.

practice, would result in such and such an undesirable condition. Such pronouncements would not be expressed simply as qualified opinions but would be buttressed by specific, detailed examples and forecasts in whatever quantity deemed necessary to persuade. Only a brave and almost foolhardy local official would resist such pressures.

While it is possible to look forward with some relish to this discomfiture of local pashas, the conclusion seems inescapable that along with the downgrading of the power of local officials would be an equally impressive downgrading of the voting power of the citizens who elected them. A situation like this is evoked: the good people of Oakdale or Sunnybrook Heights most emphatically do not want their district rezoned for, let us say, multiple dwellings. They are well organized and vociferous. Their local leaders, when apprised of their feelings, agree whole-heartedly. But they can only wring their hands and, in answer to the protests of their constituents, point out that on the basis of expert study and analysis of the local situation, which cannot in any case be refuted without the expense of a considerable amount of local money and time, no other course is open. The familiar committees of protesting local citizens will confront not their elected representatives, perennially anxious about the next election, but a panel of regional planners to whom the local problem is only a small fragment of a vast mosaic. This sort of drama is already being rehearsed all over the country in the course of road and highway planning. It is very much a part of the shape of things to come.

In sum, it appears that an inexorable consequence of establishing a national computer system along these lines is the withering away of the planning and policy-making functions of local governments. This leaves unanswered the question of what constitutes local government. Are we talking about townships, counties, cities, or States when we speak of local government? Unfortunately, the question must remain unanswered. We simply cannot tell, at this point, how far regional power will be permitted to develop; to develop the system at all, local authorities and local governments must be prepared to accept a great deal of Federal authority. The technical requirements of the system alone demand this. Also, once in operation, the system itself can develop only in the direction of more central power.

We need not suppose, however, that the seemingly omnipotent regional satraps find their situation any bed of roses either. To appreciate this, let us consider their point of view.

Under present conditions, the actual responsibilities of any regional director or commissioner are vague. This is because we lack dependable data about local conditions and have no efficient means for acquiring them. The regional officials of the older Federal agencies, with the possible exception of the Internal Revenue Service, have adjusted to this situation. They tend to counsel, exhort, advise, and recommend rather than act. When they have purely regulatory functions, such as those of the Interstate Commerce Commission or the Securities and Exchange Commission, they tend to regulate occasionally by making an example of some individual offender who makes himself too conspicuous, but are content merely to frown at others. In any case, they tend to leave matters of policy to the decision of their superiors or the courts. This is no criticism, for it is all that is expected of them. For the most part, they are supposed to curb flagrant abuses, rather than to manage efficiently.

As the newer agencies of the War on Poverty have begun to operate at the regional level, the lack of sufficient source data has taken on a more desperate aspect. These newer agencies are supposed not only to advise and counsel, but also to *plan* and, to an increasing degree, to see to the execution of their plans. Their failure to accomplish this has become notable, but at least they have a good excuse. As long as they have no reliable data, they cannot be expected to do more than score an occasional small success, just enough to keep up morale and demonstrate that under the right conditions something could be done in this or that deplorable situation. In the War on Poverty, and in the long march to the Great Society, they are just so many more "guerrillas," these agencies with portentous names.*

With the advent of the national computer system and its attendant reorganization of the Federal Government, these regional administrators and their unhappy staffs will be confronted by an entirely new situation. They will soon find themselves with a positive embarrassment of reliable data about the conditions in their regions. Most of it, moreover, will not be their exclusive property, but instead will flow by them into a central pool where it will be available to their bureaucratic friends and enemies alike. Suddenly they will be greatly pressured to come up with ambitious and workable plans. Hanging over their heads like a sword will be the example of Mayor Lindsay of New York City, who, it is said, once lost the use of some 10 million dollars of Federal anti-poverty funds for want of a plan to spend it.

These administrators not only must plan, and see their plans meticulously scrutinized as only a large computer system can do, but will also be responsible for executing these plans. Their plans and programs will have to work, and usually the first time.

But—and here's the rub—they will not have the facilities, even on a regional basis, to handle this phase completely. Regional authorities will be informed of what goes wrong in their regions. They will also have the facilities for reporting and measuring progress, or the lack

* Or "Green Berets," possibly.

135

of it, in correcting those ills. Information in both of these areas can be supplied by their local government sources in whatever detail required. This data alone is insufficient, though, for intelligent planning necessitates access to a great deal of data from other regions, and to much summary and theoretical data from more rarified planning levels. For this they must contact the National Data Center and the National Intergovernmental Affairs Council, or whatever the supreme body eventually comes to be called.

In short, regional administrators will tend to fall into the familiar pattern of "middle management"—the group whose traditional independence of action is seen by computer management experts as most likely to be reduced in importance.

The result of this situation is difficult to foresee in all of its ramifications, but it is fairly certain that these regional chiefs will be a desperate crew. Power and responsibilities they will certainly have—equivalent to that of several State governors and legislatures. But, overseeing their activities and monitoring their decisions will be an automated secretariat which will be more critical and perceptive than any electorate. This secretariat will express its desires not as "mandates," subject to varying interpretations, and often susceptible to fulfillment in principle only, but rather as detailed master plans explicated by specific directives that the regional administrator cannot ignore. He will be expected to be a trouble-shooter and a front man, and, when the plans go sour, a sacrificial victim.

This brings us to the top level, or the central control echelon, of the system. One element of this will be the National Data Center which is the system's permanent data storage facility, or memory. It will thus contain three distinct kinds of information: first, the files of source data, constantly augmented from the far-flung network of local and regional terminals; second, a collection of system operating procedures, i.e., a store of computer programs devoted to all the intricate actions that the system takes in response to source data inputs; and third, a distillation of the first two, but with something added.

The second category will be constantly augmented as new situations develop and new methods of handling them are devised. These programs will originate at all levels of the system, and, in addition to their local use, will become part of a permanent archive, available for further applications. Devising methods of making these individual programs compatible with the rest of the system, and methods of filing them so that they are accessible, will be a major function of the Data Center's human components.

The third kind of information is somewhat more difficult to categorize. Perhaps it is best described by making an extended analogy from the military art or science: in the conduct of military operations, a distinction is made between *tactics* and *strategy*. Tactics generally refers to the means employed to accomplish an objective, i.e., whether to use armored forces or paratroops, or whether to occupy a city or by-pass it. Strategy has to do with ends, goals, or objectives. Of course, both have various levels; what may appear to a lowly lieutenant as strategy may be considered as tactics by an army commander with a loftier view of the situation. In general, however, this distinction between means and ends holds up for the two.

Underlying both tactics and strategy are tactical and strategic *doctrines*—the intellectual bases upon which tactical and strategic decisions are made. Tactical doctrines are variously expressed in an army's training literature, and in the organization and armament of its forces. A well-known example is the following: at the beginning of World War II the German army's tactical doctrines called for the deployment of tanks in large concentrations—armored divisions and corps; at the same time, the French army's tactical doctrines called for the dispersal of tanks—a relative small number assigned to each infantry division. German tactical doctrine called for deep thrusts by tank forces; the French sought to employ them more as spearheads and backup forces for infantry attacks, and, more often, as mobile strong points for infantry defense.

This illustrates that tactical doctrines, while they are frequently involved and complex, are susceptible to being well codified and defined. This is distinctly less so in the case of strategic doctrines. Far more than tactical doctrines, they are products of a continuing analysis of many rapidly changing factors and unique conditions. Their resolution involves the consideration of a welter of political, economic, and social events and conditions, as well as an appreciation of the purely military. Strategic doctrines, consequently, can rarely be entirely codified, and never for long periods. Their determination, and the specific strategies derived from them, has to be a continuous process, and to the range of the considerations involved, a rather loosely organized one in which many opinions and viewpoints are expressed. It is certainly no accident, in view of this, that determining strategy has become increasingly a civilian function; like war itself, it is "too important to be left to the generals."

From this analogy, we can see that the network of local and regional systems, and the proposed National Data Center itself, correspond to the tactical aspects of the system's operations. In fact, *all* second-level computer system operations have a tactical purpose. Who, then, develops the strategic doctrines necessary to provide some point to all the activity this represents?

Senator Muskie's suggested outline for government reorganization, described in Chapter 7, specified such an agency for strategic planning: his National Intergovernmental Affairs Council (NIAC). He compared it to the Government's top agency for the development of military strategy—the National Security Council. He envisioned the NIAC as a kind of advisory council and high policy planning group chaired by the President himself, and made up of the secretaries of the various Federal departments concerned with the economic and social welfare.

Taking Senator Muskie's model as a guide, we can get a fair idea of what this socioeconomic strategy group will look like.

The United States Government Organizational Manual for 1966–1967 describes the National Security Council's function as being "to advise the President with respect to the integration of domestic, foreign, and military policies relating to the national security." We may expect the NIAC's functions to be described in similarly broad terms: it will advise the President with respect to the integration of domestic (and perhaps foreign) policies relating to the national *welfare* (or perhaps, in the words of the Automation Commission Report, "the national purpose").

The National Security Council does not have much of a staff. Aside from its august council members (the President, Vice-President, Secretary of State, Secretary of Defense, and the Director of the Office of Emergency Planning), its table of organization includes only a Special Assistant to the President and an Executive Secretary. However, the Council directs the Central Intelligence Agency, whose functions are extensive, though somewhat vaguely defined. In addition to this, the Defense Department has an Assistant Secretary of Defense for International Security Affairs whose responsibilities include "monitoring Department of Defense participation in the National Security Council affairs, including development, coordination and recommendation of the positions of the Defense member on the Council," and, "initiating appropriate actions and measures within the Department of Defense for implementing approved National Security Policies." The Department of State has no similar official, although it does have a Deputy Assistant Secretary for Politico-Military Affairs who presumably renders the same kind of service. The Office of Emergency Planning, on the other hand, appears to be almost entirely devoted to assisting the National Security Council. As a part of the Executive Office itself, it is devoted solely to nonmilitary defense research planning, including civil defense and emergency resource and manpower allocation.

On the basis of this kind of administrative support, we begin to see that the National Security Council is an extensive organization in fact, if not in principle. The proposed NIAC can be expected to take a similar form. It will certainly have a "research" facility analogous to that of the CIA (no sinister implication is intended), and it will undoubtedly be served by similar complementary organizations within the various departments whose secretaries are represented on the Council itself.

No description of the National Security Council would be complete without a reference to the constellations of private organizations—universities, foundations, and frankly profit-seeking research companies—that are at the Council's call. A complete list of these and the research projects in which they have participated obviously cannot be assembled, for many of the details of this relationship are highly classified. Its extent, however, is considerable. Most of us are acquainted with the publicity given to some of the CIA's unofficial partnerships, notably its dealings with Michigan State University. These represent only a small part of the total.

Some idea, however, of the kind of policy studies that these institutions supply may be gained from this quotation from the "advertising brochure" of one of them, the Hudson Institute, which describes itself as a "private, non-profit research organization studying public policy issues, especially those related to U.S. National security and international order. . . ." The brochure continues:

"So far, Hudson Institute's work has been primarily in the following areas: international crises, with emphasis on crisis management and the significance of crises for arms control and patterns of international relations; various aspects of civil defense; alternative future tactical and strategic nuclear postures; causes and techniques of insurgency and some of the technical and political problems of counter-insurgency warfare; the role and problems of command and control; strategic and political implications of future military technology; arms control implications of the current arms race generally and of various civil defense and ABM (anti-ballistic missile) programs in particular; alternative European futures and various possible U.S. roles and European defense policies in these alternatives; United States national interest in internation order and some of the basic political and strategic choices facing the U.S. . . ."

Listed among the Hudson Institute's clients are the Arms Control and Disarmament Agency, the Office of Emergency Planning, and the Defense Department's Assistant Secretary for International Security Affairs, as well as a host of other government agencies and other private policy-planning groups, such as the Council on Foreign Relations.

It is difficult, if not impossible, to assess the role and the responsibilities of such organizations as the Hudson Institute as they apply to the determination of strategy and strategic doctrines and policies. It seems reasonable to suppose that they are considerable, and the more so because they are so poorly defined. However, one can foresee a similar constellation of private policy-planning groups developing around the proposed NIAC. Indeed, such a development is already in progress, although it is still in an elementary stage; the Hudson Institute itself lists along with its studies in military strategy, a study devoted to "long-range issues affecting poverty in the U.S.," and among its clients, the Office of Economic Opportunity.

Given that the form of NIAC will be similar to that of the National Security Council, what will be the basis of the "advice" it offers the President? Here the analogy with the National Security Council grows weak. Defense policy and strategy, one may suppose, depend largely on data about conditions in regions not under U.S. control. Information-gathering efforts in this area must, therefore, remain diversified. No single system, or any collection of systems, can encompass them all. This is much less so in the case of data requirements of the NIAC complex. Virtually all source data required for its deliberations will be available—and much of it available only—from the National Data Center and its regional and local affiliates, or, in other words, from the national computer system. All research and study, whether official or unofficial, public or private, will begin there. The present practices of the economic and sociologic research fraternity— large inferences based on observations of small samples and even smaller populations, activities roughly analogous to a China expert's two-week visit to Hong Kong or to a single U2 flight over Cuba—will be outmoded. Any socioeconomic pundit who wants to be where the action is must obtain access to the National Data Center's files, and the wholehearted cooperation of the Center's staff as well. This is probably the most important development of the computer revolution.

The reason behind it is that, as a result of our experience with computers, we have finally learned something that we ought to have known and appreciated all along: the ultimate basis of power is knowledge. Having accepted this, we are all prepared, or at least resigned, to handing over the power to order our lives to those who presumably know more about what's best for us than we do ourselves. There is perhaps no more poignant example of this than our collective acceptance of the war in Viet Nam. President Johnson enjoys a public confidence that no other President has ever had. (How Lincoln would have envied him!) He can conduct one of the most unpromising, if not unjustified, foreign adventures that any President has ever undertaken, simply because every reasonable person is sooner or later obliged to admit that the President knows far more about the situation than anyone else, and to recognize that no one can alter this state of affairs. Therefore, he must be trusted; he must be given the absolute power of decision that the adventure requires. With none of the charisma that characterized such chieftains as Churchill and Roosevelt, with none of the reserves of mass insanity that Hitler had at his command, without taking even the most elementary steps to discourage and limit expressions of dissent, without (it would appear) even especially desiring it himself, he has become, in terms of the absolute power he can wield, the equal of the most thorough tyrants of history. The President can say to all who question him, "I know more than you do." Such is the power of information.

The Viet Nam War may be the most striking example of the power of the Presidency, but it is not the only one. In descending order are President Kennedy's decisions relative to Cuba and Berlin, followed closely by his decision to commit in excess of $50 billion of the nation's resources to putting a man on the moon. Of somewhat lesser scope than these is President Johnson's decision to subsidize the development of a supersonic transport plane to the tune of $4 to $5 billion.

The Chief Executive's omnipotence extends only as far as his omniscience is generally conceded. His decisions relative to civil rights, the War on Poverty, and much of his economic policy are variously received with faint approval or open scorn, for he cannot reasonably claim to have greater knowledge in these areas than can the average Congressman or newspaper columnist. In these matters he is, at most, only the first among equals, and sometimes not even that.

The President's monopoly on military strategy and knowledge of foreign policy, and to a somewhat lesser degree, his monopoly on knowledge of the implications of space flight, stems from two things—the Government's security laws, under which access to data in these areas is highly restricted, and the absence of any real pressure groups or lobbies in these areas, groups with sufficient resources and motivation to acquire some real and contrary knowledge of their own. With some rare exceptions, all the studies in these areas are made either by or for the Government, with the result that opponents of, let us say, the Viet Nam War, or proponents of policies of nuclear disarmament, are limited to appeals to the emotions only.

This condition most emphatically does not hold at present in areas closer to home. There is no monopoly on knowledge, or more accurately, on ignorance, of the workings of the economy, or of the problems of urbanization or of the implications of civil rights legislation and policies. This is not because we have so much knowledge, but because the Government has so little. The results of this oligopoly of ignorance are deplorable, but they at least illustrate, in a negative way this time, the awesome power of knowledge—of abundant information interpreted—and leave us with this paradox: the man whom we

141

trust to lead us in a most dangerous and uncertain war, who may have our entire existence as a species in his hands, is not at all credited with the wisdom and wit to deal with the mere nuisances of poverty, urban blight, river pollution, and others.

This is the situation now, but it will soon change. The means for ending the general state of ignorance concerning our economic and social patterns are at hand. President Johnson's successor will find that he has the same kind of omniscience in domestic affairs that Johnson now enjoys vis-à-vis military strategy and foreign policy.

What can appear along with this omniscience was described with incredible foresight by a visitor to these shores more than 130 years ago.

Wrote Alexis de Tocqueville at the conclusion of *Democracy in America:* "I think, then, that the species of oppression by which democratic nations are menaced is unlike anything that ever before existed in the world; our contemporaries will find no prototype of it in their memories. I seek in vain for an expression that will accurately convey the whole of the idea I have formed of it; the old words *despotism* and *tyranny* are inappropriate: the thing itself is new, and since I cannot name, I must attempt to define it.

"I seek to trace the novel features under which despotism may appear in the world. The first thing that strikes the observation is an innumerable multitude of men all equal and alike, incessantly endeavoring to procure the petty and paltry pleasures with which they glut their lives. Each of them, living apart, is as a stranger to the fate of all the rest; his children and his private friends constitute to him the whole of mankind. As for the rest of his fellow citizens, he is close to them, but does not see them; he touches them, but he does not feel them; he exists only in himself and for himself alone; and if his kindred still remain to him, he may be said at any rate to have lost his country." Then de Tocqueville turned to our system:

"Above this race of men stands an immense and tutelary power, which takes upon itself alone to secure their gratifications and watch over their fate. That power is absolute, minute, regular, provident, and mild. It would be like the authority of a parent if, like that authority, its object was to prepare men for manhood; but it seeks, on the contrary, to keep them in perpetual childhood; it is well content that people should rejoice, provided they think of nothing but rejoicing. For their happiness such a government willingly labors, but it chooses to be the sole agent and the only arbiter of that happiness; it provides for their security, foresees and supplies their necessities, facilitates their pleasures, manages their principal concerns, directs their industry, regulates the descent of property and subdivides their inheritances. . . .

". . . I have always thought that servitude of the regular, quiet and gentle kind which I have just described might be combined more easily than is commonly believed with some of the outward forms of freedom, and that it might even establish itself under the wing of the sovereignty of the people."

Is this the expression of only an excess of Gallic ardor and an aristocratic disdain for the fruits of the revolution that occurred in his own country, or can his "immense and tutelary power" describe our computer system?

There is no final answer to this question, of course, but perhaps, by examining it in more detail, we can at least answer a somewhat more practical and immediate one. We might phrase it this way: Given the prospect of an enormous increase in the collective intelligence of the central authority, how can we, as individuals and as free associations of individuals, best continue to match wits with it, and so avoid being reduced to helpless observers and unwitting participants in its designs for a Great Society of its own definition?

9

Living with a National Computer System (Continued)

The Government's monopoly of knowledge pertaining to military and foreign affairs seems at first to be unrelated to its impending monopoly on domestic, economic and social data. The military–foreign affairs monopoly, as noted, came into being because there are definite legal restrictions on the dissemination of information considered vital to the national security, and because of the absence of any significant number of special interest groups devoted to a free and exhaustive inquiry in these areas. Neither of these conditions are present on the domestic scene. Short of imposing an absolute dictatorship, no one can similarly restrict domestic information or outlaw special interest groups devoted to domestic issues.

If anything, the trend is toward greater dissemination of social and economic data by the Government. Recent Federal laws have made Government source data more accessible to the public, and the various Government agencies have become increasingly lavish in supplying the public with economic and social information. Progressively more publicity is given to the pronouncements of such agencies as the Council of Economic Advisers and the Federal Reserve Board which, along with the increasing amounts of data emanating from the components of the so-called Federal Statistical System, provides those outside the Government with a far better picture of economic and social conditions than ever before.

A similar trend exists in the development of special interest groups that are so necessary to the democratic process. They are more numerous than ever, are better organized and staffed, and cover more areas of interest. Far from discouraging the formation of such groups, the Government fosters and supports them. Why should we not suppose then that these trends will continue in the future?

To answer this, we might begin by asking why information on military and foreign affairs is severely restricted while information on domestic affairs is not. This is because military and foreign affairs information is generally presumed to affect the national security, and domestic information does not. The agencies of the military and foreign policy establishments are seen to have missions and responsibilities of a character entirely different from those of the domestic establishment. In a word, they are concerned with national *survival*. The domestic establishment is devoted principally to "national housekeeping"—with providing services necessary for public order but not actually for survival. We could probably manage to exist without a Post Office Department or even a Justice Department, but not without an army.

This being the case, it must be assumed that as a Government function comes to be regarded as more and more essential to national survival, access to information relative to it will be increasingly restricted. This applies even to the military establishment itself. (Strange as it may seem, until the early twentieth century, U.S. military information could be disseminated during peacetime, except on such subjects as operational codes.)

What evidence can we find to support this assumption? After national defense and foreign relations, the next most crucial area, in regard to national survival, is economic affairs. A collapse of our economy would jeopardize our national existence. If a collapse were less than total, a vigorous and healthy economic posture would still be vital to our military and foreign policy.

Is economic information subject to restrictions at all similar to that of defense and foreign policy? Obviously it is. Whole categories of economic data—too many to list—are strictly controlled by the Government. These data include, in particular, information on impending decisions and policies of such agencies as the Federal Reserve System, the Securities and Exchange Commission, the Treasury Department, and the Justice Department. They also apply to the handling and use of "private" economic information by "private" persons—for example, how corporate officials may use corporate financial data. This does not imply that such restrictions are tyrannical, unconstitutional, or in any way unjust. On the contrary, they are generally recognized as being hardly less essential to the general welfare than are restrictions on information relating to the national security.

The next area pertains to the administration of justice (whether it is less important than economic affairs is open to question). Here again are all kinds of restrictions on information, most of them hoary with tradition. They apply to everything from the handling of source data to decision-making and the determination of policy. However, some restrictions in this area are not as traditional. They well serve to demonstrate that when something becomes of serious public concern, restrictions on information concerning it are sure to follow. A specific example of this is the Department of Justice's Community Relations Service. This agency was authorized and established by the Civil Rights Act of 1964 to assist local communities in "resolving disputes, disagreements, or difficulties relating to discriminating practices based on race, color. . . ." The participants in the agency's mediation activities are bound to secrecy. They can be fined as much as $1,000 or imprisoned for revealing details of negotiations.

All this tends to support the conclusion that, in general, an agency limited to essentially "housekeeping functions" (collecting routine statistics, maintaining routine services, safeguarding Government property, and the like) can afford to be relatively open about its activities. As an agency becomes responsible for specific programs relating to the national welfare—if not to the national security—and to that catch-all, the national interest, it must increasingly limit public access to information about its activities.* At the same time it almost certainly increases its *total* output of information. With all of its security restrictions, the Defense Department practically inundates the world with information. But it is—every scrap of it—"managed information." It is directed at specific groups of people always for a specific purpose: to further the interests of the Defense Department and to enable it to carry out its mission of providing for the security of the United States. This policy probably will be adopted increasingly by other agencies as they, too, move from their present humble positions into those in which they play a major part in providing for the general welfare and achieving the national goals.

Computers, and in particular the national computer system, will be totally affected by this policy. How its technical capacities are exploited will be determined largely by the necessities that this policy defines. In summary, these are: to collect as much social and economic source data as is required in the national interest, or for the general welfare, as they are expressed in terms of specific programs to achieve specific goals; and at the same time, to restrict access to that data in the national interest.

Such a policy, applied through the national computer system, will

* President Johnson expressed this principle, in a public statement on July 4, 1966, extolling the merits of a bill permitting greater access to Federal records, with these words: "Officials within Government must be able to communicate with one another fully and frankly without publicity. They cannot operate effectively if required to disclose information prematurely or to make public investigative files and internal instructions that guide them in arriving at their decisions.

"I know that the sponsors of this bill recognize these important interests and intend to provide for both the need of the public for access to information and the need of the Government to protect certain categories of information. Both are vital to the welfare of our people."

affect two factors in the "national equation": individuals, which can be broadly interpreted as persons, families, and even companies, and special-interest groups, which can be defined as aggregations of individuals freely linked together by some common purpose or in pursuit of some common aim. Both factors, in contrast to State and local governments and their contractors, are "outside" the system.

The sources for most of the data collected by the system will be individuals. For the most part, decisions based on the data so collected will not concern individuals, at least not directly. This can be illustrated by an example of the kind of data collection effort* that, with the establishment of the national computer system, will be routine and will be applied to all areas of our lives:

Family Factors and School Dropout: 1920–1960
(Cooperative Research Project No. 2258–OE)

Purpose:

To make longitudinal analyses of the influence of social background and community climate on the educational attainment of white and nonwhite adolescent males; to examine the relation of attainment with education and occupation of family head, presence of father in the home, and number of siblings; to explore the relationship between education and first job obtained by youth on entry into the labor force; and to explore changes in the dropout phenomenon between 1920 and 1960 in relation to changes in community structure.

Methodology:

Special tabulations were prepared by the Bureau of the Census based on samples of about 5,700 boys from 14 to 17 and 22,000 males ages 20 to 61 in 1962. The data were analyzed for at least nine birth cohorts of whites and five of nonwhites.

Contractor:

Population Studies Center, University of Michigan.

This study has no specified social or economic goal or purpose. Apparently, someone simply felt that the information would be valuable at some time. Nevertheless, ultimately something more than this would probably come of it. The data might be used just to effect a change in the techniques of making such studies; that is, it might be determined that certain categories of data, number of siblings, for example, are almost irrelevant to the problem and so are not worth

---

* U.S. Department of Health, Education and Welfare: Abstracts of Research and Demonstration Projects in Social Welfare and Related Fields.

collecting, or that a better method of describing that "first job" is needed (perhaps in terms of its future prospects).

As the data are further "digested," however, and combined with data from other studies, they become part of the basis for other, more far-reaching decisions, which result, perhaps, in significant changes in broad socioeconomic policies. Conceivably, these could lead to changes in the educational structure or in the requirements for some types of jobs. (It might thus be determined that certain categories of dropouts were being denied access to certain jobs for which they are actually well suited in spite of their educational deficiencies, or it might result in policies intended to increase the likelihood of fathers remaining in homes.)

Inevitably, as such policies are put into effect, the environment of the groups studied would change, and it would be a planned, or managed, change. The groups' actions would be responsible for these changes to some degree, even though no individual, at any point in the process, was singled out and, let us say, given assistance in obtaining further schooling or a job.

Moreover, the span between the initial data collecting and the environmental change would be rather long, and a complex chain of events would link the two. When the data are collected the results might be unforeseen. The initial collection, an analysis phase, might be handled by study groups with one purpose in mind, and the subsequent policies based on the analysis decided by another policy-making group with entirely different aims. Neither might even be aware of the other's existence. The results of the new policies, that is, the resulting changes in the original environment, might be assessed by still another group.

Such a process could become so involved and its interactions so subtle that one is tempted to dismiss it altogether and to see it as actually developing in random fashion. In this instance, it is much more satisfying to focus on special cases in which the reaction to an individual data-set is immediate and clearcut, as, for example, when an individual is disqualified for a job because of a particular fact—an arrest record or membership in a certain organization—or when a motorist's license number is checked against a central file and then action is taken immediately on the basis of that check.

But no matter how subtle the process may appear, it is not at all random. It is no more so than is the process by which a piece of pie eaten at a particular meal contributes to the amount and distribution of one's body fat. It is merely convenient, in the kind of situation we are dealing with, to consider such processes as random.

On this point the members of the Gallagher Subcommittee and the experts associated with the National Data Center proposal seemed to be unable to communicate. To the Subcommittee, the only point to collecting data about individuals was to get back to them as individuals at some time. Nevertheless, if we are to believe the experts, this is not so. Existing information-handling techniques are, by and large, adequate for making decisions about particular individuals in particular situations, but are inadequate for making decisions that will affect large numbers of individuals.

We can conclude from this that, first, individuals will be called upon to supply a great deal of information about their activities, since the usefulness of that information will not be limited to making decisions about them as individuals. Each individual will be, in a sense, like someone with a rare and interesting disease, who, regardless of his otherwise humble status, can attract the attention of high-powered specialists from all over the country, or like an obscure criminal who becomes the subject of a legal decision of great consequence. Of course, since computers do not, as a rule, look at things in the same way as such human specialists as doctors and lawyers do, there will not be much of this kind of notoriety associated with individual peculiarities. The individual legal or medical victim is of interest because he is symbolic of a larger set of victims that is not immediately perceivable by humans. A computer would, however, perceive the entire set of "victims" and one individual member of it as such would be no more available or interesting than any other.

We can also conclude that it will be difficult if not impossible for any individual to know what the consequences of many of his actions will be. Seemingly trivial actions will acquire a new significance, although the individual will never know precisely what it is.

For most persons, this will be a rather novel situation. Traditionally, an individual's relationship with his environment, especially with the authorities in his environment, has been such that either there are definite, clearcut consequences of his actions or they are so delayed and so random as not to be considered consequences at all. If one violates a law, either there is a high probability of being apprehended and penalized in a definite way or there is not. Upon completing a college entrance examination with a certain score and fulfilling certain other stated requirements, one is admitted to a particular college or one is not. At least, if things do not work out this way, it is not too difficult to find out why they did not.

In effect, each individual has to avoid a certain number of actions and perform certain others. Otherwise, one can more or less follow one's fancy, secure enough in the knowledge that whatever one does or does not do is his own affair. Whether one bowls on a Sunday afternoon or visits a library instead is of no consequence since no one checks these things. No discernible relationships exist between one's actions and what happened next, and especially, none could be seen to result in changes in the individual's environment.

One of the exceptions to this clearcut state of affairs, however, is the environment of certain kinds of large organizations—particularly those with many status levels and subtle personnel evaluation policies. Persons in this environment discover that seemingly chance actions often bring about unforeseen results, not only to the individual taking the action, but also to groups of individuals with whom the individual may be linked. The same phenomenon occurs in schools. Successful individuals in this environment generally learn to be extremely circumspect, to pay great attention to small details of their actions, and to formulate elaborate theories as to the rationale by which they are evaluated. Such theories are often wide of the mark, for rarely is it in the interest of the authorities to reveal the rationale, or even to admit that it exists. Not infrequently, they may not even be aware of its existence themselves.

With the advent of a national computer system, such an environment could become the norm. The system can define many relationships in detail and collect data relevant to them. Many plans and policies can be put into effect to work subtle but far-reaching environmental changes. To many of the individuals affected, the changes may continue to appear to be random and even capricious. One school dropout may find himself virtually incarcerated; another may be left to his own devices; and still another may find himself bound for Harvard—as all three become unknowingly involved, through certain of their actions, in various phases of some elaborately designed educational experiment. The same can be said of more fortunate groups of individuals.

Not all such programs will have such spectacular results, of course. Most of us are not as glamorous as high school dropouts; our social characteristics and behavior are of interest only insofar as they relate to economic characteristics and behavior. We are more properly units in an enormous economic equation, or rather a continuing series of them. What we buy and don't buy, what we spend and save, and why, is of consuming interest on one level of economic analysis and planning or another even though our vices are of only routine concern to sociologists. Fortunately for those involved in such plans, the language of economic behavior is much more developed than that of social behavior, and the techniques for gathering economic data—again at all levels—are better understood and better developed.

Thus, our individual behavior in buying and selling an automobile, a house, or a security, in paying our debts and acquiring new ones, and in earning money and being paid, will be noted meticulously and studied exhaustively. Again, the individual's decision to buy a particular car will not in itself greatly impress economic planners. But it will categorize him among automobile purchasers. As the behavior of this group is analyzed along with that of other groups, and then related to still other sets of information at the system's disposal, certain decisions will be made, policies will be applied and restrictions will be imposed or lifted, which will ultimately affect the individual car purchaser in some respect. It is possible that he will find certain categories of cars easier for him to purchase and certain others more difficult. This effect will be no more predictable to the individual than it ever was, but the converse of this will no longer be true—the authorities can predict the individual's actions.

As more and more individual actions are noted, grouped, and related, and subsequently used as the basis for official plans and policies, the individual will be increasingly "boxed in." His environment will have been designed very much with reference to "people like him"—if not specifically for him—the groups whose actions follow a pattern similar to his.

The individual, in this situation, is faced with the constant problem of knowing "who he is." He needs to know what kind of actions tend to place him in which group, and what social and economic policies are in force at the moment for that group.

It has become a commonplace to predict that within a generation most adults will change their vocations several times in the course of their working lives as particular individual skills—and whole industries for that matter—become outmoded and replaced by new ones. Each time an individual is faced with this, he will have to apply and be accepted for some kind of retraining. During his training period, moreover, he and his family will have to be maintained in the style to which they have become accustomed, directly or indirectly at public expense. This is confidently and repeatedly predicted by forward-looking business leaders and government spokesmen.

When an individual comes up for this sort of "retread," he will not be free to choose his next career. The amount and kind of training he receives depend on how he is evaluated and categorized, and what policies are in force for the category into which it is decided that he falls. Whatever the means for evaluating him, it will not be as simple as taking a test, but will be an evaluation of his total relationship to the society and the economy. Consequently, every individual who wants to survive must, during each "employment period," do the things that will improve his next vocational evaluation, and *not* do the things that will tend to degrade it. Since the only source of the information he needs to do this is likely to be the Government, this will be quite an order.

To a somewhat lesser extent, an individual's efforts to find housing

151

will be subject to the same conditions. As the Government becomes more deeply involved in public housing for all income groups through rent subsidies, urban planning, grants-in-aid, various kinds of mortgage guarantees, special tax credits to developers, and the like, every prospective client for housing will be far more rigorously evaluated in terms of his eligibility for one or the other of the multitude of housing aids available. The prototype of this sort of evaluation exists already. Eligibility requirements are still only casually related to such things as the national economy, racial balance, and sociological factors in general. As the broader possibilities of housing eligibility requirements become manifest, individual eligibility will be determined not merely by the rough and ready test of income and credit rating. Of equal importance are factors that have some bearing on how the individual "fits" in the community. What educational styles will he tend to support and what sort will he tend to resist? What kind of business, cultural, and entertainment facilities will he tend to support and what kind will he ignore or oppose? How long is he likely to remain in the community? What sort of community groups will he join, and which will he ignore or resist? These are some of the criteria by which his eligibility will be determined. The criteria will obviously not be the same for all. For each of perhaps dozens of socioeconomic categories there will be different optimums, and for each community different "mixes" of these socioeconomic categories will be established, and, within defined tolerances, maintained.

An individual's "housing eligibility index" will be of great importance to him. It will be to his interest, naturally, to act to improve it, not to lower it. Undoubtedly he must consider not only the total amount that he spends, but also the whole pattern of his spending, which, of course, can be inspected and evaluated by the system. Does he spend an inordinate amount on entertainment, and not enough on property maintenance? Does his previous residence-choice behavior indicate that he is more interested in convenience in commuting than in good educational facilities for his children? Does it indicate a propensity to race prejudice? These are some obvious considerations. Actually, a properly programmed computer can deal with relationships that are far more sophisticated than these. His choice of magazine subscriptions, for instance, can be found to indicate accurately the probability of his maintaining his property or his interest in the education of his children. Men make their living working out the patterns of such relationships.

The difficulties this poses for the individual are sombre to contemplate. They make present-day status-strivings look like child's play. The problem, moreover, will be made even more difficult because the criteria for eligibility will not be revealed to individuals, and will tend to fluctuate constantly as economic and social conditions change and as official plans and policies respond to various pressures, or signals, from the rest of the system. A decision to introduce a new industry, or complex of industries, into an area will lead, perhaps, to decisions to alter the characteristics of various satellite communities. An unfavorable trend toward racial imbalance in a particular community might lead to alterations in the eligibility of persons in certain socioeconomic categories. And there is always the "experimental factor." This future society will be characterized by its capacity to "manage change," an essential of which is controlled sociological experiment.

The same conditions can be anticipated in education, medical care, military service, and other areas. Without intricate policies and programs of social and economic "guidance" of this sort, the stated goals and objectives of the Great Society could simply not be realized, especially as the population approaches 300 million, as automation makes its impact increasingly felt, and, with complete disregard for this, as expectations for the "good life" continue to rise.

It appears that individuals involved in these programs will seek to retain the illusion that they control the courses of their lives, but, judging by the experience of those in the school and corporate environments, even the illusion will be difficult to sustain. Every individual will be aware to some extent that his actions must be accounted for and that his performance will be evaluated in a variety of ways. He will realize that he will be placed—that is, he will place himself—in one or another of a number of socioeconomic categories, each of which is subject to a particular set of permissions and pressures. These will tend to be general rather than specific. An individual will appreciate them only insofar as they are easy and rewarding or difficult and unrewarding.

This kind of future has become the subject of a large body of science fiction, of which Aldous Huxley's *Brave New World* is perhaps the preeminent example. Generally, in these stories the rank or position of various categories of the population is clearly indicated; people are marked like members of a military organization. This, like so many intriguing notions in literature, is unlikely, however. There is little or no social gain in this device, and in a truly stratified society, there may even be a loss. At any rate, sociologists tend more and more to favor diminishing the obvious indicators of social and economic status. For example, the distinction between wage earners who are paid by the hour and salaried workers who are paid by the month or year, regardless of the number of hours actually worked, has come in for increasing criticism. Also, there is the suggestion that it would be desirable to institute formal education courses to teach lower class children the peculiarities of middle-class speech, clothing styles, and manners. Such efforts will no doubt help to soften the reactions of individuals to their being manipulated, but will also make it even more difficult for an individual to know where he stands.

But it is not deliberate attempts to conceal or complicate the workings of the system that will ultimately confound the individual, but rather the form of the system itself. For while the aims and requirements of the society necessitate a socioeconomic planning and control system and, in particular, a national computer system, their form is largely determined by how these interlocking systems can function most efficiently.

If past experience is any guide, the form of the computer system will determine the form of the more loosely defined socioeconomic planning system. The old sayings that form follows function and that computers alter organizational structures and aims are still serviceable, for, without the computer, what we have been examining would be just another attempt at a rigorously planned society ruled by a rather benevolent bureaucracy—a sort of large-scale, up-to-date Austro-Hungarian Empire. Such systems never worked well in the past or for long, and would not work here or now, whatever M. de Tocqueville might suppose. But the computer system adds another dimension. The kind of system we can now envision is analogous to a bureaucracy of almost celestial capacity. This is because the system makes it possible to discern and define relationships in a manner which no human bureaucracy could ever hope to do. It can, of course, record and store facts on a cosmic scale, but this is not its secret; we humans alone could do this if we had to. But we have never been able to divine the importance that one fact imparts to another—not, at least, in sufficient detail or time to do anything about it.

This is exactly what the system will do to perfection. Essentially it will reveal relationships by comparing separate sets of data. If, for instance, in comparing a list of doctors to a list of chess players (both drawn from the same population), it finds that a great many more chess players are also doctors than chance alone would account for, then a relationship between doctoring and chess playing is revealed. From this point it can proceed by comparing other lists, lawyers and chess players, doctors and bridge players, or chess playing doctors under 35 years of age to chess playing doctors over 35 and so on almost ad infinitum until the nature of the relationship is at least pragmatically established. Most of the system's effectiveness in doing this is due to its capacity to scan and compare the contents of incredibly large amounts of data, or long lists, so rapidly with so little error.

154

This scanning and comparing capacity will make it virtually impossible for any individual to know how the system evaluates him, or even to estimate what the system does or does not know about him. This point was brought out in Representative Gallagher's Invasion of Privacy hearings. As noted, the Subcommittee was greatly concerned that a "dossier" could be established and maintained for each individual. It was felt, therefore, that, as a precaution against the misuse of this dossier, provisions should be made for every individual to "inspect" the contents of his "dossier" in order to correct any errors or refute any derogatory information which it might contain. The discomfiture of the Government's statistical experts in the face of this proposition was almost comical. They simply could not make the Congressmen understand that their proposed system would not contain any "dossiers" to inspect. It would, to be sure, contain quantities of personal data about specific individuals, with their names or some other identifiers associated with that data, but the data itself would be scattered far and wide throughout the system. For an individual to inspect his "dossier," or for anyone else to inspect it, virtually the whole system would have to be methodically searched under the general instruction: "retrieve and print any data referenced by the name of individual 'X.' "

Even if this were to be done, and an individual were to obtain a compilation of everything the system "had" on him, all he would know is that his name had appeared at one time or another on a rather large number of "lists." He might learn, for example, that he has been listed as: a married veteran, as a nonagricultural initial employment placement (pay grade #9), as a sand and gravel industry injury case, as having paid Federal excise taxes in excess of 0.004 per cent of his gross income for the past three years, as an enrollee in a college course conducted by radio or television, as being the parent of a partially blind child, as having a net worth of between $6,000 and $8,000, as having increased his net worth at the average rate of 9 per cent for the past three years, as holding a Federally insured demand deposit of between $500 and $750 at the close of the previous calendar year, as having been examined for tuberculosis, and so on through at least several thousand categories.*

This would tell him nothing, for it would not reveal what comparisons had been made between the various lists upon which his name appeared and other lists, nor what conclusions had been drawn from whatever comparisons had been made. It would not tell him whether or not radio and TV courses were considered to be worth-

* All of these categories are based on actual data inventories presently maintained by the Federal Government.

while, or that his annual increase in net worth of 9 per cent was considered to be normal for a person of his age, occupation, and marital status.

To learn the answers independently, he would have to "audit" the system, which is analogous to auditing the books of, let us say, the Internal Revenue Service to see if one's taxes were being levied fairly. This procedure, if feasible, would be extremely expensive and would certainly invade the privacy of a great many other individuals. The individual in question would simply have to be satisfied with whatever information the authorities felt obliged to give him. At most, this might be that in regard to such and such an instance he has been classified into such and such a category for which such and such a policy is in effect. If he feels misused, he may appeal to such and such a tribunal.

In short, the individual would find that his total environment resembled that of a large, well run school, or at best, that of a large corporation located in a small town. His political rights, of course, would not be violated, but would resemble those of a small stockholder in a large, well managed enterprise. The mark of sophistication and savoir-faire in this future will be the grace and flexibility with which one accepts one's role and makes the most of what it offers.

We do not, however, exist merely as individuals, and we are not limited only to membership in groups resulting from someone else's efforts at sociological or economic analysis. An alcoholic is automatically part of one group, but if he joins Alcoholics Anonymous, he is not only in a group of his own choosing, but also qualifies his membership in the group of alcoholics.

We might, therefore, examine the possibilities of what can be defined as special interest groups—neighborhood associations, gangs, parent-teacher associations, alumni groups, societies for the preservation or destruction of this or that, and so on to such frankly self-aggrandising associations as labor unions, trade associations, professional societies, and various kinds of "rights" movements.

Organizations of this sort must have some value, because as our society becomes increasingly regimented more and more of them appear on the scene, and many that have been quiescent and traditional are becoming active. The principal purpose of such organizations is to influence public policy—to try to force some set of authorities to stop doing something and start doing something else, something more favorable to the organization's interest as the organization itself defines it. An extreme example of this is the avowed purpose of the Mattachine Society to change official policies regarding homosexual activities. This group is not concerned with how such changes will affect the functioning of society as a whole, nor whether they are

156

advisable in the light of reputable sociological theory or of various plans and conditions that the proper authorities may wish to further or maintain.

The aims of any special interest organization may be considered by those outside it to be selfish, antisocial, quixotic, or simply irrelevant, but taken altogether the activities of these myriad collections of enthusiasts represent the only real alternative to a totalitarian administration. Dictatorships frequently leave their charges in possession of the right to vote in elections. They *never* permit them the right of free association. Where such organizations flourish, freedom, initiative, and individuality flourish; where they falter, all the formal ritual of democratic government does not count for much. For an illustration of this, one need look no further than the nearest slum. The inhabitants of slums have exactly the same rights as the rest of us, but it has been observed that they do not organize spontaneously. Politicians and officials, consequently, do not fear them.

The real source of strength of all special interest groups is information and knowledge. To make their influence felt they must ultimately confront officials and the general public with the "facts." They must establish that something is being done wrong, and that the alternate method that they advocate is demonstrably better. The only substitute for this approach is one based on an appeal to sentiment, which is not very reliable.

Their fund of information and knowledge, moreover, must be their own—of their own gathering. They can never be satisfied with official presentations of or explanations for the status quo. Whether they choose to stand as supporters or critics of a particular course of action or state of affairs, they must always stand also as independent experts, ready to supply new information relative to whatever public discussion is at hand.

Until now, conditions have greatly favored the emergence and success of these special interest associations to the point where they collectively represent a kind of shadow government on every level. Every legislator and public official is acquainted with a number of them, either bearing them like a cross or using them as his hatchet men. And each special interest organization has its pantheon of heroes and villains in the public sector. The Wilderness Society matches wits with the Department of the Interior, and hectors the Senate and House Committees on Interior and Insular Affairs. The Advertising Federation of America seeks to frustrate the Federal Trade Commission and to persuade the House Commerce Committee.

The extent and effectiveness of this kind of thing are staggering. The publications of special interest groups reveal a continuous, intense preoccupation with the form and course of legislation and administration. The coverage is generally biased and not infrequently devoted to selfish ends*—but the point is, it is about all that stands between us and a completely passive and acquiescent existence as wards of the state.

This ferment is to some purpose because by and large the Government, in its attempts to order a particular course of events, still operates on a rather primitive level. Lacking reliable information, and both the means for acquiring it and for making intelligent use of what it has, its seemingly vast endeavors turn out to be no more than a conglomeration of hesitant and often short-sighted maneuverings by individual agencies that are short on money and expertise and not infrequently as much devoted to protecting their own preserves from the encroachments of their bureaucratic neighbors as to pursuing any wider purpose.

The partisans of individual privacy see this state of ignorance as the surest guarantee of security. As long as individual personal data are widely scattered and fragmented, they argue that the individual's privacy is reasonably safe, for it is too difficult for the authorities to get at it. The truth of this applies not only to personal and individual data, but also to whole categories of social and economic data of other kinds. Speaking of the trouble this causes, Dr. Edgar S. Dunn, Jr., in his review of the National Data Center proposal commented that the data handling problems of the "newly emerging welfare agencies of the Federal Government . . . when added to the usual difficulties of new program development, threaten to delay programs and render decisions more vulnerable to attack."

This vulnerability to attack, however exasperating it may be to these agencies, is precisely what makes it possible for special interest groups to grapple with such behemoths with some chance of success. Their financial resources may be slender, but they can often aspire to an edge on information, especially concerning the local situation.

But what will happen when the Government begins to pull itself together, and, in effect, closes the information gap? Before answering this let us try to see how the Government itself sees its problem. In general terms, of course, the collective viewpoint is expressed on all levels as: "We need more information." The prologue to every new plan and proposal is a call for some kind of massive study effort. The remedy for the aches and pains of every existing plan and program is the same. Every agency worthy of the name has directors of research and policy analysis. More and more of them have their own statistical programs and survey projects.

But let us go beneath all this and see what is said about the in-

---

*Jessica Mitford, in *The American Way of Death*, provides some particularly repellant examples of this.

158

formation problem itself; that is to say, not what is said about the need for information relative to some particular problem, or to some particular program, but rather about the problem of using the information once it is obtained. Not unexpectedly, Dunn has some of the most profound thoughts on this subject. He does not see the problem as solely a need for more data. As he sees it, "the central problem of data use is one of *associating* numerical records." He then provides a far-ranging analysis of this:

"No number," he writes, "conveys any information by itself. It acquires meaning and significance only when compared with other numbers. The greatest deficiency of the existing Federal statistical system is its failure to provide access to data in a way that permits the association of the elements of [different] data sets in order to identify and measure the interrelationships among interdependent activities. This deficiency has been partially overcome in a few vital areas where we need to trace and analyze the performance of the economy, by the establishment of special programs to bring together data sets in the form of national accounts, special index series, etc., but remains a debilitating constraint for most uses of data for analysis and planning. This is true of virtually all levels of use for virtually all purposes. It is a problem that plagues the research analysts inside and outside of the National Government, who, for example, are engaged in building models of the economy in the interest of analyzing and projecting the major dimensions of economic growth and stability. . . ."

The deficiency to which Dunn refers is not limited to Government agencies, of course; it is felt throughout the society. But the very lack strengthens the positions of special interest groups just as it weakens those of the authorities. Since the authorities cannot demonstrate interrelationships with any certainty, the opponents of their measures are not obliged to do so. They either appropriate official statistics and turn them to their own account or present alternate statistics of their own, and subject them both to their own interpretation without much fear of having them refuted.

As this deficiency is corrected, however, the balance will change rather drastically. Countering a proposed official policy or program will require a far greater intellectual effort than is needed under present conditions. Proposing a better approach will be even more difficult. It will not be enough to deal in such intangibles as personalities, motives, and intentions. Rather, the precise nature of a vast number of relationships must be worked out in detail and their implications ascertained and presented with great skill. In short, organizations will be faced with substantially the same problem vis-à-vis the authorities as we see in store for individuals.

A hint of what this will mean is contained in a letter released by the Executive Director of one such special interest group, Miss Helen M. Harris of United Neighborhood Houses of New York, Inc., an association of social welfare groups. Miss Harris's letter is one of resignation—in more than one sense actually—for she was resigning her post as chairman of the New York City Council Against Poverty's* Planning and Coordination Committee, and her reasons for doing so, as expressed in her letter, have much to do with the "information gap."

She discusses first the position of her late Committee:

"The truth of the matter is [that] the Committee is neither planning nor coordinating—nor can it. To plan responsibly, we should have at our disposal a map and a profile of every poverty area, with all the most up-to-date pertinent facts concerning its population, with the extent and character of its poverty, its housing, its unemployment by age groups, its incidence of school drop-outs and its resources, both public and private. We should have in addition reports on the status of all anti-poverty efforts in the area. It then might be possible to judge the projects which come before us with some regard to the *need* in a given area as against *relative* need in relation to other areas. . . .

"As it is now, with few exceptions, the Committee considers each project not on its merits but in a vacuum, sometimes giving approval to really questionable proposals simply because they are in what appears to be a sparsely served area or because heavy pressure is brought to bear. The degree and quality of the pressure, rather than the merits of the project, may thus determine its acceptance. . . ." Then, turning to the Committee's relations with officialdom, she notes that:

"Two other factors tend to negate the planning function of the Committee. The Anti-Poverty Operations Board [a municipal agency] . . . dispenses City poverty funds without regard for the Council's recommendations and on occasion has granted funds to a sponsor in the face of an adverse action by the Council. There has been little coordination between the Council and the Anti-Poverty Operations Board. Board actions as a rule are not reported to the Council or to the Planning and Coordination Committee. . . .

"To compound confusion further [the] Office of Economic Opportunity in Washington from time to time makes unilateral decisions that frustrate any attempt of the Council to allocate poverty funds planfully and responsibly. It is always a Clear Day in Washington and by some God-given extrasensory perception Office of Economic Opportunity staff [members] can see what is needed in New York City,

---

* Also a private organization.

160

which individual or group is best able to provide it and which project should be processed first. . . ."

As a superefficient computer system replaces this "God-given extrasensory perception," the position of persons like Miss Harris and of groups like hers will become, in a word, hopeless. It is not, certainly, the avowed intention of public officials to bring this about; there is certainly no conspiracy to this end. But they, too, need the maps and the profiles, etc., whose lack so distresses Miss Harris, and they mean to have them. Referring again to Dunn's review:

". . . There is," he writes, "a particularly important class of records that is missing. It can be identified by examining the problems of some of the most important Federal programs. Missing are the records which enable policy makers and planners to understand adequately how people, households, regions, activities, enterprises and administrative units are functionally related and how they change over time.

"The importance of such a capability is readily apparent. There is a large array of new and old welfare programs involved in trying to ameliorate various forms of social pathology and transform people (e.g., poverty, education, health) and regions (e.g., Economic Development Administration, Rural Redevelopment) and the activities that engage them (e.g., Small Business Administration and large elements of the agricultural program). There is a large array of old and new programs engaged in planning for and providing public facilities (e.g., highways, mass transportation, water resources, urban development and housing, etc.). In each of these programs considerable effort, planning and resources are expended for program development, in establishing the formulary for program management, and in evaluating program results. . . .

"To date, the problems have been formidable and the results unimpressive for one principal reason. The information base that exists and can be economically assessed tells us a great deal about the characteristics of people, households, activities, enterprises and their institutions at any one point, but tells us very little about how they are linked into functional networks or how they transform over time. These latter are the most relevant information resources for policy making and program evaluation in these areas. What form of job training, what form of regional assistance, what kind of road networks, what modes of mass transportation, what kind of cities are questions that need to be answered on the basis of some knowledge of functional linkages and evaluated in terms of measurement of change. The responsible planners and administrators of these programs are feeling a keen sense of frustration because of the paucity and irrelevance of much of the information available to them."

161

Dunn, of course, describes the situation in negative terms. Things bog down and go awry nowadays because of what is not available; conversely, we may assume, things will improve greatly when the missing records, and the means for making good use of them, are supplied. But, the point is, the deplorable situation that he describes so concisely will still apply to the mass of would-be policy makers and planners outside the Government. The Government will have become much smarter, but the rest of us will remain relatively ignorant. The trend in this direction is well established, of course. Dunn and the Ruggles Committee may be impressed with the Government's state of ignorance, and Miss Harris with its pretensions to omniscience, but already the Government is generally considered to be much smarter than all of us.

One of the persistent factors, for instance, in the 1966 stock market slump, was simply a vast uncertainty about the economy, and what was likely to happen next; opinions galore were available, but, as a *New York Times* article summed it up: "Economists simply do not know just how much future business activity will be influenced by the growing scarcity and increasing cost of money. They do know that changes in the money supply contribute to prosperity or recession, but they confess that there is no way of measuring cause and effect."

The general reaction to this took the form of waiting for a word from the White House. "We desperately need some positive statement of economic policy from Washington," the research director of one of the great brokerage houses is quoted as saying.* "The entire [economic] situation must be clarified before we can expect the market to change very much for the better. . . . The President will have to get into gear," says the trustee of a distinguished mutual fund.† Unfortunately, the President's sources are no better, but they soon will be.

Remarkably, these sentiments were openly expressed by the one special interest group that has always prided itself on being better informed and having better ideas on money management than anyone in government. Such intellectual preeminence has literally been its stock in trade. True, much of the uncertainty felt by these wizards was caused by the widening scope of possible Government intervention, but this is just the point: this scope has increased because the Government has increased its capacity to use economic and financial information, and already knows much more about banking and eco-

* Robert Johnson of Paine, Webber, Jackson, & Curtis quoted in *Newsweek*, Sept. 12, 1966.
† George Whitney of the Massachusetts Investors Trust, also quoted in *Newsweek*, Sept. 12, 1966.

nomic policy than Wall Street does, even though it still falls several leagues short of the omniscience that Wall Street demands of it.

As this trend continues, the role of private special interest groups will be reduced to requests for special consideration, and to offering advice "for whatever it is worth." Let us enlarge upon this point by considering a homely little example of the kind of decision-making process that largely determines the course of our lives; first, to see how the process actually occurs now, and then how, under the centralization of knowledge, the same process will occur.

In September, 1966, the Senate Banking Committee unanimously approved a bill to grant certain Federal agencies broader powers to regulate the interest rates on savings accounts in savings and loan associations and commercial banks. Among other things, the legislation enables the Federal Reserve Board to set varying maximum interest rates by region, by categories of deposits, and by "other criteria it might establish." The bill is described as an anti-inflation measure and the powers granted would run for only one year.

Represented at the Senate hearings on this bill were two groups of interested parties. One was made up of Government officials and included high ranking managers of the Treasury Department, the Federal Reserve Board, the Federal Home Loan Bank Board and the Federal Deposit Insurance Corporation. The opposing "team," as one would expect, was made up of savings and loan and banking leaders—representatives of the U.S. Savings and Loan League, and the National League of Insured Savings Associations and, offstage, the American Bankers Association.

Both groups presented their respective "cases" to the committee. The result was a compromise. The Government men wanted permanent controls; they lost on this point. The bankers wanted the controls postponed until March, 1966, in the hope that they would be unnecessary by then; they lost on this point. Also, the bankers were not granted a proposed amendment to increase Federal insurance on savings up to $20,000 instead of the limit at that time of $10,000. Presumably, however, both parties were reasonably satisfied with their efforts.

This kind of amiable contest is routine and basic to the management of our affairs. One of its most salient features is that both parties are rather evenly matched when it comes to the theories upon which their positions are based. In this particular debate both factions availed themselves of much of the same source data. Their respective conclusions, moreover, were largely conjecture. The Vice-Chairman of the Federal Reserve Board, for example, was quoted as saying, in objection to the one-year limit on the proposed controls, that this "might thwart the effective use of the new authority," and that the Federal Reserve Board *might* not be inclined to increase reserve requirements "if it knew that those requirements *might* be reversed at the end of a year." In the same vein, a spokesman for the bankers, in support of the proposed raising of the limit of insured savings, asserted that it would attract "*more*" funds to savings and loan associations.

All-in-all, neither side had much information at its disposal, other than knowing what it desired and what it would settle for. A computer would have settled their problems handily. This regretable darkness has one compensation—it affects both parties impartially. Ideally, forthcoming information should be available to both parties equally; but let us see what is likely to occur.

Suppose that it is 1979.* The National Data Center and the national computer system are in full operation. Suppose that the same issue is being considered, and by the same cast of characters. This time the Government team comes in "armed to the teeth." They have been given a detailed simulation of the probable behavior of the banking team. Their computer has been apprised of all the data available to bankers and with detailed analyses of their previous positions and policies. It has been programmed to produce a set of simulations based on the various strategies available to the bankers, with indications as to the relative probabilities of their being employed. Thus the Government team has largely anticipated in detail the arguments of the bankers. And, of course, the computer routinely provides them with rebuttals for all these arguments, using data analyses not available to the bankers themselves.

The Government team has been provided with other, although probably less detailed, simulations of the voting behavior of the Senate Banking Committee members. This is based on analyses of past voting behavior on similar issues and perhaps of conditions in their home States, and would probably include a projection of what questions they, as individuals, would be likely to ask regarding this bill, and what sort of answers they would like to hear.

Also, the Government team has an array of projections and simulations that demonstrate in exhaustive detail the correctness or appropriateness of its own proposals and recommendations. An example of this is the following: according to *The New York Times*, the immediate purpose of the bill in question is to end the competition between savings and loan associations and commercial banks for the "savings dollar." At the time of the hearings, this "rate war" had led to a considerable flow of funds from savings and loan associations into commercial banks, and, consequently, had contributed to a severe

* It would probably be closer to 1984, but the use of that date is obviously taboo in any speculations about the future.

shortage of home mortgage funds, since the commercial banks were more inclined to use these funds for other kinds of loans.

All this, in 1966, could be stated in general terms. Also, reasonably good statistics could be readily compiled to demonstrate that such a condition actually existed; or conversely, it could be refuted in general terms, and equally impressive statistics could be offered to back *this* position (assuming that such a condition conformed to reality at least to some extent). In other words, the Government's position was based on historical data, and some intelligent guesses or estimates of the future, and so was the bankers' position. What was lacking was any really credible description of what would happen next, that is, if the measures advocated by the Government were actually applied to the situation.

But armed with the proper kind of computer analysis, the Government spokesmen can describe the future implications of the savings and loan situation in terms almost as explicit as those they can presently apply to its past. They could say, with much confidence, that if their proposals were adopted, the funds available for home mortgages one year from then will be increased by 1.5 billion dollars, and that if their proposals were not accepted these funds would further be decreased by 0.6 billion dollars. They can then, if pressed to do so, demonstrate, again in terms of numbers, how this will affect employment and personal incomes; how it will affect school construction, formation of new business, and so on. They can also break these figures down by regions, States, congressional districts and others—a tactic that will be of considerable value in gaining the support of particular Congressmen. They can probably show a quantitive relationship between the availability of home mortgage funds and voting behavior, again by geographic location. In short, they have some heavy artillery at their disposal.

In contrast to all this, the other two parties to the meeting, the senators and bankers, are still obliged to rely pretty much on their prestige and wits. It might be argued that the bankers, at least, have their own computer systems and their own experts, and that they produce equally good statements of their own positions. This, however, is not to be expected, for the cost of maintaining a system that can match the Government's capabilities would simply be prohibitive, even if it were shared by all the banks and savings institutions. The Government, after all, will have a unified general purpose system whose cost will be shared by the entire Executive Branch, and by all the local governments as well. Its facilities for collecting and processing source data will make even a nationwide private banking system look puny in comparison. In fact, due to the close relationship between private and "public" banking operations, any private banking computer system is, functionally speaking, a mere subsystem of the more extensive Government system. Everything it can do for bankers, it can also do for the Government. To expect, therefore, a private system to match the Government's facilities is like expecting the American aerospace industry on its own to match the Government's space program.

This example involves the banking industry, which, as noted, has the most highly developed privately owned computer systems, and which, in all probability, will continue to lead the field for a long time. If we were to project another example from a different area, possibly a confrontation involving the Department of Health, Education and Welfare and an assemblage of private social welfare lobbies and pressure groups, the information gap would be far greater and the power even more unbalanced.

In conclusion, let us look at the third party to the kind of decision-making process being considered, the legislators who presumably have the last word concerning policies to be adopted. These gentlemen are by tradition expected to acquire somehow as much understanding of the affairs of government as the President's clerks themselves. In the past at least, many attained this eminence. A congressional committee member of long standing, who had only a modest education and only somewhat greater native intelligence, could, in a term or two, become considerably competent in some specialty of government. Quite aside from his abilities as a politician, he could be a fearsome adversary for some other public servant who had not done his homework or who had something to hide. Although it has become fashionable to judge a legislator's competence mainly by the grace with which he accepts the advice of his intellectual betters, this tradition of congressional expertise has been a good thing. It is, for example, one of the factors that has enabled this country to avoid the transformation into a kind of mandarin state, which, whatever else can be said about it, happens to be distinctly undemocratic.

Lately, however, this tradition has tended to fade. Increasingly, legislators are relying on the assistance of outside sources—not only for information, but also for decisions. The very drafting of laws is not infrequently turned over to lobbyists and to officials of the Executive Branch. In the area of information collecting itself, we have lately been treated to the curious, and perhaps melancholy, spectacle of the members of the Senate Foreign Relations Committee being obliged to rely on published newspaper articles, some even in the foreign press, as sources for their questioning of State Department officials.

In view of this trend, one wonders how these legislators will cope with the arguments of public officials supported in depth by the computer.

As we have shown, whenever they are obliged to consider a piece of legislation proposed by the Administration, or whenever they submit a draft of their own for consideration by the Administration, they will find themselves confronted by the most unimaginably lofty and dense arguments, replete with unassailable facts and assumptions and the most precise, detailed prognoses and contingencies. All of this is the product of the thousand-fold amplification of human wit that a properly employed computer system can effect.

In the face of this, what intellectual arsenal will they command? Their present mainstays, the lobbyists and pressure groups, will be nowhere near their calibre. Even their ultimate weapon, their own shrewd assessment of what their constituents want or will put up with, will be outclassed by the kind of analysis of voting behavior and motivation that a computer can provide.

An example of future trends in this respect is Secretary of Defense Robert McNamara's relations with congressional leaders. McNamara enjoys certain advantages aside from his information monopoly; he has going for him the flag, life and death, the specter of international communism, and his own stature as a man of proven brains and energy. But more important than all of this, McNamara presides over a Department that understands and uses computers and the most advanced information technology at every level. The Defense Department has pioneered in this kind of intellectual exploitation. It has, as noted, long since been functionally reorganized; it has revamped its internal communications to include a whole variety of new techniques of program reporting and evaluation (many of which have been gratefully adopted by industry), of which McNamara's highly touted "cost effectness" policies are a well-known example. Thus organized, he and his "whiz kids" are literally giants among pygmies in an intellectual contest. For this reason principally, in the art of handling legislators, McNamara and the Defense Department are the models for the rest of the Federal Government.

With this example in mind, one is forced to the conclusion that legislators will be left with the kind of roles now filled by Senator Dirksen on the one hand and Senator Morse on the other. For there will surely be, even in this super-rational future, certain residual and evanescent forces—various fears, resentments, and aspirations which even the most accomplished combine of computers and social scientists cannot cope with satisfactorily. Men of a certain sensitivity, if it is combined with the right kind of charm and presence, will capitalize on these emotions and so make their presence felt.

Beyond the legislature, the situation will be more to the advantage of the forceful and colorful leader of men—in the manner of, let us say, Jimmy Hoffa or the late Malcolm X—or, failing the presence of such titans as these, to disciplined and strategically placed groups like the Patrolmen's Benevolent Association of the New York police, or some of the associations of teachers and social workers who have learned the value of sticking together no matter what.

If another kind of future is possible, it would still have to involve computers and computer systems, including an inevitable national computer system. In addition, it would have to hold some means whereby the freedom of individuals to combine to further their own purposes would be preserved not only as a kind of ornament, but also as a way to achieve tangible results without the necessity to riot and strike.

Is such a future within the grasp of reasonable men? We cannot know until we look for it, for unlike the possible futures we have considered, present events do not reveal it.

10

•

Conclusion

In looking back over the evolution and development of computer systems, one's attention is repeatedly drawn to the large part that military requirements have played in the process. This is evident not only in a purely technological sense—to the extent that military requirements have tended to dictate the direction of hardware design—but also in the evolution of computer system applications. Again and again, as we trace the growth of computer-based management and analysis techniques, we find direct evidence of, if not a military origin, the military establishment's early support and strong participation. Along with this has been an equally impressive appreciation of the computer's potential by military authorities. From the very beginning the traditionally mossbacked armed services and the far-flung military bureaucracy that enfolds them have moved swiftly to accommodate themselves and to exploit the possibilities that the computer revolution presents. In doing so, they have become progressively more efficient in meeting their traditional obligations, and have increasingly, and to a great extent unwittingly, become the inspiration and model for the rest of the society as well. Today it can be maintained that the military establishment, which includes not only the Defense Department and the armed services but also its elaborate network of contractors and subcontractors among the universities and throughout industry, is the intellectual sword of the republic, and the true cradle of the future.

This is no longer true only of computer developments and industrial management styles. As the goals and objectives of socioeconomic planning and control become more extensive, more and more of the military vision and aptitude has been borrowed by the civilian policy-making establishment. The transaction has taken place on a variety of different levels: at the most primitive, as civilian groups have begun to employ routine data-processing equipment and pro-

169

cedures originally developed as military communications and logistic devices; at intermediate stages, as these groups have begun to employ tried and true military organization styles and military administration techniques; and in more exalted regions of policy making, where we find such spinoffs as the widespread adoption of planning and analysis techniques of military origin and the application of quasi-military strategic and tactical concepts to essentially civil programs and problems.

The results of this are seen in the new Departments of Health, Education and Welfare, and Housing and Urban Affairs, which are close cousins in terms of organization to the Departments of the Army, Navy, and Air Force. Although necessarily still in a primitive stage of development, these agencies are increasingly employing intellectual contractors such as the System Development Corporation or Basic Systems, Inc. (analogues of the Defense Department's RAND Corporation or the Air Force's MITRE Corporation) and in Senator Muskie's proposed National Intergovernmental Affairs Council with its inspiration in the National Security Council.

This is not to imply that our civilian policy and planning establishments are about to take to gold braid or jump boots, for their chosen model is much more sophisticated than this. Though authoritarian, the Defense Department is civilian, and its effectiveness has sprung from its capacity to draw on the disparate talents of cloistered Ph.D.s of the Institute for Advanced Studies *and* of the ferocious Pfc.s of the Green Berets. Its table of organization lists, for example, directors of Electronic and Information Systems, of course, and also those of such seemingly nonmilitary interests as Family Housing, Small Business and Economic Utilization, Organization and Management Planning, Civil Rights and Industrial Relations, Education, Manpower Planning and Research, Resource Analysis, Atomic Energy, Economics, Community Relations, Chemistry and Materials, and National Communications Systems. It also contains a Defense Contract Audit Agency, employing one of the largest and most sophisticated accounting systems in the world, and an Industrial College, which is described as providing for senior military and governmental civilian students courses on management policies, the conservation and management of national resources, managerial practices and problems in defense industries, national security-related economic and social policy, and other related subjects. In addition to its military law enforcement structure, it even has a kind of economic supreme court, the Armed Services Board of Contract Appeals, composed of "attorneys who have been admitted to practice before the highest court of any State and the District of Columbia," and who are empowered to decide disputes arising from its contracts with industry.

170

This is not to suggest that the Defense Department aspires to a greater role in the conduct of national affairs, as some have maintained, but rather that it is indeed a highly complex and sophisticated model of one way to manage a whole society. It is truly a society in itself, a kind of state within a state, and one that has effectively solved many of the most vexing problems that beset our civilian society. It has virtually eliminated the evil effects of race prejudice. It has no slums (and if slums seem incongruous in juxtaposition with a military establishment, one has only to look at some of the other armies of the world). Its educational system, which extends from the primary schools established for its dependents to entire departments of some of the Nation's graduate schools, runs smoothly and productively under an incredible variety of conditions. Its health and medical services operate with equal efficiency. In addition, the Defense Department is compassionate. For example, it will see to it that the humblest private is flown halfway around the world to be at the bedside of a dying relative. It does not even limit its compassion to its own; its millions having succored flooded Dutchmen, rescued Arab pilgrims stranded on the road to Mecca, dropped hay to snowbound Canadian elk, dispatched ships to the aid of Greek earthquake victims. Who, indeed, can point to a better working model of the Good Society?

Since it is such a splendid example, perhaps we can learn more from it.

As noted, our civilian economic and social planning establishment has adopted the military style for its own. It speaks of a "War on Poverty" and organizes its poverty "fighters" into "task forces" and into Job Corps, Neighborhood Youth Corps, Teacher Corps. It is invidious to compare this greater war to the Defense Department's current war effort, and to see parallels between the two, and yet they are obvious. However, to do so one must compare the War on Poverty of today with the U.S. effort in Viet Nam in 1956 or 1957. We see the same teams of expert U.S. (i.e., Federal) advisers seeking to guide local officials and forces at every level. We have the same subsequent realization that such tactics are woefully insufficient and that a progressively greater involvement and escalation will be required. Viet Nam's montagnards, its self-seeking local officials, its Buddhist monks, and all the rest of the unhappy cast are mirrored in Watts and Harlem, in the city halls of a half a hundred cities best left unnamed, and among the members of the Ad Hoc Committee on the Triple Revolution and such groups as Saul Alinsky's Industrial Areas Foundation, and to some extent, the rest of us.

How far one can develop this analogy depends largely on one's point of view concerning the practicality and the morality of both

171

of these undeclared wars. It is, admittedly, difficult to balance one's feelings about the two struggles; it is much easier to see one as the antithesis of the other. Tactically, however, they are not opposed, they appear to be similar.

This does not mean that the "War on Poverty" itself was in any way inspired by the Viet Nam War—that is the irony. It only tends to resemble the more innocent stages of the Viet Nam War because the organizations that are conducting it have, perhaps unconsciously, tended more and more to model themselves on that paragon of planning and efficiency which, under the direction of the same Commander-in-Chief, has played the major role in determining the course of the Viet Nam War.

This being the case, it may well be that in spite of its many admirable qualities, the Department of Defense is not the best model for a society to choose, even for a society with our problems. On this premise, let us see what this model lacks.

The Department of Defense certainly has that basic essential—information. It has the finest information systems on earth. And it has the capacity to use them, its resources being a generation and perhaps as much as half a century ahead of any other agency. It is preeminent also in material resources, organization, and personnel. The only quality it has been seriously accused of lacking is judgment. It doesn't seem to know when to stop. Secretary of Defense McNamara has been specifically taxed with this lack, but he is no more than an extension of his department.

To say that the Defense Department has no capacity for self-criticism and for the interplay of alternate points of view is wholly inaccurate. Like every other military organization it has an elaborate system devoted to this end. It has refined this system to the point at which it literally supports whole institutes of scholarly Cassandras who criticize and advise. In reality, its critical faculties are too well organized. There is no provision for small factions of soreheads or of selfish and nearsighted individuals to do something unreasonable—to insist on some far-out approach and to instigate and proselytize, to shrink from horror before a particular course, or to be overly optimistic about another. In short, it has no access to the kind of raucous and untidy wheeling and dealing that distinguishes the democratic process from the monarchial, the kind, for example, that distinguished the often ignoble Continental Congress from the Court of Versailles.

Any organization that adopts this model will find itself in much the same position with respect to its critical faculties, and nothing will reinforce it more than a national computer system. The Defense Department, after all, can compensate for its deficiency by relying to some extent on the larger society around it, although only through the President. The larger society, however, will not have this compensation. When its reorganization is complete, all the possibilities for intelligent dissent and for the free examination of alternatives—for knowing where to stop—will have disappeared. The only way out of this box is to forget about military analogies and adopt some others. We can do this only on one condition: we can consider only models that accept the reality of large-scale digital computer systems, and the inevitability of their evolving into a unified national system affecting every important socioeconomic area of our lives. Of necessity, any such models considered in this category are fairly primitive.

One is represented by the AFL-CIO's computer system which is used as a bargaining tool. As an organization that has been devoted to advancing its point of view in the face of powerful and determined opposition, the labor union is an appropriate place to start looking for alternatives to the compassionate-authoritarian model. Its principal opposition, it is true, has not been of an official character, at least not for some time. In industry, "management" comes nearest to official power. That is to say, management sees itself as totally involved; it is concerned with directing all the elements of the industrial situation. It wants to be formally concerned not only with profit and production, but also with the welfare of the workers. There is no pretension about this; even the most primitive employers have recognized that labor is a production factor that must be taken into account. The union, on the other hand, has never aspired to such a role. Its *raison d'être* is to represent a special interest group within management's universe. It does not, normally, see itself as a subcontractor of labor or of any other formal subsystem of the production system. It is simply the opposition, ready to drive a hard bargain. As such, it can be a model for all those special interest groups whose role it is to remain outside the central power structure in order to preserve their identity and point of view, a role that has no counterpart in the Defense Department model. (The Defense Department is, of course, involved with labor unions, but they do not constitute part of its system. It suffers them the way it suffers the French.)

In recent years, as the information revolution has had its effect on management, the unions—and the AFL-CIO in particular—found themselves in a predictable position: they were being outweighed and outgunned by management's computer systems. Management came to know much more about the collective bargaining situation than the unions did.

The AFL-CIO's Industrial Union Department now has its own

computer system. It is being used as a weapon to coordinate labor-management bargaining techniques and to analyze employment contracts. It has a data storage and retrieval capacity sufficient to enable individual union bargaining committees to learn much more about the companies they are dealing with. According to *The New York Times*, these facts include: "information on plants and employment involving such factors as the interlocking of directorates, the products produced, the profit status, the names of decision makers and the divisions of a company which are profitable and which are not."

"The Industrial Union Department," continues the *Times*, "is also analyzing thousands of representation elections conducted by the National Labor Relations Board, using such information as the numbers of workers involved, the votes, the date of certification, appeals, and unfair labor practices."

The AFL-CIO initially tested the system in negotiations between the United Electrical Workers and two corporate heavyweights (and computer-management heavyweights), the General Electric Company and Westinghouse Corporation. Indications are that the negotiations will be long and hard, but whatever the outcome, they will not be the decisive test of the union's new approach. The important fact is that it represents one possible alternative to the crushing superiority of a large-scale central computer system.

This suggests that, in the future containing the national computer system, there ought to be an alternate information system at the disposal of those who, to put it simply, do not see their interests coinciding with what the central authority sees as the general welfare. The analogy here is that of a free press, or an independent press supplementing an official one, or of an independent legal profession at the disposal of private interests as opposed to a legal profession wholly under state control (as in the case of the Soviet Union).

With such an alternate system patterns of dissent could evolve and alternatives could be explored which will otherwise be impossible. Private research into social and economic areas would be possible on a scale that is not at all feasible as long as researchers are obliged, as they will be, to rely on official sources for the source data and analytical techniques necessary to their work. Something other than becoming a government contractor will be possible for scientists of all kinds, and even relatively small organizations can participate in developing social and economic programs that touch upon their areas of interest on some basis other than as a client of the central authority.

However, this cheerful prospect is impossible. It is one thing for the AFL-CIO to aspire to match the computer capabilities of even a very large corporation; it is another for any private group to match the potential of the Federal Government. It was possible to do something like this in developing an independent press and an independent legal apparatus. Both of these, however, got their start when the central Government, and local government as well, was relatively puny. Also, neither institution is really a system, and a system is called for. We have never developed a truly private banking system, transportation system, or communications system, nor have we developed a private space exploration program, or for that matter, a private computer system development program. It is hardly likely that we can do so. There must be some other alternative.

But perhaps, in our preoccupation with such models of truculence as the Defense Department and the Viet Nam War, and with the AFL-CIO and its dealings with business management, we have overemphasized our relation to the Government as one of perpetual conflict. We are not necessarily opposed to the Government; our position is not that of the Viet Cong to the National Security Council, or even that of the United Electrical Workers to the General Electric Company. It may be more fruitful to see our position as falling somewhere between the relationship of the South Vietnamese people to the U.S. military authorities and that of the General Electric Company's shareholders to the company itself.

With this in mind, let us consider another possible model.

In August, 1966, Senator Edward Kennedy of Massachusetts addressed to the Senate* his approval and praise of those contributions of Senator Muskie in the cause of creative federalism described in Chapter 8. He then offers some further contributions himself, "directed," he says, "at one very important part of the overall problem—the need to build an effective communications system between local, State and Federal levels of government. . . ."

" . . . What I have in mind is a computer-based information system, using satellite centers, which would provide each State and local government with detailed information on which [Federal assistance] programs were available to it and which would be most appropriate for it. With a profile of each community, a satellite computer could be programmed to inform the community of what new programs are available, what programs have filled their quotas, what programs have changed, and what programs have been discontinued. In every case, the information provided would be based on the needs of the state or community in question.

"Such a system has been used with great success by the National Aeronautics and Space Administration† in their Technology Utiliza-

* See Appendix 4.

† In this analogy, we are at least *one* step removed from the Defense Department!

175

tion program to provide private industry with detailed information on technological advances that may be of benefit to particular industries."

Senator Kennedy then cites a study that was made for him by the International Business Machines Corporation to describe the kind of information the system would contain (as input data):

"1. Socio-economic data involving income distribution, education, law enforcement, health and welfare, etc.

"2. Community Resource Data involving labor force and employment, industry and trade, transportation, housing and community facilities, financial, etc.

"3. Programs Reference Data concerning the nature and purposes of [Federal] assistance programs, conditions of eligibility, information contact, authorizing legislation, and the administering agency.

"4. Programs Status Data involving the nature and extent of usage of various aid programs, the status of obligated funds, the names and numbers of communities involved, etc. . . ."

To this point, Senator Kennedy's proposal is well meaning and helpful, but hardly a definitive answer to the real problem, but there is more, and it bears close attention.

" . . . An information system of the type I propose," he went on, "need not be limited solely to offering data on Federal programs. By keeping a record of the projects and programs carried out in the various communities, it should be possible for communities to learn from the system what programs other communities are developing and profit from their experiences.

"Moreover, as experience is gained in dealing with communities, it might eventually be possible to assign to the system certain tasks of analysis and evaluation, such as the projection of socio-economic trends, analyses of cost-benefit ratios, and preparation of financial justification of projects."

With this the importance of Senator Kennedy's approach can begin to be appreciated, for he focuses on something that has been conspicuously absent in all of the "systems approaches" we have considered: the advisability of the Government's using its power and resources not only to extract information from the citizenry and to use it as it sees fit, but also to supply information. Moreover, he does not ignore the fact that the Government has a number of long-established programs devoted to disseminating information "in the public interest." He is concerned with something else: real-time information.

True, his proposal tends to limit dissemination of information to State and local governments. Also, by placing the management of the system under Federal control, there is a strong presumption that only information that is not considered embarrassing to Federal interests will be fed into the system. No bureaucracy will knowingly or willingly expose its activities or policies to potentially adverse outside scrutiny. In view of this, Senator Kennedy's proposed system seems to be no more than an effective public relations device. The information services that his system could be expected to provide amount to little more than telling people what is good for them and telling it only to the sort of people who are most likely to be the Federal Government's retainers and clients. All-in-all, the chief value of this approach, like that of the AFL-CIO's, is in the principle it happened to embody.

But there was more to it. Senator Kennedy did not neglect to consider the political and administrative realities of his scheme, although he approached these with considerable delicacy and tact.

"The system I visualize," he said, "would be decentralized in nature. But careful study would be needed to determine . . . whether the overall system would best be operated under the direction of the Department of Housing and Urban Development, the Bureau of the Budget, the Census, the General Services Administration, the Legislative Reference Service, or some other government agency."

At first glance, this appears to be almost a ritual phrase, typical of any preliminary proposal for an addition or alteration of the Federal structure, except for this: the first four possibilities are familiar arms of the Executive Branch; the fifth, the Legislative Reference Service, is not. As a department of the Library of Congress, it is fully within the Legislative Branch, and answerable only to Congress. It is, moreover, charged with providing members of Congress (and not infrequently their constituents) with a variety of information gathering and research services, much of it in response to specific queries.

Place the system that Senator Kennedy outlined under the control of an agency like this—one outside the Executive Branch—and you might have a new ball game.

" . . . The system," Senator Kennedy notes: "might be capable of providing Congress and the Administration with a better measure of the needs and performances of the cities, states and regions operating under these programs.

"This could facilitate legislative oversight [Congressional surveillance], as well as making possible speedy and more accurate adjustment of aid programs to meet existing needs."

Senator Kennedy concedes that "constructing such a system would involve certain risks to established political procedures, even though the system [to use another ritual phrase], is intended solely as an aid to decision making and not as a replacement of the decision maker." In view of this, he recommends that this aspect of the situation be

177

thoroughly studied. His choice to make such a study: the Advisory Commission on Intergovernmental Relations,* already the inspiration for much of Senator Muskie's proposed government reorganization. He particularly notes that this Commission is "not a Federal agency in the usual sense. Its members include representatives of the executive and legislative branches of all levels of government." Without speculating as to where Senator Kennedy's own preferences lie in the matter of responsibility for operating his information system (he appears to be impartial about this), let us explore some of the possibilities of control by some agency other than any in the Executive Branch.

Suppose that the system were operated by Congress's Legislative Reference Service. This immediately brings up the question of source data—the system inputs. Since the Service has no facilities for collecting this at present, and they are not provided for in the proposed system, we may assume that they will be supplied by agencies within the Executive Branch—in part from the Federal Statistical System and in part from the operating departments such as Health, Education and Welfare and Housing and Urban Development.

In regard to the first two categories of input data, i.e., socioeconomic data and community resource data, their origin in the Executive Branch poses no great problem. The agencies that presently collect these data are oriented toward disseminating it, and, as the head of one agency put it, they operate in a goldfish bowl; they could not hold back if they wanted to. As this data collection becomes more computerized and the volume and detail of source data increases, the release of data in quantity may be a problem, but whatever is released will probably be accurate and unbiased.

But as for the last two categories, i.e., programs reference data and programs status data, can we really say the same thing? Executive agencies have always resisted handing over this kind of information to the Legislative Branch or to anyone else on anything but their own terms, as the transcript of almost any Congressional committee hearing can demonstrate.

Besides the Legislative Reference Service, however, another information gathering service under the direction of Congress is the General Accounting Office. It does *not* have to rely on Executive

* The U.S. Government Organization Manual for 1966–1967 describes the Advisory Commission on Intergovernmental Relations as follows:

"The Commission was established by act of September 24, 1959 (73 Stat. 703, 5 U.S.C. 2371) to bring together representatives of Federal, State, and local governments for consideration of common problems, to discuss the administration of Federal grant programs and the controls involved in their administration, to make available technical assistance to the executive and legislative branches of the Federal government in the review of proposed legislation, to discuss emerging public problems that are likely to require intergovernmental cooperation, to recommend the most desirable allocation of governmental functions. . . ."

Branch cooperation or judgment for the sources of its information. According to a number of statutes dating back to the original Treasury Act of 1789, it is empowered to "make for the Congress independent examinations of the manner in which Government agencies are discharging their financial responsibilities," as the United States Government Organization Manual for 1966–1967 puts it. The Manual continues: "Financial responsibilities are construed as including the administration of funds and the utilization of property and personnel only for authorized programs, and the conduct of programs or activities in an effective, efficient, and economic manner.

"To carry out these functions, the Comptroller General* or his authorized representatives are authorized by law to have access to and examine any books, records, documents, papers or records—except those pertaining to certain funds for the purpose of intercourse or treaty with foreign nations—of any department or establishment."

Looking further into the description of this organization we find that the Comptroller General:

". . . is responsible for prescribing principles, standards and related requirements for accounting by the executive agencies. . . .

" . . . required by law to render decisions as to the legality of expenditures of public funds. . . . By law, the decisions of the Comtroller General are final and conclusive on the executive branch of the Government.

" . . . makes special audits, surveys, and investigations at the specific request of congressional committees, as required by law." General Accounting Office representatives may be assigned to assist specified (Congressional) committees at their request and are called upon frequently to testify before Congressional committees on various matters. As another service to the Congress, they comment on proposed legislation.

The impressive powers of the General Accounting Office stem directly from the Constitution, and from the Anglo-Saxon tradition of keeping the strings of the public purse out of the hands of the executive, whether prince or president. This same tradition places the power to levy taxes and appropriate public monies solely in the hands of the legislature, and in the matter of extracting those monies from the citizenry it makes the Executive Branch the people's bailiff and no more. The Executive Branch may thus physically collect the taxes but it cannot hold or spend them without legislative sanction.

We who have learned that information is every bit as essential to the exercise of power as is money might then ask: Why not also restrain Executive power by denying it the exclusive right to the in-

* The head of the General Accounting Office.

179

formation it also extracts from us? Or, in more formal terms: If information is as essential as money to the exercise of power, do we not provide the Executive Branch with too much power by permitting it to control the collection and use of economic and social data? More specifically, suppose we were, through our elected representatives, to divorce the present Federal Statistical System, and in its time, the National Data Center and the national computer system, from the Executive Branch altogether? What would be the result?

Let us examine the idea in more detail. Suppose we were to begin by consolidating the data gathering and record keeping functions of the Federal Statistical System, and for good measure, those of the National Archives and Records Service (presently part of the Executive Branch's General Services Administration) into a new agency, leaving in abeyance for the moment the question of what branch of the Government would control it. To this new agency, we assign the responsibility for designing and developing the National Data Center, and, ultimately the national computer system itself.

At the same time, suppose that we let the rest of the great governmental reorganization proceed as before; i.e., let the Executive Branch refashion its economic and social welfare agencies to the Defense Department model, and invent a domestic analogue of the National Security Council and so on. We also permit the Executive departments and agencies to continue to handle as much of the actual collection of information as is consistent with their missions, in exactly the same way that various agencies of the Executive Branch presently collect money in the form of taxes, duties, interest payments, fees, and even make sales (e.g., postage stamps).

The information thus collected, however, would be automatically deposited in the coffers of our independent information agency, which, for the moment, we can consider as a kind of analogy to the Federal Reserve System whose banks serve as depositories for all Federal funds. The Executive departments could, of course, draw on this "information bank," but they would be subject to such legal restrictions as Congress might enact.

The money-information analogy does not, of course, apply here completely, because information has a quality that money, unfortunately, does not: it can be infinitely reproduced. In other words, although continuously transferring their funds of information to the "bank," Federal agencies could still retain duplicates of the "funds" every bit as useful to their purposes as the originals, something which cannot be done with funds of money. With a computer system, moreover, the duplication, like the transfer, would be cheap and easy to accomplish.

This, however, is of no great consequence, for the purpose of this whole scheme is not to deny the Executive Branch the possession of the information it needs to function, but rather to deny it *exclusive* possession, ultimately subject to no accounting but its own. Most of the information collected by the Executive Branch will be about itself and its activities, most especially about how its various programs are working and about what it plans to do next; for, with the Federal Statistical System divorced from the Executive Branch, a great deal of the source data upon which Executive Branch policies are based will be fed directly to the bank, to be subsequently furnished to the Executive Branch on demand.

Besides the Executive Branch, who else would have access to the "information bank"? Ideally, the answer to this should be the Congress, the Courts, local and State authorities, and the public. For each of these groups, naturally, there must be some restrictions on access. Some of these are already provided for in a panoply of existing statutes. They include constitutional provisions, laws pertaining to all kinds of disclosure situations, and laws relating to the national security. Many more laws, and perhaps even an amendment to the Constitution itself, would probably be required to define all of the access privileges of each of these parties. In general, however, they are not too difficult to specify: they should, in sum, be consistent with the duties and rights, already well defined, of the legislature—access to sufficient information to permit it to continue to enact laws, rather than simply to ratify them; of the courts—to permit them to exercise the powers invested in them by the Constitution and the laws of the United States; of State and local governments—ditto; and of the rest of us—to permit us "peaceably to assemble, and to petition the Government for a redress of grievances."

To which branch, if not to the Executive, should this "information bank" be subject? The first that comes to mind is the Legislative Branch. Let us imagine that in this case the new agency could monitor the Executive Branch's use of information in somewhat the same way in which the General Accounting Office monitors its use of money. Even with the most sophisticated computer system, it is unlikely that this could be done as precisely as financial accounting, for although social and economic data can be organized and made far more accessible by computer processing, it is doubtful that they can ever equal the compactness of financial data. But such a monitoring capability would certainly enable Congressmen to evaluate Executive Branch goals and performance in a manner which they cannot hope to do now. They could, to a great extent, examine the premises, the basis for assumptions, on which social and economic planning decisions were based. This is dangerous; it would be much

181

easier for obstructionist and publicity-seeking Congressmen to "let the cat out of the bag," and to otherwise embarrass and disrupt carefully thought out Executive policies. Its effect on the morale of devoted and conscientious public servants might be compared to the effect of a civilian review board on the morale of the police.

This, however, is part of the price of democracy and representative government.* Whether or not the price is *too* high must be decided.

As a somewhat less risky alternative, the Judicial Branch could control the new agency. This, admittedly, departs radically from tradition, and it is likely that the Federal judiciary would not welcome the added responsibilities involved. Before dismissing the Judicial Branch as a serious consideration, however, we should consider a little-known judicial agency as a model and good precedent for what we are contemplating: the Administrative Office of the United States Courts.

Prior to 1939, the administrative machinery of the Federal court system was under the formal jurisdiction of the Executive Branch's Department of Justice, a situation that judges found increasingly illogical inasmuch as the Department was also the courts' principal litigant. This sentiment, which was, happily, shared by the Attorney General at that time, led to the passage of the Administrative Office Act. Under the provisions of the Act, control by the Executive Branch was transferred entirely to the Judicial Branch, where it has ever since been exercised by a committee of senior judges under the presidency of the Chief Justice of the United States. In turn, the committee, called the Judicial Conference of Senior Circuit Judges, oversees the operation of the Administrative Office created by the Act as a kind of minuscule Executive Branch.

The Administrative Office itself attends to all the housekeeping requirements of the Federal court system. Its responsibilities include supervising the system's nonjudicial personnel—clerks, secretaries, probation officers, commissioners, referees, and others; administering the system's finances—preparing is budget,† payment of operating expenses, purchasing supplies and equipment; and administering a

* A hint of the sort of reaction to be expected may be found in the reaction of the Administration to Senate amendments to the Administration's bill to create a Federal Department of Transportation. One Senate amendment (conceived by the Senate Government Operations Committee) required Congressional approval of transportation "standards and criteria," i.e., the determinants for allocating financial assistance to various forms of transportation activities. The Administration opposed this restriction on Executive decision-making most vigorously, and succeeded in eliminating it from the House version of the bill, although not from the Senate's.

† The Act provides that these budgets are not to be revised in any way by the Executive Branch.

continuing program of collecting data on the system's performance. Since the Judicial Branch presently has more than 6,000 employees and operates on a budget in excess of $50,000,000, this represents a respectable effort.

An essential to the Administrative Office's success has been the Judicial Conference. Originally created in 1922 to aid in improving Federal court procedures and performance, it has since evolved into a kind of "legislature" for the entire Judicial Branch. It has been instrumental in the imposing of a set of uniform rules of procedure for the Federal courts (which have since become models for revisions of State court procedures). Its prestige with Congress is such that it reviews all proposed legislation pertaining to judicial matters and reports its views to the Senate and House Judiciary Committees. It approves the annual budget drawn up by the Administrative Office; and, through its 20 subcommittees, constantly supervises the workings and evolution of not only the system's Administrative Office, but also of the entire judicial system. (Not the least of its value is that it stands as a buffer between Congress and the Administrative Office. Unlike the general run of Federal executives, the Director of the Office rarely has to face Congressional scrutiny on his own.)

Both the Administrative Office and the Judicial Conference can be of great interest because many of the conditions that brought them about and sustain them are also applicable to a national computer system. What, after all, do we expect from a judicial system? The conventional answer is "justice"; this can be explicated as "expert and impartial decisions." To this end it has been seen as no more than practical to staff the judicial system with highly trained, capable people-experts, and then to encourage them to be impartial by making them independent of the pressures of those whose objectives and goals, however legitimate, would tend to make them partial.

The imperatives of information collecting can be seen in terms comparable to those of the administration of justice. We do not, of course, expect an information system to make decisions for us, but it should supply us with expert, impartial information as a basis on which to make them, impartial or otherwise. We might well consider endowing the whole process of information collecting with some of the sacred character with which, in the interests of assuring its independence and thus its impartiality, we have surrounded the judiciary. This means establishing the senior administrators of the national computer system as independent, nonpolitical figures answerable only to their own highly developed consciences and integrity and to the Constitution and the public laws. It might then be possible to turn over the entire administration of the system to them.

183

Whether or not this could be accomplished without incorporating these men into the judiciary itself is a difficult question. If, however, it turns out that only a touch of the judicial aura would do it, this would not be the first time that the judiciary had been expanded to meet the requirements of modern civilization. We need only mention, in this respect, the U.S. Court of Customs and Patent Appeals. With this as a precedent, it might not be too far-fetched to imagine a court at the same level devoted to problems arising from the collection and use of information, and, with its judges incorporated into the Judicial Conference. Perhaps the whole national computer system could be tucked under its wing.

Another possibility is to organize the new agency outside all three branches of the Government, either as a public corporation or as a permanent body similar to some of the temporary advisory groups that occupy the interstices of the Government's three branches from time to time. Of these, the Advisory Commission on Intergovernmental Relations is probably the most independent, as Senator Edward Kennedy pointed out. In practice, however, the Federal Reserve System, although technically part of the Executive Branch, is the nearest model to the kind of independent Government body we are contemplating.

In the final analysis though, it may not really matter how the new agency is dealt with at this level. Our political system can come up with a jurisdictional formula sufficient to insure that the new agency would be independent.

Assuming its independence then, let us suppose that the agency would serve as a kind of national information bank where the vital commodity of social and economic data could be deposited and disbursed. Without stretching the Federal Reserve System analogy too far, we might note that the Federal Reserve Banks are not merely repositories for Government funds, but also serve as repositories for certain private funds. Perhaps a similar feature could be incorporated into the new agency's National Data Center. Private organizations of various kinds could thus be encouraged, or even required under some circumstances, to deposit information in the "data bank," where it could be made available, subject to certain restrictions or qualifications, to other depositors, both public and private alike.

Hopefully, this would encourage a considerable amount of private socioeconomic research of a type that is now rarely attempted. Frankly partisan organizations of all kinds might find it much to their interest to make more strenuous efforts to collect detailed, and disciplined, data in support of their positions if they were assured that it would not only find a permanent resting place, but also would be used by others. For example, the workers of an organization

184

such as the Student Nonviolent Coordinating Committee, if moved to do so, could probably compile statistics on some areas of Southern life which, when compared with similar statistics compiled by, let us say, Mississippi or even by some of the Federal agencies, would make interesting and even devastating reading.

By the same token, groups that tend to rely heavily on emotional charges and appeals with little factual basis would, with the existence of a National Data Center of this kind, be at a disadvantage. A widely publicized, ringing statement in opposition to this or in defense of that would immediately provoke a "run on the information bank" by many editors and reporters, if no one else, for supporting evidence. Anyone who expected to be taken seriously would have to have something on deposit, and what he did have must agree with other deposited data relative to the issue at hand.

Less partisan private groups would also have much to gain from their access to the Center. They, too, would find that the results of their researches would come to the attention of other researchers, legislators, and decision makers and become an added incentive to more research, and perhaps an aid to obtaining additional funds to support it. The Data Center, in effect, might lead directly to an increased demand for private socioeconomic research. At the same time, the availability of the Center's store of relevant source data would contribute to significant reductions in the costs of such private research.

Much of these benefits would accrue to private research groups in any case. Even if the Data Center were to be set up as part of the Executive Branch, a considerable participation by private research groups would be encouraged, and even sponsored and subsidized, by Executive Branch agencies, just as it is now. But private groups would not, in this case, have all of the options that would be available to them under the independent Data Center arrangement. Rather, access to the Data Center would tend with the passage of time to be determined by one's contract arrangements with Executive Branch departments, and these, inevitably, would be determined by officially determined priorities. With the independent Data Center this would be minimized.

In sum, an independent Data Center could become a major factor in reversing the present trend toward a Federal monopoly of economic and social research. The tendency for people of these disciplines to move into specialized "think factories," sponsored by universities, corporations, and foundations, and actually supported largely by Federal funds, could be replaced by an outward movement into associations with all sorts of special interest groups. Economists and sociologists could thus begin to occupy a position comparable in some respects to that occupied by lawyers and even journalists, who, in addition to being in "private practice" and on the public payroll, aid the causes of virtually every organization devoted to either supporting or opposing the established order of things.

As far as mere individuals are concerned, it is not easy to see how any kind of Data Center, independent or not, will be of much assistance to them. Of course, a relatively simple information service set-up within the Data Center could accomodate the needs of individuals. Such a service could probably provide answers to relatively routine queries concerning individual eligibilities, rights, and the like, and supply routine data to individuals about Government programs and social and economic conditions. But, beyond this, an individual alone could not expect much from the Center. The same constraints to the interpretation of individual data that would be found in a system under Executive Branch control would, it seems, be equally applicable in the case of an independent Data Center. Also, to take advantage of the Center one would require the use of a rather complex remote terminal, actually a computer of moderate capacity itself, and much more knowledge and experience in dealing with the Center than most individuals are likely to possess.

However, individuals—particularly individual companies—could avail themselves of the assistance of Data Center consultants. These men would be equipped with data terminals and the requisite knowledge to use them, and would be able to apply the Center's data resources to the solution of individual problems and the pursuit of individual goals.

There is an obvious analogy here to lawyers, and more particularly to the new breed of tax consultants, who, to assist their clients through the morass of Government tax policy, generally combine the talents and credentials of the attorney-at-law and the certified public accountant.

In summing up the effect on society of an independent National Data Center and national computer center, it is worth citing a few things that it would not, of itself, accomplish. It would not, first of all, facilitate the Government's economic planning and control. On the contrary, it would be an enormous strength to those forces opposing national economic and social development. Some groups would attempt to use the system's data resources to prove scientifically that Negroes are inferior to whites, that this or that minority is receiving more than its share of public assistance, that such and such an economic development scheme is impractical and discriminates unfairly against this or that privileged group. The conscientious Federal planner or administrator would find the meticulously reasoned basis for his projects subject to much hostile examination and criticism,

186

and he would be obliged to devote an appreciable amount of his budget to refuting them. He would also have to compete with a large assortment of do-gooders in the private sector with programs and plans of their own. It is questionable whether, in such a situation, highways would be constructed more efficiently, rivers would be cleaned up as rapidly, and specific economic and social injustices eradicated as completely.

It would not, moreover, further the harmony between factions in the private sector. All selfish interests would tend to be voiced with greater authority and would attract more adherents. For example, perhaps even an organization like the Ku Klux Klan could use the Center's data resource to, let us say, locate areas and population groups that would be receptive to its message, or proponents of more relaxed narcotics laws could present their case more persuasively. With more demands on the Data Center, the threat to individual privacy would be considerably more difficult to contain. In sum, the perils of free access to information are probably as great as the freedom to publish and proselytize.

Nevertheless, this may well be a price worth paying. Given the resources of modern technology and planning techniques, it is really no great trick to transform even a country like ours into a smoothly running corporation where every detail of life is a mechanical function to be taken care of. This has been amply demonstrated in this country since World War II by our own large private corporations, and, of course, by the greatest corporation of them all, the magnificent Department of Defense itself. To a lesser but still impressive extent it has also been demonstrated by our uncouth rivals across the Iron Curtain. In both areas, computers and computer systems have more than demonstrated their particular capacities in this respect.

But what remains to be demonstrated is that all this can be done in a manner that will preserve something else: those qualities of life in a free society that are not so easy to show on a balance sheet, nor to factor into an equation destined for a computer program.

APPENDICES

Appendix 1

The Ad Hoc Committee on the Triple Revolution Memorandum

A Letter

The following letter was sent by The Ad Hoc Committee on The Triple Revolution to President Lyndon B. Johnson. The White House reply from Mr. Lee White, Assistant Special Counsel to the President, was received shortly. The letter to the President, together with the Report, was also sent to the Majority and Minority leaders of the Senate and the House of Representatives and to the Secretary of Labor. Texts follow:

March 22, 1964

Dear Mr. President:

We enclose a memorandum, The Triple Revolution, for your consideration. This memorandum was prepared out of a feeling of foreboding about the nation's future. The men and women whose names are signed to it think that neither Americans nor their leaders are aware of the magnitude and acceleration of the changes going on around them. These changes, economic, military, and social, comprise The Triple Revolution. We believe that these changes will compel, in the very near future and whether we like it or not, public measures that move radically beyond any steps now proposed or contemplated.

We commend the spirit prompting the War on Poverty recently announced, and the new commissions on economic dislocation and automation. With deference, this memorandum sets forth the historical and technological reasons why such tactics seem bound to fall short. Radically new circumstances demand radically new strategies.

If policies such as those suggested in The Triple Revolution are not adopted we believe that the nation will be thrown into unprecedented economic and social disorder. Our statement is aimed at showing why drastic changes in our economic organization are occurring, their relation to the growing movement for full rights for Negroes, and the minimal public and private measures that appear to us to be required.

Sincerely,

Donald G. Agger	Gunnar Myrdal
Dr. Donald B. Armstrong	Gerard Piel
James Boggs	Michael D. Reagan
W. H. Ferry	Ben B. Seligman
Todd Gitlin	Robert Theobald
Roger Hagan	William Worthy
Michael Harrington	Alice Mary Hilton
Tom Hayden	David T. Bazelon
Ralph L. Helstein	Maxwell Geismar
Dr. Frances W. Herring	Philip Green
Brig. Gen. Hugh B. Hester	H. Stuart Hughes
Gerald W. Johnson	Linus Pauling
Irving F. Laucks	John William Ward

191

April 6, 1964

DEAR MR. FERRY:

The President has asked me to thank you for your letter of March 19, in which you enclose the memorandum, The Triple Revolution, drawn up by your Committee.

In recent months the President has taken a number of steps addressed to the problems discussed in your memorandum—poverty, unemployment, and technological change. He has committed this Administration to an unrelenting war on poverty and, as you are of course aware, has submitted to the Congress major new legislation requesting the necessary weapons for the prosecution of this war. On December 21 he established the Committee on Economic Impact of Defense and Disarmament. The Committee will provide central review and coordination of activities in the Executive branch designed to improve our understanding of the economic impact of changes in defense expenditures. The President has also asked the Congress to establish a Presidential commission to study the impact of technological change on the economy and to recommend measures for assuring the full benefits of technology while minimizing any adverse effects.

Rapid advances in technology and sharp changes in the direction and location of economic activity pose both challenges and problems for the Nation. Your Committee has clearly been willing to take a completely fresh look at these matters. You may be sure that the Committee's analysis and recommendations will be given thoughtful consideration by all of those in the Executive branch who are concerned with these problems.

Sincerely,

s/   LEE C. WHITE
*Assistant Special Counsel
to the President*

MR. W. H. FERRY
*The Ad Hoc Committee on The
Triple Revolution*

The Triple Revolution

This statement is written in the recognition that mankind is at a historic conjuncture which demands a fundamental reexamination of existing values and institutions. At this time three separate and mutually reinforcing revolutions are taking place:

THE CYBERNATION REVOLUTION: A new era of production has begun. Its principles of organization are as different from those of the industrial era as those of the industrial era were different from the agricultural. The cybernation revolution has been brought about by the combination of the computer and the automated self-regulating machine. This results in a system of almost unlimited productive capacity which requires progressively less human labor. Cybernation is already reorganizing the economic and social system to meet its own needs.

THE WEAPONRY REVOLUTION: New forms of weaponry have been developed which cannot win wars but which can obliterate civilization. We are recognizing only now that the great weapons have eliminated war as a method for resolving international conflicts. The ever-present threat of total destruction is tempered by the knowledge of the final futility of war. The need of a "warless world" is generally recognized, though achieving it will be a long and frustrating process.

THE HUMAN RIGHTS REVOLUTION: A universal demand for full human rights is now clearly evident. It continues to be demonstrated in the civil rights movement within the United States. But this is only the local manifestation of a worldwide movement toward the establishment of social and political regimes in which every individual will feel valued and none will feel rejected on account of his race.

• We are particularly concerned in this statement with the first of these revolutionary phenomena. This is not because we underestimate the significance of the other two. On the contrary, we affirm that it is the simultaneous occurrence and interaction of all three developments which make evident the necessity for radical alterations in attitude and policy. The adoption of just policies for coping with cybernation and for extending rights to all Americans is indispensable to the creation of an atmosphere in the U.S. in which the supreme issue, peace, can be reasonably debated and resolved.

The Negro claims, as a matter of simple justice, his full share in America's economic and social life. He sees adequate employment opportunities as a chief means of attaining this goal: The March on Washington demanded freedom *and* jobs. The Negro's claim to a job is not being met. Negroes are the hardest-hit of the many groups being exiled from the economy by cybernation. Negro unemployment rates cannot be expected to drop substantially. Promises of jobs are a cruel and dangerous hoax on hundreds of thousands of Negroes and whites alike who are especially vulnerable to cybernation because of age or inadequate education.

The demand of the civil rights movement cannot be fulfilled within the present context of society. The Negro is trying to enter a social community and a tradition of work-and-income which are in the process of vanishing even for the hitherto privileged white worker. Jobs are disappearing under the impact of highly efficient, progressively less costly machines.

• The U.S. operates on the thesis, set out in the Employment Act of 1964, that every person will be able to obtain a job if he wishes to do so and that this job will provide him with resources adequate to live and maintain a family decently. Thus job-holding is the general mechanism through which economic resources are distributed. Those without work have access only to a minimal income, hardly sufficient to provide the necessities of life, and

193

enabling those receiving it to function as only "minimum consumers." As a result, the goods and services which are needed by these crippled consumers, and which they would buy if they could, are not produced. This in turn deprives other workers of jobs, thus reducing their incomes and consumption.

Present excessive levels of unemployment would be multiplied several times if military and space expenditures did not continue to absorb 10% of the gross national product (i.e., the total goods and services produced). Some 6 to 8 million people are employed as a direct result of purchases for space and military activities. At least an equal number hold their jobs as an indirect result of military or space expenditures. In recent years, the military and space budgets have absorbed a rising proportion of national production and formed a strong support for the economy.

However, these expenditures are coming in for more and more criticism, at least partially in recognition of the fact that nuclear weapons have eliminated war as an acceptable method for resolving international conflicts. Early in 1964 President Johnson ordered a curtailment of certain military expenditures. Defense Secretary McNamara is closing shipyards, airfields, and Army bases, and Congress is pressing the National Space Administration to economize. The future of these strong props to the economy is not as clear today as it was even a year ago.

How the Cybernation Revolution Shapes Up

Cybernation is manifesting the characteristics of a revolution in production. These include the development of radically different techniques and the subsequent appearance of novel principles of the organization of production; a basic reordering of man's relationship to his environment; and a dramatic increase in total available and potential energy.

The major difference between the agricultural, industrial and cybernation revolutions is the speed at which they developed. The agricultural revolution began several thousand years ago in the Middle East. Centuries passed in the shift from a subsistence base of hunting and food-gathering to settled agriculture.

In contrast, it has been less than 200 years since the emergence of the industrial revolution, and direct and accurate knowledge of the new productive techniques has reached most of mankind. This swift dissemination of information is generally held to be the main factor leading to widespread industrialization.

• While the major aspects of the cybernation revolution are for the moment restricted to the U.S., its effects are observable almost at once throughout the industrial world and large parts of the nonindustrial world. Observation is rapidly followed by analysis and criticism. The problems posed by the cybernation revolution are part of a new era in the history of all mankind but they are first being faced by the people of the U.S. The way Americans cope with cybernation will influence the course of this phenomenon everywhere. This country is the stage on which the machines-and-man drama will first be played for the world to witness.

194

The fundamental problem posed by the cybernation revolution in the U.S. is that it invalidates the general mechanism so far employed to undergird people's rights as consumers. Up to this time economic resources have been distributed on the basis of contributions to production, with machines and men competing for employment on somewhat equal terms. In the developing cybernated system, potentially unlimited output can be achieved by systems of machines which will require little cooperation from human beings. As machines take over production from men, they absorb an increasing proportion of resources while the men who are displaced become dependent on minimal and unrelated government measures —unemployment insurance, social security, welfare payments.

These measures are less and less able to disguise a historic paradox: That a substantial proportion of the population is subsisting on minimal incomes, often below the poverty line, at a time when sufficient productive potential is available to supply the needs of everyone in the U.S.

Industrial System Fails to Provide for Abolition of Poverty

The existence of this paradox is denied or ignored by conventional economic analysis. The general economic approach argues that potential demand, which if filled would raise the number of jobs and provide incomes to those holding them, is underestimated. Most contemporary economic analysis states that all of the available labor force and industrial capacity is required to meet the needs of consumers and industry and to provide adequate public services: Schools, parks, roads, homes, decent cities, and clean water and air. It is further argued that demand could be increased, by a variety of standard techniques, to any desired extent by providing money and machines to improve the conditions of the billions of impoverished people elsewhere in the world, who need food and shelter, clothes and machinery and everything else the industrial nations take for granted.

There is no question that cybernation does increase the potential for the provision of funds to neglected public sectors. Nor is there any question that cybernation would make possible the abolition of poverty at home and abroad. But the industrial system does not possess any adequate mechanisms to permit these potentials to become realities. The industrial system was designed to produce an ever-increasing quantity of goods as efficiently as possible, and it was assumed that the distribution of the power to purchase these goods would occur almost automatically. The continuance of the income-through-jobs link as the only major mechanism for distributing effective demand—for granting the right to consume—now acts as the main brake on the almost unlimited capacity of a cybernated productive system.

• Recent administrations have proposed measures aimed at achieving a better distribution of resources, and at reducing unemployment and underemployment. A few of these proposals have been enacted. More often they have failed to secure congressional support. In every case, many members of Congress have criticized the proposed measures as departing

195

from traditional principles for the allocation of resources and the encouragement of production. Abetted by budget-balancing economists and interest groups they have argued for the maintenance of an economic machine based on ideas of scarcity to deal with the facts of abundance produced by cybernation. This time-consuming criticism has slowed the workings of Congress and has thrown out of focus for that body the interrelated effects of The Triple Revolution.

An adequate distribution of the potential abundance of goods and services will be achieved only when it is understood that the major economic problem is not how to increase production but how to distribute the abundance that is the great potential of cybernation. There is an urgent need for a fundamental change in the mechanisms employed to insure consumer rights.

Facts and Figures of the Cybernation Revolution

No responsible observer would attempt to describe the exact pace or the full sweep of a phenomenon that is developing with the speed of cybernation. Some aspects of this revolution, however, are already clear:

The rate of productivity increase has risen with the onset of cybernation.
An industrial economic system postulated on scarcity has been unable to distribute the abundant goods and services produced by a cybernated system or potential in it.
Surplus capacity and unemployment have thus co-existed at excessive levels over the last six years.
The underlying cause of excessive unemployment is the fact that the capability of machines is rising more rapidly than the capacity of many human beings to keep pace.
A permanent impoverished and jobless class is established in the midst of potential abundance.

• Evidence for these statements follows:

1. The increased efficiency of machine systems is shown in the more rapid increase in productivity per man-hour since 1960, a year that marks the first visible upsurge of the cybernation revolution. In 1961, 1962 and 1963, productivity per man-hour rose at an average pace above 3.5%—a rate well above both the historical average and the postwar rate.

Companies are finding cybernation more and more attractive. Even at the present early stage of cybernation, costs have already been lowered to a point where the price of a durable machine may be as little as one-third of the current annual wage-cost of the worker it replaces. A more rapid rise in the rate of productivity increase per man-hour can be expected from now on.

2. In recent years it has proved to increase demand fast enough to bring about the full use of either men or plant capacities. The task of developing sufficient additional demand promises to become more difficult each year. A $30 billion annual increase in gross national product is now required to prevent unemployment rates from rising. An additional $40 to $60 bil-

lion increase would be required to bring unemployment rates down to an acceptable level.

3. The official rate of unemployment has remained at or above 5.5 per cent during the Sixties. The unemployment rate for teenagers has been rising steadily and now stands around 15 per cent. The unemployment rate for Negro teenagers stands about 30 per cent. The unemployment rate for teenagers in minority ghettoes sometimes exceeds 50 per cent. Unemployment rates for Negroes are regularly more than twice those for whites, whatever their occupation, educational level, age or sex. The unemployment position for other racial minorities is similarly unfavorable. Unemployment rates in depressed areas often exceed 50 per cent.

Unemployment Is Far Worse Than Figures Indicate

These official figures seriously underestimate the true extent of unemployment. The statistics take no notice of underemployment or featherbedding. Besides the 5.5% of the labor force who are officially designated as unemployed, nearly 4% of the labor force sought full-time work in 1962 but could find only parttime jobs. In addition, methods of calculating unemployment rates—a person is counted as unemployed only if he has actively sought a job recently—ignore the fact that many men and women who would like to find jobs have not looked for them because they know there are no employment opportunities.

Underestimates for this reason are pervasive among groups whose unemployment rates are high—the young, the old, and racial minorities. Many people in the depressed agricultural, mining and industrial areas, who by official definition hold jobs but who are actually grossly underemployed, would move if there were prospects of finding work elsewhere. It is reasonable to estimate that over 8,000,000 people are not working who would like to have jobs today as compared with the 4,000,000 shown in the official statistics.

Even more serious is the fact that the number of people who have voluntarily removed themselves from the labor force is not constant but increases continuously. These people have decided to stop looking for employment and seem to have accepted the fact that they will never hold jobs again. This decision is largely irreversible, in economic and also in social and psychological terms. The older worker calls himself "retired"; he cannot accept work without affecting his social security status. The worker in his prime years is forced onto relief: In most states the requirements for becoming a relief recipient bring about such fundamental alterations in an individual's situation that a reversal of the process is always difficult and often totally infeasible. Teenagers, especially "drop-outs" and Negroes, are coming to realize that there is no place for them in the labor force but at the same time they are given no realistic alternative. These people and their dependents make up a large part of the "poverty" sector of the American population.

Statistical evidence of these trends appears in the decline in the proportion of people claiming to be in the labor force—the so-called labor force participation rate. The recent apparent stabilization of the unemployment rate around 5.5% is therefore misleading: It is a reflection of the discouragement and defeat of people who cannot find employment and have withdrawn from the market rather than a measure of the economy's success in creating jobs for those who want to work.

4. An efficiently functioning industrial system is assumed to provide the great majority of new jobs through the expansion of the private enterprise sector. But well over half of the new jobs created during 1957–1962 were in the public sector—predominantly in teaching. Job creation in the private sector has now almost entirely ceased except in services; of the 4,300,000 jobs created in this period, only about 200,000 were provided by private industry through its own efforts. Many authorities anticipate that the application of cybernation to certain service industries, which is only just beginning, will be particularly effective. If this is the case, no significant job creation will take place in the private sector in coming years.

5. Cybernation raises the level of the skills of the machine. Secretary of Labor Wirtz has recently stated that the machines being produced today have, on the average, skills equivalent to a high school diploma. If a human being is to compete with such machines, therefore, he must at least possess a high school diploma. The Department of Labor estimates, however, that on the basis of present trends, as many as 30% of all students will be high school drop-outs in this decade.

6. A permanently depressed class is developing in the U.S. Some 38,000,000 Americans, almost one-fifth of the nation, still live in poverty. The percentage of total income received by the poorest 20% of the population was 4.9% in 1944 and 4.7% in 1963.

• Secretary Wirtz recently summarized these trends. "The confluence of surging population and driving technology is splitting the American labor force into tens of millions of 'have's' and millions of 'have-nots.' In our economy of 69,000,000 jobs, those with wanted skills enjoy opportunity and earning power. But the others face a new and stark problem—exclusion on a permanent basis, both as producers and consumers, from economic life. This division of people threatens to create a human slag heap. We cannot tolerate the development of a separate nation of the poor, the unskilled, the jobless, living within another nation of the well-off, the trained and the employed."

New Consensus Needed

The stubbornness and novelty of the situation that is conveyed by these statistics is now generally accepted. Ironically, it continues to be assumed that it is possible to devise measures which will reduce unemployment to a minimum and thus preserve the over-all viability of the present productive system. Some authorities have gone so far as to suggest that the pace of technological change should be slowed down "so as to allow the industrial productive system time to adapt."

We believe, on the contrary, that the industrial productive system is no longer viable. We assert that the only way to turn technological change to

198

the benefit of the individual and the service of the general welfare is to accept the process and to utilize it rationally and humanely. The new science of political economy will be built on the encouragement and planned expansion of cybernation. The issues raised by cybernation are particularly amenable to intelligent policy-making: Cybernation itself provides the resources and tools that are needed to ensure minimum hardship during the transition process.

• But major changes must be made in our attitudes and institutions in the foreseeable future. Today Americans are being swept along by three simultaneous revolutions while assuming they have them under control. In the absence of real understanding of any of these phenomena, especially of technology, we may be allowing an efficient and dehumanized community to emerge by default. Gaining control of our future requires the conscious formation of the society we wish to have. Cybernation at last forces us to answer the historic questions: What is man's role when he is not dependent upon his own activities for the material basis of his life? What should be the basis for distributing individual access to national resources? Are there other proper claims on goods and services besides a job?

• Because of cybernation, society no longer needs to impose repetitive and meaningless (because unnecessary) toil upon the individual. Society can now set the citizen free to make his own choice of occupation and vocation from a wide range of activities not now fostered by our value system and our accepted modes of "work." But in the absence of such a new consensus about cybernation, the nation cannot begin to take advantage of all that it promises for human betterment.

Proposal for Action

As a first step to a new consensus it is essential to recognize that the traditional link between jobs and incomes is being broken. The economy of abundance can sustain all citizens in comfort and economic security whether or not they engage in what is commonly reckoned as work. Wealth produced by machines rather than by men is still wealth. We urge, therefore, that society, through its appropriate legal and governmental institutions, undertake an unqualified commitment to provide every individual and every family with an adequate income as a matter of right.

• This undertaking we consider to be essential to the emerging economic, social and political order in this country. We regard it as the only policy by which the quarter of the nation now dispossessed and soon-to-be dispossessed by lack of employment can be brought within the abundant society. The unqualified right to an income would take the place of the patchwork of welfare measures—from unemployment insurance to relief—designed to ensure that no citizen or resident of the U.S. actually starves.

We do not pretend to visualize all of the consequences of this change in our values. It is clear, however, that the distribution of abundance in a cybernated society must be based on criteria strikingly different from those of an economic system based on scarcity. In retrospect, the establishment

199

of the right to an income will prove to have been only the first step in the reconstruction of the value system of our society brought on by the triple revolution.

• The present system encourages activities which can lead to private profit and neglects those activities which can enhance the wealth and the quality of life of our society. Consequently, national policy has hitherto been aimed far more at the welfare of the productive process than at the welfare of people. The era of cybernation can reverse this emphasis. With public policy and research concentrated on people rather than processes we believe that many creative activities and interests commonly thought of as non-economic will absorb the time and the commitment of many of those no longer needed to produce goods and services.

Society as a whole must encourage new modes of constructive, re-warding and ennobling activity. Principal among these are activities such as teaching and learning that relate people to people rather than people to things. Education has never been primarily conducted for profit in our society; it represents the first and most obvious activity inviting the expansion of the public sector to meet the needs of this period of transition.

• We are not able to predict the long-run patterns of human activity and commitment in a nation when fewer and fewer people are involved in production of goods and services, nor are we able to forecast the over-all patterns of income distribution that will replace those of the past full employment system. However, these are not speculative and fanciful matters to be contemplated at leisure for a society that may come into existence in three or four generations. The outlines of the future press sharply into the present. The problems of joblessness, inadequate incomes, and frustrated lives confront us now; the American Negro, in his rebellion, asserts the demands—and the rights—of all the disadvantaged. The Negro's is the most insistent voice today, but behind him stand the millions of impoverished who are beginning to understand that cybernation, properly understood and used, is the road out of want and toward a decent life.

The Transition[1]

We recognize that the drastic alternations in circumstances and in our way of life ushered in by cybernation and the economy of abundance will not be completed overnight. Left to the ordinary forces of the market such change, however, will involve physical and psychological misery and per-haps political chaos. Such misery is already clearly evident among the unemployed, among relief clients into the third generation and more and

[1] This view of the transitional period is not shared by all the signers. Robert Theobald and James Boggs hold that the two major principles of the transitional period will be (1) that machines rather than men will take up new conventional work openings and (2) that the activity of men will be directed to new forms of "work" and "leisure." Therefore, in their opinion, the specific proposals outlined in this section are more suitable for meeting the problems of the scarcity-economic system than for advancing through the period of transition into the period of abundance.

more among the young and the old for whom society appears to hold no promise of dignified or even stable lives. We must develop programs for this transition designed to give hope to the dispossessed and those cast out by the economic system, and to provide a basis for the rallying of people to bring about those changes in political and social institutions which are essential to the age of technology.

The program here suggested is not intended to be inclusive but rather to indicate its necessary scope. We propose:

1. A massive program to build up our educational system, designed especially with the needs of the chronically undereducated in mind. We estimate that tens of thousands of employment opportunities in such areas as teaching and research and development, particularly for younger people, may be thus created. Federal programs looking to the training of an additional 100,000 teachers annually are needed.

2. Massive public works. The need is to develop and put into effect programs of public works to construct dams, reservoirs, ports, water and air pollution facilities, community recreation facilities. We estimate that for each $1 billion per year spent on public works 150,000 to 200,000 jobs would be created. $2 billion or more a year should be spent in this way, preferably as matching funds aimed at the relief of economically distressed or dislocated areas.

3. A massive program of low-cost housing, to be built both publicly and privately, and aimed at a rate of 700,000–1,000,000 units a year.

4. Development and financing of rapid transit systems, urban and interurban; and other programs to cope with the spreading problems of the great metropolitan centers.

5. A public power system built on the abundance of coal in distressed areas, designed for low-cost power to heavy industrial and residential sections.

6. Rehabilitation of obsolete military bases for community or educational use.

7. A major revision of our tax structure aimed at redistributing income as well as apportioning the costs of the transition period equitably. To this end an expansion of the use of excess profits tax would be important. Subsidies and tax credit plans are required to ease the human suffering involved in the transition of many industries from man power to machine power.

8. The trade unions can play an important and significant role in this period in a number of ways:

   a. Use of collective bargaining to negotiate not only for people at work but also for those thrown out of work by technological change.
   b. Bargaining for perquisites such as housing, recreational facilities, and similar programs as they have negotiated health and welfare programs.
   c. Obtaining a voice in the investment of the unions' huge pension and welfare funds, and insisting on investment policies which have as their major criteria the social use and function of the enterprise in which the investment is made.

201

d. Organization of the unemployed so that these voiceless people may once more be given a voice in their own economic destinies, and strengthening of the campaigns to organize white-collar and professional workers.

9. The use of the licensing power of government to regulate the speed and direction of cybernation to minimize hardship; and the use of minimum wage power as well as taxing powers to provide the incentives for moving as rapidly as possible toward the goals indicated by this paper.

• These suggestions are in no way intended to be complete or definitively formulated. They contemplate expenditures of several billions more each year than are now being spent for socially rewarding enterprises, and a larger role for the government in the economy than it has now or has been given except in times of crisis. In our opinion, this is a time of crisis, the crisis of a triple revolution. Public philosophy for the transition must rest on the conviction that our economic, social and political institutions exist for the use of man and that man does not exist to maintain a particular economic system. This philosophy centers on an understanding that governments are instituted among men for the purpose of making possible life, liberty, and the pursuit of happiness and that government should be a creative and positive instrument toward these ends.

Change Must Be Managed

The historic discovery of the post-World War II years is that the economic destiny of the nation can be managed. Since the debate over the Employment Act of 1946 it has been increasingly understood that the federal government bears primary responsibility for the economic and social well-being of the country. The essence of management is planning. The democratic requirement is planning by public bodies for the general welfare. Planning by private bodies such as corporations for their own welfare does not automatically result in additions to the general welfare, as the impact of cybernation on jobs has already made clear.

The hardships imposed by sudden changes in technology have been acknowledged by Congress in proposals for dealing with the long- and short-run "dislocations," in legislation for depressed and "impacted" areas, retraining of workers replaced by machines, and the like. The measures so far proposed have not been "transitional" in conception. Perhaps for this reason they have had little effect on the situations they were designed to alleviate. But the primary weakness of this legislation is not ineffectiveness but incoherence. In no way can these disconnected measures be seen as a plan for remedying deep ailments but only, so to speak, as the superficial treatment of surface wounds.

Planning agencies should constitute the network through which pass the stated needs of the people at every level of society, gradually building into a national inventory of human requirements, arrived at by democratic debate of elected representatives.

202

- The primary tasks of the appropriate planning institutions should be:

  To collect the data necessary to appraise the effects, social and economic, of cybernation at different rates of innovation.

  To recommend ways, by public and private initiative, of encouraging and stimulating cybernation.

  To work toward optimal allocations of human and natural resources in meeting the requirements of society.

  To develop ways to smooth the transition from a society in which the norm is full employment within an economic system based on scarcity, to one in which the norm will be either non-employment, in the traditional sense of productive work, or employment on the great variety of socially valuable but "non-productive" tasks made possible by an economy of abundance; to bring about the conditions in which men and women no longer needed to produce goods and services may find their way to a variety of self-fulfilling and socially useful occupations.

  To work out alternatives to defense and related spending that will commend themselves to citizens, entrepreneurs and workers as a more reasonable use of common resources.

  To integrate domestic and international planning. The technological revolution has related virtually every major domestic problem to a world problem. The vast inequities between the industrialized and the underdeveloped countries cannot long be sustained.

- The aim throughout will be the conscious and rational direction of economic life by planning institutions under democratic control.

In this changed framework the new planning institutions will operate at every level of government—local, regional and federal—and will be organized to elicit democratic participation in all their proceedings. These bodies will be the means for giving direction and content to the growing demand for improvement in all departments of public life. The planning institutions will show the way to turn the growing protest against ugly cities, polluted air and water, an inadequate educational system, disappearing recreational and material resources, low levels of medical care, and the haphazard economic development into an integrated effort to raise the level of general welfare.

We are encouraged by the record of the planning institutions both of the Common Market and of several European nations and believe that this country can benefit from studying their weaknesses and strengths.

A principal result of planning will be to step up investment in the public sector. Greater investment in this area is advocated because it is overdue, because the needs in this sector comprise a substantial part of the content of the general welfare, and because they can be readily afforded by an abundant society. Given the knowledge that we are now in a period of transition it would be deceptive, in our opinion, to present such activities as likely to produce full employment. The efficiencies of cybernation should be as much sought in the public as in the private sector, and a chief focus of planning would be one means of bringing this about. A central assumption of planning institutions would be the central assumption of this statement, that the nation is moving into a society in which production of goods and services is not the only or perhaps the chief means of distributing income.

The Democratization of Change

The revolution in weaponry gives some dim promise that mankind may finally eliminate institutionalized force as the method of settling international conflict and find for it political and moral equivalents leading to a better world. The Negro revolution signals the ultimate admission of this group to the American community on equal social, political and economic terms. The cybernation revolution proffers an existence qualitatively richer in democratic as well as material values. A social order in which men make the decisions that shape their lives becomes more possible now than ever before; the unshackling of men from the bonds of unfulfilling labor frees them to become citizens, to make themselves and to make their own history.

But these enhanced promises by no means constitute a guarantee. Illuminating and making more possible the "democratic vistas" is one thing; reaching them is quite another, for a vision of democratic life is made real not by technological change but by men consciously moving toward that ideal and creating institutions that will realize and nourish the vision in living form.

Democracy, as we use the term, means a community of men and women who are able to understand, express and determine their lives as dignified human beings. Democracy can only be rooted in a political and economic order in which wealth is distributed by and for people, and used for the widest social benefit. With the emergence of the era of abundance we have the economic base for a true democracy of participation, in which men no longer need to feel themselves prisoners of social forces and decisions beyond their control or comprehension.

DONALD G. AGGER, Washington, D.C.
> Attorney, Partner, de Grazia, Agger and Hydeman.

DR. DONALD B. ARMSTRONG, M.D., Scarborough, N.Y.

JAMES BOGGS, Detroit, Michigan
> Mr. Boggs is an auto worker, and the author of *Pages from a Negro Worker's Notebook,* 1963.

W. H. FERRY, Santa Barbara, Calif.
> Vice-President, Fund for the Republic, Inc., Center for the Study of Democratic Institutions.

TODD GITLIN, Ann Arbor, Michigan
> President, Students for a Democratic Society.

ROGER HAGAN, Cambridge, Mass.
> Editor, *The Correspondent,* Council for Correspondence

MICHAEL HARRINGTON, New York City
> Author, *The Other America.*

TOM HAYDEN, Ann Arbor, Michigan
> Students for a Democratic Society.

RALPH L. HELSTEIN, Chicago, Illinois
President, United Packinghouse, Food and Allied Workers.
DR. FRANCES W. HERRING, Berkeley, Calif.
Institute for Governmental Studies, University of California.
BRIG. GEN. HUGH B. HESTER (Retired), St. Petersburg, Fla.
Director of Procurement of Supplies for Gen. MacArthur's forces in the SW Pacific, 1942–47.
GERALD W. JOHNSON, Baltimore, Maryland
Journalist.
IRVING F. LAUCKS, Santa Barbara, Calif.
Former head, Laucks Chemical Company, now Consultant to The Center for the Study of Democratic Institutions.
GUNNAR MYRDAL, Stockholm, Sweden
Economist, Institute for International Economic Studies.
"I am in broad agreement with this Statement, though not entirely so."
GERARD PIEL, New York City
Publisher, *Scientific American.*
MICHAEL D. REAGAN, Syracuse, N.Y.
Graduate Program in Public Administration, Maxwell Graduate School of Citizenship and Public Affairs, Syracuse University.
BEN B. SELIGMAN, Washington, D.C.
Director, Department of Education and Research, Retail Clerks International Association.
ROBERT THEOBALD, New York City
Consulting economist, and author of many books, the latest being *Free Men and Free Markets.*
WILLIAM WORTHY, New York City
Correspondent, Baltimore *Afro-American.*
ALICE MARY HILTON, New York City
Independent consultant, problems of technology and automation.
MAXWELL GEISMAR, Harrison, N.Y.
Social critic, author of *Henry James and the Jacobites.*
PHILIP GREEN, Haverford, Pa.
Assistant Professor of Political Science, Haverford College.
H. STUART HUGHES, Cambridge, Mass.
Professor of History, Harvard University.
LINUS PAULING, Pasadena, California
Nobel laureate, Peace; Consultant to the Center for the Study of Democratic Institutions.
JOHN WILLIAM WARD, Princeton, N.J.
Professor of History, Princeton University.
A. J. MUSTE, New York City
Secretary Emeritus, Fellowship of Reconciliation.

Dr. Louis Fein, Palo Alto, Calif.
> Independent consultant, computer field.

Stewart Meacham, Philadelphia, Pa.
> Peace Secretary, American Friends Service Committee.

Everett C. Hughes, Waltham, Mass.
> Professor of Sociology, Brandeis University.

Robert L. Heilbroner, New York City
> Economist; author, *The Worldly Philosophers, The Great Ascent*.

Irving Howe, New York City
> Editor, *Dissent* Magazine.

Bayard Rustin, New York City
> Executive Secretary, War Resisters League; organizer of the March on Washington.

Norman Thomas, New York City
> Socialist leader.

Dwight Macdonald, New York City
> Writer and critic.

APPENDIX 2

Report of the National Commission on Technology, Automation, and Economic Progress

To THE PRESIDENT AND THE MEMBERS OF THE CONGRESS:

We have the honor to present the report of the National Commission on Technology, Automation, and Economic Progress. This Commission was established by Public Law 88–444, which was approved by Congress on August 5, 1964, and signed by the President on August 19, 1964.

The Commission was appointed by the President in December 1964, and the appointments were approved by the Senate on January 27, 1965. The Commission has met in monthly 2-day sessions beginning in January 1965. It has heard many witnesses; it has received reports from numerous organizations and other individuals; and it has had the assistance of a highly competent and dedicated staff.

The report is supplemented by extensive supporting documents, including reports on the many studies conducted by experts at the request of the Commission and statements made by various interested organizations and individuals. Though the Commission does not necessarily endorse the information and views of these supplementary documents, it considers them of value and has directed their publication.

The content of this report has been developed through lengthy discussions by the members of the Commission and represents their combined judgment and general agreement. It does not necessarily represent their individual endorsement of the details of each finding. On a very few of the findings, individual members have expressed their opinions in footnotes.

HOWARD R. BOWEN, *Chairman*

BENJAMIN AARON	WALTER P. REUTHER
JOSEPH A. BEIRNE	ROBERT H. RYAN
DANIEL BELL	ROBERT M. SOLOW
PATRICK E. HAGGERTY	PHILIP SPORN
ALBERT J. HAYES	THOMAS J. WATSON, JR.
ANNA ROSENBERG HOFFMAN	WHITNEY M. YOUNG, JR.
EDWIN H. LAND	

Members of the Commission and Interagency Advisory Committee

COMMISSION

Chairman

DR. HOWARD R. BOWEN, President, University of Iowa, Iowa City, Iowa

Members

DR. BENJAMIN AARON, Professor of Law and Director, Institute of Industrial Relations, University of California, Los Angeles, California

MR. JOSEPH A. BEIRNE, President, Communications Workers of America, Washington, D.C.

DR. DANIEL BELL, Chairman, Sociology Department, Columbia University, New York, New York

MR. PATRICK E. HAGGERTY, President, Texas Instruments, Incorporated, Dallas, Texas

MR. ALBERT J. HAYES, Past President, International Association of Machinists, Washington, D.C.

MRS. ANNA ROSENBERG HOFFMAN, President, Anna M. Rosenberg Associates, New York, New York

DR. EDWIN H. LAND, President and Research Director, Polaroid Corporation, Cambridge, Massachusetts

MR. WALTER P. REUTHER, President, United Automobile Workers, Detroit, Michigan

MR. ROBERT H. RYAN, President, Regional Industrial Development Corporation of Southwestern Pennsylvania, Pittsburgh, Pennsylvania

DR. ROBERT M. SOLOW, Professor of Economics, Massachusetts Institute of Technology, Cambridge, Massachusetts

MR. PHILIP SPORN, Chairman, System Development Committee, American Electric Power Company, New York, New York

MR. THOMAS J. WATSON, JR., Chairman of the Board, IBM Corporation, Armonk, New York

MR. WHITNEY M. YOUNG, JR., Executive Director, National Urban League, New York, New York

ADVISORY COMMITTEE

Cochairmen

JOHN T. CONNOR, Secretary of Commerce
W. WILLARD WIRTZ, Secretary of Labor

Members

GARDNER ACKLEY, Chairman, Council of Economic Advisers
WILLIAM C. FOSTER, Director, Arms Control and Disarmament Agency
ORVILLE L. FREEMAN, Secretary of Agriculture
JOHN W. GARDNER, Secretary of Health, Education, and Welfare

208

Donald F. Hornig, Director, Office of Science and Technology
Robert S. McNamara, Secretary of Defense
Glenn T. Seaborg, Chairman, Atomic Energy Commission
James E. Webb, Administrator, National Aeronautics and Space Administration

Introduction[1]

Future historians will probably describe our time as an age of conscious social change. The change we are witnessing includes the rapid growth of population, the massive flow of peoples from rural areas to the cities, the steady growth of national wealth and income, the rise of oppressed and submerged peoples, the spread of mass education, the extension of leisure, the venture into space, and the frightening increase in the destructiveness of military weapons. Change is worldwide in scope. Not all nations or regions are participating to the same degree or have reached the same stage, but almost no part of the world has been left untouched.

It is easy to oversimplify the course of history; yet if there is one predominant factor underlying current social change, it is surely the advancement of technology. Technological change includes new methods of production, new designs of products and services, and new products and new services. Technological change is exemplified by the automation of a machine tool, reorganization of an assembly line, substitution of plastics for metals, introduction of a supersonic transport, discovery of a new method of heart surgery, teaching of foreign languages by electronic machines, introduction of self-service into retailing, communications by satellite, bookkeeping by electronic computer, generation of electricity from nuclear energy, introduction of frozen foods and air conditioning, and the development of space vehicles and nuclear weapons.

As men have learned the power of applying thought and experiment to the attainment of human ends and have systematically exploited the possibilities of pure science and technology, a steady flow of new methods, new designs, and new products has resulted.

There has been widespread public recognition of the deep influence of technology upon our way of life. Everywhere there is speculation about the future possibilities for human life, and much public attention is directed toward scientific and technical trends. The vast majority of people quite rightly have accepted technological change as beneficial. They recognize that it has led to better working conditions by eliminating many, perhaps most, dirty, menial, and servile jobs; that it has made possible the shortening of working hours and the increase in leisure; that it has provided a growing abundance of goods and a continuous flow of improved and new products; that it has provided new interests and new experiences for people and thus added to the zest for life.

On the other hand, technological progress has at various times in history,

---

[1] This introduction was written by the Chairman at the request of the Commission, but is not part of the official report of the Commission.

209

one of them in recent years, raised fears and concerns which have led to some questioning of its benefits. One of these concerns has been the fear of annihilation by "the bomb." Another concern has been the apparently harmful influences of modern technology on the physical and community environment—leading to such problems as air and water pollution, inadequate water supply, unsatisfactory solid waste disposal, urban congestion and blight, deterioration of natural beauty, and the rapid depletion of natural resources. Another concern has been the apparently harmful influence of urban, industrial, and technical civilization upon the personality of individual human beings—leading to rootlessness, anonymity, insecurity, monotony, and mental disorder. Still another concern, perhaps the one most responsible for the establishment of the Commission, has arisen from the belief that technological change is a major source of unemployment. This concern has been fostered by the substantial and persistent unemployment during the period 1954–65. The fear has even been expressed by some that technological change would in the near future not only cause increasing unemployment, but that eventually it would eliminate all but a few jobs, with the major portion of what we now call work being performed automatically by machine.

As a nation we have willingly accepted technological change because of its many benefits, but we have never been fully successful in dealing with its problems, even when the pace of technological advance and the growth of the labor force were less rapid than today.

The relatively high postwar labor productivity, much of it due to technological change, combined with the current and future high rate of labor force growth increases dramatically the number of jobs which must be created continually to achieve and maintain full employment. During the period since 1947 output per man-hour in the private economy has increased at the rate of about 3 per cent a year as compared to 2 per cent a year in the previous 35 years. It is possible that this higher rate of productivity growth will continue, and it may even accelerate in the decade ahead. Moreover, in the next 5 years, the labor force will increase by approximately 1.9 per cent a year, and the increase beyond that time will be almost as fast. This figure compares with 1.5 per cent a year in the last half of the 1950's.

The social costs and dislocations flowing from past technological changes underscore the need to prepare for the changes that lie ahead. For instance:

> Modern farm technology—ranging from the cottonpicker and huge harvesting combines to chemical fertilizers and insecticides—has resulted in rapid migration of workers to the cities and has contributed to serious urban problems.
>
> The technological revolution in agriculture has compounded the difficulties of a large section of our Negro population. Pushed out of rural areas, many of them have migrated to cities in search of livelihood. But they have arrived just when deficient economic growth rates have increased the competition for available jobs, and when advancing technology has been reducing the numbers of the semiskilled and un-

skilled manufacturing jobs for which they could qualify. Despite improvements in the past 2 years, there are 700,000 fewer factory production and maintenance jobs than at the close of the Korean War.

The closing of obsolete plants and facilities as a result of technological and economic changes has thrown some whole communities—particularly one-industry communities—into economic distress. The fact that coal mining employment fell by 46 per cent in 7 years between 1947 and 1954 illustrates the problem. Appalachia is evidence of our failure to cope with it.

Technological change has upset the delicate balances of our environment. Pollution of air and water bedevil our metropolitan areas in which 70 per cent of our population lives, while the growing urban population has intensified problems of urban transportation, housing, education, health, and public services.

Despite the great wealth that technology enables us to produce, in 1963 nearly 35 million Americans were still below the poverty level (7.2 million families and 1.8 million persons living alone). Approximately half of these people lived in family units whose breadwinners were employed full-time.

Technology is not a vessel into which people are to be poured and to which they must be molded. It is something to be adapted to the needs of man and to the furtherance of human ends, including the enrichment of personality and environment.

Technology has, on balance, surely been a great blessing to mankind—despite the fact that some of the benefits have been offset by costs. There should be no thought of deliberately slowing down the rate of technological advancement or hampering the freedom of discovery. The task for the decades ahead is to direct technology to the fulfillment of important human purposes. Much of this technology will be derived from the social sciences and the humanities as well as the physical and biological sciences. It will be concerned with such values as individuality, diversity, and decentralization rather than conformity, massive organization, and concentration. It will be directed toward human, environmental, and resource development rather than the proliferation of conventional consumer goods. It will seek to make work more meaningful rather than merely more productive.

In the new technology, machines and automated processes will do the routine and mechanical work. Human resources will be released and available for new activities beyond those that are required for mere subsistence. The great need is to discover the nature of this new kind of work, to plan it, and to do it. In the longer run, significant changes may be needed in our society—in education, for example—to help people find constructive and rewarding ways to use increasing leisure.

Our problem is to marshal the needed technologies, some of which are known and some not yet known. If we are to clean up our environment, enhance human personality, enrich leisure time, make work humanly creative, and restore our natural resources, we shall need inventiveness in the democratic decision making process as well as in the needed technologies. We shall also need to find creative combinations of public and private initiative, as some of the goals of the future may not be achievable through private initiative; leadership will be required by government— Federal, State, and local—with important roles to be played by universities and nonprofit institutions.

It was in the setting of the considerations outlined above that the legislation establishing the Commission was enacted in August 1964. Since that time, conditions have changed and public concerns have been modified. As a result of the tax cuts and other fiscal policies adopted beginning in early 1964, unemployment has been reduced from 5.4 per cent to about 4 per cent at present. With the intensification of the war in Vietnam, the prospects are for still further cuts in unemployment, and concern is expressed about inflation. However, despite the recent improvement in the employment situation, the basic issues which the Commission was asked to consider are just as relevant and urgent as they were a year ago; and they will continue to be relevant and urgent for many years. The Commission's basic recommendations have not been altered by the turn of recent events.

In the legislative charge (as expressed in Public Law 88–444 creating the Commission), the Congress gave the Commission the following mandate:

a. To identify and assess the past effects and the current and prospective role and pace of technological change;
b. To identify and describe the impact of technological and economic change on production and employment, including new job requirements and the major types of worker displacement, both technological and economic, which are likely to occur during the next 10 years; the specific industries, occupations, and geographic areas which are most likely to be involved; and the social and economic effects of these developments on the Nation's economy, manpower, communities, families, social structure, and human values;
c. To define those areas of unmet community and human needs toward which application of new technologies might most effectively be directed, encompassing an examination of technological developments that have occurred in recent years, including those resulting from the Federal Government's research and development programs;
d. To assess the most effective means for channeling new technologies into promising directions, including civilian industries where accelerated technological advancements will yield general benefits, and assess the proper relationship between governmental and private investment in the application of new technologies to large-scale human and community needs;
e. To recommend, in addition to those actions which are the responsibility of management and labor, specific administrative and legislative steps which it believes should be taken by the Federal, State, and local governments in meeting their responsibilities (1) to support and promote technological change in the interest of continued economic growth and improved well-being of our people, (2) to

212

continue and adopt measures which will facilitate occupational adjustment and geographical mobility, and (3) to share the costs and help prevent and alleviate the adverse impact of change on displaced workers.

The Commission was asked to concern itself with only the next decade. It has not attempted to deal with the distant future. Nevertheless, the scope of the mandate was wide and the issues both complex and difficult. But the Commission has attempted, within the limits of its 1-year life, to answer the questions raised and to offer recommendations as requested.

HOWARD R. BOWEN, *Chairman.*

THE PACE OF TECHNOLOGICAL CHANGE* [2]

It has become almost a commonplace that the world is experiencing a scientific and technological revolution. Stock phrases—knowledge explosion, second industrial revolution, automation revolution—express this belief. According to one extreme view, the world—or at least the United States—is on the verge of a glut of productivity sufficient to make our economic institutions and the notion of gainful employment obsolete. We dissent from this view. We believe that the evidence does not support it, and that it diverts attention from the real problems of our country and the world. However, we also dissent from the other extreme view of complacency that denies the existence of serious social and economic problems related to the impact of technological change.

There is no doubt that the pace of technological change is uneven from decade to decade and century to century. Past trends and current prospects suggest that the present is, and the near future will be, a time of rapid technological progress. The combination of increased expenditure on research and development, extended and deepened education, continued urbanization, and improved communications has led to spectacular accomplishments in science and engineering. But this is as far as we are prepared to go. It is beyond our knowledge to know whether the computer, nuclear power, and molecular biology are quantitatively or qualitatively more "revolutionary" than the telephone, electric power, and bacteriology.

Our study of the evidence has impressed us with the inadequacy of the

* For general comments on report by several Commission members, see pp. [215–216].

[2] Studies were prepared for the Commission's consideration on most of the major points in this report. The Commission appreciates the efforts of the experts who prepared these studies and has directed their publication in volumes supplementary to the report. We believe the information and views provided in them are of value, but we endorse the findings of none.

The (†) symbol in footnotes throughout the report is used to indicate studies prepared for the Commission.

In relation to this section, see Bureau of Labor Statistics, *Industry Productivity Projections: A Methodological Study* (†); Frank Lynn, *An Investigation of the Rate of Development and Diffusion of Technology in Our Modern Industrial Society* (†); and Edwin Mansfield, *Technological Change: Measurement, Determinants, and Diffusion* (†).

basis for any sweeping pronouncements about the speed of scientific and technological progress. There are, however, a few measurable aspects of the process about which reasonable statements can be made. Our broad conclusion is that the pace of technological change has increased in recent decades and may increase in the future, but a sharp break in the continuity of technical progress has not occurred, nor is it likely to occur in the next decade.

There appears to be no direct method of measuring the rate of technological change through the number of significant innovations or their economic effects. Therefore, indirect measures must do. The most useful appear to be indexes of productivity and productivity growth, particularly output per man-hour (the volume of final output of goods and services produced in a year divided by the number of man-hours worked in the year). Output per man-hour is not, of course, a measure of technical progress alone. It depends also upon the education, skill, and health of workers and managers and upon the plant and equipment with which they work. Nevertheless, any great change in the overall rate of technological progress capable of having major effects on the economy is most likely to be reflected in output per man-hour.

The most inclusive useful index of productivity is output per man-hour in the whole private economy. In the 35 years before the end of the Second World War, output per man-hour in the private economy rose at a trend rate of 2 per cent a year. But this period includes the depression decade of the 1930's. Between 1947 and 1965 productivity in the private economy rose at a trend rate of about 3.2 per cent a year. If agriculture is excluded, the contrast is less sharp, with the rate of increase 2 per cent a year before the war, and 2.5 per cent after. . . .[3]

Some attempts have been made to refine a measure of the effects of technological change by allowing for the influence of better educated workers and increasing capital investment. The results are necessarily imprecise, and show, as would be expected, that not all the gain in productivity can be attributed to changing technology. They do suggest, however, some acceleration in the rate of progress, and give a picture consistent with the simpler index of output per man-hour.

If this increase in the rate of productivity growth does not square with the assumption that a veritable technological revolution has occurred, the increase itself is nevertheless substantial. Growth at 2 per cent a year doubles in 36 years; growth at 2.5 per cent a year doubles in 28 years; growth at 3 per cent a year doubles in about 24 years. The notion that the product of an hour of work can double in 24 years—not much more than half a working lifetime—is quite enough to justify the feeling of continuous change that is so much a part of the contemporary environment. The time scale has indeed shrunk visibly.

One other important aspect of innovation is at least partially amenable to measurement. The economic impact of a scientific or engineering discovery

[3] We give the figure without agriculture not to suggest that agricultural productivity does not matter, but only to isolate the productivity trend in "industry." For manufacturing alone, the postwar rate of productivity gain was 2.6 per cent per year.

begins not when the discovery is first made, not even when it is first commercially introduced, but only later when the resulting new product or new process receives widespread commercial acceptance. The process of development and diffusion through industry takes time—sometimes a long time. The steam locomotive and the diesel coexisted for at least 30 years; the DC–3 introduced in the 1930's is still flying. Studies made for the Commission confirm the common belief that things happen faster nowadays: the lag between discovery and commercial application has shortened. It is nevertheless still substantial.

Lynn concluded from an examination of a limited sample of 20 major technological innovations during the last 60 to 70 years that every step in the process of technological development had accelerated. The typical time between a technical discovery and recognition of its commercial potential had fallen from about 30 years before the First World War to 16 years between the wars, and 9 years after the Second World War. The additional time required to convert these basic technical discoveries to initial commercial application had decreased from about 7 years to about 5 years. . . . The rate at which new technologies diffused throughout the economy after their introduction had speeded up considerably between the early part of the century and the interwar period, with only slight further acceleration after 1945. Technological innovations with consumer applications were developed and diffused nearly twice as fast as those with industrial applications. The implied shrinking of the time scale is quite consistent with the productivity figures already given.

Mansfield's findings were based upon a survey of 12 important technical innovations in 4 major industries. He found only a slight and unclear tendency for innovations to spread more rapidly than in the past, but his estimates of the amount of time involved are not very different from Lynn's. Mansfield calculates the average time lag between invention and innovation in his sample at about 14 years, with another 1 to 15 years before one-half the firms in an industry had imitated the innovation.

No small number of case studies can be conclusive; but there is certainly evidence of a faster rate of technological development. The process, however, is still a fairly long one. Our studies suggest that major technological discoveries may wait as long as 14 years before they reach commercial application even on a small scale, and perhaps another 5 years before their impact on the economy becomes large. It seems safe to conclude that most major technological discoveries which will have a significant economic impact within the next decade are already at least in a readily identifiable stage of commercial development.

We find, in summary, evidence of enough increase in the pace of technological and economic change that there is no ground for complacency. Our society has not met the challenge of technical progress with complete success. There is much to be done.

General Comment on Report by Mr. Beirne, Mr. Hayes, and Mr. Reuther, joined by Mrs. Hoffman and Mr. Young

We have concurred in this report because we believe that on the whole both its analysis and its recommendations are sound—although some of the recommendations could be more forcefully stated and we would have liked to have certain additional recommendations included.

We feel obligated to state regretfully, however, that in our opinion the report lacks the tone of urgency which we believe its subject matter requires and which its recommendations reflect.

The more than 50 per cent increase in the trend rate of productivity advance in the post-World War II period compared to the prewar period, and a similar increase in the rate of labor force growth in the years ahead as compared to the 1950's, give new dimensions to the two major challenges that face us. The first is to provide productive employment and adequate incomes for all who are willing and able to work so that all may participate in the creation and sharing of the abundance that our developing technology makes possible. The second is to carry out programs and policies in both the private and public sectors to insure the fullest utilization of our productive potential to make life for all our people far better than most would have dared to dream just a few decades ago.

We agree that the problems flowing from technological change during the next decade will not be unsolvable economically. The obstacles to their solution are essentially political. The fundamental political problem is the lack of a sense of urgency in many quarters in dealing with human problems—meeting individual and social needs and the improvement of the quality of life in our society—comparable to the sense of urgency that moves our Nation to swift, determined, and vigorous action when we face a military challenge.

It is our profound conviction that no person or family should suffer hardship that it is possible for us as a nation to avoid. American Negroes, who have already waited 300 years, must not be made to wait any longer for the full equality that can be theirs only under full employment. Conscience and compassion should be no less compelling and courage should be as great in our pursuit of the rewarding purposes of peace as in our military efforts.

It is, therefore, our hope that this report will be read and understood as an agenda for action—a call for the full mobilization of America's resources in the building of a truly Great Society.

General Comment on Report by Mr. Sporn, joined by Mr. Haggerty

Perhaps it is inevitable in the nature of the assignment given this Commission that the major emphasis of this report should be on the problems associated with technological change and their possible solutions. However, I believe that this report fails to give adequate emphasis to the positive contributions of technology. Technological progress in the United States has played a major role in bringing this Nation the highest standards of material welfare more broadly disseminated throughout its population than has ever before been achieved by any society in the history of the world.

Automation represents a logical extension of this 200-year-long history of technological progress that carries the potential for continuing to enhance the productive capabilities of our society and to make possible the continuing expansion of the material, social, and spiritual welfare of the Nation and of the world. It does not represent a radical departure from past experience, but its continued development is essential to expand the capabilities of our society and to disseminate more widely rising levels of human well-being.

The material and spiritual wealth made possible in large part by technological progress has raised our standards of expectations and performance so that our society is no longer willing to accept the inevitability of the hardships of dislocations that often accompany the change characteristic of a dynamic society. However, this cannot stand as an indictment of technology, but only as a challenge to the dynamism, strength, and adaptability of the Nation's political, social, and economic institutions to develop and facilitate the widespread introduction of new technology and the wider dissemination of its benefits. In this context it is imperative that our society, while continuing to pursue vigorously a course of uninterrupted technological advance, undertake without delay vigorous programs to relieve individuals of the adverse impacts of the dislocations stemming from advancing technology. Thus resistance to change can be reduced and further technological progress promoted.

TECHNOLOGICAL CHANGE AND UNEMPLOYMENT

The language and legislative history of Public Law 88–444 leave no doubt that Congress was seriously concerned with the role of technological change and the high levels of unemployment which persisted in the United States after 1953. At the end of the Korean War, unemployment began to creep upward from an average level of some 3 per cent of the civilian labor force; it rose and fell with economic conditions, but stalled at higher levels at the peak of each succeeding business cycle. The explanation was sought by some in the dramatic technological changes that had occurred during the 1950's. It was not the first time that the possibility of persistent technological unemployment had been the focus of public discussion.

We believe that the general level of unemployment must be distinguished from the displacement of particular workers at particular times and places, if the relation between technological change and unemployment is to be clearly understood. The persistence of a high general level of unemployment in the years following the Korean War was not the result of accelerated technological progress. Its cause was interaction between rising productivity, labor force growth, and an inadequate growth of aggregate demand. This is firmly supported by the response of the economy to the expansionary fiscal policy of the past 5 years. Technological change on the other hand, has been a major factor in the displacement and temporary unemployment of particular workers. Thus technological change (along with other forms of economic change) is an important determinant of the precise places, industries, and people affected by unemployment. But the general level of demand for goods and services is by far the most important factor determining how many are affected, how long they stay unemployed, and how hard it is for new entrants to the labor market to find jobs. The basic fact

217

is that technology eliminates jobs, not work. It is the continuous obligation of economic policy to match increases in productive potential with increases in purchasing power and demand. Otherwise the potential created by technical progress runs to waste in idle capacity, unemployment, and deprivation.

A. General Levels of Unemployment

Changes in the volume of unemployment are governed by three fundamental forces: the growth of the labor force, the increase in output per man-hour, and the growth of total demand for goods and services. Changes in the average hours of work enter in exactly parallel fashion but have been quantitatively less significant. As productivity rises, less labor is required per dollar of national product, or more goods and services can be produced with the same number of man-hours. If output does not grow, employment will certainly fall; if production increases more rapidly than productivity (less any decline in average hours worked), employment must rise. But the labor force grows, too. Unless gross national product (total final expenditure for goods and services corrected for price changes) rises more rapidly than the *sum* of productivity increase and labor force growth (again modified for any change in hours of work), the increase in employment will be inadequate to absorb the growth in the labor force. Inevitably the unemployment rate will increase. Only when total production expands faster than the rate of labor force growth *plus* the rate of productivity increase and *minus* the rate at which average annual hours falls does the unemployment rate fall. . . .

In the late 1950's, productivity and the labor force were increasing more rapidly than usual, while the growth of output was slower than usual. This accounts for the persistence of high unemployment rates.

. . . In this period output per man-hour in the private economy rose at a trend rate of 3.2 per cent a year. . . . (For purely statistical reasons the figure is lowered to 28 per cent when Government employees are included in any calculation of the rate of growth of output required to reduce unemployment.) The labor force had been growing only at about 1 per cent a year from 1947 to 1953, a reflection of the low birth rates of the 1930's; between 1953 and 1960 it speeded up to 1.5 per cent. Average hours worked per year have been declining slowly and sporadically for a long time, with the average yearly decrease about 0.3 to 0.4 per cent. . . . The growth rate of output, which had been as high as 5.2 per cent a year between 1947 and 1953, slowed to 2.4 per cent between 1953 and 1960. . . . An increase in unemployment was the immediate result. Yet, an addition to the GNP growth rate of only 0.4 per cent a year would have prevented unemployment from rising.[4] Since the end of 1960, the growth rate has averaged slightly more than 4.5 per cent a year, enough to reduce the unemployment rate from 5.6 to 4.1 per cent at the end of 1965.

Except for the recession years of 1949, 1954, and 1958, the rate of economic growth throughout this period exceeded the rate of productivity

[4] Assuming a rate of productivity increase no higher than that actually recorded.

218

increase and employment rose. But in only 6 of the past 12 years was the growth rate high enough to offset both productivity increase and labor force growth. In the other 6 years unemployment rose. . . .

But if part of the national purpose is to reduce and contain unemployment, arithmetic is not enough. We must know which of the basic factors we can control and which we wish to control. Unemployment would have risen more slowly or fallen more rapidly if (1) productivity had increased more slowly, or (2) the labor force had increased more slowly, or (3) hours of work had fallen more steeply, or (4) total output had grown more rapidly. These are not independent factors, however, and a change in any of them might have caused changes in others.

A society can choose to reduce the growth of productivity, and it can probably find ways to frustrate its own creativity. We believe this choice to be utterly self-defeating in its impact on living standards and wages. Although a reduction in the growth of productivity at the expense of potential output might result in higher employment in the short run, the long-run effect on employment would be uncertain and the long-run effect on the national interest would be disastrous. It may be possible to slow the growth of the labor force by encouraging later entry, earlier retirement, lower participation by some groups, or reduced hours of work. In the past, rising productivity has been realized partly through higher incomes and partly through reduced working time and shorter working life. This pattern is likely to continue.

Despite rapid increases in productivity, economic growth consistent with the 2.9 per cent unemployment rate of 1953 or the 4.3 per cent rate of 1957 would not have been difficult to achieve or sustain; they would have been considerably less than those actually experienced between 1947 and 1953 or between 1960 and 1965. The high unemployment that led to the formation of this Commission was the consequence of passive public policy, not the inevitable consequence of the pace of technological change.

When Public Law 88–444 was passed, the national unemployment rate was 5.1 per cent. As this report is finished it is 4.0 per cent. The experience of the economy during the life of this Commission is the best evidence that economic growth can continue to offset the growth of productivity and labor force and reduce unemployment further. We believe that continued reduction in unemployment is a feasible task and a matter of urgency for our society. We recognize that the task is a challenging one under the circumstances of the coming years.

We do not expect output per man-hour in the whole—private *and* public—economy to rise during the next decade at a rate substantially faster than the 2.8 per cent a year characteristic of the postwar period. Some moderate acceleration may take place in the longer run. The growth of the labor force, however, is predictable and dramatic. The labor force will increase approximately 1.9 per cent a year during the next 5 years, and almost as fast in the following 10 or 15 years. We expect a continued slow and irregular decline in hours of work. It follows that the output of the economy—and the aggregate demand to buy it—must grow in excess of 4 per cent a year just to prevent the unemployment rate from rising, and even faster if the unemployment rate is to fall further, as we believe it should. Yet our economy has seldom, if ever, grown at a rate faster than 3.5 per cent for any extended length of time. We have no cause for complacency. Positive fiscal, monetary, and manpower policies will be needed in the future as in the past. The Nation should not be lulled into forgetfulness by a short-run need for increased defense expenditures.

B. Displacement of Workers Through Shifts in Employment Among Industries and Occupations[5]

Hidden beneath national averages is continuous movement into, out of, between, and within labor markets. In 1964, for instance, the average number of persons in the labor force was 74 million, with about 70 million employed and 3.9 million unemployed. But that is only part of the story, for in the same year:

> 87 million people were in the work force at some time,
> 85 million different people held jobs,
> 43 million entered or reentered the labor force,
> 42 million left the labor force permanently or temporarily,
> 1.7 million looked for work but did not work at all,
> 14.1 million different people experienced some unemployment,
> 8 million or more changed jobs voluntarily or involuntarily.

The unemployment rate by State ranged from 2.9 to 7.9 per cent, by broad occupations from 0.5 to 10.6 per cent, by broad industry group from 2.3 to 9.9 per cent, by age from 2.7 to 17.8 per cent, and by race from 4.6 to 9.8 per cent. About 1 out of every 15 persons moved his place of residence. None of these figures includes the vast amount of constant change in jobs and job content which is always going on within firms.

Some of the 14 million who experienced some unemployment in 1964 were new entrants to the labor force. Others were laid off only temporarily. But between one-third and one-half of those unemployed were permanently or indefinitely severed from their jobs; they were forced to find new employment, remain among the unemployed, or withdraw from the labor force. Thus the average number unemployed during a year understates the actual volume of involuntary displacement that actually occurred.

There are many causes of displacement. The demand for a product may decline, perhaps in a general cyclical downturn, perhaps because consumer tastes change. A new product or a newly invented process may capture a market from an existing producer. A company or an industry may change its location, perhaps in search of lower wage rates or raw material sources, or because a technological change in transportation affects the relative advantages of being near raw materials sources or near markets. An employer may find himself in an unfavorable competitive position because of technological backwardness, his own inefficiency, or for reasons beyond his

---

[5] In relation to this section, see Bureau of Labor Statistics, *Disemployment of Labor at the Establishment Level* (†); William Haller, Jr., *Technological Change in Primary Steelmaking in the U.S., 1947–65* (†); Walter R. Butcher, *Productivity, Technology, and Employment in U.S. Agriculture* (†); and Joseph P. Newhouse, *Technological Change in Banking* (†).

control. A major technological development may displace an entire occupational group within a plant. An accretion of small changes may increase productivity more rapidly than output rises and attrition can absorb.

Displacement is implicit in the natural history of economic development, as the example of the United States shows. In the most primitive stages of growth, the labor force is concentrated on producing food and fibers; as the economy becomes more productive, there is a shift to the production of manufactured goods; then, as basic physical needs are satisfied, larger portions of the labor force are transferred (or displaced) to the production of a variety of services. . . . in this country in the course of the last 35 years. . . . [there] were broad shifts among the major [industrial] sectors, and within these, large-scale displacement occurred in some industries and rapid employment growth in others. It is as true for an industry as it is for the economy as a whole that employment grows if sales and production rise faster than productivity. If they do not, employment falls. . . .

Industry-by-industry accounts of postwar developments in output, productivity, and employment must be interpreted in the context of national totals. An industry whose productivity kept pace with the average for the whole private economy would have experienced an 81.2 per cent increase in productivity between 1947 and 1965. Even in an industry with an average productivity increase, therefore, employment would have fallen if production had not been growing, or had grown only slowly. On the other hand, industries whose production had grown rapidly, even if productivity growth had also been fast, would have increased their employment. Since 1947, employment in the total economy has risen by 21.7 per cent. Most industries, therefore, have registered substantial increases in employment.

Technological change has also been a major source of occupational displacement, though not the only one. Innovation can destroy an occupation, create an entirely new one, or transform radically the content of what appears on paper to be the same occupation. In some cases, the change is clearly associated with technological developments: among the losers were farmers and farm workers, coal miners, lumbermen, and railroad employees; among the gainers were office machine workers and electronic technicians. In other cases, the main cause of change was not technological, for example, elementary school teachers, stock and bond salesmen, taxicab drivers and chauffeurs, porters, bartenders, milliners, and athletes.

Employment shifts, whether by industry or occupation or by establishment, are only an indication, not a measure, of the displacement of individuals. Employment changes within an establishment may not enter the statistics at all. Jobs may disappear but the workers may be absorbed in other parts of the establishment. Employment in one firm may decline but be offset by increases in another, leaving industry totals unaffected. There are, however, offsetting forces. Some workers quit voluntarily, retire, or die. A fall in employment which does not exceed this attrition rate need not result in displacement. On the other hand, some of the voluntary quits may be in anticipation of layoffs and therefore represent a hidden displacement.

Nor is there a good measure of the distress caused by displacement.

221

Everything depends on the difficulty with which a new job is obtained, its location, and relative attractiveness. If the economic environment is favorable and the displaced worker has attractive skills, the distress need not be great. If the contrary, the human costs of displacement may be high. Under the best of circumstances a loss of accumulated job rights and a lower wage are likely consequences. The most serious adjustment problems have resulted when massive displacement has occurred among workers with overspecialized skills in isolated areas without alternative sources of employment. Coal miners are a prime example. The most profound of all displacements has been that in agriculture, where, in the postwar period, a 5.7 per cent annual rate of productivity increase accompanied by only a 1.4 per cent increase in farm output has reduced farmowners and farmworkers from 8.2 million in 1947 to 4.8 million in 1964, or 42.3 per cent. Those who left by the door marked "education" entered a new productive life. Too many, suffering from deficient rural educations, lacking skills in demand in urban areas, unaccustomed to urban ways, and often burdened by racial discrimination, exchanged rural poverty for an urban ghetto. How many of the 4.8 million workers who remain in agriculture are underemployed is conjectural, but the number is probably high.

C. Influence of Skill and Education on Unemployment[6]

Occupational changes in the period of rapid productivity growth since 1947 exhibit a few easily identifiable broad trends. Very highly skilled employment has increased rapidly: Professional and technical workers were 6.6 per cent of the total in 1947 and 12.2 per cent in 1964; the number of unskilled laborers, by contrast, fell as a per cent of the total, but not absolutely. In the same span of years there has been a visible shift from manual to white-collar work: In 1947 manual workers were 41 per cent of the total, and white-collar workers 35 per cent (the remainder were service workers, farmers, and farm laborers); by 1964, the percentage of all workers in manual occupations had fallen to 36, while white-collar occupations expanded to employ 44 per cent of all workers. . . .

However, the meaning of this trend in terms of skill is far from clear: Many manual jobs are highly skilled, many clerical and sales jobs are unskilled; the requirements are different, but not easily compared.

Unemployment has been concentrated among those with little education or skill, while employment has been rising most rapidly in those occupations generally considered to be the most skilled and to require the most education. This conjunction raises the question whether technological progress may induce a demand for very skilled and highly educated people in numbers our society cannot yet provide, while at the same time leaving stranded many of the unskilled and poorly educated with no future opportunities for employment.

[6] In relation to this section, see James R. Bright, *The Relationship of Increasing Automation to Skill Requirements* (†); and Morris Horowitz and Irwin Herrnstadt, *Changes in the Skill Requirements of Occupations in Selected Industries* (†). See also *Automation: Impact and Implications, Focus on Developments in the Communications Industry*, prepared by the Diebold Group, Inc., for the Communications Workers of America, AFL-CIO, April 1965.

No confident answer can be given to this difficult and complex question. Our society is extending secondary and higher education to larger and larger fractions of the population, and, therefore, it is necessary that the number of suitable and rewarding jobs should increase correspondingly. Otherwise a different kind of frustration would result. We must, then, ask a much more subtle question: Is the demand for highly educated people outrunning the supply, and is the supply of unskilled workers outrunning the demand? It is intrinsically difficult to establish any answer because occupational content can change while the occupational title remains the same, and because it is often unclear which occupations make greater demands in skill and education. Even if we were confident that there were imbalances between skills demanded and skills supplied, it would not follow that the source of the imbalance is technological. Japan and Western Europe operate sophisticated industrial economies with educational profiles far inferior to our own, and there is reason to believe that a highly automated economy could be engineered to fit a variety of educational profiles. But that is not our problem. In the shorter run, whatever the general trend, there is no doubt that technological change may increase, decrease, or simply change the skills required in particular jobs. The result may be displacement.

There is little doubt that the occupational structure of the American labor force is changing and will continue to change. Perhaps the main reason for this is the rapid growth of those industries—education, finance, insurance, health, and business services—which employ predominantly white-collar and professional workers. Another reason is the rapid improvement in educational attainment itself. Technological change within industries does not seem to be the major factor, except as regards the declining employment of laborers. Whether changes in the demand for different skills are to a substantial extent placing the new jobs beyond the reach of those losing other jobs can best be assessed by examining the relationship between educational attainment and educational requirements.

Here, too, the evidence is at best fragmentary, but the Commission is impressed with labor market developments during the business expansion following the tax reduction of early 1964. As the general unemployment rate has fallen, the improvement has been greatest for those with the least education. In 1965, the unemployment rate for those with 8 years of schooling or less fell from 7.6 to 5.9 per cent; for high school graduates with no further education, from 4.8 to 4.1 per cent; and for a college graduate, only from 1.5 to 1.4 per cent.

It is the proper function of a market to allocate resources, and in this respect the labor market does not function differently from any other. If the available resources are of high quality, the market will adjust to the use of high-quality resources; if the quality is low, methods will be developed to use such resources. In an efficient market, the choice between low-skill and high-skill manpower and between labor-intensive and capital-intensive production methods is made on the basis of relative costs. Although employment of unskilled, untrained labor can be encouraged by lowering its cost relative to that of skilled, trained labor a better way would be to generate higher rates of economic activity. (In the same way, labor and machines "compete" with each other.) In a slack labor market employers must have some means of selecting among numerous applicants, and it is not surprising that educational attainment is often used as a convenient yardstick, regardless of its direct relevance to the requirements of the job.

We have found it useful to view the labor market as a gigantic "shapeup," with members of the labor force queued in order of their relative attractiveness to employers. If the labor market operates efficiently, employers will start at the head of the line, selecting as many as they need of employees most attractive to them. Their choice may be based on objective standards relating to ability, or on dubious standards of race, sex, or age; wage differentials may also be important; and formal education may be used as a rough screening device. The total number employed and unemployed depends primarily on the general state of economic activity. The employed tend to be those near the beginning and the unemployed those near the end of the line. Only as demand rises will employers reach further down the line in their search for employees.

If the relative disadvantages of the unskilled and uneducated have increased in recent years, the main reason is that the economy is less, not more, likely to run out of skilled and educated men and women. Thus the important factor is the impressive gain in the educational attainment of the labor force. . . . The proportion of workers aged 18 years and over who have completed 4 years or more of high school has risen from 43.3 to 57.5 per cent since 1952; those with 4 years or more of college, from 8 to 11.6 per cent. . . .

Differential levels of educational attainment by age and color are particularly noticeable. Every age group has shared in the upgrading, but in 1965, 70.2 per cent of workers age 18 to 34 years had completed at least 4 years of high school, while only 46.3 per cent of those in the 45–64 age group had done so; 11.7 per cent of the younger age group had completed 4 years or more of college, compared with 10.3 per cent of the older. The disadvantage associated with color is shocking: Of all nonwhites in the labor force 18 years and older in 1965, 37.6 per cent had only elementary school educations, 37.5 per cent had completed high school, and only 7 per cent had at least 4 years of college. The comparable figures for white workers were 21.6, 60, and 12.2 per cent. . . .

The gap between white and Negro educational attainment measures not only the long oppression of the Negro but an economic loss to them and to American society. The problems are especially severe among older Negro workers, but the gap exists at all ages. It must be closed.

It is inevitable in a society where educational standards are improving that the young will be better educated than the old. But the educational disadvantages of Negroes are not inevitable, although they are real and tragic. And because workers of low educational attainment are the least desirable to employers, nonwhite and older workers are concentrated at the rear of the line, not only because of their lower educational attainment, but also because of direct discrimination. Nevertheless, whatever the level of economic activity, whatever the extent of the pressures of demand on employers to seek further down the education and skill ladder, and whatever other hiring standards are used, education and training can improve the ability of people with competitive disadvantages to compete effectively in the labor market.

There is ample justification for increased education and training efforts. Quite aside from the purely personal cultural aspects of education, the level of training and skill affects the overall efficiency of the economy and the flexibility of the labor force, as well as the relative place in line of labor force members. In recent years, economists have produced evidence that the rates of return for investment in education are comparable with those earned on other investments. And cost-benefit analysis of training programs under the Manpower Development and Training Act has shown that the strictly economic returns alone were large enough to pay for the investment.

But a sharp distinction is necessary: The individual's education and skill are important determinants of his relative ability to compete for jobs. The education and skill of the labor force is important to the economy's viability. Technology determines, in part, the skills required and the educational component of those skills. But the availability of skills and the educational level of the labor force are also determinants of the technological changes which occur. Together, education, skill, and technology, along with other factors, determine the structure of employment and unemployment. They do not determine the level of either.

Manpower policy—training, retraining, and education combined—has made progress in recent years. As this report is being prepared, there is yet another urgent reason why such efforts should be increased. Expansionary policy and the demands of the war in Vietnam have combined to push the economy forward and reduce unemployment among nearly all groups in the labor force. The economy has thus come closer to the point where inflationary pressure—in both labor and product markets—becomes a danger. The Commission does not believe that the toleration of unnecessary unemployment is an acceptable way to relieve inflationary pressure. We believe that the tightening of labor markets calls not for relaxation but for an expanded effort to upgrade the unemployed through education and training. Manpower policy is triply productive as it enriches the prospects of the disadvantaged, adds to the productive capacity of the Nation, and helps relieve inflationary pressure.

D. The Impact of Technological Change Upon Employment: The Next 10 Years[7]

In asking us to identify the "new job requirements and the major types of worker displacement, both technological and economic, which are likely

[7] In relation to this section, see Bureau of Labor Statistics, *America's Industrial and Occupational Manpower Requirements, 1964–75* (†); Bureau of Labor Statistics, *Technological Trends in Major American Industries* (†); Eugene Schwartz and Ted Prenting, *Automation in the Fabricating Industry* (†); Thomas Stout, *Manpower Implications of Process Control Computers* (†); Merrill Flood, *Commercial Information Processing Networks—Prospects and Problems in Perspective* (†); Paul Armer, *Computer Aspects of Technological Change, Automation, and Economic Progress* (†); and U.S. Department of Commerce, National Bureau of Standards, *The Role of the Federal Government in Technological Forecasting* (†).

to occur during the next 10 years," Congress was reflecting concern that unemployment might continue to creep inexorably upward, that occupations might change and disappear too rapidly for educational institutions and individuals to adjust, and that those without education and skills would be left further and further behind. Our assessment of the past and present effects of technological change have, by implication, already answered some of these questions. If unemployment does creep upward in the future it will be the fault of public policy, not the fault of technological change.

We requested from the Bureau of Labor Statistics a projection of manpower requirements in 1975. The structure of employment a decade ahead can be projected to a first approximation from present trends and foreseen technological developments. The level of employment depends primarily upon public policy, and the Bureau of Labor Statistics has made its projections upon our assumption that neither public opinion nor our public officials will allow a recurrence of slow growth of demand. We also asked experts to project for us the likely progress of some of the more dramatic of the new technologies. All of these projections are contained in the supplementary material to this report. We provide here only a summary.

1. Given the projected growth of the labor force, the assumptions imply that 88.7 million persons would be gainfully employed in 1975, about 18.3 million more than in 1964—an average increase of nearly 1.7 million annually. (This compares with an average annual employment increase of 1.1 million between 1960 and 1965, and 1.8 million between 1964 and 1965.)

2. While it is possible to assume a variety of patterns of economic growth, depending on shifts in investment and consumer expenditure patterns, and changes in emphasis in Government programs, the type of economy projected in this report is one characterized by an extension of the basic patterns which developed in the postwar period. Farm employment is expected to decline by about 1 million and all other employment is expected to increase by more than 19 million, for a net employment gain of 18.3 million. For nonfarm "goods producing" industries—manufacturing, mining, and construction—a moderate increase in manpower requirements[8] of 17 per cent is projected, a rate of increase somewhat faster than during the 17-year period 1947–64. . . . Requirements in the "service producing" sector as a whole—trade, finance, government, services, and transportation and public utilities—are expected to increase by 38 per cent, somewhat faster than over the past 17-year period, and more rapidly than the goods producing industries.

3. The effect of these industry employment trends will be to continue recent trends in the industrial composition of the economy. Government and services will increase sharply as a percent of the total; contract construction and trade will also increase their share. On the other hand, the relative importance of manufacturing and transportation and public utilities will decline slightly, and the relative size of agriculture and mining will

[8] It should be noted that the following discussion of industry employment trends is geared to estimates of wage and salary employment, whereas the overall figures on farm and nonfarm employment cited above relate to total employment, including wage and salary workers, private household workers, the self-employed, and unpaid family workers.

continue to decline sharply. Taking the broad "goods" and "services" sectors as a whole (and including in goods agriculture, with its self-employed as well as its wage and salary workers) the goods sector will decline from about 41 per cent of all jobs in 1964 to 36 per cent in 1975; the service sector will increase its share of manpower requirements from 59 to 64 per cent. (If self-employed persons in nonagricultural industries were added to the above comparison, the services sector would have a slightly larger share in both years.)

4. The occupational requirements of the economy will change substantially as a result of both the differential growth rates of industries and the technological developments and other factors affecting the occupational requirements of each industry. . . . Concern has been expressed that the impact of technological and industrial change will drastically curtail employment opportunities for less skilled workers. The principal conclusion of the BLS study, which takes into account the major technological changes in American industry that can be identified and makes a careful appraisal of their potential effects on employment, is that the overall demand for less skilled workers will not decrease over this 11-year period, although it will decline somewhat as a percentage of the total. Needs for laborers (except farm and mine) in 1975 will be roughly the same as in 1964, although they will decrease from 5.2 to 4.2 per cent of total manpower requirements. Over 3 million additional service workers will be required, and their share of total jobs will rise from 13.2 to 14.1 per cent. Nearly 2 million more operatives will be needed; their share will, however, decline from 18.4 to 16.7 per cent. An overall decline of more than 900,000 in the employment of farmworkers is expected, and the share of farm jobs in the total is expected to decline from 6.3 to 3.9 per cent.

The greatest increase in employment requirements will be for professional and technical workers; more than 4.5 million additional personnel will be required. The white-collar group as a whole is expected to expand by nearly two-fifths and to constitute 48 per cent of all manpower requirements in 1975. The blue-collar occupations are expected to expand at less than half this rate, and will make up about 34 per cent of all requirements. A rapid expansion in requirements for service workers is anticipated—a 35-per cent increase in employment.

5. These changes in occupational requirements have significant implications for certain groups in the labor force. If nonwhites continue to hold the same proportion of jobs in each occupation as in 1964, the nonwhite unemployment rate in 1975 will be more than five times that for the labor force as a whole. In 1964, the unemployment rate of nonwhites was 9.8 per cent, about twice that for whites. If trends in upgrading the jobs of nonwhites continue at the same rate as in recent years, the nonwhite unemployment rate in 1975 would still be about 2½ times that for the labor force as a whole. Thus nonwhites must gain access to the rapidly growing higher skilled and white-collar occupations at a faster rate than in the past 8 years if their unemployment rate is to be brought down to the common level.

If all occupations have the same composition by age in 1975 as in 1964, opportunities for younger workers (aged 14–24) will be substantially fewer than the number in this age group seeking work. The unsatisfactory current relation of youth unemployment to total unemployment will worsen unless utilization patterns change. There is here a clear need for action.

It is at best difficult to separate the technological from other causes of the structural changes we have been describing. To the displaced employee, or even to the maker of public policy, the precise causes of displacement and unemployment may not even seem important. Because society gains from the flexibility and responsiveness which are the sources of displacement, it is society's responsibility to see that alternative opportunities are available and that blameless individuals do not bear excessive costs.

CREATING AN ENVIRONMENT FOR ADJUSTMENT TO CHANGE: *Employment and Income*

We have stated the view of the economic role of technological change to which the Commission has come in the course of its deliberations. Our assignment includes also an obligation to make recommendations to management and labor and to all levels of government to "facilitate occupational adjustment and geographical mobility" and to "share the costs and help prevent and alleviate the adverse impact of change on displaced workers." Our recommendations flow logically from the view we have already adopted.

Constant displacement is the price of a dynamic economy. History suggests that it is a price worth paying. But the accompanying burdens and benefits should be distributed fairly, and this has not always been the case. The costs of displacement to employees do not exhaust the total costs of technical and economic change. Business firms, labor unions, schools, government agencies and other institutions, as well as persons, develop some vested interest in the status quo. An economic or technological change that represents progress to society as a whole may, in a nation devoted to political and industrial democracy, be resisted by persons and institutions to whom it appears a threat. Though public policy has less obligation to the perpetuation of institutions than to the protection of individuals, there is a public interest in reducing resistance to progress.

Our analysis of the economic impact of technological change suggests the following organization of our recommendations for facilitating adjustment to change.

1. For those with reasonably attractive skills and no other serious competitive handicaps, ample job opportunities and adequate incomes can be assured by management of the total demand for goods and services.

2. For those less able to compete in the labor market, productive employment opportunities adapted to their abilities should be publicly provided.

3. Under the best of circumstances, there will be some who cannot or should not participate in the job economy. For them, we believe there should be an adequate system of income maintenance, guaranteeing a floor of income at an acceptable level.

Our recommendations which relate to employment and income are discussed in this chapter. We reserve to the next chapter those recommendations which relate to information and mobility, education and training, and to the regional context of technological displacement.

A. The Management of Total Demand

It is the unanimously held conviction of the Commission that the most important condition for successful adjustment to technological change is an adequate level of total income and employment. We recognize that this is not the end of economic policy, but we are confident it is the beginning. We have noted that the unemployment problem we contemplated when we first met has diminished in the course of 1965. The sequel to the Revenue Act of 1964 has clearly demonstrated that Federal fiscal and monetary policy can bridge the gap between the current level of private spending and the level of total demand needed to reduce unemployment. During the life of the Commission the very groups disproportionately burdened by unemployment—the young and inexperienced, the undereducated, the unskilled, Negroes, production workers—have profited more than proportionately from the healthy growth of total employment. Many of them have benefited from such innovations in manpower policy as the Job Corps or the Neighborhood Youth Corps. This, too, is a source of satisfaction and an incentive to do better.

We believe that the potential for general expansion of demand and employment has not yet been exhausted. We recognize that as labor markets and product markets become tighter and production comes closer to capacity in important industries, the beginnings of inflationary pressures emerge. It is not our business to predict what will occur during the next 12 months either in Asia or in the domestic economy. We urge, however, that the toleration of unnecessary unemployment is a very costly way to police inflation. It deprives the country of valuable output, and it sacrifices the poorest and least privileged among our citizens. It is preferable to press carefully ahead with the expansion of total production and employment, and simultaneously to redouble private and public efforts in the manpower field to relieve shortages in skilled and trained labor as they arise and develop effective means of combatting other causes of inflation.

As we write, events in the economy and elsewhere are moving rapidly; there is considerable uncertainty about the size of the economic and manpower burden of military operations in Vietnam. Under the circumstances, we can make no attempt to suggest the precise direction that fiscal and monetary policy should take in the near future.[9] We urge most strongly, however, that economic policy aim resolutely and watchfully at a reduction in the general unemployment rate to 3.5 per cent or below by the beginning of 1967. No good is done our economy or our country by recoiling from that task prematurely. For the longer run, we believe it to be of the highest importance to the future of democracy in the world that this country never present to its neighbors the spectacle of wartime prosperity yielding to peacetime unemployment.

[9] In relation to this, see George L. Perry, *Employment, Output, and Policy Requirements for Full Employment* (†).

Some combination of tax reduction (leading to higher private spending) and increased public expenditure will be required to stimulate the economy when stimulus is needed. The choice between them depends upon our national priorities; a balanced policy will in the long run surely include both. We believe that the Nation faces a backlog of public neglect as the aftermath of a sequence of depression, war, and high defense spending. The needs in education, health, transportation, pollution control, resource development, and similar areas in the public domain are obvious to us and, we believe, to the public generally, though we may differ about the precise orders of priority. It is possible that international conflict may temporarily drain into military uses some of the resources that might be devoted to improving the American environment. If not, or when it no longer does so,* it is our considered judgment that major attention should be given to public investment expenditures, some of which we will mention later in this report. No easy short-run conclusion is possible on the basis of the facts available to us. Since the rewards are so great in employment for the disadvantaged, we wish to lend our weight against any easy deflationism. Every bit of employment and output counts.

B. Public Service Employment

We are not impressed with a 4 per cent unemployment rate, or a 3 per cent, or any other unemployment rate, as an ultimate goal of economic policy. We take seriously the commitment of the Employment Act of 1946 to provide "useful employment opportunities for all those able, willing, and seeking to work." This cannot mean literally zero unemployment since, in a free economy, there will always be some turnover, voluntary and involuntary. Indeed, there is some evidence that the highly mobile American economy generates more voluntary turnover than the other major industrial economies. It does mean limiting unemployment to the minimum amount necessary for the smooth functioning of a free labor market. It would probably mean the disappearance of long-term unemployment for those genuinely in the labor force. We recognize that to expand demand through gross monetary and fiscal policies sufficiently to eliminate all but short-term frictional unemployment would place the price level under heavy pressure. Both those price pressures and the frictional level of unemployment itself can be reduced by appropriate programs of education, training, and labor market improvements. But these too have their limits.

In terms of our image of the labor market as a queue, fiscal and monetary policies begin at the front of the queue and work toward the rear. Education and training and labor market policies affect not only relative places in the line, but the depth to which general economic policies can reach without generating inflation. Yet when all that is done, there remains another possibility: to begin at the rear of the line and create employment opportunities tailored to the abilities of those with serious competitive disadvantages.

We are impressed with the extent to which recent policy has been designed

* For comment by several Commission members, see p. 236.

to do exactly that. The Neighborhood Youth Corps and several other provisions of the Economic Opportunity Act, for example, represent a new departure in U.S. employment policy. New Deal public works programs provided sorely needed employment and created valuable facilities during a period of mass unemployment. The new programs are different; they are aimed specifically at those left behind in an otherwise prosperous economy. They recognize the anomaly of excessive unemployment in a society confronted with a huge backlog of public service needs in its parks, its streets, its slums, its countryside, its school and colleges, its libraries, its hospitals, its rest homes, its public buildings, and throughout the public and non-profit sectors of the economy. They recognize that employing the unemployed is, in an important sense, almost costless. The unemployed consume; they do not produce. To provide them meaningful jobs increases not only their income but that of society. Much of the work that needs doing calls only for limited skills and minor amounts of training. Some of it is manual in character; some of it is subprofessional.

The principle of such public service employment has been implicitly endorsed in existing programs. We recommend that the concept be expanded and made explicit as a permanent, long-term program. The necessary steps are as follows:

1. The major resources must come from the Federal Government but the jobs need not. . . . [in] some areas of the economy . . . important social needs are now inadequately met, if indeed they are met at all, and . . . useful employment . . . could be made available to people with relatively low skills. Many of these jobs are in the State and local sector of the public economy. Were it not for the endemic financial stringency at those levels of government, the employment might already have been provided, though perhaps without effort to allocate the jobs to the rear of the queue. A Federal funding agency could provide program approval and financial administration. State and local governments and certain kinds of nonprofit institutions as well as Federal agencies could submit proposals demonstrating ability to use the available labor productively without reducing existing levels of employment or subverting prevailing labor standards.

2. The sponsoring institutions should treat the new employees as regular employees, integrating them with existing work forces and enforcing regular standards of performance. The wages paid should be in no case lower than the Federal minimum wage, with the possible exception of a partial exemption for youth. The public service employment program should be coupled with basic education, training, and counseling to raise the productivity of the employees and assist them to move on to better jobs. With this assistance, the opportunity for higher incomes would provide the necessary incentive to seek other jobs. Since the jobs would provide services for which society has growing needs, no element of make-work would be involved.

3. All the relevant questions cannot be answered or even foreseen before more experience has accumulated. But one of the proposed program's advantages is its flexibility. It can be readily adapted to unemployment levels,

fiscal requirements, and other factors. Indeed we suggest that the operation of the program might be keyed to specific localized unemployment problems by region or by demographic group. The administration, job development, and recruitment cannot occur overnight. The first step is to make explicit the concept already implicit in existing programs by recommitting Federal policy to the Employment Act's promises of a job for "all of those able, willing, and seeking to work." Then the amount of employment provided can be expanded as rapidly as possible, holding open the possibility of delay or contraction if changing circumstances or adverse experience require.

We therefore recommend (1) that public service employment opportunities be provided to those unsuccessful in the competition for existing jobs; (2) that a 5-year program be established, with the amount of public service employment increased each year, depending upon previous experience and labor market conditions; (3) that an initial sum of perhaps $2 billion be appropriated to provide about 500,000 additional full-time public service jobs; and (4) that the program be coupled with a serious attempt to learn more about the nature and causes of "hard-core" unemployment by case and survey methods.

C. Income Maintenance[10]

We are convinced that rising productivity has brought this country to the point at last when all citizens may have a decent standard of living at a cost in resources the economy can easily bear. We believe that nearly all should, and wish to, earn their own support, for the dignity and self-respect that come from earning one's own living can hardly be achieved otherwise. Most of our recommendations are directed to making it possible, or easier, for people to adjust to a fast-changing technological and economic world without major breaks in the continuity of employment. But the problem of income maintenance is broader than the problem of displacement from employment.

The war on poverty has made it abundantly clear that the road to a satisfying life through work is not open to everyone: not to families without breadwinners, not to those whose productivity is reduced by physical or mental incapacity, not to people too old to work. They are not necessarily victims of technological progress. Nevertheless, income maintenance for them must also be considered in this report, not only for the sake of completeness, but also because technological advance is the source of the productive capacity which permits us, as a nation, to tackle the problem. Our concern here is for economic progress, not fear of technological change.

WAGE-RELATED SOCIAL INSURANCE PROGRAMS

Most people who spend the greater part of their adult life working can protect themselves against loss of income due to death, disability, old age, or unemployment through social insurance programs. In these programs,

[10] In relation to this section, see Sar A. Levitan, *Programs in Aid of the Poor* (†); and Jack Stieber, *Manpower Adjustments to Automation and Technological Change in Western Europe* (†).

benefits are related to wages and are paid as a matter of right; they do not require a means test. During fiscal year 1964–65, social insurance programs paid over $28 billion in benefits to approximately 20 million people. Payments went to the poor and nonpoor alike. No more than half the total went to persons with incomes below the poverty line.

Improvement in our unemployment insurance system could directly facilitate adjustment to change. In his study for the Commission, Stieber reports:

> Unemployed workers receive a higher proportion of former earnings in all countries studied (Great Britain, France, West Germany, Sweden, and the Netherlands), with the possible exception of Great Britain, than in the United States. Insurance payments almost always average more than 50 per cent of earnings, and often reach 80 to 90 per cent in some countries. This compares with the average of about 35 per cent of former earnings in the United States as a whole, though some States pay considerably more.

In June 1965, the Commission publicly took note of the inadequacies in our present system of Federal-State unemployment insurance, unanimously urging in a letter to congressional leaders that:

> Benefit levels must be increased; benefit periods must be lengthened; coverage must be extended; Federal standards must be provided to assure that workers unemployed by factors incident to a national economy, receive adequate protection regardless of the State of residence; a permanent Federal program for protection of the long-term unemployed must be added. Supplementation of the public system by private agreement must be encouraged by removing restrictions which exist, including regulations in certain States which eliminate or reduce benefits to those receiving supplementary unemployment benefits, severance pay, early retirement, and similar private payments.

Particular attention must be given to the needs of those with long records of steady employment who suddenly find themselves permanent victims of economic or technological change.

Average Old Age and Survivors and Disability Insurance benefits per individual recipient are currently less than $1,000 a year. We find this inadequate; we recommend that benefit standards be lifted.

Benefits under Workmen's Compensation are also in need of reform. Federal legislation is needed to establish minimum standards for Workmen's Compensation. There is also a serious lack of general protection against loss of income due to temporary disabilities arising from nonoccupational accidents or sickness.

PUBLIC ASSISTANCE

Public assistance programs as part of an income maintenance system provide minimum income support, usually but not exclusively for families without an earner, on the basis of proved need. Recipients of public assistance do not receive benefits as a matter of right, as in the case of social insurance. They must be able to demonstrate under rigid criteria an absolute need of income for subsistence. Special programs supported by Federal, State, and local governments have been established for the aged, the blind, the totally disabled, and families with dependent children. Although public assistance programs have provided needed support for many—nearly $6 billion was paid during fiscal year 1964–65 to over 9.4 million persons —they leave much to be desired.

In principle, welfare payments are limited by a strict means test to the difference between some minimum standard and a family's resources from earnings. This has the absurd consequence that additional earnings are taxed 100 per cent. Unless the family can earn enough to dispense with public assistance entirely, it loses a dollar of welfare payments for every dollar it is able to earn. It would be hard to imagine a system less consistent with our society's high valuation of work and self-help.

The "man in the house" regulation in the program for Aid to Families with Dependent Children has received more attention. In many communities, payments cannot be made to households with an able-bodied adult male in residence. Consequently, fathers are encouraged to desert their destitute families so that they may be eligible for public assistance.

Perhaps the system's most serious faults are the stringency of need tests and the small size of payments. The average payment per recipient (children and adults) under the program of Aid to Families with Dependent Children is $34 a month. Though families may receive public assistance from other sources as well, the system is hardly generous. There is wide variation among the States, with some paying as little as one-quarter of the national average of $34 per month.

Less than one-quarter of the 35 million people now living in poverty receive any type of public assistance payment and less than one-third of the 15 million children living in poverty benefit from public assistance.

It is not for this Commission to make detailed recommendations in the field of income maintenance and social insurance. We feel strongly, however, that a better integrated and more comprehensive system of social insurance and income maintenance is both necessary and feasible at this stage in our history. We recommend that Congress undertake a detailed review of the entire system, including both its coverage and its financing. There is danger, in our view, that reliance on a narrow payroll tax base makes the system more and more regressive as incomes rise and other taxes are reduced.

The Commission recommends also that Congress go beyond a reform of the present structure and examine wholly new approaches to the problem of income maintenance. In particular, we suggest that Congress give serious study to a "minimum income allowance" or "negative income tax" program. Such a program, if found feasible, should be designed to approach by stages the goal of eliminating the need for means test public assistance programs by providing a floor of adequate minimum incomes. A minimum income allowance would complete the symmetry of our tax system, under which tax payments are related to income, family size, medical, and other costs, by acknowledging the continuity beyond zero tax rates. It seems

234

anomalous to us that a family of five now pays the same tax—zero—whether its total income is $500 or $3,500.

Concrete proposals for such an income allowance program have been advanced by Milton Friedman, Robert Lampman, James Tobin, and others. Under any version of the minimum income allowance, persons with incomes below an acceptable standard would receive a tax rebate or cash allowance, just as persons with incomes above exemption levels pay taxes. Some proposals would cost as little as $2 billion per year while others would cost over $20 billion per year, depending on the level of income floor established and the care that is taken to see that no payments go to those with incomes above the "poverty line." All schemes share the feature that payments by the Federal Treasury are based on declarations of present or past income. Federal income tax returns could be used as a basis for determining qualification. Income statements could be filed quarterly, semi-annually, or annually, and payments could be made monthly.

Income maintenance payments under any such scheme should be designed to eliminate the gap between reported income and an explicit minimum. Most other systems result in some payments to those not poor. The incentive to work can be preserved by a schedule reducing the allowance partially for an increase in earned income.

Estimates relating a tax allowance schedule to total budgetary costs are based on complex assumptions which cannot be explored here. Some proposals relate the tax allowance schedule to unused exemptions and deductions, while others relate payments to the poverty-income gap. It has been estimated that it would cost $2 billion annually to pay nontaxable families an allowance equal to 14 per cent (the lowest bracket rate in the present income tax law) of their unused exemptions and deductions. The net cost of eliminating 50 per cent of the poverty-income gap is estimated to be between $5 and $8 billion per year.

There are many problems so far unresolved in connection with any system of income allowances or negative income taxation. It will be necessary to decide what forms of personal income are to be counted as reducing eligibility, and how the system is to be integrated with existing categories of social insurance and public assistance. For example, Congress might decide that beneficiaries under Old Age Survivors and Disability Insurance should not be eligible for income allowances; but in that case Congress should see to it that minimum OASDI benefits do not fall short of the income guarantee promised by the allowances. Some government transfer payments, like veterans' pensions and unemployment compensation, are intended to be compensation earned by past services or past contributions. Recipients of such payments should therefore presumably be eligible for income allowances, but the amount of those payments would presumably count as income in determining eligibility. Some forms of public assistance, on the other hand, would be replaced by a system of income allowances. Congress could ignore public assistance payments entirely, letting State and local governments decide at what level they will supplement the allowances under the negative tax program. Although this approach would permit continued inequality among States, the income allowance would provide a floor now lacking.* By relieving the States of part of the burden of public assistance, the minimum income allowance would stabilize or even reduce a source of rapidly rising demand on their limited fiscal resources. If adopted, it would seem appropriate to introduce an income maintenance program in stages, as it becomes necessary to counter the fiscal drag in the present tax-transfer structure. This is one of the few ways in which those with the very lowest incomes can share directly in tax reduction.

Comment noted on page 230 by Mr. Beirne, Mr. Hayes, and Mr. Reuther, joined by Mr. Bell and Mr. Young

It is our considered judgment that urgent social needs must be met, even if meeting them requires some reallocation of the resources left available for nonmilitary purposes after fulfilling the requirements of the Vietnam situation.

Comment noted on this page by Mr. Beirne, Mr. Hayes, and Mr. Reuther, joined by Mr. Young

We are fully in accord with the recommendation that the minimum income allowance program "should be designed to approach by stages the goal of eliminating the need for means test public assistance programs. . . ." Experience, unfortunately, indicates that the States too often reduce welfare payments when other sources of income are available to welfare recipients. We therefore would urge that pending the full development of the minimum income allowance program, reasonable Federal minimum standards be established for all welfare payments to which the Federal Government presently contributes, and that a national general assistance program conforming to those standards be created for all those in need who do not fit into the categories covered by the present federally aided welfare programs. Consistent with the minimum income allowance recommendation, minimum benefits under the wage-related social insurance programs should be raised above the poverty level.

FACILITATING ADJUSTMENT TO CHANGE: *Public Policies*

. . .

The preceding chapter has expressed the firm conviction of the Commission that the most important way to facilitate adjustment is to assure workers that jobs or income will be available in case they are displaced from present employment. The Commission has recommended: (1) fiscal policy calculated to provide at all times a brisk demand for labor; (2) direct employment of any long-term residue of unemployed workers; and (3) income maintenance for families with inadequate earnings. These basic policies are indispensable. But many other things could be done to increase the efficiency of the economy and reduce the burden of displacement and frictional unemployment. The purpose of this chapter is to identify and discuss these policies under the general headings of education and training, matching men and jobs, and regional adjustment.

* For comment by several Commission members, see below.

236

The Commission is fully aware of the significant progress that has been made in our society toward reducing frictional unemployment. Many important aids to adjustment have been developed through public policy. Examples are improvements in education, retraining, and relocation assistance. Similarly, through private initiative, many methods of softening the blow of change have been devised, among them, severance pay, early warning, company assistance in retraining and placement, and vesting of pension rights. In recent years, the pace of progress in this direction has quickened substantially. Disturbed by the economic and human costs of persistently high unemployment, the Nation in both public and private sectors has sharpened old tools and developed new ones. Many of the new policies and techniques are in an experimental stage and their capacity is not equal to the need, but the Commission recognizes and commends the progress, and its recommendations are made in light of that progress.

A. Education and Training[11]

The encouragement of an adaptable labor force fostered through education and training is second in importance only to provision of adequate employment opportunities in the facilitation of adjustment to technological and other change. We wish to emphasize at the outset that we regard the goals of education as far transcending economic objectives. These goals go beyond economic progress to the development of individuals as persons and as responsible citizens. A clear division of education into its "economic" and "noneconomic" aspects is impossible. For example, broad general education has close relevance to the preparation for vocations, and training that is intended to be technical or vocational may have equal relevance to the development of individuals as persons and as citizens. Our discussion of education tends, therefore, to be relatively broad.

From the purely economic point of view, education has three principal effects: (1) It can increase the versatility and adaptability of people with respect to vocations and thus increase their capacity to adjust to change; (2) it can open up increasing opportunity to persons who might otherwise have difficulty in finding and holding employment; and (3) it can increase the productivity of workers at any level of skill or ability. Though education is much more than a means of economic progress, it is a decisive factor in the economic advancement of any country.

Education is a source of versatility and adaptability because it provides basic knowledge and skills that are usable in a wide variety of situations. Such knowledge and skills include the ability to communicate through the written and spoken word, the ability to calculate, familiarity with basic science, habits of rational thought, and an understanding of society. This kind of versatility derives largely from general education in the sciences, mathematics, language, literature, art, and social science. Education also helps people to adapt when it offers them, throughout their lives, the

[11] In relation to this section, see Howard Jones, et al., *Education in the U.S.: Status and Prospects* (†); Don D. Bushnell, et al., *Computer Technology and Educational Progress* (†); and James D. Finn and Gabriel Ofiesh, *The Emerging Technology of Education* (†).

training they need for new kinds of jobs. Education helps people adapt when it gives them the ability to keep abreast of labor market information about new opportunities in unfamiliar industries or in distant parts of the country. Education—both general and vocational—can clearly increase the productivity of workers at all levels of skill and ability by imparting new, or renewing old, skills and abilities.

Education can open new opportunities to those persons at the end of the queue who have difficulty in finding and holding jobs. Some people are handicapped by discrimination based on race or religion or national origin, some by cultural deprivation, and some by physical, emotional, or mental disorders. Education, combined with counseling and with understanding and receptivity on the part of employers, can help such people to compete for jobs. These measures can be effective, however, only if there are jobs available. Otherwise, the upgrading of those at the end of the queue will merely move them up the line in preference to others. The solution of unemployment need not await the provision of adequate education to all, as desirable as that goal is.

It is our firm conviction that educational opportunity should be open to all. A first principle of a progressive and humane society is that no person shall be deprived by financial barriers or by barriers of ethnic or national origin, religion, age, place of residence, or background, of the opportunity for maximum growth and development through education. This is a goal to be pursued continually with both quantity and quality of education in view. The need is greatest among the culturally deprived, and special emphasis should be given to education for these groups. Significant progress toward this goal has been made in recent years, but neither accomplishments to date nor concrete plans for the future are sufficient to achieve fully what must clearly be a national goal of highest priority.

We welcome the substantial progress of recent years. Between 1957 and 1958, and 1964 and 1965, total educational expenditures have increased from $21 billion to $39 billion. The recent surge of Federal educational legislation portends further progress in the near future. This legislation includes the National Defense Act, the Education Facilities Act, the Vocational Education Act, the Higher Education Act, the Primary and Secondary Education Act, the Manpower Development and Training Act, and others. Notable progress has also been made through the efforts of State and local governments and private educational institutions.

The educational needs of our society include more extensive and better education at all levels, from nursery to the university. Within this broad field, we offer several specific recommendations.

1. High-quality compensatory education should be available to every child whose life opportunities would be improved by it. Perhaps the most serious deficiency in our educational system has been the inadequate opportunities available to those in greatest need, namely, children of families and communities where there is cultural deprivation, segregation, or isolation. The Economic Opportunity Act and the Elementary and Secondary Education Act are a beginning. However, the first effort of

Operation Head Start was but a skirmish. Significant at it was, its main effect was to demonstrate the inadequacy of available facilities. No one believed, of course, that a brief summer's experience could compensate for years and even generations of cultural disadvantage. In the future, the program must provide longer sessions with better facilities and larger numbers of experienced and qualified teachers. According to the Office of Economic Opportunity, at least 100,000 additional classrooms and 133,000 teachers would be necesssary by 1970 to provide compensatory full-year education from ages 3 to 5 for all who are in need of it.

2. The quantity and quality of primary and secondary education, especially in low-income urban areas and rural backwaters, should be improved. There is a wide gap between educational standards in high-income and low-income areas. It should be eliminated by providing excellent education in the underprivileged and depressed areas.

3. High school graduation should become universal. During the recent years of high unemployment, justifiable concern about high school dropouts has mounted. It is generally accepted that those with less than a sound high school education are unprepared for both employment and life. Progress is being made. The percentage of each population cohort completing high school has increased from 51 per cent in 1940 and 59 per cent in 1950 to 77 per cent in 1964. The gap should continue to be closed. To accomplish this, both the problem of motivation and inadequate family income must be faced realistically. Otherwise, economic improvement may actually increase the number of dropouts as jobs become more easily available. The task is neither easy nor cheap, but experimentation has suggested answers, for example, ungraded classrooms with increasing individual attention, work-study arrangements, and income-maintenance policies to make it unnecessary for young people to neglect their education because they must augment family incomes.

4. For most secondary school pupils, vocational training should be deferred until after high school. The high school should emphasize broad general education in language and literature, mathematics and science, history and social studies, and the arts. These subjects are an essential foundation not only for personal development and citizenship but also for most vocations. General education is especially necessary in a rapidly changing economy in which versatility and flexibility are at a premium. The training for many—perhaps most—specific jobs can and must be done on the job as a responsibility of the employer. However, there are some pupils whose greatest potential can be realized through occupational-vocational-technical education. Such education, with a parallel program of general education, can equip them with both job skills and a solid foundation for the adaptability necessary in a dynamic society. It can help implant the important understanding that education is a continuing process of self-renewal indispensable for continuing adaptability in a changing world. The design of occupational-vocational-technical education to achieve these purposes represents a significant challenge to the educational community.

5. A nationwide system of free public education through 2 years beyond high school (grade 14) should be established. The key institutions would

be area technical schools and community colleges. The public vocational-technical schools would provide training in trade, technical, and business occupations at the skilled worker level. The community colleges would provide liberal education as well as technical and semiprofessional training. The two types of schools might in many instances be merged into a community education center offering both the theoretical foundation of trade, technical, and business occupations and the opportunity to "learn-by-doing" while pursuing liberal education or semi-professional training. Most of the students in both types of institutions would be high school graduates, though provision could also be made for former high school dropouts, college transfers, and adults. Remedial courses could be provided for those whose earlier preparation had been inadequate and for continuing education for adults with adequate educational foundations.

6. All qualified students should have realistic access to university education. General education should be emphasized in the undergraduate years. With a nationwide system of community colleges, the standards for entrance to the university should be established at a level appropriate to work of true university grade. The university is an institution of strategic importance to technological advancement, both as an educational and as a research institution.

7. No qualified student should be deprived of education at any level because of his family's lack of financial resources. Our recommendations for full employment and income maintenance and for free public education through 2 years beyond high school should make education for every young person financially possible through grade 14. At college or the university, support for both tuition and maintenance when needed should be available through scholarships, loans, and work. We recognize that there will also be cases in which qualified students are prevented from completing high school or college because their earnings are needed by their families. Until adequate income maintenance programs are available, additional assistance will be necessary in these cases.

8. Education, training, and retraining should be available to individuals throughout their lives. The ability to manage change—whether to keep up with new developments in a profession or to retool for a new job—requires that continuous education be available when needed. Access to education governs the pace at which new knowledge can be absorbed, adjustments made to new technologies, and solutions reached to related social, political, and economic problems. The lifelong learning process has both a formal and an informal side. Learning occurs not only in the class, the extension course, and the lecture series; it also takes place in individual reading, television programs, and instruction on the assembly line. The system of public education, however, should provide a comprehensive program of educational opportunity for persons of all ages and of varying educational attainments. A system of education that is open ended, with freedom for mature students to enter, leave when alternative experiences seem more fruitful, and then reenter, can be a reality through the coordinated efforts of public schools, community colleges, vocational schools, universities, and employers. The lifelong learning process, which must be in a fundamental

240

sense a program of self-education, can be materially aided by formal educational programs. But above all, starting at the earliest levels the educational process must seek to impress upon the individual the need to assume responsibility for continuing self-education and self-renewal for meaningful adaptation to a changing environment.

9. A special need is to provide more extensive education opportunities for adults whose basic education is deficient. Many are virtually illiterate or otherwise seriously handicapped educationally. It must be recognized that every effort to improve the education of those now in school will increase the disadvantages of those with substandard education. About 30 million members of the present work force are without high school diplomas, and 8 million have not completed eight grades. One-sixth of American youth cannot qualify for military services because they are unable to pass a seventh grade equivalency examination. Two-thirds of the heads of poor families have less than an eighth grade education. The Welfare Administration of the Department of Health, Education, and Welfare estimates that the great majority of those eligible for its training programs are in need of basic education. Many other indications of the need for adult education could be cited. Yet the opportunities for adult basic education are few, the problems of motivation are practically unsolved, and new approaches and techniques are needed. Recent developments in educational technology appear to have special applicability to the needs of the adult learner. Imaginative efforts in many communities indicate that obstacles can be overcome. Experience has shown that employees are more likely to take advantage of supplementary education if provided at the workplace.

10. The Manpower Development and Training Act has made a start in the retraining of employees and the unemployed. But the program must still be described as experimental in scale; we recommend that it be expanded. Stieber points out that training allowances under the U.S. program are far smaller relative to wage rates than those in European retraining programs. With labor markets tightening, retraining has added urgency.

11. The laws of some States prevent unemployed workers from receiving training while drawing unemployment insurance. Such laws should be changed by Federal and State action. In the long run, unemployment insurance funds would probably be saved by offering a monetary incentive (over and above unemployment insurance benefits) for training to be at least equal to the added clothing, meals, transportation, and tuition costs involved.

12. Training and retraining for most jobs occur at the workplace as a responsibility of the employer. The members of the Commission have been impressed by the extensive and increasing amount of training and education that occurs within private business, and also by the relative speed with which new jobs can be learned by American workers. Effective as on-the-job training is for the teaching of specific skills, it is limited in its ability to review and improve basic education. The community must take major responsibility for the latter. However, added incentives could be given to encourage workers to undertake educational programs outside

241

working hours.[12] One promising approach would be for management and labor to develop programs under which workers would be encouraged to engage in full-time education during periods of layoff and during negotiated sabbatical leaves.

13. It has been far too common in the tradition of mass free education to ascribe inadequacies to the individual student rather than to adapt educational techniques to meet the needs or to overcome the limitations of individuals. Reducing economic barriers helps those who can succeed in the well-established techniques of formal education and training. They do nothing for those in and out of school who cannot make effective use of established patterns and approaches to education. The task of expanding educational opportunity must also focus on adjusting the system to meet the needs of those who cannot make effective use of existing educational methods. A considerable amount of experimentation and research in applying computer and information technologies to educational problems is under way. Much of what is being done bears on compensatory educational techniques for disadvantaged people in the labor force and on the development of a system of continuous, lifelong education.

Through newer techniques, a wider variety of individual learning behaviors and motivations can be recognized and accommodated. The new technologies can also relieve teachers of mechanical and administrative chores so that they can spend more time helping individual students. New information technologies are also being applied to keeping curriculums up to date in a wide variety of subject matter areas. The experimentation with new educational technologies has thus far been limited in scale, but the results have been exciting in regard to expanding educational opportunity to those who have heretofore been regarded as poor learners or poorly motivated.

14. In retrospect, one of the highest return investments we as a nation have made was the GI bill following the Second World War and the Korean War. Not only did we aid veterans to make up lost years but we brought about a veritable social revolution. Men and women whose backgrounds precluded the possibility of higher education and advanced training were lifted into totally unexpected positions in life. And in simple monetary terms, the investment has already been returned in taxes on their higher incomes. The lesson should not be forgotten or neglected.

The Commission regards universal and widespread education as one of the most important goals for America. Heartening progress is under way. But enormous tasks lie ahead before the potential inherent in our human resources is realized, and before the promise of equal opportunity in a democratic society is fulfilled. The Commission feels strongly that educational programs of high quality should be available to *all* youth. By high quality we refer to programs with adequate resources, well-trained teachers, suitable buildings, and appropriate curriculums and educational methods.

[12] Great Britain recently passed the Industrial Training Act which imposes a training tax on all employers that is rebated to those who establish approved training programs. Small employers may pool their training efforts in order to obtain the rebate. No experience has yet been accumulated.

B. Matching Men and Jobs

Adjustment by workers to technological and other change would be helped by improved operation of the labor market. Frictional unemployment can be minimized only if workers seeking jobs and employers seeking workers can be brought together efficiently.

The labor market is a complex market, or group of markets, including all classes of workers from the unskilled to professionals and executives. The labor market for most occupations is local, but there are regional and even national markets in some occupations. There is a tendency for markets to widen as mobility increases. In many cases, necessary or desirable adjustments to change involve long-distance moves, even coast-to-coast, and require a communication system that is nationwide.

LABOR MARKET INFORMATION

The first requirement for an orderly labor market and satisfactory adjustment to change is adequate information. Alternative employment opportunities are real to the individual only if he is aware of their existence. Displaced workers, those vulnerable to displacement, and those who want to improve their standing in the labor market can make reasonably appropriate decisions only if they have information, not only about present opportunities but about the future outlook for alternative occupations.

The job seeker, whether unemployed or seeking better employment, has little information available concerning alternative job openings. Many placement agencies, labor unions, trade associations, and other organizations are involved in the process of matching men and jobs. Most of them serve limited clientele, usually skilled and professional workers and executives. Only the public employment services are available to all and serve the full range of occupations. Yet they have information available only on those job openings which are listed with them by employers; and employers can learn from the public employment service only of that minority of workers who are registered there. Most information concerning job opportunities passes by word of mouth through an informal but effective grapevine, but the information provided is of limited scope.

The Bureau of Labor Statistics makes reasonably accurate long-range projections of national employment trends by occupation and industry. The U.S. Employment Service and its affiliated State agencies supply increasing amounts of information about local employment trends. But there is simply no place in any local labor market, let alone on a regional or national basis, where individual job seekers or employers can discover the full range of possible jobs or employees available. The outlook for employment at the local and regional level and the probable durability and potential of any choice made is usually unknown to the individual. The adjustment process can be improved considerably through provision of more and better information concerning present opportunities and their future promise. Some of the needed improvements follow.

1. To give job seekers and employers access to specific job openings and potential employees, the Commission recommends that a computerized nationwide service for matching men to jobs be established. The technical

243

feasibility of such a system has been established in studies sponsored by the Commission. With local centers feeding into regional centers information relevant at that level, and these in turn feeding into a nationwide job and manpower bank, the service could provide detailed information on the manpower requirements of job vacancies and the personal characteristics of job seekers.[13] The technological knowledge is available for the development of the equipment and the costs are within reason. Problems relating to the most effective methods of coding and similar problems remain to be worked out, but these can be solved if the commitment is made to develop the system.

The proposed communication system could be organized in several ways. It could be a nonprofit public service corporation with joint public and private ownership, or a part of the U.S. Employment Service. Each has advantages and disadvantages. The question of the appropriate form of organization is subsidiary to the basic recommendation that the system be established. However, some of the Commission members prefer the first possibility. The Commission believes that it would be sound policy for employers to list all or most job openings through some generally available mechanism. The proposed system would strongly encourage such listing. An obvious beginning would be for the Federal Government to list all of its openings with the system through the U.S. Employment Service.*

The operation of the system, if it were organized as a joint public-private corporation, would be as follows: Every employer could, if he wished, have in his own establishment a terminal giving access to information concerning the detailed characteristics of all job seekers. Employers could themselves choose whom to interview rather than depend upon others to refer prospective employees. Small businesses might have access to the system through jointly operated terminals or by placing job orders with the employment service. The job seeker would participate in the system either directly or through his own chosen representative—the public employment service, a private employment agency, either fee-charging or eleemosynary, a labor union, or some other agency which, through its own terminal, would have access to the requirements of prospective employers. Either employer or employee could place any desired restriction upon use of the information supplied, and appropriate safeguards could be established to guard against invasion of privacy.

If the communication system were a separate enterprise, the public employment service would be relieved of a purely mechanical function and allowed to focus all of its resources upon the needs of the unemployed and those seeking better jobs. The job seeker, in turn, could pursue his job search in an orderly fashion under the auspices of the public employment service or other employment agency. Alternatively, the operations of the public employment service might be computerized with local systems linked

[13] In cooperation with the U.S. Employment Service, the State of California has experimented with a computerized system and further experimentation is now contemplated on an interstate basis.

* For comment by several Commission members, see p. 250.

into a national system. The question of the appropriate ownership of the employment information system is separate from the desirability of the system itself. We recommend its careful study.

2. To warn of vulnerability to displacement and aid rational choice among alternatives as well as provide businessmen and public officials with better tools for long-range planning, short- and long-term forecasts of local and regional occupational demand and manpower availability should be improved and made more readily available. A focal point should be established in each community, probably in the local public employment service, where national trends and information from local businessmen, public officials, universities, and other sources can be translated into 1 to 10 year forecasts of likely local and regional manpower and employment developments. Not only employees and employers but those concerned with counseling and guidance, educational and urban planning, and economic development would be assisted by such guides to future prospects.

THE PUBLIC EMPLOYMENT SERVICE

The public employment service is federally financed but State operated. Some States operate imaginative, efficient employment services; others appear to have less effective services. There is need for high nationwide standards. Moreover, labor markets are not necessarily organized according to State boundaries. While the markets for some skills are intrastate, many labor markets overlap State boundaries and many are regional or national. Interstate cooperation among the State services exists at present, but appears sporadic and slow. State salary structures impede recruitment of quality personnel. The present system is not well suited to innovations like the computerized job information service which should operate on a nationwide basis. For all of these reasons, we believe the public employment service should become a Federal agency and then be provided with the resources to do its job.*

GEOGRAPHIC RELOCATION

While encouragement of labor mobility is essential, emphasis should be placed on attempts to rehabilitate economically distressed areas through regional planning and Federal financial and technical assistance. Efforts should be made to bring jobs to areas where workers live and to utilize fully existing social investments in community facilities, schools, churches, etc.

The availability of alternative sources of employment may be of little value to the displaced employee if they are too far away. The problems of depressed areas have received considerable attention in the past few years but are still far from solution. Economic and technological changes leave regions and their people isolated, stranded, unemployed, and poor, their resources and social investments underutilized or abandoned. The initial approach, appropriately, was to attempt to bring the jobs to the people, many of whom had been isolated from the economy's mainstream by the vagaries of technological change. The public obligation to give a geo-

---

* For comments by Commission members, see p. 250.

graphical dimension to the freedom of occupational choice was first recognized in the labor adjustment provisions of the Trade Expansion Act. Subsequently, positive support was provided in the 1963 Amendments to the Manpower Development and Training Act. Not as a general policy but as an experiment and as a demonstration, the Secretary of Labor was authorized to provide grants and loans to cover the direct costs of workers moving from labor surplus areas to promised jobs in more favorable economic areas.

At first, the program was burdened by the generally high levels of unemployment. As labor markets have tightened around the country, the availability of relocation assistance is demonstrating its value. Much should be learned from the current experiments in the design of a permanent program.

In such relocation efforts, careful consideration must be given to the total consequences. There are values in stable communities; when it is possible, economic development should be promoted in declining areas. We commend the continuing experimentation which is going into the rehabilitation of Appalachia and other depressed areas.

To people whose experience and resources are limited, fear of the unknown is probably a more important obstacle to geographical mobility than the financial cost of moving.[14]

Another important obstacle to the geographical matching of men and jobs remains almost unnoticed. Part of labor displacement results from the tendency of industry to follow the movement to the suburbs, while the poor, many of whom have been victims of technological change in agriculture, remain trapped in the central city. If one is too poor to own and operate an automobile it may be literally true that "you can't get there from here."[15] A solution to this problem is essential, not only for adjustment to technological change but for the attack on poverty and the reduction of riots and strife.

[14] A successful relocation program will require advance information on the nature of job opportunities, housing, and transportation. It may be necessary to meet the losses entailed in selling a house in an area of falling employment. Such losses are frequently absorbed by firms transferring their managerial personnel or engineers and scientists, but seldom for industrial workers.

The worker and his wife will need an opportunity to visit the prospective community. Counseling will be needed at both ends of the transfer, as well as assistance in finding housing and fitting into the community. For many, close followup for substantial periods may be necessary to prevent discouragement. New jobs must be found when others are lost. All these and moving costs, too, will often be necessary. Even then relocation will make a marginal, though worthwhile, contribution to adjustment.

[15] One member of this Commission, before the Los Angeles riots, had some of his students conduct an experiment in the Watts area. They were instructed to travel by public transportation from the center of Watts to various areas of employment throughout the city. Most of the trips involved several bus changes and at least 1½ hours of travel *each way*. It was literally impossible to get from Watts to one important employment area by public transportation in time for work in the morning.

The process of successful adjustment can also be impeded by any number of social barriers which bar certain workers from certain jobs. These practices include discrimination based on race, age, or sex and arbitrary control over hiring or training, as in certain apprenticeship programs. Such practices cannot be condoned for they prevent the Nation from fully using its human resources or using them efficiently. The government has through legal and administrative actions attempted to eliminate these practices. However effective it has been, the road to realistic solutions is a long one.

This Commission has taken special cognizance of the civil rights "revolution." The heart of the problem faced by Negroes as they strive to enter the mainstream of American economic life is employment opportunity. That this also lies at the heart of adjustment to technological change is no surprise. Therefore, it is clear that a healthy, rapidly growing economy is a necessary condition for Negro progress. However, by itself it is probably not enough. For more than 300 years, the Negro has been systematically denied his rightful place in American society. This denial has taken its toll in many ways. In order to develop and use fully the potential of America's Negroes, special programs will be needed—programs which systematically attempt to compensate as rapidly as possible for 300 years of systematic denial. The cost of these programs will be high, but it will be small in relation to the human costs of 300 years of deprivation, and it will also be small in relation to the benefits society will reap. It is probably fair to consider such expenditures in much the same light as we considered expenditures for returning GI's after the Second World War. Only now are we fully recognizing the benefits of this investment. The same will be true of the special programs which will permit Negroes their rightful place in a democratic society.

C. Facilitating Regional Adjustment*

All regions have not shared equally in the unprecedented economic growth that this Nation has enjoyed since the end of the Second World War. The economies of many regions have, in fact, declined, leaving pools of unemployment, poverty, and hardship. In a dynamic economy characterized by technological change as well as by shifts in demand, depletion of resources, and other locational factors, such geographic inequities can perhaps be expected—but this does not lessen the hardships involved. Following are some examples of the regional changes that occur and problems that result:

 a. The introduction of improved coal-mining equipment plus the increased use of petroleum and natural gas as a source of energy contributed to the problems of Appalachia.

---

[16] In relation to this section, see M. T. Puryear, *The Negro in the American Economy* (†).

* For general comments on this section by several Commission members, see pp. 250–252.

b. The development of new agricultural machinery and chemistry resulted in the emergence of large, highly mechanized and industrialized farm operations which reduced labor requirements in predominantly agricultural areas.

c. The replacement of steam locomotives by diesel engines destroyed the economy of communities whose function was the repair and maintenance of steam-operated railroad equipment.

When the impact of economic and technological change has caused certain regions to fall behind the progress of the Nation as a whole, the Federal Government has found itself with new responsibilities. Usually the forces impinging upon the declining regions are beyond their control. In addition, various Federal programs have sometimes unwittingly contributed to regional problems. For instance, Federal housing policies have contributed to urban "sprawl" and the defense and space programs have redistributed manpower resources, concentrating scientists and engineers particularly in only a few regions. The resources and too often the leadership available at the regional level are limited. In recent years Congress has provided assistance to "distressed areas" through the Area Redevelopment Administration, the Manpower Development and Training Act, the Economic Development Administration, the State Technical Services Act, and the special program for Appalachia. But so far, the Federal Government has found it difficult to cut through the layers of State and local governmental structure involved to get to the heart of the problem of local economic growth.

There are no easy solutions to the problems posed by regional economic dislocation. In the final analysis, however, the Nation is faced with the choice of rebuilding and assisting distressed communities until they become self-sustaining, or of abandoning them altogether. As a wealthy nation, we do have the resources, and assistance to such communities can be considered an investment in the Nation's future. This Commission believes that a concerted effort to revitalize potentially viable communities is required. Such assistance should be designed to encourage self-help within the community, and should be formulated with the needs of the entire regional economy in mind. The types of assistance needed include the following:

1. A comprehensive economic analysis must be the first step. Such an analysis must clearly identify the current and likely future problems which face each region and the resources available to meet these problems.

2. Wherever possible, new technological developments should be used to stimulate regional economic growth. Information about new technology must be made available to each region, and each should be assisted in applying this information. The recently enacted State Technical Services Act may help in this regard, although more emphasis on a regional rather than State orientation appears to be required.

3. Assistance in the form of venture capital is required to permit each region to take full advantage of the opportunities presented by technological change. Such capital is needed to encourage entrepreneurship and to

stimulate the development of new industry based on the emerging technologies.

4. Direct financial assistance is needed to help distressed communities update and improve education, highway, and service facilities (water, sewage, etc.). Improved schools and other institutions for upgrading human resources are particularly important. When developed as part of an overall plan, the improvement of such facilities could provide both the physical base and the stimulus for self-sustaining economic growth of the community.

A better understanding of what constitutes an "economic region" and an administrative framework capable of approaching the problem on a broad regional basis is required in dealing with the problems of regional economic growth and adjustment. The boundaries of economic regions must generally be drawn without regard to State lines. At the present time the Federal Reserve System seems to offer the most viable mechanism for developing and implementing regional programs. Federal Reserve Districts have several advantages as bases for regional development programs: the Federal Reserve Districts approximate existing regional economies; they are already established; and since the Federal Reserve System is closely associated with private banking institutions, it could effectively stimulate the application of private funds to the development of local and regional economies. Specific recommendations in this respect include the following:

1. Each Federal Reserve bank should establish a regular program of regional economic analysis as a means of continually evaluating the problems and opportunities facing the region. The Federal Reserve banks of Boston and Minneapolis, which have conducted such programs in the past, have successfully demonstrated the role the Federal Reserve System can play in the formation of regional economic goals and the policies to meet those goals.

2. It is recommended that each Federal Reserve District establish an "advisory council for economic growth" composed of leaders from business, labor, government, the universities, and other interested groups within the district. The council's activities should include the identification and interpretation of all factors affecting or likely to affect the economic well-being of the district. On the basis of this analysis the council should prepare comprehensive program and policy recommendations directed at both public and private institutions within the district; the council itself would have no action authority.

3. Capital banks should be established within each Federal Reserve District to provide venture capital and long-term financing for new and existing companies. It is suggested that these venture capital banks be financed with private funds insofar as possible.

4. Regional technical institutes should be established within each region to keep abreast of new technological developments. Innovations applicable to such regional needs as pollution, transportation, education, and health, as well as those offering opportunity or threat to the region's economic struc-

249

ture would be of particular interest. An important function of these institutes would be to assist new and existing firms to take maximum advantage of the opportunities offered by technological advance.

5. A high-level Federal executive is needed within each region to coordinate the efforts of various existing Federal programs at the regional level. This regional Federal executive could also serve as a focal point for Federal contacts with State and local programs.

The Nation can meet its goal of maximum economic growth and its commitment to provide all of its citizens with the opportunity to share in the national prosperity only when the resources available in all sections of the country are utilized to their full potential. The recommendations outlined are designed to meet this goal.

Comment noted on p. 244 by Mr. Hayes and Mr. Reuther, joined by Mr. Young

We share the view that the President should be urged to issue an Executive order under which all Government procurement contracts would require the contractors to list with the public employment service all job openings to be filled by new hires.

The steps proposed in the report to encourage voluntary listing of other employers' job openings with the service should be given a trial. If, however, they fail to achieve comprehensive listing of job openings, we will need legislation directed toward that end. Such legislation should deny experience-rating tax benefits under the unemployment insurance laws to employers who refuse to list their job openings with the service.

Where union hiring halls or other union-management arrangements are in operation, they would be acceptable in lieu of listing with the service.

Further, a new Federal standard should be adopted for the State unemployment insurance laws which would prevent the States from requiring claimants to make an independent search for work in addition to registering for employment with the service.

At present, the service is the victim of a vicious circle. The "independent search" requirement herds workers to the hiring gates of employers, thus relieving them of the necessity to list their job openings. Qualified workers not claiming unemployment insurance do not register with the service because employers do not list openings with it. Many employers do not list their openings because the service cannot provide such qualified workers.

Comment noted on p. 245 by Mr. Sporn

I fully agree with the need for raising the level of performance of many of the State employment services. However, the basis for choosing federalization of the State employment services as the means to that end, here developed, is that State operation yields differing degrees of effectivness among the States. This would appear to provide the most convincing argument for continuance of State-operated employment services. There would thus be assured the continued diversity of approach and experimentation, with the

250

excellent performance of some acting as a spur and encouragement for others to meet or surpass the standards of excellence clearly demonstrated as possible. It is disappointing to have the report take a defeatist position and advocate federalization. I am fearful that such a step would discourage experimentation and would assure uniformity but on a general level of mediocrity.

Comment noted on p. 245 by Mr. Haggerty

I am in general agreement with Mr. Sporn's comment on this point. I am particularly concerned that federalization could interfere with the flexibility of the State system which allows it to respond to local needs. But I would emphasize the need for a strong Federal role in the interstate aspects of employment service activities.

Comment noted on p. 245 by Mr. Sporn

The problem of the economically distressed regions that have failed to participate adequately in the Nation's economic growth and development is one that merits a great deal of effort to find a solution. I strongly endorse such efforts as those being made by the Appalachian Regional Commission. I regret, however, that I am compelled to dissent from the superficial analysis and bromidic prescriptions for the problems of regional economic distress presented in this report.

I can see no merit in the suggestion that the Federal Reserve Districts and the Federal Reserve banks assume responsibility for regional economic development programs, nor has there been any evidence that regional technical institutes can contribute significantly to the development of economically distressed areas. Indeed, while technological change may account for some regional dislocations, such dislocations can be traced, in far larger measure, to other causes. For example, in Appalachia the difficulties of the coal industry are largely attributable to the rise in the level of economic well-being and the consequent shift in consumer preference for fuels other than coal that are more attractive and less burdensome to use. That the coal industry, in the past 4 years, has been able to reverse its decline and grow by about 25 per cent is largely attributable to the introduction of new technology that has made possible lower costs and lower prices.

While I concur with the intent of this section to promote greater regional development efforts, I believe that this complex subject requires far more study and careful analysis than is presented here. There is a great deal of diversity among regions, and even in the case of Appalachia, the region is characterized more by diversity among its several parts than by any uniformity. The solution of regional problems, therefore, requires earnest and careful study and the development of programs at the regional and local level to develop solutions suited to the particular conditions in each case. I am, therefore, compelled to dissent from the analysis and recommendations presented here because I believe that they can only result in misguided efforts that would fail to contribute to the solution of the problems of economically depressed areas, and could even intensify their distress.

251

While we do not associate ourselves with Mr. Sporn's comment on this subject, we do share his opposition to the suggestion that the Federal Reserve Districts and the Federal Reserve banks are the appropriate units for regional development purposes. In addition, we believe that intensive study should be given to regional development experiences in other countries with a view to learning what might be applicable to the United States.

FACILITATING ADJUSTMENT TO CHANGE: *Private Policies*

The emphasis placed thus far on public policy is not intended to imply that the Federal Government has the sole responsibility for adjustment to technological change, for such adjustments occur constantly without governmental assistance. Indeed, one of the principal strengths of our private enterprise system is its flexibility in permitting changes to occur. To be sure, the Government's role in this connection is important: to provide a favorable environment for change and to act cooperatively with private parties when its assistance is needed. But in the final analysis, the parties themselves must make the decisions and work out the detailed problems of adjustment. It may be added that the private sector accounts for more than four-fifths of wage and salary employment and an even greater proportion of total employment.

Most changes are of manageable proportions; they involve a relatively small number of persons and have their own unique characteristics and requirements. Thus they do not lend themselves easily to imposed governmental solutions, which by their very nature must be comprehensive and general. On the other hand, an effective private adjustment program may receive substantial support from available public resources.

The presence of privately developed programs decreases the pressure for general legislation. Simple mechanisms which can be applied flexibly to individual situations are preferable to legislation, and for this reason public policy in recent years has concentrated on giving administrative and financial aid to private adjustment mechanisms.

In effect, governmental policy has provided more, not less, private flexibility in coping with the adjustment requirements of technological change. This orientation is designed to meet the mutual needs of management and labor and deserves their joint support.

A responsible private manpower policy—an essential element in the successful adjustment to technological change—must necessarily do more than cushion the adverse impacts of change. It must also exploit the considerable opportunities created by technological change to develop new and more rewarding jobs for the people it displaces.

The recommendations in this report are directed at developing a society in which as many people as possible contribute creatively to change and share in its benefits. Such a society is both desirable and attainable, not in spite of modern technology, but indeed, because of it. Thus, these recommendations are not intended to substitute government fiat for private judgments; rather, they are designed simply to assist employers and employees to work out their own adjustments.

A. Requirements for Adjustment

Whatever the characteristics of a given situation brought about by technological change, an adequate adjustment program must satisfy certain basic requirements. First, those displaced should be offered either a substantially equivalent or better alternative job or the training or education required to obtain such a job. This objective cannot be achieved unless displaced workers have access to the full range of available alternatives. Second, they should be guaranteed adequate financial security while searching for alternative jobs or while undertaking training. Third, they should be given sufficient financial assistance to permit them to relocate their families whenever this becomes necessary. Fourth, they should be protected against forfeiture of earned security rights, such as vacation, retirement, insurance, and related credits, resulting from job displacements.

Many private adjustment programs, formal as well as informal, go far toward meeting these basic requirements. To illustrate, 40 per cent of the approximately 8 million persons who changed employers in 1961 experienced no unemployment in the process. Even that figure is probably understated because it excludes successful job changes within a given company. Another 25 per cent were employed again within 4 weeks. Job changes were attributable about equally to three causes: voluntary moves to improve status, involuntary loss of jobs, and shifts resulting from illness or from other personal reasons.

It is difficult to estimate how many persons are covered by adequate adjustment programs. Beyond the well-known formal and collectively bargained programs, much is undertaken by managements on their own initiative or in conjunction with public agencies and community service organizations. Qualitative assessment is also difficult. Because of the dearth of available information, we suggest that the Department of Labor and the Department of Commerce systematically investigate and report publicly on successful private adjustment programs developed through either collective bargaining or the unilateral efforts of management. This would not only add to the present store of general knowledge about the adequacy of adjustment coverage, but also would permit more extensive communication about effective adjustment programs among and between employers, employees, and unions.

As increasing attention is given to adjustment programs, standards of adequacy are bound to rise; today's more advanced ideas will be commonplace tomorrow. We may expect not only wider variety in the methods of adjustment, but also greater flexibility. For example, employers should be encouraged to give employees a chance to try new jobs without forfeiting their rights to old jobs. Assurance to workers that they are not limited to one irrevocable choice among several alternatives may remove a major cause for resisting adjustments to change.

253

B. Methods of Facilitating Adjustment to Change

There is general agreement that wherever possible reductions in the work force necessitated by technological change should be accomplished by attrition. The extent of reliance on attrition, however, could be increased by better manpower planning.

One of the main objectives of manpower planning is to obviate the need for sudden and substantial layoffs and ease the impact on those who must be displaced. By studying attrition ratios and the age structure of the work force and by attempting to project manpower requirements, employers could do a better job of integrating hiring and layoff policies with the introduction of change. For instance, to the extent that necessary adjustments are made in a period of generally good economic conditions when job alternatives are relatively abundant, the burden of unemployment during less prosperous times is correspondingly reduced. Conversely, when obsolete work and manning patterns persist in an expanding economy, managements are more likely to eliminate jobs during a business downturn, with the result that a displaced employee must look for alternative jobs when they are least available and when his resources are likely to be least adequate.

Because laid-off employees need time to explore alternative job opportunities, Government agencies, unions, and others have increasingly emphasized the need for an "early warning system" which will alert employees to the possibility or inevitability of future compulsory job changes. Formal arrangements for advance notice do exist, but the notice periods are generally relatively short. Managements have been reluctant to enter into formal advance notice agreements for several reasons: fear that the firm's competitive position may be endangered, concern that employees will seek other jobs before the change is actually effected, and apprehension that such advance notice will cause a serious decline in worker productivity. Recent research suggests that employer fears of premature job-changing are largely unfounded, especially if employees must forego severance pay and related assistance should they depart before jobs have been terminated. Fear of reduced employee morale and efficiency also seems unwarranted, especially when managements combine advance notice with assistance to affected workers seeking new jobs.

Although employers must take the initiative in giving advance notice of their own planned technological changes, the broad dissemination of information about general technological developments throughout an industry or region would alert employers, unions, and employees alike to the possibility and timing of changes. Such a general sharing of information could be effected through periodic conferences between Federal, State, and municipal government officials, employers, and unions about the state of technology in various industries and would assist all parties to prepare for impending changes.

The value to employees of advance notice of technological change can be greatly enhanced if it is accompanied by assistance in finding alternative jobs or securing additional training or education. Employees should be

254

given either time off with pay to look for other jobs or financial assistance while they upgrade their skills through additional training or education. Employers willing to lend this type of assistance might well make it dependent upon the employees' commitment to stay at their present jobs through the transitional period.

Alternative or additional assistance can take the form of counseling, job referral service, or on-the-job training, with the last, in particular, offering great potential benefit to employers, employees, and the community at large. It is now generally conceded that the most efficient method of training workers for existing job vacancies is by instruction on the job. However, sufficient knowledge about the potential capacities of employees is lacking; consequently, many are not given training for jobs at the highest levels of their capabilities. The most frequently cited example of this deficiency in current adjustment programs is management's failure to promote more blue-collar workers to white-collar jobs, even though many skilled craftsmen are quite capable of learning work now assigned to junior engineers and white-collar technicians. To the extent that this condition prevails, employers waste existing human assets while substantially raising recruitment costs. To the extent that assistance measures outlined above prevent unemployment, individual managements and the community as a whole would benefit from reduced unemployment insurance costs and, in even greater measure, from the establishment of a more equitable system of sharing the costs of progress.

C. Protecting the Earned Benefit Rights of Displaced Employees

The United States does not provide by law that private as well as public employment automatically carries such benefits as paid vacations and holidays, sick leave, severance pay, and the like. Traditionally, we have relied upon the enlightened self-interest of individual employers or the pressures of collective bargaining to secure these and related benefits for employees. Even in the few instances in which nonwaivable rights have been established by law, some classes of employees remain uncovered.

The principal device developed by American unions to protect the job interests of those they represent is seniority—a system of employment preference based on length of service. Employees with the longest service are given the greatest job security and the best opportunities for advancement. In addition, rights to certain benefits and the amounts of some of them are determined on the basis of seniority. More than any other provision of the collective agreement, seniority affects employees' economic security. In industries characterized by a steady reduction in total employment, length of service is the principal protection against job loss. In cases of mass layoffs, an employee's chances of being retained or recalled will very likely depend upon such factors as the basis for determining seniority preference (e.g., plant, departmental, or craft), the provision for trial periods to "make out" on a new job, and the extent to which "bumping" is permitted.

The seniority principle has become so important that it is embodied in virtually every collective agreement, and it undoubtedly has exercised considerable influence on personnel policies of many unorganized firms. And although it is a creation of a collective agreement and lacks independent legal status, seniority is almost universally regarded by employees as a valuable property right.

It should not be surprising, therefore, that unions usually insist upon the strict enforcement of seniority provisions in their collective agreements, especially in respect to layoffs and recalls. Seniority, however, does not create jobs and therefore cannot be relied upon as the sole protection against technological change. Because of the heavy reliance placed on private arrangements to provide certain benefits and protections to workers, loss of a job usually also entails loss of vacation eligibility, loss of various forms of insurance protection for the worker and his family, and, frequently, loss of pension rights as well.

The loss of pension rights is particularly serious since the worker cannot relive the years during which he accumulated the pension entitlement that vanished with his job. Private pension plans now cover approximately 25 million workers.

These plans differ widely, however, not only in formal structure, but also in eligibility requirements, benefit levels, methods of funding, and vesting provisions. Many assert that pension benefits should be "portable" in order not to inhibit labor mobility, and that in any event pensions are a form of deferred wages which "belong" to employees. These claims have led to frequent demands for compulsory minimum vesting as a condition of approval for any pension plan by the Internal Revenue Service, without which employer contributions cannot be deducted as a business expense. Such a proposal is included in the 1965 Report of the President's Committee on Corporate Pension Funds and Other Private Retirement and Welfare Programs. Opponents argue that the added expense it entails will discourge the kind of experimentation that has brought such vitality to the private pension movement in this country. Whatever the merit of opposing arguments, the most recent survey by the U.S. Bureau of Labor Statistics showed that more than two-thirds of private pension plans, covering 60 per cent of employees with private pension rights, included some form of vesting. The Commission takes no position on the adequacy of the pace of this development but hopes that the movements toward portability and vesting will continue.

Of equal or greater concern in the administration of private pension plans are eligibility requirements, investment policies, funding arrangements, and disclosure of relevant information to plan participants. The last problem is at least partially covered by the Federal Welfare and Pension Plans Disclosure Act and by similar laws in some States; but unduly restrictive eligibility requirements and unsound investment policies sometimes lead to the disappointment of legitimate expectations on the part of employees. We favor whatever legislative or administrative measures may be necessary to promote greater equity and security in the establishment and administration of private pension plans. Specifically, we recommend that careful study be given to a legislative system of reinsurance for private pension plans similar to the reinsurance of bank deposits through the Federal Deposit Insurance Corporation.

Although not as widespread as pension plans, profit-sharing arrangements are gaining increasing favor in the American economy, especially among unorganized employers and usually for salaried workers only. As in the case of pensions, employer contributions must be irrevocable; but profit-sharing, which is geared to the actual business performance of the enterprise, permits greater flexibility in the employer's commitment while at the same time allowing for more rapid and substantial increases in the equity of employees of a successful firm. By their very nature, however, profit-sharing plans cannot guarantee the kind of security afforded by pension plans.

An increasing number of workers, both organized and unorganized, participate in group plans for life and health insurance at substantially reduced rates. Severance of employment may present the employee with the equally impractical choices of forfeiting these benefits or converting them to individual policies at prohibitive cost. Increased efforts should be devoted to making such benefits portable, especially among employers in a given industry or area. Similarly, provisions of the type incorporated in some collective agreements to continue the life and health insurance coverage of employees during temporary periods of unemployment should be encouraged, as should arrangements for areawide or industrywide coverage for health and welfare plans.[17]

D. Hours of Work, Leisure, and the Adjustment Process[18]

Full employment is not the only requirement for free choice between work and leisure. Under present practices, the tendency is to force choice between an arbitrary pattern of work and no job at all. Industry needs to develop a more flexible system of determining work schedules. The increasing numbers of youth and women in the labor force indicate the rising demand for part-time jobs. Insofar as any industry can develop its program of production to accommodate itself to employ even a small percentage of

[17] It has been suggested that the investment tax credit under the Internal Revenue Act be used as a device to facilitate adjustment of displaced persons and to protect them against some of the consequences of loss of security and accumulated job rights. The proposal is that one-half of the investment credit that each firm is entitled to be placed in reserve in a Government trust fund to meet the needs resulting from disemployment of a firm's employees. Some of the possible benefits might be supplementation of unemployment compensation, retraining allowances, wages of a lower-paid new job or inferior fringe benefits, an annuity equivalent of lost pension rights, or relocation costs. At the end of 5 years, any unused portions of the trust fund account would be returned to the appropriate firms. Thus, the firms would be given a financial incentive to plan their operations to minimize dislocations. The proposal envisions that if the temporary diversion of part of the investment credit reduced the incentive to new investment, the size of the credit would be increased. This proposal would require more study than this Commission can give it. We do commend it to the Treasury, the Council of Economic Advisers, and other appropriate agencies for study. For a fuller description of the proposal, see UAW, AFL–CIO, Use of Investment Tax Credit to Facilitate Adjustment (†).

[18] In relation to this section, see Myron Joseph, Hours of Work Issues (†); and Juanita Kreps and Joseph Spengler, The Leisure Component of Economic Growth (†).

its work force on a part-time basis, it needs to implement the concept. We should, and no doubt will, continue to use a portion of rising productivity to add to leisure. Such increased leisure can take a number of forms: periodic extended vacation periods; more holidays; earlier retirement, including "phased retirement" which permits gradual reduction in length of the workday or workweek commencing a few years before actual retirement; sabbatical leaves to provide opportunities for extended physical rest, personal reappraisal, retraining, and additional education; and, of course, reduced hours of work.

As yet, however, no serious attempts have been made to come to grips with the problem of introducing flexibility into weekly work schedules. Compulsory overtime work is still a feature of employment in many industries; compulsory payment of overtime for work performed on Saturdays and Sundays as such is even more common.

During the course of the Commission's deliberations, we received a special request from the President to consider the question of "appropriate periods of work—daily, weekly, annually, and over a lifetime." Accordingly, we devoted many hours of research, consideration, and debate to that question and to the separate though related issue of overtime penalties. Having done so, we must report our inability to reach agreement on any meaningful recommendations in respect to these problems or to achieve any substantial modification of widely divergent views held by various Commission members. Under the circumstances, we unanimously agree that no useful purpose would be served by documenting our differences, and we pass on to matters on which consensus has been achieved.

E. Collective Bargaining and the Management of Change

Collective bargaining has proved to be an excellent vehicle for the effective management of change; it permits those directly affected by the change to deal with it firsthand and with a familiarity that takes into account peculiarities and problems peculiar to an enterprise. Especially in recent years, some managements and unions, occasionally but not usually with the help of outsiders, have developed with varying degrees of ingenuity and success plans to facilitate change.

We doubt, however, that facilities of the Federal Government have been used as frequently or with as much imagination as the circumstances permit. We recognize, of course, the very proper desire of employers and unions to be masters of their own destinies to the full extent permitted by law. There need be no conflict, however, between governmental assistance and private autonomy. The power to decide can and should remain with those who must live with the decisions that are made; but greater use of government research would contribute considerably to the soundness of private judgments.

Despite its many successes, collective bargaining has often failed, and sometimes has failed spectacularly, to deal effectively or even responsibly with the management of change. It has been argued, not unreasonably, that the failures are the fault of the parties, not of the system.

Procedurally, the process of collective bargaining on basic issues has tended to stagnate during the life of the agreement and to accelerate frantically in an atmosphere of crisis immediately preceding contract renewal. Happily, employers and unions in a number of industries are abandoning this pattern in favor of more or less continuous discussion. Basic issues such as adjustment to technological change cannot be resolved, however, by a small team of negotiators working themselves into a state of physical and mental exhaustion for a few months every 2 or 3 years. These issues must be dealt with patiently, carefully, and above all, continuously, until satisfactory solutions emerge. This kind of bargaining calls for ability of the highest caliber on the part of leaders of both labor and management.

All of our recommendations presuppose the desirability, if not the necessity, of a continuing expansion of the economy. In such a climate management and labor, by the skillful use of various adjustment programs, can take the important steps necessary to eliminate wasteful and useless work practices. If technological change can be viewed as an opportunity to be readily embraced rather than as a cataclysm to be avoided at all costs, then the workers' defense mechanism described by Veblen as "the conscientious withdrawal of efficiency" will gradually give way to a spirit of accommodation and cooperation.

F. *Other Private and Public Efforts to Manage Change and Facilitate Adjustment*

Although development of private adjustment programs is principally the responsibility of the parties immediately involved, useful assistance can be obtained from outside private organizations as well as from government.

Increased management awareness of, and concern for, adequate solutions to adjustment problems is reflected in the STEP (Solutions to Employment Problems) program of the National Association of Manufacturers. Member companies are surveyed to ascertain the types of programs being used to deal with manpower problems; each program is verified by members of the STEP staff and evaluated in terms of its potential usefulness to firms seeking solutions to similar problems; then the case studies are summarized and circulated among member firms. Such a program can prove to be very valuable to the overall manpower adjustment capability of the Nation by emphasizing the problem-solving approach to adjustment situations and by greatly increasing communication relating to such problems among managements. STEP is also exploring ways to facilitate the development of community-based approaches to the solution of manpower problems whereby effective programs are developed through linking private and public resources to existing and emerging problems.

Another example of a well conceived approach to the solution of manpower problems is the National Skills Bank of the National Urban League, a computerized file of the capabilities of Negro jobseekers. The plan has emphasized detailed descriptions of each applicant's work capabilities and potential through testing and intensive interviewing, and has been effective in opening up a greater range of jobs. Although this program was directed mainly at trained persons whose skills were underutilized, the Urban League has also used it to screen people who need training and other remedial help and to refer them to available programs. Like the STEP program, the National Skills Bank attempts to bring both public and private resources in local communities to bear on manpower problems.

These new programs emphasize the need for longer range and more systematic planning to prevent adjustment situations from becoming adjustment problems. And because most adjustment situations are relatively small, there is every reason to expect that such an approach can prove effective. Large displacements sometimes occur, however, and demand extraordinary efforts to deal with them. The closing of a large plant or the sudden cancellation of a major Government contract can throw thousands of workers in a single community out of jobs overnight. The United States is the only industrialized country that permits the closing of large plants without notice. We have previously urged that employers give as much notice of such closing as possible; we also recommend that the Federal Government follow a like course in announcing contract cancellations.

When disastrous situations of this type do occur, the Federal Government should coordinate and expedite both public and private job and retraining alternatives for the unemployed. The value of such a service can be tremendous. It makes possible the rapid search for alternative jobs, the prompt establishment of necessary training programs, the establishment of an emergency food program from Federal surplus supplies, and the negotiation of agreements with financial institutions for temporary postponement of debt repayments by displaced employees. In short, a wide variety of resources must be effectively brought to bear in a very short time, and this requires coordinators well-trained in advance with a working knowledge of the range of resources available, the kinds of problems to be solved, and the necessary administrative procedures involved.

G. The Adjustment to Change for Minority Groups

The adjustment to technological as well as to economic and social change presents special problems for Negroes and other minority groups. No set of measures promoting public and private adjustment will suffice if the avenues to education, jobs, advancement, and the highest achievements of our society can offer are impeded by discrimination. Not until unions, employers, and private and public institutions are able to overcome the insidious vestiges of discrimination based on race, color, sex, religion, or national origin can the adjustment process be considered adequate for such groups.

At present the economic opportunities of Negroes are barred by exclusive hiring practices, discriminatory promotion policies, and unreasonable and unnecessarily restrictive hiring requirements. Some unions refuse to admit more than a few Negroes to membership, thereby excluding Negroes from apprenticeship programs and from many highly skilled jobs in some industries. Too many employers still fail to provide opportunities for Negroes in executive training and development programs and thereby foreclose advancement in the ranks of corporate management. In the process of adjusting to change, every form of discrimination based on race, color, sex, or religion must be overcome.

260

Its proponents have always asserted that by precept and example collective bargaining has benefited unorganized workers as well as union members. Many individual employers and unions as well as the AFL–CIO were speaking out against racial and ethnic discrimination in employment before the Civil Rights Act of 1964 was passed, and they played major roles in bringing about the enactment of that Act and other civil rights legislation. Moreover, the AFL–CIO and many of its affiliates have supported a wide range of other legislation beneficial to the economically and racially disadvantaged groups in our society. However, even in those international unions whose dedicated opposition to discrimination in employment is unchallenged, adherence to these principles is not always as steadfast at local levels where regional and cultural influences sometimes outweigh organizational commitments. National multiplant corporations encounter similar problems with some of their local plant managers. It must be noted that some unions and some employers, and even some Federal, State, and local agencies, have a record of discrimination against Negroes and other minority groups that is a mockery of the basic principles of industrial democracy. All too belatedly, some leaders of management and organized labor are seeking to make up for decades of indifference or outright hostility toward these minorities. To a degree, shifts in their attitudes have been compelled by Title VII of the Civil Rights Act of 1964 and by similar State enactments. We recommend the strengthening of the enforcement provisions of this legislation.

Literal adherence to the letter of the law, however, is simply not enough. Negroes and ethnic minorities in this country have been so conditioned to patterns of discrimination in employment that many will not take the law at its face value and risk the humiliation of being rejected for employment or union membership on the irrelevant and invidious grounds of race, color, or national origin. They need and are entitled to an affirmative assurance. It is not enough for employers, including Government agencies, to establish a policy against discrimination in employment; they should go into the Negro, Mexican-American, and Puerto Rican communities and actively recruit employees from among them. They should also lower minimum standards of employment for certain jobs with unnecessarily and unreasonably high requirements. Such a shift in policy could, by itself, make available thousands of jobs now out of reach of culturally deprived groups, including many native white Americans.

In addition to initiating these changes through collective bargaining, those unions and managements which have not already done so must take steps to assure that national policies against discrimination are effectively implemented at the local level. Experience demonstrates that active cooperation of managements with unions greatly facilitates the elimination of discriminatory practices at the plant level. Although some progress has been made in opening skilled trades apprenticeship programs to members of minority groups, much more remains to be done. Like many employers, a number of unions continue to tolerate differing degrees of adherence to national policies in various parts of the country; but discrimination is a national evil that must be eliminated on a national basis.

We believe that employers and unions alike have an affirmative duty to make special efforts to aid Negroes and members of other minority groups in obtaining more and better jobs. Such efforts will not in themselves redress the injustices which these disadvantaged citizens have already suffered; but surely they are the very least we should expect from those who profess a belief in democracy.

What has been said about racial and ethnic minorities applies, though to a lesser extent, to women and to older workers. Though discrimination against them is more easily masked and often justified by plausible reasons, no one can deny that there is widespread prejudice against employment of women and older workers as such. Such prejudice has no place in a society dedicated to providing every person willing and able to work with a useful and suitable job.

H. The Government as a Model Employer

Change and adjustment are not confined to the private sector. Just as public policy urges greater private labor and management responsibility for facilitating adjustments, so should government assume like responsibility for managing the introduction and adjustment to changes affecting its own employees. The public pressure for increased efficiency in government operations is constant and insistent; but there is little or no corresponding pressure to improve adjustment programs. We believe, however, that the Federal Government, with 2.5 million civilian employees, has a particular obligation to be a model employer in the management of change. We also believe the Federal Government could be a more positive influence by encouraging its contractors to make adequate provisions for displacement.

Federal protection of the earned worklife credits of its employees is, for the most part, excellent. Pension rights are vested after 5 years. Life and health insurance can be transferred to private carriers when an employee leaves without having to take new physical examinations. However, should an employee choose to continue his vested pension rights after leaving Federal service, he loses the family survivorship benefits which would ordinarily apply. In transferring life and health insurance he loses the benefit of low group rates. Ways should be explored to correct these deficiencies.

In respect to information about alternative job opportunities, Federal practice leaves much to be desired. For example, the Federal Government does not list all job vacancies with the public employment service; yet it urges private employers to do so. Indeed, there is no central file of available jobs for the Federal establishment. Although the Civil Service Commission is taking steps to correct this by establishing new information centers in place of outmoded departmental boards of examiners, we feel that function should be assigned to the U.S. Employment Service along with adequate funds to support the activity.

The Federal Government has attempted to increase occupational mobility by review and change of occupational codes and by breaking down tasks along work-function lines. Subprofessional careers have been opened up to people who previously were confined to blue-collar jobs. However, the

Government should reinforce this program by extending its internal training and retraining efforts. The effectiveness of on-the-job training has been noted elsewhere in this report, and those observations apply with equal force to public employment. Moreover, there should be a concerted effort to ensure that training and education resources are not disproportionately allocated to those in higher grade and skill levels. Frequently, lower level employees are not even aware of the resources available to them; and even when they are, their desires for self-improvement and advancement are usually given a much lower priority than those of higher rated employees who have already achieved substantial success within the framework of the existing system.

This suggests a built-in bias or distortion in the way we look at the problem. It is not enough simply to help those who have already done well to do better; for this does nothing to correct whatever weaknesses and discrimination there may be in our methods of defining, recognizing, and rewarding achievement. We must also expand the opportunities for further development and advancement for those who have been relatively less successful but who have the desire to move ahead and the willingness to work toward that goal. In providing such opportunities and carefully monitoring the results, the Government may gain information about our present criteria of "success" that may be of considerable value to the whole society.

Education and training budgets of agencies are frequently among the first to feel the effects of economy drives. The Congress, which has given such extensive recognition to the value of education and training elsewhere in the economy, should seek to help agencies sustain their budget requests for training programs. Moreover, it should seriously consider removing the job-relatedness restrictions on payments to employees for courses taken on their own time. As matters stand, this feature tends to exact a relatively tight interpretation of the law for those in relatively low-skilled jobs, and a relatively loose interpretation for those in professional and related jobs. State and local governments should also conduct themselves as model employers in regard to adjustment to change.

I. The Government as an Experimenter in New Adjustment Techniques

The Federal Government is in an excellent position to experiment with new methods to increase worklife flexibility and adjustment techniques. It is a major contributor to advanced research in education and training technologies as well as in computer technologies.

Earlier in this report we emphasized the need for an improved system of job information and for increased access of people to such a system. Accordingly, recommendations were made for a national computerized man-job matching system and a reorganized and improved public employment service. Recent experience has demonstrated, however, that expanding and centralizing job information centers does not in itself insure that all people wanting work will come to such centers. Many people in disadvantaged groups either fear or distrust all governmental offices; some may simply not know how to read well enough to be aided by printed information. Therefore, we suggest that the Federal Government explore new methods of disseminating information to those who need and want work, but cannot or will not go to places where such information is normally given.

The Federal Government should also take the initiative in expanding employment opportunities by removing what may be rather arbitrary entrance requirements for low-skilled jobs. In a recent experiment it removed the requirements of a written test and a clean police record for some 2,000 jobs in the Washington, D.C., area. Initial reports suggest that the experiment was highly effective, but only after considerable effort was made to get the job information to the potential candidates. All Federal employees will benefit from the removal of functionally meaningless barriers between jobs. The absence of formal academic credentials should not, in itself, deny a person access to more rewarding work if he has the present ability or potential to render good service.

Reducing artificial barriers to achievement of more rewarding careers would be greatly enhanced by more experimentation in the Federal Government with new educational technologies. Experimentation elsewhere has demonstrated that the new technologies hold the potential for reducing training time and adapting training programs to a variety of individual learning behavior. The problems and needs of older workers, particularly those at lower skill and occupational levels, presents an especially important area in which the Federal Government could be in the forefront of experimentation. Recent developments suggest that there are new ways to recognize individual potential and to help people realize a much higher degree of attainment in relatively shorter periods of time. Some of the experimentation with new methods could be directed at helping to meet the more critical manpower needs of the Federal Government, especially where normal sources of supply are inadequate.

TECHNOLOGY AND UNMET HUMAN AND COMMUNITY NEEDS:
General Considerations

Technology has the potential, whose beginnings we already see, to realize a persistent human vision: to enlarge the capacities of man and to extend his control over the environment. Where technology has changed the productive process, its fruits have been visible in the higher standards of living of people. But the meaning of technology is not only that it produces *more* goods, but that in reducing their cost, it provides the solid foundation for creating "social equality" among groups. As Joseph Schumpeter put it in his usually pungent way, "The capitalist achievement does not typically consist in providing more silk stockings for queens but in bringing them within the reach of factory girls in return for steadily decreasing amounts of effort."

In directing the attention of this Commission to the impact of technology on society, the Congress wisely did not limit its instructions to the immediate tasks of assessing the impact of technology on employment and recommending measures for easing the adjustments to change; it also asked us to explore the future. In the light of the technological and social changes

264

expected over the next decade, we were asked to define "those areas of unmet community and human needs toward which application of new technologies might most effectively be directed," to assess "the most effective means of channeling new technologies into promising directions," and to recommend administrative and legislative steps "to promote technological changes in the continued economic growth and improved well-being of our people."

In effect, we are being asked, *What can our society have? How does society decide what it wants? How can it get what it wants?* In short, we are being asked to deal with the quality of American life in the years ahead. This is a task we approach with awareness of the complexity of the problems.

A. The Possibilities Available

In the 20 years since the end of the Second World War, the annual output of the American economy has increased from $212 to $676 billion. (If adjusted for price changes, the real increase, in 1965 dollars, is from $394 to $676.) The important point is that a 3 per cent annual increase in output per man-hour *doubles* the national product in about 24 years, or in little over half of an individual's working lifetime. This dramatic increase provides us with an unprecedented array of choices.

The fruits of our technology and our increasing productivity can be distributed in differing proportions in three ways: They can directly aid the individual by increasing his income, shortening his hours, or improving his worklife; they can be used for communal and social needs to improve the environment, health, and education of the people; and a portion can be used to aid other peoples.

If all the productivity gains in the next 20 years were taken solely in the form of added income, the average per capita earnings would move from its present $3,181 to $5,802, an increase of 82 per cent. In the unlikely event that we choose to use all our gains for more leisure, then, according to Kreps and Spengler, "the workweek could fall to 22 hours by 1985; or it would be necessary to work only 27 weeks of the year; or retirement age could be lowered to 38 years." We might also apply the savings from productivity to improve the nature and conditions of the work environment itself—to reduce monotony, enlarge jobs, encourage variety and rotation; in short, to increase the satisfactions in work.

We can also use the gains of productivity to satisfy unmet community needs by larger public investment (choices that would have to be made communally). New educational technologies can increase the effectiveness of learning. Centralized, computerized diagnostic services are only one example of potential health technologies. Efficient transportation and communication, clean air and water, comfortable housing, attractive and efficient cities can all be had, though not without large cost and not, perhaps, simultaneously and immediately. Through new technological means—machine technologies and intellectual technologies—we can improve the quality of American life.

A third area is our relation—and responsibility—to less advantaged countries. Their problems are vast. Some are threatened directly by famine, if not simply incredibly poor diets. Technology, which is one of the chief means of increasing productivity, can find its greatest applications in these countries. The question of how much aid can be given and how much can be used lies outside the charge of this Commission. However, we do feel that some share of national income and some direct application of our technologies will be committed for the foreseeable future in loans and aid. And this, too, is an option before us.

B. The Matrix of Decisions

There are two questions before us. One is: What proportions of national income and increased productivity should go for what ends? The second is: How adequate are our mechanisms for making such decisions and assessing the consequences?

There is a widely held belief—derived from our experience in military and space technology—that few tasks are beyond our technological capability if we concentrate enough money and manpower upon them. The problems, however, are not wholly congruent. Although we do possess many sophisticated tools, the social, political, and economic institutions which must use these tools have to answer different kinds of questions, for we are not always as agreed upon economic and social values as we may be on defense and space goals. Moreover, our relative affluence and technical sophistication should not lead us to believe that we can attain all our goals at once. Their cost still exceeds our resources. A study by the National Planning Association on the realization of national goals agreed upon by the Commission created by President Eisenhower showed that even with a 4 per cent annual increase in national product we would, in 1975, fall short by $150 billion a year of the possibility of satisfying all those goals at the same time. Thus we will continue to face the need to set priorities and to make choices.

We cannot set forth in this report what the specific priorities should be. We are concerned with *how* we decide what to choose. Congress has asked us: "How can human and community needs be met?" But there is a prior question: "How can they be more readily recognized and agreed upon?"

What concerns us is that we have no such ready means for agreement, that such decisions are often made piecemeal with no relation to each other, that vested interests are often able to obtain unjust shares, and that few mechanisms are available which allow us to see the range of alternatives and thus enable us to choose with a comprehension of the consequences of our choices.

One of the difficulties is that economic goods are of two types: individual goods and social goods. Individual goods are divisible; that is, each person or household buys particular objects and individual services on the basis of free consumer choice. Social goods are not divisible into individual items of possession; they are communal services (e.g., national defense, education, beautification of landscape, flood control, etc.). They are not sold to individual consumers nor adjusted to individual tastes. The nature and amount of the goods must be set by a single decision, applicable jointly to all persons. Social goods, therefore, are subject to communal or political rather than individual demand.

Individuals have their own scale of values against which they assess relative satisfactions against costs and make their purchases accordingly. Public life lacks such intimate measures. We cannot individually buy in the marketplace our share of unpolluted air, even if we are willing to pay the price. The availability of higher education in the marketplace alone would deny many families the possibility of such education, and could also deny society some of the social benefits which a more educated, and therefore more productive, citizenry might create. We lack an effective social calculus to give us true valuation of the entire costs and benefits of individual and social purchases. Thus, there is no mechanism by which we can consider the different combinations of private consumption and public services and decide which may be desirable.

The Commission has no pat solution for improving the decision-making process, but we have three suggestions which we believe worthy of consideration. First, the undertaking of technical research and development on our unmet human and community needs would itself demonstrate the possibilities open to communities and thus lead to action. For example, a research effort which resulted in a new, integrated concept of water supply, desalination, and waste disposal might prompt political action, just as the potential of space and rocketry research resulted in the decision to embark on the man-on-the-moon project. Second, efforts should be made to improve our capability to recognize and evaluate social costs and social benefits more adequately and to supply better information to the public and political leaders on cost-benefit relationships. Third, a majority but not all the members of the Commission suggest that improvement in our decision-making apparatus might be achieved by the encouragement of an appropriate body of high prestige and distinction which would engage in the study of national goals and in the evaluation of our national performance in relation to such goals.[19]

It is to the elaboration of these considerations, technological and social, that we now turn.

APPLYING TECHNOLOGY TO COMMUNITY NEEDS

Our "unmet human and community needs" are vast, even in the wealthiest society the world has ever known. In fact, it has been the expectation of rising standards of living that has lifted our aspirations, broadened our options, and led us to reject things as they once were. It has been estimated, for example, that about 20 per cent of our people live in poverty. But this statistic obscures an important social consideration. It is a definition of poverty by 1964 standards. If we applied 1947 standards, perhaps only 15 per cent of the people would be considered poor today. In the same way we will no longer accept the kinds of housing and urban services that were characteristic of American cities 20 years ago. It is the nature of the

[19] Mr. Sporn wishes to call attention to his comment on p. 293.

American experience to upgrade constantly the notion of what constitutes a decent minimum and, correspondingly, poverty.

In a predominantly private enterprise society, unmet needs tend to be of two kinds: (1) The private needs of low-income people who are unable to buy housing and necessary services; and (2) the public needs of all, which are not readily available in private markets. Some kind of minimum income maintenance has been discussed elsewhere in this report as an answer to the first. We limit ourselves here to the second category.

The list of public needs which have not been adequately met is a long one. While the lists of different persons might vary somewhat, there is a general consensus on a number of "human and community needs." Most of them are related to the growing problems of urbanization: education, health, crime, low-income housing, air and water pollution, mass transportation, and waste disposal—problems arising out of the fact that a preponderant part of our population now lives in cities, and that many cities have been unable to expand the range of necessary services to meet the needs of the new numbers.

Why have not these needs been met? Our conviction, growing out of the spectacular achievements in military technology and our success in the conquest of space, is that the obstacles are not primarily technological. This does not imply that specific technologies are available in each area, although in many cases they are. Just as the concentration of research efforts produced such radically new innovations as intercontinental ballistic missiles and Polaris submarines, concentrations of similar scale on more difficult economic and social problems could contribute to meeting our human and community needs if the political consensus could be implemented.

However, more than a generalized agreement is necessary if these concerns are to be translated into programs. We need criteria to recognize which technologies can give us adequate performance, and we must identify the barriers to change and devise strategies for overcoming them.

We have selected health and the urban environment as among the most important areas where new technologies can make a substantial contribution. Each of these has distinctive problems of its own, yet they are also inextricably linked.

A. Health Needs[20]

During the past few years, the Nation has taken important steps toward improvement of the health of the population. Especially important is the legislation enacted in 1965, including the Medicare program; the Heart Disease, Cancer, and Stroke Amendments; the Clean Air Act Amendments; the Solid Waste Disposal Act; the Water Quality Act; the extension of Hill-Burton programs for improving hospital facilities, equipment, and administration; the continuance of Federal support for expansion of medi-

---

[20] In relation to this section, see James Dickson, M.D., *The Life Sciences, Technology, and Unmet Human and Community Needs* (†). We are also indebted to George Reader, M.D., New York Hospital-Cornell Medical Center, and Michael E. DeBakey, M.D., Baylor University College of Medicine.

cal research projects; provisions for training health manpower; support for local community health protection programs; and the development of health research and information services such as provided by the National Library of Medicine.

However, the medical system of the United States faces critical problems. As a nation, we have been devoting a rising percentage of our GNP to medical care, but the population per physician has remained essentially constant (790 to 780 per physician between 1950 and 1961). Medicare and other legislation will increase the demand for hospital services. There are still vast needs of other groups to be met. Many studies have shown that the socially deprived have poorer health than the rest of society: infant and maternal mortality are greater, life expectancy is less than the norm. The poor, the crowded, and ethnic and racial minorities tend to have the most illness. It is difficult to sort out the many reasons: lack of education, lack of opportunity, lack of access to medical care, inadequate housing and food—all these contribute to an environment conducive to disease, as well as to low income. One of our great lags is in maintaining the health of the people of working age as compared with other countries. The mortality rates for males in the working years in the United States is higher than those in Western Europe. . . .

The tasks that lie ahead include not only the implementation of the programs recently passed, but a broader effort to achieve the following goals: (1) Fuller access to diagnostic and patient care facilities by all groups in the population; (2) broader and bolder use of the computer and other new health technologies; (3) increased spread and use of health statistics, information, and indexes; and (4) new programs for training health manpower.

ACCESSIBILITY OF DIAGNOSTIC AND HEALTH CARE FACILITIES

If we want to make progress in providing the fundamentals of adequate care in the treatment of disease and disability, these questions cannot be avoided: (1) Are there sufficient physicians, nurses, and other health workers? (2) Is adequate care available to all segments of the population? (3) Is there adequate emphasis on prevention of disease and maintenance of health at all ages? (4) Is there a properly staffed health department? (5) In each community, rural as well as urban, are there adequate numbers of hospital and nursing home beds? (6) Is modern equipment available for diagnosis and treatment? (7) Is there a coordinated effort to move patients through the health care process back to active life smoothly, economically, and efficiently? Regretfully, in most communities these questions must still be answered in the negative.

One major barrier to achieving more adequate health care is that there are not enough physicians and other health care personnel. It is possible, however, to develop technologically sophisticated ways of efficiently screening large numbers of people to detect certain abnormalities. An example is the automated multiphasic screen through which hundreds of patients can pass each hour, at a minimal expenditure of professional time. Patients found to have an abnormality can be referred to a planned program of study and followup where nonprofessional personnel under appropriate

269

supervision can further analyze causes of disability. A voluntary medical diagnostic screening system, when further developed through research, has the potential of improving diagnosis of many illnesses and ensuring better use of medical manpower.*

Although computer-aided diagnosis is primarily confined to research efforts at this time, the results give promise of providing a useful operational tool for the physician in the next decade. The computer will not replace the judgment of the physician. In fact, if we rely on medical technology alone medical care would be depersonalized. Rather the computer will be a valuable aid to the physician in arriving at a diagnosis, much like a consultant who suggests one or more tentative diagnoses. More important, in a program of preventive medicine and increasing medical care, the computer in the 1970's should be able to digest facts about the present medical status of individual patients (the majority of whom are healthy) and separate out those cases warranting the further attention of a doctor.

THE SPREAD OF HEALTH TECHNOLOGY

Substantial advances have been made during recent years in the development of new and advanced equipment for health technology. These include new laboratory and X-ray equipment for use in diagnosis, new operating room equipment to facilitate lifesaving surgery, new instruments for improved postoperative care, and electronic computers for use in the day-to-day operation of hospitals.

The use of computer systems promises considerable help both in reducing clerical loads and in aiding diagnoses. Today many hospital nurses spend as much as 40 per cent of their time doing clerical work. Location of terminals at each nursing station and at other locations throughout the hospital connected to a central computer would allow for the rapid processing of admittance, pharmacy orders, laboratory tests, and medical records; this would not only reduce the clerical load of administrative personnel, but also of doctors and nurses. So far, these new technologies are available and in use mainly in large medical centers. The rate at which their adoption spreads will probably remain slow unless programs for promoting their widespread use are put into effect.

More could be done with larger information systems. Regional health computer centers could provide medical record storage for perhaps 12 to 20 million people and give hospitals and doctors in an area access to the computer's diagnostic and other capabilities via telephone line connections. Such regional health computer systems could provide regional data processing for automated clinical laboratories, automation of certain aspects of medical diagnosis, storing and rapid recall of individual health records, and collection and evaluation of important medical statistics. They could help provide better care to everyone regardless of geographic location, reduce unit costs, thereby relieving the economic load on the Nation, and provide for a more efficient use of manpower to alleviate the manpower problem that will be intensified by regional medical programs and Medicare.

Therefore, it would be desirable to undertake research and development

* For comment by Commission members, see p. 277.

to test the feasibility and cost of regional health computer systems. Centers could be integrated with individual hospital information systems and with the National Library of Medicine's system of national medical information retrieval and dispersal (MEDLARS).

INDEXES OF PROGRESS

It is important that we improve our health statistics and provide comprehensive indexes of progress. The most accurate measures we now have of progress in community health are infant and maternal mortality rates. Mortality rates for other age groups and causes of death also provide valuable information. Disease surveys may provide baselines, too, from which progress may be measured from year to year. Systematic and regular applications of these various indexes and accumulation of this information within a national institute would probably allow us to evaluate the progress toward health goals and help establish the relationship between improved medical diagnosis and care and better community health.

NEW PROGRAM FOR MANPOWER

The gap between the technological potential and our ability to apply it effectively is partly due to the lack of a significant improvement in the proportion of physicians to population. We have also not developed the proper manpower training programs for the new technologies. We have continued to hold on to our traditional and basic training programs in the various health and medical fields without analyzing the new technologies available and the real possibility of training new categories of manpower who can perform many of the functions now carried out by highly skilled and scarce professional personnel.

One solution lies in restructuring our training programs in accordance with current scientific and technological developments. The only solution, in the long run, is an increase in the number of trained medical personnel, physicians, nurses, and medical technicians in all categories. For this we need an extensive planned program of government support for the creation of more schools, expansion of enrollments, new methods of instruction, redefinition of how modern knowledge and technology can be most effectively applied, and, as seems likely, training of new categories of health personnel to supplement and complement those already in existence.

B. The Urban Environment

At the turn of the century, well over one-half of all Americans lived in rural areas. Today, nearly three-fourths are urban dwellers. Most of the population increase in the coming decade will take place in the suburbs; for every new person coming into the central city, two or three will be added in the suburbs. The density and social complexity of these and future urban environments defy any historical precedent.

In the past, changes in transporation performance characteristics were the strategic variable in determining the scale of urbanization. The limits to urban growth in the 19th century were set at first by natural waterways and canals, later by railroads and steamships. Since the First World War the automobile and the truck, running on great new ribbon highways, have greatly advanced the pace of urbanization and changed its nature.

271

In the coming decade, cities, suburbs, and metropolitan areas are likely to figure prominently in national policy. As suburbs spread out from central cities, the expansion of dwelling space is merging to form a new social and economic unit—the megalopolis. The 500-mile coastal stretch from southern New Hampshire to northern Virginia makes up a northeast megalopolis whose main outlines are clearly visible. Similar developments are under way around the Great Lakes and on the west coast. Growth of the megalopolis will intensify the need to develop the common use of water, land, recreational resources, and transportation systems for large areas cutting across the boundaries of existing State and local governments.

Spending in these areas is already vast. Total private and public spending for urban facilities in 1962 was estimated at $64 billion. This massive investment in housing, school facilities, shopping centers, and highways is greater in the aggregate than the expenditures for national defense in the same year. However, much of this spending was frequently unrelated to an overall program for meeting the needs of metropolitan areas, and the result has been that the cities still find themselves with congested traffic, polluted air, and drab housing projects.

Interested as we are here in the application of usable technologies, we confine our remarks to transportation, air and water pollution, and housing.

TRANSPORTATION[21]

Our extensive transport facilities have made us a highly mobile people, and our growing mobility has resulted in rapidly changing patterns of population distribution and industrial location. With mobility, however, there have also been problems. Our cities are heavily congested, the trip from home to work is burdensome and time-consuming, the accident toll on the highways is hideously heavy, and the costs of delays in terminal areas are high for all forms of transport.

The potentials of new transportation technology point toward the solution of many of these problems. Yet these possibilities are not being realized, due in large part to unresolved organizational, administrative, and financial difficulties. The problem is aggravated by the failure to look at transport technology as a whole. We have fragmented systems in which rails are separated from trucks, rigid governmental regulation is imposed, and differential subsidies are given to different modes of transport.

New innovations and proposed systems are emerging although resources available for carrying out far-reaching research and development are meager. These new approaches have been developed or proposed with the recognition that the consumer's final choice of transportation is governed by his assessment of the speed, comfort, proximity, safety, privacy, and frequency of alternative services. It seems clear that the recently authorized high-speed ground transportation research and development was long overdue. We believe that similar R. & D. programs closely coordinated should supplement the urban transportation demonstration activity currently being carried out by the Department of Housing and Urban Development.

[21] In relation to this section, see Edward W. Hassell, U.S. Department of Commerce, *The Role of Technological Change in Transportation Policy* (†).

The specific technologies need not concern us here. Our interest is in how to choose among available technologies and how to bring them into application. We recognize that the economic cost factor, in the end, is the decisive one. But for us to have a true picture of the economic costs, none of these technologies can or should be considered in isolation. A wide variety of advanced systems require exploratory and advanced development before their relative merits can be determined. In some cases experimental applications may be necessary to test consumer acceptance and modal preferences. The majority of these systems requires an effort far greater than could be supported by a single sector of our economy or geographic area. This is the rationale for the Federal support of a systems research program directed towards particular multistate regions. We recommend that this competence be broadened to permit the determination of national transportation requirements and the evaluation of alternative proposed programs.

AIR POLLUTION[22]

Pollutants which contaminate our air have increased substantially. The growth of population in urban areas has concentrated the discharge of waste products into a small sector of the atmosphere, thereby intensifying the problem of air pollution. Unless the same technological skills which have given us the many new amenities of modern living are effectively directed toward curbing this ugly byproduct of our technological progress, pollution threatens to exact an ever more exorbitant toll on public health and welfare.

Regretfully, there are no complete technological "cures." While further research will increase their efficiency and reduce their costs, effective technological control measures are not available for many types of air pollutants. Particular contaminants can be removed by devices using filtration, electrostatic precipitation, or centrifugal force. Smoke pollution from domestic, commercial, and industrial incinerators, boilers, and heating systems can be greatly reduced by improved fuels, better stoking and combustion equipment, and education as to proper firing practices. But the only effective answer to air pollution is prevention.

Precise and accurate information on the effect of various pollutants on the environment is meager. This deficiency needs to be remedied if we are to develop wise air pollution control policies and regulations. We therefore urge an enlargement of current research to develop greater knowledge and understanding of the effects of various pollutants on the human, animal, and vegetable ecology upon which to base balanced programs of air pollution control.

Growing public concern has been reflected in various legislative actions. The Congress passed the Clean Air Act of 1963 by substantial bipartisan majorities, and amendments to the act were passed in 1965. The Secretary of Health, Education, and Welfare has issued standards for controlling the discharge of pollutants from gasoline or diesel-powered motor vehicles. There is new activity, too, at the State level: legislatures in more than half

[22] In relation to this section, see Department of Health, Education, and Welfare, Public Health Service, Division of Air Pollution, *Technological Change As It Relates to Air Pollution* (†).

the States are currently considering measures designed to strengthen air pollution control. Although laggard in the past, many States have shown interest in sharing in the new Federal program grants.

By far the most important barrier today to effective control is economic. The enforcement of an air pollution control law costs money; and the installation of remedial measures at the source of pollution costs even more. At all lower governmental levels, air pollution must compete with a host of other problems, from slum clearance to road building, for a share of available funds. Companies, keenly aware of their competitors and of their obligations to stockholders, are understandably reluctant to invest unilaterally large sums for equipment from which, in most cases, no competitive advantages or production gains can be expected. The point, of course, is that industry and consumers are not often called upon to pay for the direct costs they generate. Some way must be found to assign costs of air pollution to the sources of pollutants, whether they be industrial, municipal, or individual.

In the long run, the operation of the economic marketplace must act to reduce air pollution at its source. Since the automobile is one of the major contributors to the problem, the Federal requirement that antipollution devices be installed on all cars produced in the 1968 model year and thereafter is a welcome beginning.

WATER RESOURCES AND WATER POLLUTION[23]

Since our Nation's inception, water has been one of its most abundant and vital resources. Over the years we have made great strides in controlling and directing its course, reducing the national catastrophes caused by floods, and opening up new geographic regions previously undeveloped for lack of water. At the same time, however, we have been unbelievably irresponsible in contaminating our water resources to the point where we are now faced with a problem of limited supply.

Traditionally, we have discharged pollutants into rivers to let them wreak havoc on the natural and human environment and then we have attempted to purify the water again before reusing it downstream. Fortunately, river basins are endowed with a natural cleansing ability for some types of pollutants, and location of water treatment plants has traditionally taken full advantage of this self-purifying capacity.

However, as our population density has increased, the natural cleansing ability of streams has been exceeded. In addition, our technologically advancing industries have discharged new types of pollutants which not only are less susceptible to natural cleansing, but often reduce the stream's ability to cleanse.

Yet existing technologies can provide a solution and already; in some of our river basins, water is being reused several times. Technologically there is no limit on the number of times this process can be repeated. It is still

[23] In relation to this section, see Department of Health, Education, and Welfare, Federal Water Pollution Control Administration, *Water Pollution Control System* (†); and Department of Health, Education, and Welfare, Public Health Service, Division of Environmental Engineering and Food Protection, *Report on the Solid Waste Problem* (†).

possible to return most of our rivers, streams, and lakes to their natural condition. The problem is in part one of decision and authority, although a good deal more needs to be known about the effects of many pollutants.

Water pollution control cannot be accomplished piecemeal, since we must control pollution at all points along the stream if contamination is to be eliminated. One means to check pollution is to ask municipalities and firms responsible for such effects to bear the costs of filtration. The Ruhr, flowing through West Germany's most dense industrial region, is at present less polluted than it was 20 years ago. This happy circumstance is the result of a cooperative arrangement between 259 municipalities and 2,200 industries along the river which have developed a system of effluent fees calculated to encourage the construction of waste disposal systems. In this case, the entire cost of pollution is assigned to the source.

The Federal Government should encourage, and, if necessary, require the establishment of effective river basin authorities at the State or regional level, depending upon geographical location. These agencies should have authority to make and enforce comprehensive plans for an entire basin, regulate the discharge of pollutants from private and public establishments, maintain water treatment facilities, and impose user charges for water treatment facilities upon those who discharge wastes.

HOUSING[24]

The housing industry has been frequently criticized for its technological backwardness. The issue is incredibly complex; for the "blame," such as it is, rests on many: the industry, its unions, its suppliers, the mortgage bankers, and consumers, who seem to prefer styles of housing which do not lend themselves to the most advanced techniques. For those who can afford the housing they prefer, there is little reason for public concern. It is upon those with low incomes that the high cost of housing imposes its burdens.

According to the 1960 Census of Housing, about 6.3 million households with incomes under $4,000 and an additional 2.2 million households with incomes over $4,000 lived in units that needed complete replacement. There are approximately 1.5 million new housing units built each year, but population growth, demolition of old structures, migration to other sections of the country, and other losses account for almost all of this construction. Even if we were to increase construction by over 30 percent, a majority of the 8.5 million substandard units would still be standing by 1970.

If housing needs of moderate-income families are to be met and a high volume of housing production is to be sustained, then what is needed now is a direct attempt to reduce housing costs through exploration of advanced technological potential. Recent years have seen many improvements in building materials, but few in building techniques. The typical construction firm is too small to conduct its own research. While the structure of the industry provides pressure to reduce the costs of doing things the traditional way, there is little pressure for new methods. The use of power equipment

[24] In relation to this section, see Department of Housing and Urban Development, *Technology, Automation, and Economic Progress in Housing and Urban Development* (†).

in site preparation, the hoisting of materials, and improved hand tools have increased efficiency but have made no basic change in methods. Complex patterns of special interests, fragmented local governments, and lethargy perpetuate outmoded building codes which stand in the way of whatever incentives to innovation exist.

It is clear that we cannot adequately rehouse America by existing methods. This can only be done, we believe, if advanced production techniques are introduced and combined with adequate community planning which fits the single-family house, the multiple units, and the high-rise apartments into an integrated and esthetic design. Advanced production techniques need not, as some fear, promote monotony or drabness. For example, mass-produced modular units could be turned out in different colors and textures and put together in a great many different ways to create a pleasing variety of modes and designs. Careful site planning could assure privacy and individual variation. We have, we feel, the possibility of creating a human environment which would enhance beauty and pleasure. The architectural imagination and the technical capabilities are present. What is needed is a leadership which would remove organizational barriers. The Federal Government, acting with those private industries and entrepreneurs who can revolutionize the patterns of production, has an opportunity to provide that leadership in several ways:

1. As it has in agriculture, the Federal Government should actively stimulate research in housing and community development through research grants and through its own building activities. It should also support basic research to establish performance criteria (e.g., moisture resistance, insulation, lighting, etc.) for housing and housing components.

2. Where advanced production techniques require large markets (for tooling, etc.), the Government can provide incentive for private industry research by offering initial markets in federally supported public housing for the most promising innovations. These could serve as demonstrations of new possibilities. In the construction of new buildings and houses, for example, the Federal Government could adopt the approach used by the several California school districts which are part of the School Construction Systems Development Program. By taking bids on 22 schools at a time, a large enough market was created through this program to induce manufacturers to make new products and designs to meet the schools' specifications; thus, building designs (e.g., structural systems, lighting-ceilings, air conditioning) were not limited by existing equipment and processes. The Federal Government has a variety of opportunities to stimulate and demonstrate the creative use of new technology.

3. The Federal Government can take the lead in modernizing local building codes and removing obstacles to new technologies. The research and development of new materials and methods of residential construction cannot be adapted to mass production so long as there are thousands of different local building codes in the United States. Even in a single metropolitan area, there may often be 50 or more local building codes. A substantial proportion of all construction, including housing, is either federally financed

or insured. The Federal Government should, in consultation with the States and the contruction industry and building trades unions, develop an acceptable model code. It should then give financial aid, insure building loans, or build its own facilities only in those localities which modernize their building codes in line with the model national code. In this way, Government action could break down one of the most important obstructions to action.

4. The creation of mass production housing and the undertaking of large-scale urban reconstruction will create a new industry and many new jobs. Increased demand for community facilities and other construction associated with higher demand for housing made possible by technologically induced cost reductions will add to rather than diminish demand for conventional construction skills. In the event that new techniques introduced cause certain crafts to suffer, it may be necessary to explore the costs of a federally subsidized system of retraining, severance pay, and retirement costs for technologically displaced building trades workers.

Comment noted on p. 270 by Mr. Sporn, joined by Mr. Haggerty

I agree with the first sentence of this paragraph. The logical conclusion to be drawn is that there is a need to develop programs for training adequate numbers of physicians and other health care personnel. But the suggestions drawn in the following four sentences are so technically premature that I cannot join the Commission in taking the position indicated.

TECHNOLOGY AND THE WORK ENVIRONMENT

Despite the contributions of technology to higher standards of living, we have not yet found ideal solutions to the monotony and drudgery of some work processes. No one disputes that to the greatest possible extent work should be pleasurable and meaningful; the question is how to achieve this goal. Among the necessary preconditions are sufficient affluence to permit experimentation and an understanding that all human beings do not react in the same way to identical work situations. Beyond that, however, must come the realization that machines can now be designed to serve the needs of those who operate them and that in this creative synthesis of human and purely productive needs we can achieve not only more efficient production but also more satisfactory personal development. Acceptance of these values, far from inhibiting new developments and increased production, will tend to free our society from the limiting concept that efficient production can only be equated with maximum detailed breakdown of work elements. Today it is possible to view jobs as broad entities in which the human personality may be considered just as vital a component as the nonhuman mechanism.

The task of introducing this new approach requires extensive preparation. It cannot be accomplished by men accustomed to dealing with these problems in traditional ways. We must look to our universities and engineering schools as well as to industry to train a new generation of men who view the processes of production and employment as an integrated whole, with men and machines interacting with each other.

277

A. Humanizing the Environment Work[25]

We do not propose any plan or blueprint for the "humanizing" of work. No single design is possible. We do seek to call attention to the kinds of changes necessary if the values of technology are to be realized within the productive process as well as in its products. Work becomes more meaningful when people can relate to a total process or product and understand their own work in the scheme of the whole. Some are happier on a job when they have opportunities to interact, to mingle and talk to each other; others may prefer to work alone. Within productive limits, workers should have some share in determining work methods in planning of changes, particularly technological ones, which affect their jobs.

Much of this can be justified in simple dollars-and-cents terms: industry has found that considerable savings have often been realized when job design has been reorganized to take into account the needs of the men on the job. But even when the reorganization of the work process may itself increase costs, it is the recognition of the human needs which are important. And if productivity in the past has been oriented to the increase in the amounts of goods, some of its savings in the future can be utilized to bring a greater satisfaction in work for the individual.*

B. The Flexible Lifespan of Work

In the coming "postindustrial society," a man may have to go through two or three work cycles of retraining or of new careers because of the continuing needs for new skills to keep abreast of new technologies and new intellectual techniques. Education for change has become a new watchword, almost a new cliché of the time.

The saving grace of American society has been its adjustability, fluidity, flexibility, and responsiveness to change. An educational system providing free education through the high school years has produced a skilled and literate labor force which has allowed industry to introduce new and complicated techniques with speed and facility. We believe that the opportunities should be extended, where possible, throughout the worklife of all Americans, both to upgrade skills and to allow for a changeover of careers and work patterns. To this end, we would specify two objectives:

1. *A flexible worklife.* The possibility should be explored of a system whereby individuals could continue their education by allowing them to "charge off" or earn tax credits for that education which is necessary for the development of new skills.** Where industry is forced to lay off individuals temporarily, firms should be encouraged to use these "intermissions" as training and study periods; the costs of providing schooling could be met by government grants or tax credits or by arrangements with government services such as manpower retraining. Pension plans and similar measures

---

[25] In relation to this section, see Charles R. Walker, *Changing Character of Human Work Under the Impact of Technological Change* (†).

* For comment by Commission members, see p. 280.
** For comments by several Commission members, see p. 280.

278

that root employees to a firm should be made more flexible through shorter vesting periods or pooled funds to allow people to move more freely when they want to. In short, adaptability to the technological society is one of the great needs in coming decades, and it should be the effort of government, industry, and labor to adopt measures which can help achieve that objective.

2. *Flexible retirement*. The idea of a fixed retirement age makes little sense in a society so diverse in its work and skills. In certain occupations, notably the intellectual ones, age and its experience is a resource that should not be wasted; in those industries involving heavy-duty work, an age balance weighted toward the older side may be a constant drag on productivity. We need to establish flexibility in the patterns of retirement as in education.

There is no single blueprint. In some industries early retirement is being and should be encouraged. In others arrangements should be made, perhaps, for a combination of part-time work and supplementary pay schemes (drawn from unemployment insurance funds) to allow a man to "phase out" his retirement.

The conception that a man after 65 should be completely out of the labor market may in itself be a disservice to vigorous individuals who want and need to work. These are matters of company policy and collective bargaining. But in this light, and assuming a firm national commitment to full employment, Social Security restrictions on earnings after 65 should be reviewed with an eye to allowing more part-time employment.

C. A Single Standard of Pay

The industrial revolution, despite sometime pious disavowals, did turn labor into a "commodity," no more so than by instituting the practice of paying production workers by the piece or by the hour (and sometimes, even as today, by the *tenth* of an hour worked). At the same time, white-collar workers and other technical and administrative personnel are paid by the week, the month, or the year. Thus an old status distinction and social stigma is still being reinforced.

Whatever the initial logic, the time may be near to end an invidious distinction which has denied workers a sense of full participation in the social enterprise. What once may have been difficult is today more manageable. In the emerging economy, the majority of workers are in service and white-collar jobs, and the relative number of blue-collar workers is declining. In the changing nature of work, it is more and more difficult to measure the contribution of the single worker in the productive process, and the concept of "the piece" or "the hour" loses meaning where work is a team affair and production processes are continuous.

The established differences in the treatment of the two groups have adversely influenced the willingness of many wage earners to approach the idea of change with an open mind. The proposal to put all workers on a weekly or monthly salary—with its implications of greater continuity of employment, closer equalization of fringe benefits, and abolition of divisive class distinctions within the enterprise—is worthy of the most careful consideration by employers and unions. Among other things, such a step would tend to break down barriers between present groups of salary and wage earners on issues of mutual concern and make possible a more fruitful collaboration.

We believe, therefore, that industry and unions should begin to discuss the question of paying all workers by the same standard, and of extending to blue-collar employees the usual prerogatives (sick time, jury duty, funeral leave) which most salaried employees enjoy today.

We recognize the many difficulties standing in the way of such an effort. For purposes of overtime and cost measurement, firms often have to keep records of hours worked. But this is true of salaried employees as well who, though often subject to the same accounting, are paid by the week or the month rather than by exact hours worked. We see little justice in a system whereby a production worker is laid off or works "short weeks" when the schedule so dictates, while officeworkers and clerks receive full salaries, whatever the flow of work.

These issues fall into the difficult realm of values which cannot be imposed by fiat. The effort to realize them has to be made with due regard for the differences and variabilities of industries and the manifold administrative and economic problems which such charges would entail. An effort to impose a total blueprint disregarding the complexities would be disastrous. Such a recognition of difficulty should not prevent us from beginning and assessing the results. These ideas and efforts are not new. Steps towards humanizing work, increasing flexibility of worklife, and creating a single standard of pay have been made by dozens of large and progressive American corporations. We propose that such steps, already taken, be extended, and that these objectives, pioneered by a few, become stated declarations of public policy.

To say that these are matters of public policy does not mean that they are, therefore, matters for legislative or governmental action (although in some instances legislative policy may stand in the way of certain actions). The reorganization of work and the single standard of pay are questions which devolve on industry and labor, and are a legitimate instance for collective bargaining. All such improvements require a give-and-take on both sides.

To declare these matters of public policy is, however, to declare them matters of community conscience, requiring us to set up public standards by which we can judge ourselves. There is another and larger implication. For if such a step is taken, it would demonstrate to all other countries that the American way can give a new meaning and substance to that ancient phrase, "the dignity of work." It would indeed be a landmark in the history of work and of civilized society.

Comment noted on p. 278 by Mr. Haggerty, joined by Mr. Sporn

Any effort to improve the work environment at the expense of overall productivity is unsound because, in effect, the institution is deliberately choosing to be less competitive. I doubt the wisdom and the probability of success of such efforts.

Our private enterprise industrial institutions not only are, overall, the most effective in the world, but also provide the best work environment. This is not to deny either the need or the opportunity for improvement in both the level of effectiveness and quality of work environment which exists.

I am in no way pessimistic about our ability to continue to improve the work environment. In fact, I believe the greatest opportunity for improvement in effectiveness for any institution lies in improving the work environment in the most direct and meaningful way possible—by increasing use of the new relatively untapped imaginations and energies of all the men and women who make it up. We in the United States have done a better job of organizing work than has been done anywhere else in the world, but we still use the abilities of most individuals in only a very limited way, and our industrial institutions are still far from having achieved a theoretical maximum. I believe we are more than an order of magnitude, probably many orders of magnitude, away from the level of effectiveness which we can achieve. We will continue to gain in effectiveness as we improve our knowledge and use of technology, and especially as we learn to improve the management of our industrial organizations so as to equate more nearly the personal goals of each of the men and women who make up an organization with the goals of the organization itself.

Comment noted on p. 278 by Mr. Sporn, joined by
Mr. Beirne, Mr. Haggerty, Mr. Hayes, and Mr. Reuther

The implications of this tax proposal need much more clarification and analysis. It would appear to offer benefits inversely related to need, with those in the lowest income brackets and in greatest need receiving little or no benefit.

Improving Public Decision Making

Given our technological capability and our relatively abundant resources, why have we not been more successful in meeting our human and community needs?

The market, when it is free, provides a basic mechanism for consumers to determine what is to be produced. Legislative decisions on public spending in response to national or local needs provide for communal services. We do not question the validity of these economic and political mechanisms in allowing for the greatest variety of free choice for the consumer and democratic participation by the voters. We feel, however, that in the "accounting systems" which guide such choices there are various inadequacies, that local governmental units are not drawn along the functional lines necessary to meet modern needs, and that decisions are made piecemeal, often without regard to context or to the effect on other decisions. This is why, so often, there are unintended consequences of social actions.

In an effort to improve the means of public decision making, we propose that the Government explore the creation of a "system of social accounts" which would indicate the social benefits and social costs of investment and services and thus reflect the true costs of a product. We argue that the present system of local government is too fragmented to meet pressing

281

urban needs, and that some form of comprehensive government reorganization along metropolitan or regional lines is necessary lest control of local government pass by default into Federal control. We believe that a new intellectual technique, that of systems analysis, can provide a new approach to meet government planning needs. And finally we propose that the Federal Government encourage by demonstration grants and by its own procurement policy socially desirable technological innovations.

A. A System of Social Accounts

We have learned in recent years how to chart economic growth and identify the kinds of policies which may be necessary to stimulate growth. We have begun to perfect an economic reporting system and to establish economic indicators that measure national performance. But we do not have, as yet, a continuous charting of social changes, and we have been ill-prepared (in such matters as housing, education, or the status of the Negro) to determine our needs, establish goals, and measure our performance. Lacking any systematic assessment, we have few criteria which allow us to test the effectiveness of present policies or weigh alternatives regarding future programs.

The development of national economic accounting provides us with an instructive picture of the workings of a modern economy. It allows us to create economic models for such policy planning as national income and employment forecasting, regional industrial forecasting, water use and transportation planning, and urban land use forecasting and planning. The impetus to this accounting grew out of the depression experience. The needs of the 1930's led to the Government's collection of national income data, and thus facilitated macroeconomic analysis on an aggregate, national basis. In effect, the government's decision about the type of data to be collected shaped in considerable measure the subsequent direction of economic theory and practice.

But two problems arise if the economic accounts are to be used to assess social policy. One is the limitations of gross national product as a measuring instrument. GNP measures only market transactions. Services performed within a household are not "valued." Neither are those performed in government, since it, too, is not part of the market. GNP does not adequately reflect improvements in products, the introduction of new products, or the side effects in the form of social costs or benefits. If a new product replaces an older one but the price remains the same, there will be no increase in *measured* GNP. Moreover, the sense of progress can be exaggerated by the "additive" nature of GNP accounting. Thus, when a factory is built, the new construction and the new payrolls are an addition to GNP. If, at the same time, the factory pollutes a stream and builds a filtration plant to divert the wastes, these expenditures, too, become an addition to GNP. In the financial sense, more money has been spent in the economy. But the gross addition simply masks an "offset cost," not a contribution to economic progress.

The second problem is that while the economic data are highly relevant to the formation of economic policy, they are less applicable to recent problems of social change. National economic and census statistics, aggregated as they are, tell us little about pockets of poverty, depressed communities, sick industries, or disadvantaged social groups. National data, averaged out, provide few clues or little information relevant to regional or local problems. In the integration crises and antipoverty programs of the 1960's, the Federal Government found itself lacking the necessary information for making effective policy decisions in response to these new social problems. The need for this kind of data is urgent. And just as the development of economic accounts influenced a new body of theory, the collection of new social data could influence decisively the development of social science for the next generation.

What would a system of social accounts allow us to do? The word "accounts" is perhaps a misnomer. Sociologists have been able to establish few completely consistent sets of relationships (such as, say, between unemployment and delinquency), and even where such relationships can be established, it is difficult to state these in measurable terms. Yet the need to make these explorations is necessary.

A system of social accounts, if it could be established, would give us a broader and more balanced reckoning of the meaning of social and economic progress and would move us toward measurement of the utilization of human resources in our society in four areas:

1. The measurement of social costs and net returns of economic innovations;
2. The measurement of social ills (e.g., crime, family disruption);
3. The creation of "performance budgets" in areas of defined social needs (e.g., housing, education);
4. Indicators of economic opportunity and social mobility.

Eventually, this might provide a "balance sheet" which could be useful in clarifying policy choices. It would allow us to record not only the gains of economic and social change but the costs as well, and to see how these costs are distributed and borne.

The following elaboration is meant to be illustrative rather than prescriptive, to suggest the range of problems and the scope of application.

SOCIAL COSTS AND NET RETURN

Technological advances create new investment opportunities which are expected to be paid for out of the enhanced earnings they produce. But clearly there are losses as well: e.g., the displacement created by technological change, particularly where the advanced age of the workers or the particular skill displaced make it difficult to find employment at a previous wage. Or, a new plant in an area may create new employment opportunities, yet its byproducts—water pollution and air pollution—may create additional costs for the community. Thus, there is often a divergence between the private cost borne by an entrepreneur and the social cost of production. Such items as maintenance of the unemployed, provisions for the victims of industrial accidents or occupational diseases, and costs of access roads are borne in part by the employer and by the community as "social overhead costs."

283

National economic accounting does not directly assign the costs generated by one group which are borne by others (e.g., the costs to the community of strip mining which gouges out a countryside). Social accounting would permit us to make such assessments, and, where possible, against the firms responsible. On the other hand, certain costs of technological innovation—e.g., severance pay or maintenance of workers on a firm's payroll—may be so large as to inhibit the introduction of useful technological devices. Thus such costs might be borne better by the community than by a firm itself.

These are questions of public policy. But they can only be decided when we have a clearer picture of the actual social costs and returns. The problem is not only one of social costs unfairly generated and widely borne, but the broader cost matrix which would allow us to balance gains against costs.

THE MEASUREMENT OF SOCIAL ILLS

Every society pays a huge price for crime, juvenile delinquency, and disruption of the family. There are no simple causes of such social ills such as unemployment. Yet such ills and social tensions have measurable effects on the economy, from the loss of able-bodied workers because of mental illness to direct losses of property from thefts and riots. Although data on crime, health, dependent children, and the like are collected by Federal agencies, there is rarely any effort to link these problems to underlying conditions, nor is there a full measure of the cost of these ills. Systematic analysis of such data might suggest possible courses of remedial action.

PERFORMANCE BUDGETS

The American commitment is not only to raise the standard of living, but to improve the quality of life. But we have too few yardsticks to tell us how we are doing. A system of social accounts would seek to set up "performance budgets" in various areas to serve as such yardsticks. A series of community health indexes would tell us how well we are meeting the needs of our people in regard to adequate medical care. A national "housing budget" would reflect our standing in regard to the goal of a "decent home for every American family." It would also enable us to locate by city and region the areas of greatest needs and so provide the basis for effective public policy.

INDICATORS OF ECONOMIC OPPORTUNITY AND SOCIAL MOBILITY

More than 25 years ago, Gunnar Myrdal, in *An American Dilemma*, wrote: "We should . . . have liked to present in our study a general index, year by year or at least decade by decade, as a quantitative expression of the movement of the entire system we are studying: the status of the Negro in America. . . . But the work of constructing and analyzing a general index of Negro status in America amounts to a major investigation in itself, and we must leave the matter as a proposal for later research."

Almost three decades later, we still have no "general index" of the status of the Negro in America. In a strict methodological sense, no comprehensive indexes are possible, perhaps, but specific indicators can be assembled. Thus, where once it seemed impossible to conceive of a "value" figure for "human assets," the creation of recent years of a "lifetime-earning-power index" gives us a measure to reflect the improvements in income which come with increased education, improvement in health, and reduction of discrimination. Data on social mobility can measure the extension of equality of opportunity and identify the barriers (e.g., inadequate school opportunities) to that equality. Economists have a term "opportunity costs" which allows us to calculate not only direct costs, but the gains foregone from the use of those resources if they had been employed elsewhere. "Social opportunity costs" may allow us to reckon the possible gains in the utilization of unused human resources, and to weigh, in terms of social costs and social benefits, alternative social policies.

Many sources for the kind of data necessary for social accounting exist in government today. Other data (such as indicators of economic and social mobility and performance budgets), while available in fragmentary form in social agencies and university research groups, would have to be organized as regular time-series within the Government. But though a system of social accounts involves data gathering, the problem is primarily one of interpretation and synthesis. It can, therefore, be best combined with an existing economic data-gathering and interpretation body. For that reason we recommend that the Council of Economic Advisers take over the task of seeking to develop a system of social accounts.

B. The Fragmented Nature of Our Government Structure

The proliferation of government, especially at the local level, has created serious problems in the coordination of public programs, in reducing public accountability, in making decisions affecting multiunit areas, and in contributing to wide disparities between available financial resources and community and human needs. The problem is indeed complex. In 1962, the San Diego metropolitan area had 11 municipalities; the Phoenix area, 17; the Houston area, 25; the Cleveland area, 75; the St. Louis area, 163; the Chicago area, 246; and the New York metropolitan region, 1,400 local governments. Small villages, school districts, towns, counties, and even States have lost much of their original relevancy as operative entities.

One consequence of this multiplicity of governments is the continuous deterioration of services in our major cities. The list of problems is usually long—their severity varying with the particular area—and includes air and water pollution, inadequate mass transportation, insufficient recreation areas and open spaces, inadequate waste disposal systems, water supply problems, growing slums, and increasing ugliness. The citizenry is aroused to action only when a critical condition develops—unbearable smog, serious commuting problems, water crises, etc.—and then ad hoc measures are invoked; but these only postpone a future reckoning.

The need is to define problems in functional terms. It has been argued that local governments should be reorganized so that areawide functions are handled by areawide units (metropolitan districts, counties, interarea compacts), while local functions would be maintained by local bodies. Such steps, while necessary, may still be inadequate because of the disparate tax powers of different units and the inadequate tax base of most local governmental units.

The continuous growth and emergence of community and human needs will undoubtedly create greater pressure for governmental reorganization.

The failures of local authority have already been indicated by the absorption of local decision-making powers by State and national bodies. Continued local inaction can only result in the greater concentration of power over local decisions in the hands of Federal and State officials. If this situation is to be avoided, local leaders must take the initiative in experimenting with new ideas and patterns of government for meeting their needs.

C. Systems Approach[26]

The technological advances which may be possible in the future will come not only from machines, but from what has been called the "intellectual technology"—the application of new computer-using intellectual techniques (systems analysis, simulation, and operations research)—which not only gives us greater precision in specifying the relevant variables of a problem, but also enables us to recast our way of looking at them. Much of this, as it applies to social and economic actions, has been called the systems approach.

The systems approach has been applied previously in the development of military projects and space systems. It appears to be applicable to social problems, since these, like large-scale space and weapons projects, are complex, require a multidisciplinary approach, and involve the organization of technological or quantitative factors.

The approach has two main features. First, objectives are stated clearly in performance terms rather than in particular technologies or preexisting models. Thus, we would want to define a transportation problem in overall terms of the different numbers of passengers and the different amounts of freight that have to be moved varying distances over different time periods, rather than, how do we seek to rescue a "sick" railroad, etc. In such systems analysis one seeks, then, the best "mix"—of cars, trucks, trains, airplanes—in order to find the most efficient combination. The advantage of specifying objectives in systems terms is that it forces decision makers to so delineate the factors that a rational comparison of alternative solutions is possible.

The second feature of the systems approach is its emphasis upon the interrelations within a system. The usual approach has been to divide a problem into more manageable subproblems. We divide a city's traffic problem from its housing, school location, and industry location problems. Yet clearly the change in traffic flows and densities will affect residential patterns and industry concentration. Since any one problem is so directly linked with others, it has to be viewed in its entirety. In short, what a systems approach implies is comprehensive planning so that we can trace out

[26] In relation to this section, see Abt Associates, *Report of a Survey of the State of the Art: Social, Political, and Economic Models and Simulations* (†); Ronald P. Black and Charles W. Foreman, *Transferability of Research and Development Skills in the Aerospace Industry* (†); State of California, Department of Finance, *The Four Aerospace Contracts: A Review of the California Experience* (†); Richard D. Duke, *Urban Planning and Metropolitan Development, The Role of Technology* (†); and Interagency Task Group on Technological Forecasting in the Federal Government, *The Uses of Systems Analysis in Manpower Adjustment* (†).

the effects, progressive and regressive, of any set of choices and decisions upon all other relevant decisions.

The systems approach is neither radical nor new. What is new are the dimensions of the problems and the possibilities, because of refinements in technique, to apply this approach to situations never before thought solvable in these terms. Over the past few years, the Department of Defense has used the systems approach most effectively. "Program-budgeting," a systems approach to the functional grouping of tasks developed by the Rand Corporation, has been applied by Secretary McNamara to the reorganization of defense forces. Tools such as operations research, cost-benefit analysis, statistical decision theory, and simulation are now part of the intellectual armory of planners. In August 1965, President Johnson ordered the Bureau of the Budget to install this new approach to resource management into all cabinet-level agencies of Government. These efforts are exemplary, but it seems highly unlikely that a sufficient number of analysts combining both technical knowledge of the problem at hand and a thorough understanding of strengths and weaknesses of analytical techniques will be available for some time to come.

There is a strong need for the development of systems analysis capabilities in individual branches of the Government and in the Congress. Beyond this there is the broader question of how these different intellectual resources, which are being employed primarily to deal with the programs of the agencies, can be coordinated and used for the analysis of the various social problems that confront us.

One of the most useful applications of a systems approach would be in urban resource allocation and operations management, where a coordinated approach is necessary if urban life is to be viable. In the last few years, a number of such efforts, beginning with the creation of metropolitan and regional models and simulating a set of alternative changes, have begun to show the value of this approach.

In the 89th Congress, bills have been introduced into the Senate and the House which would authorize the Government to make research grants to States and universities for the application of systems analysis and systems engineering in the areas of community needs. While we cannot necessarily pass upon the specific bills themselves, we do believe that new programs may be required to bring systems analysis to bear on the problems and needs of the community.

D. Federal Promotion of Research and Experimentation[27]

One of the important ways in which decision making could be improved would be to increase Federal Government support for experiments in the application of technology to social problems.

The Federal demonstration grant may prove to be a useful means of stimulating research in a number of fields, for example, the testing of consumer responses to new modes of high-speed railroad transportation in the

[27] In relation to this section, see James Alcott, *The Social Consequences of Technology, A Report on the Engineering Foundation Research Conference, July 26–30, 1965* (†).

northeast corridor. A comprehensive program of demonstration grants could be effective in stimulating the tryout of new ideas in city planning and community organization. One can envisage an experiment where a single large community might be designed from "scratch" by urban planners, economists, and engineers; much as New Haven has done, some large community might invite the cooperation of a team of operations analysts operating under a Federal demonstration grant to work out a set of proposals for the community's problems. These grants could serve as test or pilot models which would ultimately find their way into official policy and practice when they proved useful and workable.

A second type of experiment would be to utilize the vast purchasing power of the Federal Government to set up new standards and promote technological innovations. In fiscal year 1964, the Federal Government purchased directly $34 billion of goods and services, of which $26 billion was spent by the Department of Defense. Almost 15 per cent of the total volume of all building and construction in the United States was accounted for by Federal procurement. In such products as fuels and lubricants, construction equipment, and photographic services, the Federal Government accounts for between 7 to 9 per cent of the total sales of these items in the United States.

In this respect, the Federal Government could be a major innovator if the existing practices of Federal agencies in a position to use their purchasing power were modified. It would obviously not be realistic to impose a complete change in Federal procurement policy, but the possibility of setting up some experimental design should be explored.

In modifying Federal purchasing practice, primary emphasis should be placed on performance criteria rather than product specification alone for items or services to be purchased. By emphasizing only "product specification," Federal procurement policy often limits the number of bidders and suppliers to a specific item; by calling for "performance criteria," the Government would specify the general end result without limiting the design to preexisting products.

By emphasizing "performance criteria," the Federal Government could encourage industry to innovate; it could encourage cost reduction; it could serve as a "pilot customer" by creating new markets with sufficient volume to encourage industry to free itself from local restrictions (e.g., building codes); it could set industry standards which would enable all firms within an industry to incorporate new features in their designs.[28]

[28] If the Federal Government adopts this approach, the ability of procurement divisions to frame specifications in performance language will need to be strengthened by a staff of technological experts which would aid purchasing agents. The staff need not (and often should not) be a part of the specifying agency. An interagency pool could be created which would serve all Government departments. Technical competence already exists in the National Bureau of Standards, the Atomic Energy Commission, and the NASA laboratories.

The Department of Defense and NASA, in much of their contracting, use specifications to achieve performance criteria. While a product is often specified, the details are not spelled out, and the emphasis is on the statement of performance. In fact, in most Federal procurement dependent on advanced technologies where the state of the art is still fluid, constantly improved performance is called for.

The adoption of minimum safety standards on automobiles is a timely example of Government procurement power. In 1965 the Congress directed the General Services Administration to set up safety standards for automobiles purchased by the Government as a means of inducing manufacturers to incorporate such features in all automobiles. Federal procurement requirements provided an opportunity for the entire industry to act.

Finally we propose the provision of Federal funds to universities and other organizations for the improvement of research techniques and their experimental application to urban problems. In our history we have had two spectacular examples of such help, and with magnificent results. In the field of agriculture, the creation of the land-grant colleges under the Morrill Act established a pattern of research and, through extension services, help to farmers, which have largely been responsible for our extraordinary advances in agricultural productivity. In the physical sciences, the maintenance of Government-supported materials research centers and a large number of federally financed interdisciplinary programs have been major resources not only for the advances in scientific knowledge but, equally, in the strengthening of national security itself. We propose that the Government experiment with the formation of university institutes or interdisciplinary programs, adequately financed and fully integrated with the educational function of the university, which would serve as laboratories for urban problem analysis and resources for local communities that would want to use their advice and services.*

E. The Generation and Transfer of Technology[29]

The evidence is overwhelming that technology stimulates the rate and volume of economic growth, and that the infusion of new technology can speed the rate of economic growth. It is evident that increases in GNP are related to expenditures for research and development. R. & D. expenditures are still rising rapidly. In 1965, a total of about $21 billion will be devoted to R. & D., about $15 billion of which will be spent or supplied by the Federal Government. The way in which R. & D. is spent is important both for the pace of technological advance and for the determination of the areas where technology will—and can—be applied.

Four questions of policy arise in relation to R. & D. expenditures and the uses of technology for economic growth and social needs:

1. Is there some "optimal limit" to the amount of R. & D. expenditures, based on our ability to develop enough well-trained research manpower, to use these expenditures well?
2. Are there significant "imbalances" in the present pattern of R. & D. expenditures, particularly by the Federal Government?
3. What can be done to stimulate the greater use of R. & D. by lagging industries?
4. What kind of Federal policy is necessary for the dissemination of

* For comment by a Commission member, see p. 293.

[29] In relation to this section, see Richard L. Lesher and George J. Howick, *Background, Guidelines, and Recommendations for Use in Assessing Effective Means of Channeling New Technologies in Promising Directions* (†).

technological knowledge to potential users—problems ranging from the organization of comprehensive information retrieval systems to the direct assistance of communities, small business, and other industries in gaining access to publicly available technological knowledge?

A determination of an optimum research and development expenditure is a most difficult question. Private industry has a basic market test of its ability to devote some portion of its capital investment for research and development; at some point R. & D. has to "pay off" or the company cuts its expenditure in a specific area. What the limit of Federal expenditures should be, however, is difficult because we have no test of the potentialities of R. & D. In some areas (e.g., defense or basic research) one may want to encourage experimentation, even where there is no immediate possibility of payoff (either in profitabilty or in new knowledge) because of the intrinsic worthwhileness of such experiments. It has been suggested that precise figures should be gathered which show the annual employment of scientific manpower and dollars in relation to the putative national goals they serve. Such a report might provide the framework for a more detailed consideration of the kinds of Government expenditures on R. & D.

The question of imbalances in existing spending is one which involves political judgments. Over half the Federal budget is devoted to defense and it is, therefore, not surprising that the largest part of Federal R. & D. funds are in support of defense objectives. But we also feel that other areas—principally housing, transportation, and urban development—have been neglected in federally supported R. & D. efforts, and considerably more has to be done in these fields.

It has been argued that some industries have lagged technologically because of the disproportions in R. & D. spending or the failure to apply in other areas technologies developed for one area. The concentration of research and development in a few industries is not, per se, evidence of misallocation. Technological opportunities are greater in some fields than in others, and uneven distribution of R. & D. does not itself indicate inefficient resource allocation within industry. Nor is there evidence that increased R. & D. would necessarily stimulate change in all industries.

The relevant question is whether it is possible to help potential users who are unable for a while to help themselves. Government support of research and development in agriculture and aviation has reaped rich economic rewards. In areas where market criteria cannot generate sufficient incentives for adequate research and development—such as weather forecasting, public health, education—the Federal Government has a recognized responsibility. And where R. & D. benefits are insufficiently realized through private capabilities, it is the task of public policy to provide incentives. The responsibility is not necessarily that of doing research or even financing it, but of providing incentives for getting it done.

The transfer of technologies developed in Federal laboratories and agencies for industrial and consumer use requires a more forthright and unified Government policy than exists at present. Technology transfer—

using new technology for purposes other than the specific ones for which it was developed—is not given much attention in many Government agencies. Locating the technology and identifying new and different uses require the assignment of competent persons within the agencies for such tasks and the cooperation of the many different scientific and technical missions.[30] Until this task is given a higher priority, there will be gaps in the collection of important technological information.

The other side of the coin is the reporting and dissemination of such information to potential users. There, too, a national policy is necessary. The Government can engage in a variety of activities, from the simple publication of documents (placing the burden of discovery on the potential user) to such more active roles as centralizing all bibliographical citations in an information retrieval system, the creation of technical consulting services (available, for example, to small businesses), or the use of governmental facilities by nonprofit institutions for the adaptation of new technologies for commercial purposes.

Given the range of possible activities, we cannot within our limited purview define the exact limits of governmental involvement. Certainly, it would seem that the Federal Government has a legitimate role developing weather satellites and medical research equipment. But we cannot say that it is an obligation of Government to assist all claimants or engage in partnership with profit or nonprofit organizations to develop all new technologies or devices originated by Government for civilian use. These are questions to be decided on the broader base of national goals. As a minimum we do feel that the Government has a responsibility for making available for nongovernmental utilization the results of Government-performed research and other research that was substantially funded by the Government. The issue, in the future, will be a vexing one, and more detailed study is needed.

F. Conclusion: The Attainment of National Goals

Ours, like most modern societies, is becoming "future-oriented." We have become increasingly aware of the multiple impacts of social change—

[30] Some pioneering efforts are under way. The Department of Commerce, through its Institute for Applied Technology, has established the Clearinghouse for Federal Scientific and Technical Information. Its ultimate mission is to provide a central source to any user for all unclassified Government scientific and technical information. The Committee on Scientific and Technical Information (COSATI) under the Federal Council for Science and Technology has established subpanels which are studying operational techniques and systems, information science technology, education and training, international information activities, information generation, information users, and nongovernmental information relationships. Individual agencies are also increasing their attention to this subject. The Science Information Exchange has elicited the cooperation of most segments of the Government community sponsoring and conducting research in the life sciences. NASA has deployed technology utilization offices in its various installations to seek out important research and development results. NASA has also placed legal responsibility on its contractors to report the new technology resulting from work done under NASA support. The Atomic Energy Commission has encouraged its scientists and engineers to report civilian applications of nuclear technology they generate. Finally, the State Technical Services Act will improve the flow of information to small and medium sized businesses.

of which automation, one of the concerns of this Commission, is a prime example—and in so doing, we realize that we have to plan ahead. We have to anticipate social change. We need to assess its consequences. We have to decide what policies are necessary to facilitate—or inhibit—possible changes.

There are, broadly speaking, two kinds of social change. One derives from the aggregate of millions of individual decisions, each shaped by varying cultural and social values. Of this, population is a prime example. The decisions of individual men and women—when to marry, how many children to have, when to have them—are decisions which no social agency can or should control, though their consequences are important for government and business planning, and we do seek to anticipate them.

The second kind of change results from the conscious social choices of Government. The decision to resist aggression in Korea, to launch a space program, to extend civil rights, to open a "war" against poverty, were decisions with enormous consequences for the lives of all of us. The social map of the United States in recent years has been reworked more by Government decisions in regard to spending in science, research, defense, and social needs than by any other combination of factors.

In this second kind of change we are able, in the felicitous phrase of Dennis Gabor, to "invent the future." Since social change is increasingly a matter of conscious decisions and social choices, and given the huge resources we possess, we can decide what kind of future we want and work for it. In effect, we can spell out national goals, and seek to meet them within the framework of our capacities.

The basic decisions on policy, of course, are made by the President and the Congress operating within the framework of constitutional processes and individual liberties as interpreted by the courts. And this system has been the political mainstay of a free society. Our concern is to strengthen this system at a time when social and technological change begins to confront us so directly and when we need some means of assessing the consequences of such changes in a comprehensive way.

Forecasting the future is not a task for government alone. In fact, the concentration of forecasting mechanisms entirely in the hands of government, particularly at a time when such forecasting becomes a necessary condition of public policy, risks one-sided judgments—and even suppression of forecasts for political ends.

Along with forecasting there is a need to set national goals and to enlarge the participation of all sectors in the public debate which would be necessary in the statement of priorities. For this reason the Commission, while not endorsing any specific format, feels that some national body of distinguished private citizens representing diverse interests and constituencies and devoted to a continuing discussion of national goals would be valuable. Such a body would be concerned with "monitoring" social change, forecasting possible social trends, and suggesting policy alternatives to deal with them. Its role would not be to plan the future, but to point out what alternatives are achievable and at what costs.*

* For comments by several Commission members, see p. 293.

The discussions of the Commission, in effect, have been a forum bringing together representatives of industry, labor unions, voluntary associations, universities, and the public in a spirited debate, based on factual data where possible, on policy issues which involve a clarification of national goals. None of us, we have learned, is committed to doctrinaire solutions. We begin with a bias to the free market and the free society, but we have also recognized that where the market economy is incapable of providing certain services, public agencies must undertake such functions. Equally, we have agreed that certain communal needs can only be met by Federal expenditures, even though the operative activities need not be in the hands of Government agencies. But in all this, we have become aware of differences in value, and of the need to find some basic agreements in order to be able to carry forward the charge given to us by the President and the Congress.

We must find new means of making our institutions flexible and adaptable while maintaining the mechanisms of free choice and democratic participation.

Our recommendations, Mr. President, have been made with those objectives in mind.

Comment noted on p. 289 by Mr. Sporn

I am not aware of any solid basis for characterizing the contribution of Government-supported materials research centers and interdisciplinary programs as "spectacular" or "magnificent" or comparable with the contributions of the land-grant colleges and the agricultural extension services. This suggestion needs much more study before it is implemented. It is to be hoped that recognition of the need and of their own responsibilities in our society will stimulate at least one or more universities and private foundations to undertake such a program on their own. The results could then provide some basis for judgment whether Government financial support for an enlarged effort would be justified.

Comment noted on p. 289 by Mr. Sporn

I strongly disagree with the suggestion that a national body such as the one suggested here would improve the Nation's decision-making apparatus. While I believe it may be desirable from time to time to establish ad hoc commissions to serve limited purposes, the establishment of a single official agency with responsibility for the study of national goals, the "monitoring" (sic!) of social change, and the evaluation of national performance seems to me to represent the denial of the essence of a free society. I fully agree with the need "to enlarge the participation of all sectors in the public debate which would be necessary in the statement of priorities," but the establishment of any select body to study national goals and priorities on a continuing basis is in conflict with the need and desire for fuller participation of all sectors of our society, and would ultimately thwart the goals of a free people. The genius of our free society rests on the participation of its many diverse interests through discussion and debate of national goals and the evaluation of national performance. There are numerous private and public groups, including busi-

293

ness, labor, the academic community, the Congress, and the Executive branch of the Government, that are continually exploring these questions. It is essential that such diversity continues to be encouraged and that any temptation to delegate to a select elite the responsibiliy for such study be resisted if a healthy, free society is to be preserved.

Comment noted on p. 292 by Mr. Beirne, Mr. Hayes, and Mr. Reuther, joined by Mr. Bell and Mr. Young

We regret that the report does not explicitly recommend implementation of the purpose outlined in this sentence. Implicitly, the sentence calls for indicative planning or programming of the kind carried out in an increasing number of other democratic countries. It is our firm conviction that some form of democratic national economic planning is essential in the United States in order to assure not only sustained full employment but proper allocation of economic resources to assure prompt meeting of our most urgent national needs in both the public and private sectors.

The blind forces of the marketplace are no longer adequate to cope with the complex problems of modern society. The accelerating pace of technological and economic change continually generates a host of new problems at the same time as it opens up vast new vistas of opportunity. The problems and opportunities can both be foreseen, at least over relatively short time spans. What we are able to foresee we should be able to deal with rationally. Planning provides the mechanisms for rational action to make the most effective use of our resources both to solve problems and to make the fullest use of opportunities.

Economic planning, in essence, involves an evaluation of national needs in relation to the resources available to meet them and the establishment of an order of priorities and a set of policies to meet those needs. In a free society, the order of priorities ought to be determined on the basis of the broadest possible consensus. This would require enlisting in the planning process the democratic participation of representatives, at every level, of the major interest groups, as well as government representatives. It would also require the services of experts in economics, science and technology, education, housing, health, manpower problems, etc.

The planning we envision involves no compulsion. It would seek, rather, to establish a common framework of assumptions upon the basis of which both governmental and private organizations would determine their separate policies and action. Thus, through voluntary action based upon common premises, decisions made in the public sector would tend to mesh with those in the private sector and the decisions of separate firms and industries within the private sector would mesh better with each other.

Planning, moreover, would impose a valuable new discipline upon government, requiring it, at frequent intervals, to review and coordinate all its activities in the light of the goals of a plan.

We would urge strongly that intensive study be given to planning mechanisms now employed in Western European countries and Canada with a view to designing and putting into effect democratic national economic planning machinery suitable to the political and economic environment of the United States.

SUMMARY OF MAJOR CONCLUSIONS AND RECOMMENDATIONS

The issues discussed in this report are complex and diverse. A brief summary of major conclusions cannot do justice to the report and is certainly not a substitute for the full text with its supporting evidence and argument. Once the text has been read, however, a summary may serve a useful purpose in crystallizing the major points and pointing up the recommendations which have been made. The principal conclusions and recommendations follow:

1. There has been some increase in the pace of technological change. The most useful measure of this increase for policy purposes is the annual growth of output per man-hour in the private economy. If 1947 is chosen as a dividing point, the trend rate of increase from 1909 to that date was 2 per cent per year; from 1947 to 1965 it was 3.2 per cent per year. This is a substantial increase, but there has not been and there is no evidence that there will be in the decade ahead an acceleration in technological change more rapid than the growth of demand can offset, given adequate public policies.*

2. The excessive unemployment following the Korean War, only now beginning to abate, was the result of an economic growth rate too slow to offset the combined impact of productivity increase (measured in output per man-hour) and a growing labor force.

3. Since productivity is the primary source of our high standard of living and opportunity must be provided to those of the population who choose to enter the labor force, the growth of demand must assume the blame for and provide the answer to unemployment. But it must be realized that the growth rate required to match rising productivity and labor force growth rates is unprecedented in our history, though not in the history of other industrial economies. There will be a continuing need for aggressive fiscal and monetary policies to stimulate growth.

4. To say that technological change does not bear major responsibility for the general level of unemployment is not to deny the role of technological change in the unemployment of particular persons in particular occupations, industries, and locations. Economic and technological changes have caused and will continue to cause displacement throughout the economy. Technological change, along with other changes, determines who will be displaced. The rate at which output grows in the total economy determines the total level of unemployment and how long those who become unemployed remain unemployed, as well as how difficult it is for new entrants to the labor force to find employment.

5. Unemployment tends to be concentrated among those workers with little education, not primarily because technological developments are

* Mr. Beirne, Mr. Hayes, and Mr. Reuther wish to call attention to their comment on the pace of technological change on p. 215.

changing the nature of jobs, but because the uneducated are at the "back of the line" in the competition for jobs. Education, in part, determines the employability and productivity of the individual, the adaptability of the labor force, the growth and vitality of the economy, the quality of the society. But we need not await the slow process of education to solve the problem of unemployment.

6. The outlook for employment and adjustment to change in the next decade depends upon the policies followed. Uneven growth and decline of occupations and industries could, but need not, cause serious difficulties for the economy as a whole. The number of unskilled jobs will not decline, though unskilled jobs will continue to as a proportion of all jobs. Growth patterns in both the economy and the labor force provide an important warning: Unless Negroes and, to a lesser degree, youth, are able to penetrate growing occupations and industries at a more rapid rate than in the past, their high unemployment rates will continue or even rise. Our society must do a far better job than it has in the past of assuring that the burdens of changes beneficial to society as a whole are not borne disproportionately by some individuals.

7. The more adequate fiscal policies of the past two years have proven their ability to lower unemployment despite continued technological change and labor force growth. Economic policy must continue, watchfully but resolutely, to reduce the general unemployment rate. We must never again present the spectacle of wartime prosperity and peacetime unemployment. The needs of our society are such that we should give major attention in our fiscal policies to public investment expenditures.

8. With the best of fiscal and monetary policies, there will always be those handicapped in the competition for jobs by lack of education, skill, or experience or because of discrimination. The needs of our society provide ample opportunities to fulfill the promise of the Employment Act of 1946: "a job for all those able, willing, and seeking to work." We recommend a program of public service employment providing, in effect, that the Government be an employer of last resort, providing work for the "hard-core unemployed" in useful community enterprises.

9. Technological change and productivity are primary sources of our unprecedented wealth, but many persons have not shared in that abundance. We recommended that economic security be guaranteed by a floor under family income. That floor should include both improvements in wage-related benefits and a broader system of income maintenance for those families unable to provide for themselves.

10. To facilitate adjustment to change as well as to improve the quality of life, adequate educational opportunity should be available to all. We recommend compensatory education for those from disadvantaged environments, improvements in the general quality of education, universal high school education and opportunity for 14 years of free public education, elimination of financial obstacles to higher education, lifetime opportunities for education, training, and retraining, and special attention to the handicaps of adults with deficient basic education.

11. Adjustment to change requires information concerning present and future job opportunities. We recommend the creation of a national computerized job-man matching system which would provide more adequate information on employment opportunities and available workers on a local, regional, and national scale. In addition to speeding job search, such a service would provide better information for vocational choice and alert the public and policymakers to impending changes.

12. The public employment service is a key instrument in adjustment to technological and economic changes. But it is presently handicapped by administrative obstacles and inadequate resources. We recommend the now federally financed but State-administered employment services be made wholly Federal. This would bring them into harmony with modern labor market conditions. Then they must be provided with the resources, both in manpower and funds, necessary to fulfill their crucial role.

13. We recommend that present experimentation with relocation assistance to workers and their families stranded in declining areas be developed into a permanent program.

14. Displacement, technological and otherwise, has been particularly painful to those blocked from new opportunity by barriers of discrimination. The Commission wishes to add its voice to others demanding elimination of all social barriers to employment and advocating special programs to compensate for centuries of systematic denial.

15. Technological and economic changes have differential geographic impacts requiring concerted regional efforts to take advantage of opportunities and avoid dislocation. We recommend that each Federal Reserve bank provide the leadership for economic development activities in its region. The development program in each Federal Reserve District should include: (1) A regular program of economic analysis; (2) an advisory council for economic growth composed of representatives from each of the major interested groups within the district; (3) a capital bank to provide venture capital and long-term financing for new and growing companies; (4) regional technical institutes to serve as centers for disseminating scientific and technical knowledge relevant to the region's development; and (5) a Federal executive in each district to provide regional coordination of the various Federal programs related to economic development.

16. The responsibility of Government is to foster an environment of opportunity in which satisfactory adjustment to change can occur. But the adjustments themselves must occur primarily in the private employment relationship. The genius of the private adjustment process is the flexibility with which it accommodates to individual circumstances. Our report suggests areas for consideration by private and public employers, employees, and unions. We also recommend study of a reinsurance fund to protect pension rights and modifications of the investment tax credit to encourage employers to provide appropriate adjustment assistance. We also advocate a positive program by employers and unions to provide compensatory opportunities to the victims of past discrimination and stronger enforcement provisions in civil rights legislation relating to employment. Federal, State,

and local governments are encouraged to conduct themselves as model employers in the development of new adjustment techniques.

17. Technology enlarges the capacities of man and extends his control over his environment. The benefits of increased productivity can and should be applied to combinations of higher living standards and increased leisure, improvements in the work environment, increased investment in meeting human and community needs, and assistance to less advantaged nations.

18. As examples of possible applications of new technologies to unmet human and community needs, we recommend improvements in health care, transportation, control of air and water pollution, and housing.

(1) To improve health care, we recommend: (a) Fuller access to diagnostic and patient care facilities by all groups in the population; (b) broader and bolder use of the computer and other new health technologies; (c) increased spread and use of health statistics, information, and indexes; and (d) new programs for training health manpower.

(2) To aid the development of an efficient transportation system we recommend: Federal support of a systems research program directed toward (a) the problems of particular multistate regions, (b) the determination of national transportation requirements, and (c) the evaluation of alternative programs.

(3) For air pollution control, we recommend: (a) Enlargement of research efforts to learn and understand the effects of various pollutants on living organisms; and (b) assignment of pollution costs to the sources of pollutants.

(4) To control water pollution, we recommend: The establishment of effective, amply empowered river basin authorities.

(5) To encourage improvement in housing technology, we recommend: (a) Federal stimulation of research; (b) use of federally supported public housing to provide initial markets for new housing technologies; (c) promulgation of a national model building code by making available Federal support and insurance of housing and other construction only in those communities which put their building codes in harmony with the national code; and (d) provision of adjustment assistance to any building crafts destroyed by technical change.

19. We also recommend: (1) Increased use of systems analysis in resolving social and environmental problems, (2) the use of Federal procurement as a stimulus to technological innovation through purchasing by performance criteria rather than product specification, (3) provision of Federal funds to universities and other organizations for the improvement of research techniques and their experimental application to urban problems, (4) the formation of university institutes integrated with the educational function which would serve as laboratories for urban problem analysis and resources for local communities wanting their advice and services, and (5) increased efforts to make available for nongovernment use results of Government performed or funded research.

20. Finally, we recommend: (1) Efforts by employers to "humanize" the work environment by (a) adapting work to human needs, (b) increasing the flexibility of the lifespan of work, and (c) eliminating the distinction in the mode of payment between hourly workers and salaried employees, (2) exploration of a system of social accounts to make possible assessment of the relative costs and benefits of alternative policy decisions, and (3) continuous study of national goals and evaluation of our national performance in relation to such goals.

APPENDIX 3

The National Data Center Proposals

Report of the Committee on the Preservation and Use of Economic Data to the Social Science Research Council, April 1965

Members of the Committee

RICHARD RUGGLES, *Chairman*
RICHARD MILLER, *Secretary*
EDWIN KUH, Massachusetts Institute of Technology
STANLEY LEBERGOTT, Wesleyan University
GUY ORCUTT, University of Wisconsin
JOSEPH PECHMAN, Brookings Institution

SUMMARY OF REPORT

During the past four years the Committee on the Preservation and Use of Economic Data has met with a considerable number of Federal agencies concerned with the collection and use of data in machine readable form. The prime concern of the Committee has been the development and preservation of data for use in economic research. Although considerable progress has been achieved in specific areas, the Committee has concluded that three more general lines of action are required. Specifically, these are (1) the Federal Government should undertake the establishment of a Federal Data Center; (2) procedures should be established to insure the development and preservation of import data; and (3) research institutions and universities should develop an organization for coordinating their requests for economic data.

First, the Committee urges that the Bureau of the Budget, in view of its responsibility for the Federal statistical program, immediately take steps to establish a Federal Data Center. Such a Federal Data Center should have the authority to obtain computer tapes and other machine readable data produced by all Federal agencies. It would have the function of providing data and service facilities so that within the proper safeguards concerning the disclosure of information both Federal agencies and users outside of the Government would have access to basic data. The Federal Data Center would require computer facilities, and it would need to be staffed with personnel capable of understanding the data problems in the various areas. In view of the importance of the Federal Data Center, the Committee suggests that the Center be established with specific responsibilities for these functions and interagency authority to carry them out.

Second, the Committee urges that the Office of Statistical Standards of the Bureau of the Budget place increased emphasis on the systematic preservation in usable form of important data prepared by those agencies engaging in statistical programs. In both the initial budget for statistical programs and the subsequent review of ongoing work, the Bureau of the Budget should see that provision is made for the development of computer tapes of important data, together with the supplementary material required for interpretation.

Third, the Committee recommends that at an early date the Social Science Research Council convene representatives from research institutions and universities in order to develop an organization which can provide a clearinghouse and coordination of requests for data made by individual scholars from Federal agencies. In addition, such an organization would serve the Federal Government in an advisory capacity and provide a mechanism for the development of data tapes needed for research purposes in specific areas of economic research.

The Background and History of the Committee

In December 1959, the Executive Committee of the American Economic Association devoted a part of its annual meeting to the consideration of the preservation and use of data for economic research. The AEA Executive Committee recognized that research in the social sciences in general, and in the discipline of economics in particular, to an increasing extent requires large systematic collections of microdata for the formulation and testing of hypotheses, and that collections of microdata are research tools for the social scientist much in the same way that books and manuscripts are for the humanities and laboratories are for the scientist.

Although the AEA Executive Committee agreed that the problem of developing and preserving important bodies of microdata was extremely important, they concluded that it was not feasible for the American Economic Association to undertake an effort in this area, since the organizational structure of the association makes it difficult for subcommittees to carry out substantive work of this nature. The Executive Committee therefore recommended that the Social Science Research Council set up a Committee on the Preservation and Use of Economic Data to study this problem and undertake any program of action which it might deem desirable.

Creation of the SSRC Committee

Accordingly, in December 1960 the Social Science Research Council arranged an exploratory discussion of the problem of data preservation and use, drawing on social scientists from universities and the Federal Government. This discussion revealed that although there was a large area of common interest among the various social sciences, there were also wide differences in approach and areas of concern when any specific aspect of data preservation and use was being considered. It became obvious that the problem was too broad and diverse to be solved by any simple general solution, and that a more concerted and focused attack on specific parts of the problem would have to be undertaken.

For this reason, a small committee was then appointed to explore the problems arising in the field of economic data alone. This committee consisted of individuals who were acquainted with the statistical work being done within the Federal Government, and who were also doing research using large bodies of empirical data. At the outset the newly constituted Committee on the Preservation and Use of Economic Data recognized that in order to maximize the effectiveness of its effort it should concentrate its attention on those areas which would yield the most valuable research materials per unit of cost. By definition this immediately excluded information which was widely scattered throughout the Government or stored in bundles in warehouses, and it suggested that attention should be focused on those bodies of information which were currently available in machine readable form. The Committee was concerned with the archival problem, as well as the problem of making existing data currently available to research workers, and for this reason it proposed to examine the disposal policy of the various Federal agencies as well as to try to develop methods whereby machine readable data could be made directly available to scholars engaged in economic research.

Committee Activities, 1962–1964

During the 3 years from 1962 through 1964, the Committee undertook to study, on an agency-by-agency basis, the problem of providing access to specific bodies of information. Meetings were held with a considerable number of independent agencies in the Departments of Commerce, Labor, Treasury, Agriculture, Interior, and Health, Education, and Welfare. In addition, the Committee kept in close contact with the Bureau of the Budget and the National Archives. In some cases, arrangements were made to create and make available specific bodies of information, and substantial progress was made in developing awareness of the general problem of preservation and use of data by the Federal agencies. Representatives of the National Science Foundation attended many of these meetings.

Despite the progress which was achieved in specific areas, however, the Committee, at the end of 3 years' operation, concluded that some more general solution was required. Such a solution would require that the Federal Government develop (1) a systematic policy insuring the preservation of important data, and (2) mechanisms whereby data could be made available for research purposes to universities and research institutions. In addition, the Committee also recognized that the universities and research institutions themselves should develop a more systematic and coordinated program of data development.

This report is intended to set forth the conclusions of the Committee with respect to the problems inherent in the preservation and use of economic data collected by the Federal Government. In addition, Part II will consider the problem of data development facing universities and research institutions, and make recommendations as to steps which can be taken in this area.

Decentralization of the Federal Statistical System

The statistical system of the Federal Government is highly decentralized. In contrast with many other countries, the United States does not have a central statistical office which is responsible for the recordkeeping of the Nation. Instead, each of the large number of administrative and regulatory agencies undertakes to provide much of the information which is required for its own operation. Thus, for example, the Bureau of Labor Statistics collects information on wholesale and retail prices, wage rates, employment, and a wide variety of other data relating to the role of labor in the economy. The Office of Business Economics provides data on the national income accounts, showing the progress of business activities and the functioning of the economy. The Federal Trade Commission and the Securities and Exchange Commission collect quarterly financial reports on manufacturing corporations. The Department of Health, Education, and Welfare collects the basic statistics on education and health.

In a great many instances, these statistics themselves are a byproduct of the regulatory process. Thus the Internal Revenue Service processes personal and business income tax returns and provides statistical tabulations of these returns which constitute a basic statistical source. Similarly, the Social Security Administration, in carrying out its administration of the social security program, has large bodies of information on wage and salary payments to individuals. However, one Federal agency, the Bureau of the Census, performs many of the functions normally undertaken by a central statistical office. The Census Bureau is responsible for comprehensive data on population, housing, agriculture, manufactures, retail and wholesale trade, transportation, and government bodies. This information provides other agencies with basic information about the American economy and its functioning. Thus, for example, census data provide much of the information behind the national income accounts and the detailed data about specific States and cities. To an increasing extent, the Census Bureau is undertaking special services and tabulations for other Government agencies. Certain tasks formerly undertaken by other agencies, such as the collection of foreign trade statistics and labor force surveys, have become a regular part of the census program.

Responsibilities of the Office of Statistical Standards

The Office of Statistical Standards of the Bureau of the Budget has the function of improving, developing, and coordinating Federal statistical services. There are two specific ways in which the Office of Statistical Standards can enforce coordination and maintenance of high statistical performance. First, all survey forms which are sent out by the Federal agencies for the collection of data must have the approval of the Office of Statistical Standards. Second, since it is a part of the Bureau of the Budget, the Office of Statistical Standards participates in the review of budget requests of the various agencies for statistical activities. Both of these instruments are important, but unfortunately the task of coordination is so great that it is difficult to insure the comparability of data among various Federal agencies.

Responsibilities of National Archives

The National Archives and Records Service has the responsibility for promoting improved current records, management, and disposal practices of Federal agencies, and for selecting, preserving, and making available to the Government and the public the permanently valuable noncurrent records of the Federal Government. Before the advent of the computer, the National Archives was concerned primarily either with the basic original records or documents obtained by the Federal agencies, or with the analytic or statistical end products. The problems of intermediate worksheets and data in semiprocessed form were left largely to the discretion of the individual agencies involved. Thus, for example, with respect to the corporate tax records of the Internal Revenue Service, the National Archives has preserved in warehouses bales of tax returns filed by corporations going back to 1909. In addition, National Archives has also preserved the statistical tabulations of tax returns. With the development of machine readable data, however, it is becoming increasingly obvious that bodies of information in machine readable form which are intermediate between the original records obtained by a Federal agency and the final statistical tabulations may be more worth preserving than the original records themselves. There is a growing recognition by the National Archives of this fact. The Committee was very much impressed by the active interest which the staff of the National Archives showed in this problem. However, again the problem is so vast that it may require completely new procedures and policies in the future.

Impact of the Computer on Data Processing

Data processing methods have undergone a systematic evolution which has had far-reaching implications for the Federal statistics system ever since the original punchcard equipment was introduced. Early computers were to some degree a logical extension of this punchcard equipment. Although the UNIVAC Model I pioneered by the Bureau of the Census in the early 1950's represented a monumental step forward, it was only the modest beginning of what has turned out to be a completely new technology. Each succeeding generation of computers incorporates improvements in the size of memory, the speed of computation, and the density of data storage on tape such that the capacity and speed of operation have been increased many times over. By now the technological revolution has become so great that a reexamination of the organization of the Federal statistical system is urgently needed.

INCREASE IN EFFICIENCY

From the outset, the computer, like other forms of automation, has reduced the amount of labor required in the processing of data. Before their introduction, a large organization of clerks and punchcard machine operators was needed to handle the huge volume of punchcards required for any substantial statistical operation. Sorting, tabulating, and computing

304

were relatively lengthy processes. Even for minimal tabulations a great many steps were requested. It is true, of course, that the computer has made necessary the development of specialists who could write programs for data processing, but once a program is written and proved out, it can be used to process large masses of information rapidly and with a small staff.

REDUCTION IN PROCESSING TIME

Equally important, the time required for data processing has also been substantially reduced. Operations which formerly took 7 to 8 months to carry out now have been reduced to a matter of weeks. In the processing of the 1960 population census, the time required for certain steps was reduced from several years to several months. This shortening of time has not only meant an increase in efficiency in terms of overhead and other fixed elements in the program, but it has also resulted in making important information available more promptly. This reduction of the timelag between the collection of information and its availability greatly affects the usefulness of the information.

IMPROVEMENT IN DATA QUALITY

The computer has also made possible new kinds of analysis which could not have been done before because of the cost and time required to carry out the necessary computations. First, it has become possible to examine and edit much more carefully than was possible heretofore. Computers can "wash" the information, and find inconsistencies which would have gone unnoticed in hand editing. Editing instructions to test the reasonableness of the basic information can be built into the processing programs. Thus, in the case of census data for manufacturing establishments, the computer can spot errors in reporting wage bills and manhours by computing average hourly earnings. Where the resulting figures are outside a reasonable range, the original information can be questioned. Other kinds of inconsistencies can be tested in a similar way, and for each individual report the computer can make literally thousands of tests to determine which figures are out of line and which specific items should be corrected. For some Federal agencies, the ability of the computer to make such consistency checks is very important. Thus the Internal Revenue Service uses computers to check the internal consistency of items contained in each individual tax form. Such an operation is basic to one of the major administrative functions of this agency, but before the introduction of the computer it was too expensive and time consuming to be feasible. In such uses, the computer is adding a new dimension to the work and increasing the overall efficiency of the agency.

DATA REDUCTION AND TABULATION

Even with quite sophisticated punchcard equipment the difficulty of handling large masses of information made it imperative to reduce the information as quickly as possible to a more manageable volume. In the past this generally led to the development of a given set of tabulations, which became the final form of the data and which were all that was available to prospective users. Under these circumstances, the primary focus of attention by the producers of data was on the final published form of tabulation which was to result from the data processing. Once these tabulations

305

were finished, there was little or no thought of utilizing the original reports for alternative analyses, since the cost and time required for additional data processing were too great. With the dramatic reduction in cost and time which the computer has yielded, however, the focus of attention is shifting to the basic information. It is now possible to use the same basic data again and again for different analytic purposes. From the point of view of analysis, the original unaggregated microinformation offer greater potential than tabulations of a more aggregative nature. Where relationships of data inherent in the basic reporting unit are important, aggregate tabulations often hide more than they illuminate.

NEW TYPES OF ANALYSIS

The ability of the computer to carry out detailed and complex computations on great numbers of individual cases at very high speeds has made it possible to make types of analysis which are not feasible without it. For example, prior to the introduction of the computer, aggregated tabulations of individual tax returns were used to estimate the impact which proposed changes in the tax law might have on total tax revenue and on particular classes of taxpayers. With the introduction of the computer, however, it became possible to develop a much more reliable method. A sample of 100,000 tax returns was obtained, and a computer program developed to recompute each tax return individually according to the proposed revision of the law, and thus show for the sample as a whole the exact impact of the change. This method not only provides a cumulative measurement in terms of total tax revenue, but also permits an analysis of which classes of taxpayers are affected, and by how much.

COST OF ELECTRONIC DATA PROCESSING

Despite the very marked increase in the amount of data processing being done in Federal statistical agencies as a result of the introduction of the computer, the cost of data processing has become a smaller percentage of the total cost of obtaining information, and it represents a very small fraction of this total cost. In many cases the cost of the field survey may account for as much as 95 per cent of the total cost, and processing the data less than 5 per cent.

DATA STORAGE

The problem of storing basic statistical information has also been greatly reduced. A computer tape today will hold information equivalent to over 100,000 punchcards, so that a relatively small number of tapes may contain information which formerly would have occupied a great deal of space. Before the development of efficient tape storage, past data could not be kept for long periods by Government agencies, since room had to be made for the continuous inflow of new punchcards. For the first time it has now become feasible to keep the original information in machine readable form at very low cost.

INCREASED USE OF DATA

An important aspect following upon computer development has been the increasing use of basic computer tapes by others than the agency collecting and processing the original information. Prior to the computer, when the focus of data processing was the production of tabulations which would satisfy all users, Federal agencies often published massive detailed tabulations which could be used by groups outside the agency for a variety of statistical purposes. With technological advances in both computers and printing, even more massive detail is being produced. As one small example, in the IRS statistics of income series the report on individuals for 1960 consisted of 165 pages, and 233 pages for 1961: on business it was 192 pages for 1960–61 and 274 pages for 1961–62. Aside from the cumbersomeness of the sheer volume of printed material, users of statistical information are now finding that the published tabulations are costly to use and often are unsuited for particular analyses which they wish to make. Even where a specific tabulation is exactly in the form desired, the user may find it necessary to put the data back into machine readable form before he can manipulate them. For these reasons, there has been an increasing tendency for Federal agencies to supply outside users with computer tapes of information to avoid the expense of recording the data. To an increasing extent, Federal agencies are considering the preservation of and accessibility to computer tapes to be a direct substitute for printed publication to make more detailed tabulations available to research users of data. Statistical programs are no longer viewed simply as projects involving the gathering, processing, and disseminating of information. Instead Federal agencies are developing the ability to tap into a source of information at one or more points in the processing stage, where data are in the form (after editing but before too much aggregation) and on the medium of recording (magnetic tape, not original schedules or printed reports) which are needed.

INTERAGENCY USE OF DATA

The ability of the computer to handle and interrelate large bodies of information has encouraged different Federal agencies to bring together information which they collect on related economic units. The recent development by the Bureau of the Census of enterprise statistics is an example. This set of information was created by linking the establishment data collected by census with corporation tax data obtained by the Internal Revenue Service. Previously, given the costs of processing and storage, only already tabulated sets of information could be brought together, and in most cases it was impossible to reconcile different sets of related data precisely. A byproduct of interagency cooperation has been an improvement in the comparability of classification systems, techniques, and methodology. In order to collate data from different sources, Federal agencies have found it necessary to use identical classification systems and to treat similar cases in a uniform manner. Information required as a basis for major legislative and executive policy decisions necessitates drawing on many kinds of data. The increasing ability of the various Federal agencies to integrate their basic data at a primary level will provide more reliable and meaningful information for policy purposes.

Current Problems of the Federal Statistical System

Although the development of the computer has solved a great many problems in the processing and handling of data, these very advances have raised problems which were not serious before, and until these problems are faced, the Federal statistical system will not reach its full potential.

PRESERVATION OF DATA

One of the first problems raised by the development of the computer is the preservation policy of the different Federal agencies. As already indicated, the information collected by the Federal Government represents a large investment of human and material resources both on the part of the Government in obtaining the information and on the part of the respondents in providing it. Before computers were developed the preservation of most of this information was not feasible because of the high cost of storage and the impossibility of low-cost retrieval. Now that large volumes of basic data can be kept conveniently and inexpensively in the form of computer tapes and processed at low marginal cost, the question of what should be preserved must be faced as a matter of national policy. Under the present decentralized Federal statistical system, it is extremely difficult to maintain a coherent and consistent policy with respect to the preservation of machine readable data. The various agencies are primarily responsible for day-to-day operations, and cannot give high priority to long-run considerations. There is no adequate mechanism for insuring that these agencies are following optimal policies with respect to the preservation of important information. In view of the large number of organizations involved, it is inevitable that unless the situation is regularly reviewed by some group within the Federal Government which considers this problem to be a major responsibility, a satisfactory solution cannot be achieved. For this reason, the Committee urges that the Federal Government develop procedures and mechanisms for insuring the adequate preservation of important data produced in any of the Federal agencies.

DATA ACCESS

The problem of access to information is a very real one. At the suggestion of the Committee on the Preservation and Use of Economic Data, the Bureau of the Budget and the National Archives jointly undertook a survey of machine readable data held by various Government agencies. The survey covered some 20 agencies in the Departments of Agriculture, Labor, Interior, Treasury, Commerce, and Health, Education, and Welfare, and the Board of Governors of the Federal Reserve System. Over 600 major bodies of data were listed in this preliminary survey. These data are stored on approximately 100 million punchcards and 30,000 computer tapes. The decentralized nature of the Federal statistical system makes it extremely difficult for users outside the Government, and even in other Federal agencies, to find out what data exist on various topics and how to obtain access to them. Different agencies have completely different policies with respect to access, and an outsider must know precisely whom to contact with respect to each specific kind of information. Most Federal agencies process data as an activity which is ancillary to their primary responsibilities, and therefore they find it inconvenient and costly to respond to specific requests for information which would necessarily disrupt and delay their own work. Even in the case of agencies such as the Bureau of the Census where an effort is made to respond to legitimate requests for information, it is often difficult to fit outside requests involving data processing into a work program in which the various stages of processing censuses or surveys have been carefully scheduled and timed. In other words, the present Federal statistical system is primarily geared to the production and processing of information for immediate administrative use or publication. Thus the present organization of Federal statistical operations does not lend itself to optimal use of the vast amounts of existing information, despite the fact that this use could be achieved at low data processing cost.

DEVELOPMENT OF USABLE DATA

Another major problem arising from the lack of supervision and coordination of data preservation techniques is that even where important data are involved, Federal agencies often fail to develop clean edited tapes and to provide supporting information about the data contained on the tapes. Under present circumstances, such inadequacies are quite understandable. In the processing of basic information, operating agencies are mainly concerned with achieving the results necessary for specific tabulation or given computations. It is unavoidable in this process that substantial errors will be found. Sometimes these arise from transcription or classification errors, or from errors in programing. For the purposes of the operating agency, errors can often be patched up on an ad hoc basis, but doing so leaves the original tapes with the errors in them. It is usually quite possible to correct such errors when they are known to exist. On investigation, however, the Committee found that due partly to the fact that it was not necessary for immediate purposes and partly to lack of proper budget allocation agencies often neglect this task, even though its cost would not amount to more than 4 or 5 per cent of the total computation cost, and in most cases would be less than 1 or 2 per cent of the total budget for the project. In addition, agencies often do not provide sufficient information on the layout, classifications, and definitions of data contained in a tape. As a result, even for the agency's own purposes it becomes very difficult to go back after a few years and make use of the information, unless it happens to be in the same format and classification system employed for current data processing. The turnover of personnel within Federal agencies often makes it impossible to trace back precisely what was done in the original coding of the schedules or programing. In view of these circumstances, what is needed is some system which will insure that for important data all Federal agencies will provide clean, edited data with accompanying information describing layouts, coding, and programing, so that these tapes can be served by both the agency itself and by other groups. Given the presence of day-to-day business, the shortage of funds which often occurs at the end of a project, and the priority of other major responsibilities, Federal agencies cannot be expected to devote the required effort to the development of clean data tapes unless some specific procedures are developed to insure this result.

DISCLOSURE

In addition to the problem of physical access to data, there is another factor which may prevent the utilization of data in their original form. A considerable portion of the information collected from individuals and businesses is obtained with the understanding that such information will

309

be considered confidential and will not be available to other Federal agencies or anyone else. Thus, for example, in the case of the Annual Survey of Manufacturers, the data reported on the activities of manufacturing establishments constitute a confidential report to the Census Bureau and are protected by law from use by such agencies as the Internal Revenue Service for checking tax returns, or even by Congress in its investigations. It is recognized by all concerned that Federal agencies should not violate the confidentiality of their data by making them available to outside research workers or other agencies. However, it is often possible to disguise the information in such a way that specific data cannot be traced to any individual respondent. For example, the Census Bureau in the last few years has made available a sample of information on 100,000 individual households, giving considerable detail about the age, education, income ownership, occupation, etc., of the individuals in the household. In this sample the omission of detailed geographic information makes it impossible to trace the data to any specific individual. By using a similar approach the Internal Revenue Service developed a sample of 100,000 personal income tax returns. As in the case of the Census sample, data on individuals were provided without disclosing information that could be traced to any particular individual. For other types of data, the problem is somewhat more difficult. Thus, for example, merely indicating the size and industry of a manufacturing plant may be enough to identify it and so constitute disclosure, even if no additional identifying information is given. In many instances, however, there are ways in which such information can be utilized without disclosure. Since for most research purposes it is not necessary to present information on individual cases in the final results, it is often possible for researchers to provide computer programs which can be used directly upon the basic data under the auspices of the Federal agency responsible. Again, however, few Federal agencies are in a position to take the time and trouble to fill out such individual requests, even in those cases where the research would be valuable and outside financing is available.

Conclusion

In summary, therefore, because of the decentralized nature of the Federal statistical system and the pressure of the primary functions of the agencies, neither outside scholars nor Federal agencies are able to utilize efficiently the large amount of information which has been obtained at public expense.

Proposal for the Establishment of a Federal Data Center

For the reasons outlined above, the Committee on the Preservation and Use of Economic Data urges that a Federal Data Center be established by the Federal Government to preserve and make available to both Federal agencies and non-Government users basic statistical data originating in all Federal agencies.

NEED FOR INTERAGENCY AUTHORITY

The first and most basic requirement of a Federal Data Center is that it should have the authority to obtain computer tapes produced by other

Federal agencies. The exact timing of the receipt by the Federal Data Center of such tapes will differ from agency to agency, and will depend on the kind of information involved. As a general rule, however, the Federal Data Center should obtain copies of the data when a clean, edited tape of the basic information first becomes available. Fortunately, because of the nature of computer processing, duplicate copies of the basic computer tapes can be produced at low cost, so that both the agency concerned and the Federal Data Center can simultaneously have the basic information available to them. In this connection the Federal Data Center should keep track of statistical projects underway in the Federal Government and make sure in advance that the budget for each project includes the proper provision for making clean, edited tapes and providing the necessary accompanying information on classification and programing. It should be the task of the Federal Data Center to follow statistical projects and to see that the clean, edited tapes are made available within a reasonable period.

NEED FOR COMPUTER CAPABILITY

The Federal Data Center will require substantial computer capability if it is to provide access to information by outside users and by other Federal agencies. It is important that the Federal Data Center should not only furnish basic information but also, on a reimbursable basis, it should make production runs and furnish aggregated tapes or results to scholars so as to eliminate many problems of disclosure. In a great many instances the Federal Data Center will find it advisable to develop new tapes combining information from various bodies of material produced by different Federal agencies. For example, the very considerable interest in data on specific regions or cities by State and local governments for programs such as urban redevelopment, welfare, and education, makes it desirable to combine various kinds of information pertaining to a specific area on a systematic basis. In many cases such information about communities and their characteristics does not violate any disclosure rules. These data are useful not only for purposes of public policy but also to business groups interested in market research and in planning long-run investment. It is important that the Federal Data Center be staffed with computer analysts who are subject specialists so that they can understand the nature of the data with which they work and can anticipate the analytical problems of the agencies and research organizations that want to use the data.

NEED FOR SERVICE FACILITIES

A Federal Data Center would provide servicing facilities, so that Federal agencies and individuals could obtain specific information directly, and it should publish descriptions of the data available. In this sense the Federal Data Center would serve somewhat the same role as the Library of Congress, inasmuch as it would be responsible for providing a systematic and comprehensive coverage of the material available in its areas of competence. It would also, of course, be serving the same function in the statistical area as Archives now does in the area of basic records and documents. It would insure that the most useful information was preserved in a usable form, and that duplicative and unwanted data did not clog the system. Finally, the

Federal Data Center would provide basic information about the American economy as a primary objective rather than as a byproduct of the administration or regulatory function.

NEED FOR NEW ADMINISTRATIVE ARRANGEMENTS

Although the functions described above for the Federal Data Center are in part covered by the activities of existing Federal agencies, no single agency is currently combining all of these necessary functions. The Office of Statistical Standards of the Budget Bureau does have the responsibility for the supervision and coordination of Government statistical activities, but it is not an operating agency. The National Archives also has interagency authority, but it has not been involved in the field of data processing and does not as currently organized have the ability or authority to undertake the task of selecting, monitoring, and controlling machine readable data on the scale required. Finally, other statistical agencies of the Federal Government have the ability to handle, process, and combine masses of statistical data in an imaginative and productive manner, but these agencies lack interagency authority to obtain each other's records. Furthermore, although these agencies have been making an effort to provide reasonable access to their data the fact remains that they have major responsibilities for collecting and processing basic information on a continuing basis, and these responsibilities, which have first priority, make it difficult for them to devote adequate attention to individual requests.

NEED FOR EARLY AND POSITIVE ACTION

In view of these considerations, the Committee concludes that immediate action should be taken by the Federal Government to establish a Federal Data Center and to insure the orderly preservation of important data. The Bureau of the Budget has been given the responsibility of developing programs and issuing regulations and orders for the improved gathering, compiling, analyzing, publishing, and disseminating of statistical information for any purpose by the various agencies in the Executive Branch of the Federal Government (see sec. 1 of Executive Order 10253, June 11, 1951). The Committee therefore urges that the Bureau of the Budget immediately take steps to establish a Federal Data Center which would have the functions described above. It should be recognized, furthermore, that the nature of such a data center is so different from anything now in existence that it may well require additional legislative authority so that its responsibilities can be well defined and recognized by all Federal agencies. It is very important that the Federal Data Center be conceived as a new and independent function, rather than an extension of present activities by any single Federal agency which has major responsibilities of another kind. In the development of the Federal Data Center it is to be expected that the Bureau of the Budget would consult with the various Federal statistical agencies involved with policymaking groups within the Federal Government such as the Council of Economic Advisers, and with congressional groups such as the Joint Economic Committee, as well as with research institutions and universities. It is to be hoped that this planning and preparatory work can begin immediately.

In addition to the early development of a Federal Data Center, the Committee urges that the Bureau of the Budget place increased emphasis on the systematic preservation of important data by those agencies engaging in statistical programs. Specifically, the Bureau of the Budget should see that funds are budgeted for the development of clean tapes of important data together with the supplementary material required for their interpretation. The subsequent review by the Bureau of the Budget of ongoing statistical programs should make certain that the important data are in fact preserved in usable form. These procedures will be necessary even after the Federal Data Center is established, and they can be initiated immediately.

Finally, as an emergency stopgap measure, the Bureau of the Budget should undertake a current evaluation of the preservation policies of the various Federal agencies and together with the agencies make a joint determination of what sets of data should be preserved, and in some cases how these data can be put into a more usable form. In connection with this, it is also suggested that the Federal Government undertake to collect and publish at regular intervals an inventory of machine readable data held by the various agencies.

PART II. THE ROLE OF RESEARCH INSTITUTIONS AND
UNIVERSITIES IN THE PRESERVATION AND USE OF ECONOMIC DATA

Use of Data in Economic Research

Economic research has undergone striking changes during the last decade, due mainly to the advent of the computer. However, the present organization of the profession and its lack of access to major data sources impose serious obstacles in the way of optimal use of this new research development.

RESEARCH TECHNIQUES AND THEIR DEVELOPMENT

Prior to the development of the computer, empirical research in economics was largely confined to the use of aggregative economic data in fairly simple models. Price indexes, production indexes, national income accounting, and industry statistics were used not only as frameworks for classifying information, but also as a means of data reduction. The limited capability of economists to process information forces them to deal with aggregations, which often obscured interrelationships among basic variables. With the development of the computer, however, low-cost data processing has been made available to economists, and as a result for many types of economic problems research technology has undergone substantial change. Economists can now specify and develop sets of data which are tailored to the research which they are undertaking. They can also process large quantities of data on a case-by-case basis, so that complex interrelationship can be studied at a microeconomic level. The use of simulation techniques on a large scale makes it possible to test the sensitivity of models to different assumptions, and to variations in specific parameters. For the first time, it has become possible to make use of the large bodies of existing information, which can be quite powerful in testing as well as suggesting theoretical hypotheses.

313

There are currently in research institutions and universities many research projects each of which involves a large number of scholars. The Brookings-SSRC model of the U.S. economy, the Harvard economic research project on input-output studies, the simulation studies at the University of Wisconsin, and the research on consumer behavior at the University of Michigan are all examples of large-scale projects using large bodies of data processed on high-speed computers. Other institutions where computer facilities exist are also carrying out research of this type. The value and productivity of this research depend in large measure on the character and quality of data available. It is not only major research projects carried out by teams of scholars that have changed, however; individual research by specialized scholars working in a particular area has also been affected. In many universities and research institutions, there is no more than one economist for a given specialty, and for this reason he must do his research as an individual scholar. It is still true that many economists engage in research on an individual basis, but where before the computer the cost of processing data and making computations was beyond the resources available to the individual scholar, today this is not as true. The existence of bodies of data and the computer is extending the horizon of such scholars and is placing in their hands powerful research tools. An increasing number of substantial and valuable research projects is being undertaken because information is available on a highly disaggregated basis in machine readable form.

Access to Data by Economists

The use of the computer as a basic tool in empirical economic research does, of course, require that there exist bodies of suitable data in machine readable form. Without appropriate data, the economist with a computer would be in the same position as a biologist with a powerful microscope but no biological specimens. With limited or inferior data he will be constrained to results of limited usefulness or doubtful reliability.

LARGE-SCALE RESEARCH PROJECTS

For the most part, large-scale economic research projects have a considerable advantage in obtaining the kind of information they need. However, even in these cases, the Committee has found that the situation is far from satisfactory. Federal agencies are not organized to provide data, and therefore delays and administrative difficulties may make it impossible to obtain the desired information. The problem of disclosure of basic information poses additional difficulties, and Federal agencies may use these difficulties as a convenient excuse at times when they regard themselves as fully preoccupied with their own problems, although devices could be worked out to safeguard the confidentiality of the data. Where cooperation is required between two Federal agencies for the development of interrelated data, the difficulties are generally so great that research institutions hesitate to undertake the task.

INDIVIDUAL RESEARCH

The problems facing the individual research worker are many times greater than those faced by large-scale projects. First, it is often quite difficult for an individual to find out what information exists and what form it is in. Second, making arrangements with Federal agencies often requires substantial time and effort, and usually agencies are not receptive to the individual scholar unless he is well known. The cost of having the Government prepare data in a form suitable for research purposes is very high indeed, because it must be done on a special ad hoc basis which disrupts the agency's operations. For these reasons the individual researcher is usually not in a position to obtain specially developed bodies of material. However, tapes of standard or multipurpose information specifically designed to be sold for research purposes can be developed. As one example, the 1-in-1,000 sample of the population census prepared by the Census Bureau has provided many universities and research institutions with a set of basic information which can be used in a large variety of research projects. Over the long run, the individual research scholar may have to come to depend upon such standard bodies of data much in the same way as he previously depended upon published tabulations.

Data Access from the Point of View of the Federal Government

As has already been indicated, the various agencies of the Federal Government have administrative and regulatory responsibilities which constitute their major functions, and the production of statistical information and the data underlying it is usually ancillary to these major functions. Demands for data by a large number of organizations, including not only research economists but also State and local government groups, business, and other Federal agencies, often place a severe and unwanted burden upon data processing facilities and the time and energy of specialized personnel. Even when such work is done on a reimbursable basis, limitations of staff due to overall personnel and budgetary considerations and the ability to hire people make the filling of special requests a burden. Outside requests for data are often uninformed, unreasonable, and in view of the Federal agency, not worth while. Few outsiders can know enough about the data, their nature and characteristics to make sensible requests, or to have a realistic appreciation of the analytic limitations which the data impose. As already indicated, the disclosure problem is formidable and causes considerable uneasiness on the part of the responsible people in the data producing agencies, but it also may be very useful as a shield to protect them from the nuisance of dealing with individual requests. The problem, as seen by the Federal Government as a whole when contemplating a request for data, could be reduced if research workers asking for data could get together and coordinate their requests.

Economies of Scale and the Need for Coordination

Many of the requests for basic information on a specific subject by different research scholars are duplicative. However, since each research project will be designed in somewhat different terms and has different objectives, it is inevitable that the independent requests for information will not be identical. On the other hand, it is also quite possible that, if careful consideration were given to the matter, general master tapes might be designed in specific areas which would meet the needs of a large number of research projects. One of the difficulties with published information is that different research workers want different types of aggregations and classifications. Since it is now possible to provide data on a disaggregated basis, these differences are no longer relevant, and it becomes necessary only to specify the basic items of information to be included in the body of data.

This basic similarity in the demand for information on a given topic implies that considerable economies of scale could be achieved by coordination. If a single master tape would fully satisfy the demands of each user, designing special tapes for each user would be unnecessary. For this reason, the Committee has undertaken a preliminary survey of 10 major areas of economic data to see whether or not it would be possible to conduct sets of such basic tapes in these areas. On the basis of this examination it is the Committee's considered conclusion that this construction not only is feasible from the point of view of economic research needs and objectives, but also would go a long way toward improving access to major bodies of data for scholars, and toward reducing the costs and alleviating the burden placed on the Federal statistical agencies.

Development of Tapes for Specific Research Areas

The Committee circulated to a group of research scholars working in various areas copies of the preliminary inventory of machine readable data recently collected by the Bureau of the Budget and the National Archives. In a large number of cases, these scholars prepared suggestions as to bodies of data currently in existence, which should be developed and made available to universities and research institutions on a low-cost basis. Included among the suggested data files are some which are currently available to research scholars and which certainly should remain available. For example, the Bureau of the Census has developed a program of making available for purchase large bodies of unpublished data in the form of computer tapes. The Internal Revenue Service and the Bureau of Labor Statistics have also developed specific tapes for sale. However, even where unpublished material is available on computer tape, it is often not in a form which is directly useful to the research worker. Data reduction to prevent disclosure or to select a manageable sample of data may be necessary. It would also be very useful if the research community could be better informed about what tapes exist in the various Federal agencies, and the cost of obtaining them.

A number of different data characteristics which are important for research purposes have been mentioned by research workers. (1) They point out that sets of data that are continuous over time are particularly valuable. This is especially true where information relating to a specific reporting unit is obtained at regular intervals so that changes taking place at the micro level could be observed. (2) Even where continuous reporting by individual units is not available, sets of information for different periods which permit cross section analysis are very useful for research purposes since they permit examination of changes in structural characteristics and behavior. (3) It is emphasized that sets of data covering a wide range of items for a single reporting unit are more valuable for many purposes than larger sets of information which report on a smaller number of variables. In a great many cases it is the interrelationships among variables at the individual reporting unit level that are important for research purposes. (4) Sets of information which it is possible to match with other kinds of information are particularly important, even where the information contained in such sets of data may be quite narrow. Thus, for example, if a set of data tapes includes a social security number or some other identifying characteristic which would permit matching with similarly identified collateral information from another source, the tape is that much broader in its coverage. (5) Many sets of data are useful not because they are in themselves unique bodies of specialized information, but because they are already in a machine language and are capable of being manipulated at low cost, so that it is often easier and cheaper to use them than to have recourse to data already in tabulated form.

Proposal for an Organization on Economic Data

In view of the increasing importance and usefulness of machine readable data for economic research, the Committee recommends that economic research institutions and universities develop an organization to coordinate the requests by research scholars for economic data and to aid the Federal Government in the development of data for research purposes.

USEFULNESS OF FEDERAL ECONOMIC DATA

The inventory of machine readable data held by the various agencies of the Federal Government and the results of examination of the inventory by research scholars in various areas has convinced the Committee of the potential usefulness of such information for economic research. Out of the 600 items listed in the inventory, over 75 bodies of data can be identified as of prime importance for general research in the 10 areas listed. There is no doubt that this list would be considerably expanded if the scholars consulted had had available more detail on the exact contents of the different bodies of data. Furthermore this preliminary inventory was far from complete in its coverage of Federal agencies. Since there is such a large body of highly useful data, therefore, the Committee believes that research institutions and universities should encourage the Federal Government to undertake the establishment of a Federal Data Center.

NEED FOR COORDINATION

There is a substantial and growing demand from scholars in research institutions and universities for bodies of machine readable data held by the Federal Government. These demands are highly duplicative in nature, but completely uncoordinated. It is quite likely that in many instances it would be possible to obtain agreement from scholars working in a given research area as to what sets of information would be most useful if developed by the Federal Government. Such sets of information would satisfy the needs of many research analysts, so that Federal agencies would not be faced with many different requests. From the point of view of the community of research scholars, there would be considerable advantages in providing a clearinghouse for information concerning economic data, since it is so difficult for the individual research scholar to discover what information exists in the different Federal agencies, who should be contacted, and how problems relating to the confidentiality of data may be solved.

NEED FOR DATA DEVELOPMENT

It is not sufficient, however, merely to provide a clearinghouse and to coordinate individual demands for data. In a great many instances the research community should take an active role in advising the Federal Government how to develop and exploit a given body of economic data. The existence of a body of information can often stimulate valuable research activity. Thus, for example, the 1-in-1,000 sample of the population census was not developed as a response to specific research demand by scholars outside of the Government, but rather it was developed by the Census Bureau because they recognized the potential worth of this type of data. Those scholars who were consulted about specific research areas, furthermore, emphasized the need to integrate the different bodies of data collected by different agencies. Although the Federal Government is continually taking steps to improve the comparability of classifications used by the different agencies, the task of integrating bodies of data is still a formidable one requiring substantial effort. For these reasons, research institutions and universities should actively participate with the Federal Government in planning the development of economic data in specific areas.

NEED FOR A COORDINATING ORGANIZATION

In view of these specific tasks facing economic research institutions and universities, it is important to establish some continuing organization. The Committee recommends that institutions outside the Government which have a sizable staff engaged in economic research involving the computer processing of large bodies of machine readable data join to form a coordinating organization on economic data. The function of such an organization would include the servicing of individual research requests for economic data by providing a clearinghouse and information about the availability of data. Second, the organization should undertake an active program of data development in conjunction with the Federal Government.

ORGANIZATIONAL STRUCTURE

Although the organization might have a larger membership which would draw on its clearinghouse and information services, it would be desirable to establish an executive committee so that periodic working meetings could be held to determine matters of policy. If there is to be continuity in the organization, furthermore, there will have to be a permanent secretariat which can function on a day-to-day basis. In view of the importance of the Federal Government as a data source, it is recommended that this secretariat be located in Washington. Finally, it is also recommended that the proposed organization develop working subcommittees of scholars concerned with specific subject matter areas so they can advise the Federal Government on data development and the establishment of procedures for coordinating demands for data.

NEED FOR EARLY AND POSITIVE ACTION

The Committee urges that at an early date the Social Science Research Council convene representatives from research institutions and universities currently engaged in research projects involving the use of empirical information, in order to develop an organization which can coordinate requests for economic data. The group which is convened should give specific consideration to (1) how the research interests of all nonprofit research organizations and universities can be facilitated; (2) what kinds of services can be provided for nonprofit research institutions and universities; (3) what kinds of coordination are considered to be desirable; (4) how the proposed organization is to be established, staffed, and financed; (5) in what way the proposed organization can assist the Federal Government in the establishment of a Federal Data Center; and, (6) in what way the proposed organization can provide the Federal Government with advice concerning the preservation and development of basic data.

The formation of a coordinating organization should not, however, be delayed until solutions are found to all of these questions. There is an urgent need for an organized group with staff support to follow through on the problems outlined in this report. Such a group would be useful to the Bureau of the Budget in carrying out the suggestions contained in Part I of this report. Further delay may result in the loss of valuable data which could be saved by prompt action. Furthermore, in order to provide for the orderly flow of data in its most useful form 2 or 3 years hence, steps must be taken now to establish procedures for projects which are already in their formative stages and which, unless properly conceived, may in 2 or 3 years time present the same sort of problems which are now encountered. Finally, the very rapid growth of research needs and the large quantity of machine readable data generated tend to produce a large number of ad hoc solutions which will make future coordination more difficult. Adequate consideration of how to meet the needs of various groups in the immediate future may forestall the development of inappropriate partial solutions.

Appendix

PRELIMINARY EVALUATION OF PUNCHCARD AND COMPUTER TAPES OF ECONOMIC DATA HELD BY FEDERAL AGENCIES

Although it has not been possible to compile a comprehensive listing of the comments received from research scholars, the Committee has made a summary listing of some of the punchcards and tapes mentioned by research workers in specific areas. In some cases, the items discussed include tapes which can be purchased from Government agencies as well as those which are currently unavailable. In a few cases, sets of information not included in the inventory of tapes were also mentioned. . . .

1. Population

The census of population data are not only basic to the study of demography, but also provide valuable information on individuals and households necessary for research on housing, employment, education, health, and consumer behavior.

CENSUS OF POPULATION SAMPLES

The Bureau of the Census has prepared 1:1,000 and 1:10,000 samples of the census of population on both punchcards and computer tapes which are available for purchase. These bodies of data were warmly received by the profession and many research centers have purchased these sets of data. Many Ph.D. theses, as well as other research projects, are using this sample.

VITAL STATISTICS

The Public Health Service provides annual statistics on births, deaths, marriages, and divorces, which are all very useful for simulation models involving population projections.

2. Housing and Real Estate

Data relevant to research on housing and real estate are included in the material discussed under the headings of population, consumer behavior, agriculture, banking, and taxes. In addition, however, specific housing information is collected by a number of Federal agencies. Some of these agencies, such as the Federal Housing Administration, the Federal Deposit Insurance Corporation, and the Federal Home Bank Board, were not included in the inventory of machine readable data and so are not referred to in this evaluation.

INVENTORY OF HOUSING

The Bureau of the Census provides a number of different series relating to this topic. The survey of inventory change and residential financing of housing units, the housing vacancy survey, and the housing sales survey are all very useful, but for many purposes some data selection might be required to reduce the number of tapes.

BUILDING PERMITS

A number of different census surveys are available on building permits. Building permits issued monthly and annually, building permits used, non-permit construction starts, and the construction progress report are all relevant and important for the analysis of the construction industry.

PRICES OF HOUSING

The Bureau of Labor Statistics price data on housing include consumer price data on housing and rents. These tapes are in addition to the information on consumer expenditures included under consumer behavior, and if available in regional detail, would provide valuable information on the relative demand and supply of housing.

FARM REAL ESTATE

The Department of Agriculture provides information on farm real estate values. In addition there are two surveys, farm real estate market survey, and farm building survey, which would be very useful.

OTHER DATA

Financial information provided by the FHA series on insured home mortgage terminations, and data on individual parcels given by the census of government-assessed valuations, would be particularly valuable. Although the "County and City Data Book" is published, the computer tapes of this information which are now sold by the Census Bureau are very useful for research.

3. Labor Force and Wages

Information on the labor force, employment, earnings, and labor unions are provided by several Federal agencies. These data are often needed in a highly disaggregated form so that they can be related at a detailed level to other regional, industrial, and demographic information.

LABOR FORCE

The basic data in this area is provided by the Census Bureau in the Current Population Survey, and high priority should be given to making this available. In addition, the Social Security Administration provides useful samples of employer-employee records, and continuous work histories. Some sample of the summary earnings record tape would also be desirable. Finally, the Bureau of Employment Security of the Department of Labor gives data on the employment and wages of workers covered by unemployment insurance, labor turnover, and the characteristics of the insured unemployed. Given the current interest in the problem of unemployment data these sources are very important.

WAGES AND HOURS

The Bureau of Labor Statistics collects the basic information in this area in its survey of industry employment, payrolls, and hours. The data on wages and related benefits for 82 market areas also are highly important. Since census data on industry and trade also contain employment and wage data it will often be found useful if these various bodies of data are available in a form that can be interrelated.

UNIONS AND PENSION PLANS

The characteristics of labor unions together with their financial data provide the basic information on labor unions. Pension and welfare plans are covered by additional Bureau of Labor Statistics surveys. The growing importance of pension and welfare funds both as a source of funds in the economy and in terms of effects on the future income of the aged make this information particularly valuable.

4. Education

The increased interest in education and the magnitude of expenditures on education make it imperative that adequate data on this topic be available for research purposes. Much of the basic information is contained in the population census and other surveys where data are provided on the age, sex, and educational attainment of individuals. However, the Office of Education of the Department of Health, Education, and Welfare, provides a considerable amount of specialized information.

PRIMARY AND SECONDARY SCHOOLS

The inventory of schools for resource evaluation provides basic data on primary and secondary schools. Additional surveys of nonpublic schools are carried out on a periodic basis. Expenditures by type per pupil and data on various aspects of the curriculum such as science and mathematics and foreign languages furnish valuable information on the extent of educational benefits in different areas.

HIGHER EDUCATION

There is a considerable body of information available for colleges and universities in machine readable form. Data on plant and equipment, enrollment, residence and migration of students, earned degrees, faculty, and financial statistics are available. The survey of scientific and technical per-

321

sonnel made by the Bureau of the Census is pertinent here. All these bodies of information are important to research projects on the role and development of higher education in the Nation.

5. Health

In view of the development of both private and public health plans, economic research on health has become very important. The Public Health Service has since 1959 provided a series of continuing surveys and a number of special purpose supplements, all aimed at establishing basic and comprehensive data for research in the health field.

HEALTH INTERVIEW SURVEY

This survey together with the personal health expenditure survey should be made freely available to research workers with proper measures developed to safeguard the confidentiality of the original records.

6. Consumer Behavior

The field of consumer behavior has been intensively studied by economists for several decades. Consumer expenditure studies, analyses of purchasing intentions, and the financial characteristics of households are all important.

CONSUMER EXPENDITURE

The Bureau of Labor Statistics survey of urban consumers and the Department of Agriculture survey of rural consumers constitute the most recent basic data in this area. The committee has already indicated that these sets of data should be available for research purposes.

PURCHASING INTENTIONS

The quarterly survey of the intentions of households collected by the Census Bureau constitutes a body of information which is very useful in the study of consumer behavior.

FINANCIAL CHARACTERISTICS OF HOUSEHOLDS

The 1963 survey of financial characteristics was made by the Bureau of the Census for the Federal Reserve Board. These data are valuable for research not only on consumer behavior, but also on the role of the household sector as a source of financing in the economy.

7. Agriculture

Agricultural economic research has for many decades been a major concern of many colleges and universities in the United States. It is difficult at this juncture to specify just what categories of data would be of particular interest to the various research groups in these institutions. Nevertheless it is apparent that questions of land use, conservation, productivity, farm management, and many other topics are very important.

The inventory of machine readable data in the Department of Agriculture covers six areas: (1) Forest Service, (2) Commodity Exchange Authority, (3) Statistical Reporting Service, (4) Agricultural Stabilization and Conservation Service, (5) Agricultural Marketing Service, and (6) Economic Research Service. There are, of course, several classes of users for this information. On the one hand, there are research groups interested in the economic conditions in agriculture within specific regions of the country, and for these groups highly detailed information of a sample nature is often very useful. Other groups are more interested in the total national picture, and the functioning of agriculture as a sector in the economy. These groups want comprehensive tabulations, some of which are supplied by the Bureau of the Census.

FOREST SERVICE

The Forest Surveys are often based on a two-stage sampling scheme using aerial photographs. They are of interest primarily to those analyzing regional forest problems. Over 20 of these surveys were listed by the research workers consulted as having considerable priority. With respect to larger bodies of data, the National Compilation of Forest Survey Statistics is a very important set of data, containing information on ownership, size, forest type, species, and timber products.

AGRICULTURAL PRODUCTION

The basic information on farms, farm characteristics, livestock products, crops, fruit, etc., is provided by the Census of Agriculture. The Department of Agriculture also has tapes on the June–December enumerative survey, providing acreage reports for crops and reports on livestock. Both of these sets of data are important in the analysis of agricultural output.

AGRICULTURAL MARKETING

The data provided by the Commodity Exchange Authority showing futures transactions and trading data are useful in market pricing studies. In addition, some of the data provided by the Agricultural Marketing Service on such things as fruits and vegetables, slaughtering, and milk provide information on specific commodities in considerable detail.

FARM MANAGEMENT

The Economic Research Service of the Department of Agriculture provides a great deal of information about the status of farmers and farm management. Over 30 sets of data were listed as being particularly important for research on such topics as the financial condition of the farmer, transportation, housing, real estate and land use. In addition, gross income, cost of production, machinery costs, and fertilizer costs and benefits are all topics of research interest for which important sets of data exist.

8. Business and Industry

As already indicated, reports on specific business or industrial establishments might result in disclosure of confidential information. However, highly disaggregated data for regions and industries can often be presented without disclosure. In addition, samples may be developed which would not violate confidentiality, and fuller and more detailed data could be kept in a similar form by government agencies for those research projects which require processing of the original reports.

MANUFACTURING AND MINERAL INDUSTRIES

The census of manufactures and mineral industries for 1947, 1954, and 1958 and the annual survey of manufactures should be made available in as disaggregated a form as the disclosure rules will permit, and specific samples of data should be integrated with the census of manufactures data and the Internal Revenue data to provide more comprehensive and complete coverage of the manufacturing and mineral industries.

TRADE AND SERVICES

The economic censuses of wholesale and retail trade, transportation, and services should be treated in a manner similar to that described for data on manufacturing and mineral industries. In addition, the monthly surveys in this area should be developed into systematic sets of samples available over time.

BANKING AND FINANCE

In the preliminary inventory of machine readable data in the Federal Government, the Federal Reserve Board was the only financial institution included. It is probable that when the survey is extended to other Federal financial institutions, many important bodies of data will come to light. In the material examined in the current inventory, member bank loans to commercial and industrial borrowers and small business financing experience obtained by the Federal Reserve Board represent valuable research materials for analyzing business financing.

9. Government Finances and Taxation

A large body of information is available on the income and expenditures of Federal, State, and local governments, and Federal tax returns of individuals and business. These data are a very valuable source of research material.

GOVERNMENT FINANCES

The Census of Governments financial data provides information on about 91,000 government bodies. These data are valuable for comparative research on State and local governments, and when used together with other regional information provide material for analysis of regions and standard metropolitan areas.

TAXES

The Internal Revenue Service and the Brookings Institution have created in recent years tax models for individuals, for corporations, and for partnerships. All these tax models have been found to be extremely useful for research purposes. Additional tapes have also been prepared for fiduciary returns, estate taxes, and gift taxes. It is recommended that tapes be prepared on returns showing capital gains and losses, and that continuous income histories covering both individuals and corporations be developed. Finally, a considerable number of scholars consulted by the Committee emphasized that it would be highly productive if the tax records could be matched with social security records, the census of population, the census of manufactures, and the financial reports of the Federal Trade Commission and the Securities and Exchange Commission.

10. Foreign Trade and Payments

Considerable progress has been made over the last decade in the development of data on foreign trade. Imports and exports on a commodity and country basis are available in considerable detail on a monthly and an annual basis.

EXPORTS AND IMPORTS

The Bureau of the Census processes the basic foreign trade data. Export and import data are available for both waterborne and airborne trade for various levels of commodity and country detail. Such data are useful for a wide variety of purposes.

CAPITAL FLOWS

Analysis of direct foreign investment and short-term capital flows is important for understanding the balance of payments of the United States. Some of the required data now obtained by the Treasury, the Federal Reserve Board, and the Department of Commerce are in machine readable form. However, a great deal of other important data still are not in this form. A significant contribution would be made as a first step by putting all balance-of-payments material on tape.

11. Other Areas

There are, of course, other areas of data which deserve special attention. For example, data on the natural resources of the United States are very important for studies of conservation and research on the future growth of the economy. Special topics such as research and development expenditures by government and industry, studies of pollution, highways, railways, and impacted defense areas all require and often produce special sets of data which should not be overlooked.

Statistical Evaluation Report No. 6—Review of Proposal for a National Data Center

(A Report Prepared by Edgar S. Dunn, Jr., Consultant to the Office of Statistical Standards, Bureau of the Budget)

PREFACE

This report, "Review of Proposal for a National Data Center," is the sixth of a series presenting the results of a comprehensive review and evaluation of some aspects of the statistics program of the Federal Government. It was prepared by Edgar S. Dunn, Jr., Resources for the Future, Inc., as consultant to the Bureau of the Budget.

The proposal which Mr. Dunn has reviewed stems from the work of a committee established by the Social Science Research Council to study the problems of the preservation and use of economic data. In the spring of 1965 that committee made its report to the SSRC, which presented it to the Director of the Bureau of the Budget. In its report, the Committee on the Preservation and Use of Economic Data, known as the Ruggles Committee, summarized its recommendations as follows: "First, . . . that the Bureau of the Budget, in view of its responsibility for the Federal statistics program, immediately take steps to establish a Federal Data Center. . . . Second, that the Office of Statistical Standards . . . place increased emphasis on the systematic preservation in usable form of important data prepared by those agencies engaging in statistical programs. . . . Third, that

325

at an early date the Social Science Research Council convene representatives from research institutions and universities in order to develop an organization which can provide a clearinghouse and coordination of requests for data made by individual scholars from Federal agencies."

In asking Mr. Dunn to examine the proposal, and to study ways of implementing it, we were concerned primarily with the first two of these recommendations. But, while the Ruggles Committee represented the interests of the academic and social science research community, we were concerned with the use of statistical data for research, policy and decisionmaking at all levels, both within and outside Government. Mr. Dunn wisely extended it to include consideration of the relationships between the collecting and compiling processes on the one hand and preservation and accessibility for further use on the other hand.

We are indebted to Mr. Dunn for this analysis and report. We are also indebted to the many persons with whom he consulted, particularly those mentioned in his letter of transmittal who assisted by their thoughtful analysis of particular aspects of the entire problem and the preparation of the important appendix material.

RAYMOND T. BOWMAN,
Assistant Director for Statistical Standards.

November 1, 1965.

DR. R. T. BOWMAN,
Assistant Director for Statistical Standards,
U.S. Bureau of the Budget,
Executive Office Building, Washington, D.C.
Dear Ray:

Transmitted herewith is the final report containing my review of the proposal for a National Data Center.

In seeking to identify ways of implementing this proposal I undertook an intensive period of study and review covering the last 6 months. I had the benefit in this effort of the advice and counsel of numerous others. This assistance was engaged in the following way. I divided the problem into parts that could be considered simultaneously. One part consisted of an informal ad hoc committee which met with me on a number of occasions to discuss the feasibility of establishing a referral-reference function in relation to the files of the Federal statistical system. Joining me in this discussion were Joe Daly and Ed Goldfield of the Bureau of the Census, Bob Steffes and Rudy Mendelsohn of BLS and Ezra Glaser of the Patent Office. In a second initiative Mendelsohn undertook a more intensive study based upon the earlier survey of machine readable records conducted by OSS to try to get a better fix on what it will take to establish an archival function. He in turn was assisted by many people in the agencies. Lastly, the National Bureau of Standards was used as a vehicle to assemble a small group of knowledgeable people in an attempt to specify more clearly the essential elements of a data service center required to provide a range of facilitating services. Ezra Glaser, Marshall Wood, and

Dave Rosenblatt were the principal contributors to this effort although conversations included Sam Alexander and other members of his staff. Paul Krueger and I also participated in this effort.

In addition, I have engaged in many discussions of substantive issues with a number of knowledgeable people in the Federal agencies (both statistical agencies and program agencies) and in the universities.

I particularly want to acknowledge the invaluable assistance that I have received from Paul Krueger on your staff. He has given me continuous support, assistance and encouragement. He has joined me in many of the meetings and discussions with the aforementioned and has made his own valuable contribution to the thinking process.

The form and content of the report, of course, remains my own responsibility. I believe that the general conclusions and recommendations are sound and supported in whole or in part by the informed judgment of many others beside myself, but I do not attribute the views of this report specifically to any one or all of its many contributors.

In writing the report I have incorporated material included in earlier memorandums as well as sections that contain explanation and argument that is superfluous from the point of view of the informed staff member of the Office of Statistical Standards. I did so because I assumed that this report might be used in whole or in part to communicate elements of this problem and the recommended solutions to more than one group. I attempted, therefore, to include a comprehensive discussion of the problems and opportunities.

The report makes clear that my own understanding and evaluation of this problem has modified somewhat in the course of the study. I now feel that the production standards and practices are a more important element in both problems and solution. This, as well as other considerations, leads me to be less sanguine about the possibility or the desirability of keeping the issues of organization in the background. I think that there might be some benefit in our discussing this and several related issues on an informal basis.

Let me say that I have enjoyed working with the Office of Statistical Standards on this problem. I hope that the results are constructive in serving your needs and objectives.

Sincerely yours,

EDGAR S. DUNN, JR.

SUMMARY

The Ruggles Committee Report recommending the establishment of a National Data Center is only one of the more manifest expressions of concern, dissatisfaction and frustration that have been surfacing among the groups that use numerical records for research, planning or decisionmaking at all levels. The problems at issue go far beyond the forms of discontent generated by special interests or marginal interests not served by public policy. They result from major changes on both the demand and supply side of the information process since World War II. Many people in this wider circle are attached to a rather naive data bank concept of the solution that does not incorporate an adequate appreciation of the basic problems in data use and data generation.

The Problem

The central problem of data use is one of associating numerical records and the greatest deficiency of the existing Federal statistical system is its failure to provide access to data in a way that permits the association of the elements of data sets in order to identify and measure the interrelationship among interdependent or related observations. This is true at virtually all levels of use and for all purposes from academic model builders to business market researchers.

There are a number of characteristics of existing programs and procedures that stand in the way of an effective association of numerical records for purpose of analysis.

(1) Important historical records may be lost because of the absence of consistent policy and procedure for establishing and maintaining archives.

(2) The absence of appropriate standards and procedures for file maintenance and documentation lead to low-quality files that contain many technical limitations to effective association of records.

(3) Many of the most useful records are produced as a byproduct of administrative or regulatory procedures by agencies that do not recognize a general purpose statistical service function as an important part of their mission.

(4) Record association requires a good deal of intelligence about the compatibility of records in several dimensions and the circumstances that condition their availability. There exists no organized reference capability for performing the kind of reference service essential for the Federal system or even within individual agencies.

(5) Production procedures for collecting, coding and tabulating data that were appropriate when developed now lead to several types of record incompatibility that block the kinds of record association in usage that is required by current policy problems and made possible by computer technique.

(6) There are identifiable gaps in existing data records that stand in the way of bringing together records of greatest relevance for today's problems. Some of these gaps are more apparent than real and reflect the effect of the other obstacles to effective record association.

(7) The structural problems of concern to today's policymakers and the effort to bypass problems of record incompatibility force the utilization of data at levels of disaggregation that place severe strains upon regulations restricting the disclosure of information about individual respondents. Technical possibilities for using the computer to bypass these disclosure constraints have not been generally developed and made available by the agencies.

(8) There are new possibilities for more efficient management of large-scale numerical files in terms of storage and retrieval; new possibilities for rearranging files in more useful form; new possibilities for retrieving in

the form of maps, graphs, charts and other media in addition to the traditional tabular forms; new possibilities for building in disclosure controls and disclosure bypasses; new possibilities for matching records to assure compatibility. These potentialities require the expenditure of time and effort on system design and software development that few agencies can justify.

The Stakes Are High

The stakes associated with even a partial resolution of these problems of file availability and compatibility are very high. This rests in part upon an unexploited joint demand for information and in information service capability. In the Federal domain alone large amounts of money are being ineffectively spent in an effort to deal with these problems. The amount of overlapping and resource waste is substantial. The stakes are also high because the improvement in the utility of the information base could have an unmeasurable but substantial effect upon the quality of public administration.

The Solutions Are Not Simple

The solution to these problems do not rest, as some think, in bringing a large number of tapes into a common repository. Nor does it rest upon the fact that many different uses impact upon the same data sets making them "general-purpose" records susceptible to central management. General-purpose files are always put to special-purpose uses. What makes a record a general-purpose record is for it to be constructed on the basis of standards, maintained in effective condition and serviced by institutional arrangements and a technical system capability that will allow it to be combined successfully with other records in a wide variety of ways that will meet the special requirements of a wide range of users. Thus the solution to the problems will require program modification on a broad front involving all of the agencies as well as an emergent data service center.

RECOMMENDATIONS

Accordingly, it is recommended that a National Data Service Center be established with the capability to:

1. Manage archival records;
2. Develop referral and reference services;
3. Provide explicit facilitating services for users including:
   a. File rearrangement, cost tabulation and extended output options;
   b. Tape translation and file modification;
   c. Record matching;
   d. Disclosure bypassing; and
   e. Standard statistical routines.
4. Develop computer hardware and software systems essential to above;
5. Provide staff support to work in conjunction with the Bureau of the Budget to develop and establish and monitor standards essential to the system capability; and
6. Establish a research capability directed to an analytical evaluation of

user requirements for the purpose of designing and developing the system components essential to perform these services.

The National Data Service Center would perform these services for:

1. Archival records under direct management control of the Center;
2. The current and accumulated records of administrative and regulatory agencies;
3. As a system resource to be used in connection with the current records of any agency not in a position to meet the needs independently.

Resource Requirements

Figures are offered that represent estimates of program costs for several components of these functions but it is pointed out that there are joint-product, joint-cost relationships between these service activities that make these estimates questionable as a guide to overall program costs. A judgment is made that the range of services and program adjustments required (including resources for modifying agency programs to be consistent with system requirements) would call for expenditure of between $1 and $2 million annually during the first year or two and rising to the neighborhood of $10 million annually over a period of 5–10 years. A serious problem will be the assembly of the kind of intellectual resources required.

Issues of Organization

All of this really raises the issue of what kind of Federal statistical system we want to develop in the next generation, and encompasses a number of issues of organization and mission that will need to be addressed in a broad context. Further progress on the whole effort must depend on some understanding of the issues at the top policy level and some preliminary policy decisions to guide the direction of further effort.

Priorities

If an effort is made to undertake this kind of system development there are certain immediate requirements that need to be fulfilled.

a. A continuous focus of leadership needs to be established.
b. This focus needs to be provided with staff support providing the kind of research-analytic capacity that can evaluate use requirements as a guide to specifying program options and reduce these options to specifications, costs and a logical order of time phasing.
c. Begin under existing authority to:
  (1) Develop the standards for archives and compatible statistical building blocks, and
  (2) Begin work on the 9,000 tape nucleus archive identified in Appendix B. The Bureau of the Budget should give serious consideration to requesting funds to support these efforts in the fiscal 1967 budget.

Introduction

The assignment leading to this report originated 6 months ago in the form of a request to seek out and identify ways of implementing the proposal for a National Data Center presented by the Subcommittee on the Preservation and Use of Economic Data of the Social Science Research Council (the Ruggles Committee). During the interim the proposal and the problem set to which it was addressed has been intensively reviewed. I have had the benefit in this effort of the Council and effort of numerous others as indicated in the covering letter.

In order to identify the program options that might satisfy the intent of the Ruggles Committee proposal, it was necessary to try to specify more precisely the problem set at issue. This has led to a characterization of the problem and attendant proposals in a somewhat broader context than the Committee report but in a way that seems consistent with the intent and the leadership council of that group.

It is important to note that the report of the Ruggles Committee is only one of the more manifest expressions of concern, dissatisfaction and frustration that have been surfacing among the groups that use numerical records for research, planning, or decisionmaking at all levels. The Committee Report is a good representation of the interests and the concern of the academic social science research community. There are other loci of discontent. The newly emerging welfare agencies of the Federal Government (OEO, EDA, the Department of Urban Affairs, the new programs in education and health in HEW, etc.) are experiencing great difficulty in assembling the statistical data that will guide them in analyzing their missions, establishing standards for performance and formulary for guidance, and support of administrative decisions and evaluating results. Their problems in this regard, when added to the usual difficulties of new program development, threaten to delay programs and render decisions more vulnerable to attack. A wide assortment of groups associated with making policy and planning for public facilities at all levels are becoming increasingly vocal about this concern. These are the groups that plan for roads, schools, hospitals, urban and regional development, etc. As business management turns increasingly to supplement its internal sources of information with the intelligence afforded by public agencies, they, too, are becoming aware of some of the inadequacies and anomalies of the information base.

Public needs for general purpose statistical information have never been satisfied and, indeed, never will. There are serious and legitimate issues of policy about how far down the scale one goes before general purpose becomes special purpose and about the levels of support for public information services that are appropriate. However, the problems that are at issue at the present moment go beyond the forms of discontent generated by marginal interests not served by current public policy. They are the product of fundamental changes on both the demand and supply side of the information process that have come to a head since World War II.

The most dramatic and obvious change on the supply side results from

331

the advent of the large-scale computer. The economic feasibility and technical capability of producing, managing, and utilizing large numerical files has been multipled by factors of a thousand in some technical applications and often by factors of 10 and a hundred in the economic and engineering dimensions of program planning. These are order of magnitude changes in capability that have come with revolutionary speed. They not only represent important and discontinuous changes in scale but also changes in kind because program options become technically feasible that were unthinkable as recently as 10 years ago.

Less commonly noted has been an increasingly dramatic change in information requirements on the demand side. In part, this is a consequence of the technical capabilities offered by the computer as well. The user can now handle data matrixes of a size and complexity formerly unmanageable and can use analytical techniques of a computational dimension formerly impossible. In part, however, the changes in information requirements stem from radical changes in demand factors distinct from these responses to expanded technical capability. Public policy in recent years has turned increasingly to a concern about the problems of social structure as they relate to public welfare and public policy. The issues of poverty, education, health, area depression, urban organization, etc., all require an increase in relevant detail for sub-system components of the total economy or total culture. At the same time the analytical disciplines in the social sciences and management analysis and control have been turning increasingly to quantitative methods and procedures.

As a result of these processes the users are increasingly finding that their needs for data are not satisfied by traditional documentary formats and the producers of data are finding the need to make data available more commonly in machine readable form—often in an organization and a format unique to the purpose. The producers and users of data find their requirements and their missions intersecting in ways unknown a short time ago. Neither can continue to live the independent life formerly customary. The computer and other dimensions of social change have performed a shotgun wedding and both parties are in the process of discovering their incompatibility.

The procedural and program difficulties that led to this report are the product of this incompatibility. It is not uncommon in cases of this type for the assessment of difficulty to be one-sided. The community of users has been sensitive to and vocal about many of the limitations of the producers of general purpose data—their mission concepts and institutional forms. The producers, in turn, can perceive many inadequacies on the part of the users. This report continues to be one-sided in emphasis because it addresses itself primarily to the problems of use. The charge that framed it was couched in terms of the missions of the producing agencies of the Federal statistical system. It would be very worthwhile for some group to produce a companion evaluation of the anomalies in the production and usage of statistical information that arise from the practices and concepts of the user groups.

It is sometimes true that people who have concerned themselves with this

332

problem are content with a superficial level of diagnosis and prescription. There is considerable attachment to the notion that most of our problems can be solved by computerizing all of the data we have in the backroom. This may be characterized as the "naive data bank" notion and its widespread acceptance is a source of some concern. I should emphasize here that this is not a characteristic of the Ruggles Committee Report which was produced by knowledgeable and sophisticated people. However, the tendency to see the solution to the problems in relatively cheap technical programs has led to some misinterpretation of the Ruggles Committee Report on the part of both those looking for additional support for data bank schemes and those reacting to the naive data bank concept. These evaluations and solutions are not based upon an adequate understanding and appreciation of the realities of the production processes essential to data generation or the institutional forms appropriate to their purpose.

The Ruggles Committee Report gave us a healthy beginning toward an evaluation of this problem in realistic terms. However, this group did not have the time or staff resources to spell out the total problem set in a way that seems essential to support a more detailed consideration of program options. There is also a tendency in this Report to see the problem primarily in terms of the accessibility of existing records and the solution in terms of the extension of user services. There is much that is valid in this representation but it gives insufficient attention to the important fact that accessibility is bound up with all of the production procedures and is inseparable in a number of fundamental respects from the issues related to the quality and scope of the existing records. It seems useful, therefore, to attempt a more precise formulation of the problem set to the solution of which the data center concept is addressed.

The Problem

The central problem of data use is one of associating numerical records. No number conveys any information by itself. It acquires meaning and significance only when compared with other numbers. The greatest deficiency of the existing Federal statistical system is its failure to provide access to data in a way that permits the association of the elements of data sets in order to identify and measure the interrelationship among interdependent activities. This deficiency has been partially overcome in a few vital areas where we need to trace and analyze the performance of the economy, by the establishment of special programs to bring together data sets in the form of national accounts, special index series, etc., but remains a debilitating constraint for most uses of data for analysis and planning. This is true for virtually all levels of use and for all purposes. It is a problem that plagues the research analysts inside and outside of the National Government who, for example, are engaged in building models of the economy in the interest of analyzing and projecting the major dimensions of economic growth and stability. It has been the principal obstacle to the administration's attempt to build a postattack revaluation and recuperation model. It is just as serious a problem for the uses that do not take the form of integrating data sets into a complex and formal model structure.

The organization like EDA that wishes to establish a measurable test of eligibility for its program benefits faces the same problem. The business analyst who simply wants to identify a variety of characteristics of the firms and households that form his principal markets often faces the same problem. The State Governor who wants to evaluate elements of his own program or the problems of his State by comparing them with the problems and programs of other States faces the same problem.

While the general problem is one of associating numerical records in use, it is understood better if we can visualize it in terms of its problem subsets. There are a number of distinct obstacles to file association that need to be identified before we can talk about solutions and program options. Consider the following:

THE ARCHIVAL PROBLEM

This is the problem that initially interested the Ruggles Committee and the door through which they entered their concern with some the broader issues of file management. The problem arises from the fact that the statistical agencies are oriented primarily to producing data publications and often leave their records improperly documented for further proceeding and analysis. Worse still, useful records are sometimes destroyed. These things occur because the existing system has no standards for identifying the files significant for preservation or for essential levels of file documentation. It provides no financial or organizational mechanisms for their maintenance. The decisions about the significance of archives is left to functionaries with little knowledge of their value in use and who must allocate funds for their documentation and preservation in competition with agency missions defined by previous policy in more restrictive terms and considered primary by agency personnel.

This, obviously, constitutes a major obstacle to the association for records for anyone who needs to work with data with any significant historical dimension.

PROBLEMS OF FILE MAINTENANCE

Closely associated with the archival problem are some of the more fundamental problems of file maintenance. The utility of a file and its capacity for association with other records rests on more than the existence of a tape and a document that identifies its content sufficiently well for the data to be retrieved. Many additional problems stem from the low quality of file maintenance.

A couple of the more gross and obvious defects are associated with the fact that there are still important records that do not exist in machine readable form. Amongst the files that do exist on tape, some are in a mixed binary mode and some in a decimal mode making data association impossible without expensive and time-consuming mode translation. This is often true even between records of the same agency.

More subtle defects in file maintenance are uncovered when the need for data association requires bringing the detailed data into accord with summary or published data. Often in the rush to meet production goals, agencies have pushed work through the processing stages of screening, reconciliation, estimation and summary in great haste without correcting prior files when-

334

ever errors or discrepancies are found. For example, corrections made "at the summary level" are not carried back into the micro-detail. Indeed in some instances corrections have been made only in the published data, leaving both the summary and the detailed machine records uncorrected. Occasionally, summary data may no longer be in machine records and must be recreated by reprocessing the detail files or by keypunching and processing the new records. In some surveys, standards for screening data for creditability may have been coarser than appropriate for other uses.

The urgency to release results may also leave a disarray from the viewpoint of good file record and format management required for the files to be reused. There may be no uniform position in the records for like data and duplication of the same data can occur. For archival purposes a uniform record for the same data is essential and elimination of duplication economical. Also, the tape records may contain excess information. Certain codes and indicators used in the initial processing have no meaning in the archival context and the files must be purged of the excess information. Files may have interspersed alphabetic information useful only in the narrow survey context and which add complexity to programing efforts when used in other contexts. The absence of clear identifiers as part of the tape must be corrected to facilitate use of such tapes.

The requirements for simple access as well as the association of records are often stymied by the limitations of standards and procedures for routine file maintenance. Mr. Mendelssohn, who was loaned to OSS by BLS to conduct a detailed review of the condition of the more important data files that might form an archival or file management center, concluded that the loss of data because of the failure to support good file management is distressing. (Appendix B.) The report of the study group formed at the National Bureau of Standards also emphasized the problem of file maintenance (Appendix C) as did the Ruggles Committee Report.

THE REFERENCE PROBLEM

One of the serious obstacles to the fullest utilization of the information resources of the Federal statistical system and to the effective association of its records in use is the absence of any clearly defined reference function. The inadequate nature of this kind of service is directly traceable to the production orientation of the agencies stemming from their primary missions as data publishers. The reference function has generally been thought of as the responsibility of the documentary centers. To the extent that the agencies attempt to provide occasional referencing assistance, the task falls to an individual whose primary mission is defined in terms of the publication mission. The inadequate nature of this service is also traceable to the fragmented nature of the records of the Federal statistical system growing out of the divided responsibility for their generation and maintenance. The reference problem is made especially complex because of the decentralized character of the Federal statistical program. No agency has been in a position to perform a reference service in relation to the total file. The problem is becoming more acute as records are frequently demanded in disaggregate or special form not met by traditional documentary formats and are frequently used in ways that require extensive knowledge and understanding about the compatibility of records in several dimensions and the circumstances that condition their accessibility.

THE PROBLEM OF ADMINISTRATIVE RECORDS

Some of the most useful general purpose numerical records are generated as a byproduct of administrative and regulatory procedures of Federal agencies. These agencies rarely interpret their missions to include the capacity to provide general purpose statistical services. Even when they might like to do so they experience serious difficulty because of the traditions, program priorities, budgetary procedures, and legislative authorities peculiar to their agency. Users who need to acquire from these agencies, and especially those who need to match these records with other files, find their task difficult. There is an important need to provide for the management and servicing of these records for general purpose statistical use.

THE DISCLOSURE PROBLEM

The legal and administrative regulations on the disclosure of information supplied by individual respondents are becoming increasingly restrictive to the user. Only rarely is this because policy or research requires specific information about individual respondents per se. It is usually because of the need to associate sets of data in the interest of determining the interrelationship between two or more variables. The strain upon disclosure arises because matching several sets of data for consistency at levels of aggregation appropriate to the problem requires a retreat to elemental units in the process of constructing the necessary aggregates. It is not widely understood that the interest in micro-data and the existing pressures and constraints do not grow out of an interest in information about the specific respondent.

The fact that the strains upon the disclosure rules usually are of this form is fortunate because there are possible a number of servicing procedures based upon computer technology that can satisfy the needs of the user in most cases without violating disclosure regulations. Currently, however, the agencies of the Federal statistical system have only a very limited capability for performing the kinds of services that would lead to disclosure bypasses. The usage of the data is, thus, severely constrained, and valuable information is lost by aggregation at too early a stage in the analysis.

PROBLEMS STEMMING FROM THE PROCEDURES USED TO GENERATE DATA

It would be a mistake to conclude that the serious obstacles to effective use of the Federal statistical system under modern conditions is solely a product of its present inability to perform a series of user oriented services. Some of the most serious anomalies arise out of current practice in the production of data.

We have already seen how constructing legitimate disclosure bypasses forces one back to a manipulation of highly disaggregated components or even respondent units as building block elements. The collection and tabulation procedures of the agencies generate constraints on data use that lead in a similar direction. This arises out of some fundamental problems in dealing with the coding and classification of original source data.

As has been noted, a common form of information usage in analysis re-

336

quires the matching of an attribute for two or more statistical sources or the association of two different attributes. This may require matching between different historical sets or between the files of different programs or agencies. This association of records is rendered difficult or impossible by at least three classes of record incompatibility that stem from current production practice. One difficulty in associating records from the different sources stems from the noncompatibility of classification of the data by several collection agencies and information systems. In the process of condensing and summarizing source records from initial respondents, information is tabulated on the basis of classification schemes that group items into classes. Often these classifications are inconsistent. This is sometimes the result of the failure to develop general purpose standard classification codes applicable to all programs for these intermediate aggregates. It is often a result of the fact that standard codes are applied differently by different agencies so that there is no assurance that each agency (or program) will assign the same respondent to the same cell. Either of these cases often makes a comparison of the cells meaningless or difficult for purpose of analysis.

A further difficulty grows out of the fact that the basis for classification applied by the collection agency in defining the cells may be inconsistent with the analytical or descriptive requirements of the user.

When either type of problem occurs, one solution is to return to the initial respondent unit or some other disaggregate building block and reconstruct consistent boxes of data. This yields the same class of bypass procedure identified with the disclosure problem. At this point one may encounter another common problem in the form of the noncompatibility of the definitions of the respondent unit. This is a class of noncompatibility that not only renders questionable the comparison of seemingly similar cells for different systems (as in the other two classes of incompatibility) but may render difficult or even impossible the reconstruction of compatible cells.

The anomalies that grow out of these compatibility problems can be tackled in two ways. One often hears it proposed that general purpose standards for the classification of intermediate aggregates be considerably extended and aggressively applied to all agencies. This may not be the most fruitful line of approach. Existing standards may possibly be improved and made more general-purpose by a more intensive analysis of user requirements and a concern with the issue is not unimportant. However, an attempt to force all uses into a common standards mold for intermediate aggregates has attendant disadvantages from the point of view of the user as well as the producer and the agency vested with the responsibility of formulating standards. General purpose classifications for intermediate aggregates always require some compromises in taxonomy that reduce the utility of the data for special purposes. Furthermore, a great deal of the data generated by the Government comes from programs that have a special purpose mission and restrictive legislative authorities and requirements that go with it. Forcing on these agencies a rigid application of general purpose codes for intermediate aggregates may be impossible and even

337

undesirable because they conflict with special purpose missions. It does not appear to be a helpful possibility that all data sets can be arrayed in compatible boxes that will anticipate all uses. The attempt to deal with standards in this context will place impossible strains and burdens upon the machinery for making and enforcing policy with respect to standards.

A more fundamental way to handle this problem may be a progressive move in the direction of compatible building blocks that can be reassembled to provide compatible and relevant aggregate sets for special uses and can be used as a bypass for disclosure problems and other procedural obstacles. This suggests that the problem of standards of greatest importance in the emergent situation is the need for uniform identification, definition and coding of the respondent unit as a basic building-block unit. The absence of a uniform system of coding and classification for geographical areas is also a serious deficiency and is an important part of this same problem. This also suggests the importance of procedures for assuring that every agency puts each respondent in the same cell and that an important criterion for evaluating existing standards for intermediate aggregates is the extent to which they can serve as useful intermediate building blocks that obviate the necessity for returning to the respondent unit for many programs.

Unless something of significance is done to modify current practice in these production procedures, the matching of data from diverse sources will remain generally impracticable and often impossible.

ASSOCIATIVE RECORDS THAT DO NOT EXIST

Many of the most important analytical and policy issues of today require the association of existing records with records that do not exist. There are serious gaps in the public record of social activity.

There is a particularly important class of records that is missing. It can be identified by examining the problems of some of the most important Federal programs. Missing are the records that enable policymakers and planners to understand adequately how people, households, regions, activities, enterprises, and administrative units are functionally related and how they change over time.

The importance of such a capability is readily apparent. There is a large array of new and old welfare programs involved in trying to ameliorate various forms of social pathology and transform people (e.g., poverty, education, health), and regions (e.g., EDA, rural redevelopment), and the activities that engage them (e.g., Small Business Administration and large elements of the agricultural program). There is a large array of new and old programs engaged in planning for and providing public facilities (e.g., highways, mass transportation, water resources, urban development and housing, etc.). In each of these programs considerable effort, planning, and resources are expended for program development, in establishing the formulary for program management, and in evaluating program results. Indeed, Federal legislation in these areas impose planning requirements as a condition of grants-in-aid and other forms of assistance upon State and local governments and other State, local, and regional activities in at least a dozen large programs.

To date, the problems have been formidable and the results unimpressive

338

for one principal reason. The information base that exists and can be economically assessed tells us a great deal about the characteristics of people, households, activities, enterprises and their institutions at any one point, but tell us very little about how they are linked into functional networks or how they transform over time. These latter are the most relevant information resources for policymaking and program evaluation in these areas. What form of job training, what form of regional assistance, what kind of road networks, what modes of mass transportation, what kinds of cities are questions that need to be answered on the basis of some knowledge of functional linkages and evaluated in terms of measurement of change. The responsible planners and administrators of these programs are feeling a keen sense of frustration because of the paucity and irrelevance of much of the information available to them. Some of the records they need to associate to resolve these issues do not exist.

The information gap related to these requirements reveals two elements of significance for the present evaluation:

First, a large part of the apparent gap in the kind of information needed is a direct function of the same system anomalies outlined above. In many cases, the problem does not rest upon the fact that the relevant attributes of people, activities, or institutions are not included in existing records. It rests with the fact that these attributes cannot be associated in functional configurations or traced through a historical sequence. We see the evidence of this in the widespread current interest in what is characterized as "longitudinal" data (the ability to trace attributes of the same respondent through time in order to identify transformations—i.e., from and to movements in relations to places, activities, occupations, institutional affiliation, welfare categories, etc.). Therefore, many of these requirements could be met if the problem of file compatibility could be resolved through an extension of the servicing capability and some modification of the production practice of the Federal statistical system. This underscores the observation made in the introduction that the problems of file accessibility cannot be successfully separated from all of the issues related to the quality and scope of the files. In a fundamental way, file accessibility is the issue of file compatibility which is inseparable from the production practices that determine the organization and quality of the file. It is important to note that steps that can be taken to improve file compatibility and accessibility will substantially increase the effective scope and utility of present files without a change in the size of the files or the attributes of the respondents they contain though additional resources might be required.

Second, although a significant part of the gap in information is a function of file incompatibility, there are also gaps which result from missing attributes.

For example, some attributes of the population may appear only infrequently with the decennial census and be needed for intercensal periods for vital program planning and evaluation. Other attributes may not appear in any records under existing information programs. Some notable gaps appear in the fields of transportation and construction and in connection with some of the important welfare attributes of people.

The following observation is pertinent here: The system, as it currently operates, provides no authority or mechanism for the review of the statistical program and the allocation of its resources in the light of the most important changes in information requirements. The decisions about programs that determine the scope and quality and accessibility of the records are primarily made upon the basis of technical problems, cost considerations, respondent pressures, etc., that impact directly upon the production process of the individual program and agency. There is no systematic way for the requirements side of the problem to enter the decision process.

POTENTIALITIES FOR SYSTEM DEVELOPMENT ARE BEING MISSED

The new technology is making feasible a number of possibilities for greatly improving the utility of existing records. There are new possibilities for more efficient management of large-scale numerical files in terms of storage and retrieval; new possibilities for rearranging files in more useful form; new possibilities for retrieving in the form of maps, graphs, charts, and other media in addition to the traditional tabular forms; new possibilities for building in disclosure controls and disclosure bypasses; new possibilities for matching records to assure compatibility, etc.

One aspect of the service potential inherent in the new technology deserves some elaboration. The association of records in analysis usually carries with it a computational burden. This may take the form, for example, of computing the ratio of two data sets or making seasonal adjustments or computing coefficients in the analysis of variance. All of these derived numbers form a latent set implicit in the original source data. The computational capacity of modern computers is such that computations of this kind can often be made as fast or faster than the tape can be passed through the machine. Once a system has been developed for providing such a service, the marginal cost of generating these numbers when the tapes are being passed for retrieval is close to zero. Adding this kind of system capability can have the effect of increasing the effective size of the files of the Federal statistical system tenfold with latent numbers involving some computation.

These potentialities require the expenditure of time and effort on system design and software accumulation that few agencies can justify in terms of their current program levels or even appreciate in terms of their existing individual program missions.

THE PROBLEM OF FILE FRAGMENTATION

This is not a problem that is conceptually distinct from the others. Instead, it intersects the entire problem set being discussed and forms a part of the explanation for some of these anomalies. Currently, files are being generated and managed by more than 20 different agencies. It is precisely this division of responsibility and fragmentation of resources that inhibits system development and generates many of the problems of file compatibility. But apart from the way this problem invades all of the others, it imposes additional constraints because of the procedural, bureaucratic, and sheer time and space restrictions upon file usage.

The Stakes Are High

The stakes associated with even a partial resolution of these problems of file availability, accessibility, and compatibility are very high. This is apparent even if we restrict our view to the significant Federal programs mentioned above. There is manifest in these programs an impressive and unexploited joint demand for information. This jointness has two important aspects. Even where the attributes of the numerical files of importance to these agencies are disjoint, they require the same servicing capabilities in the statistical system in order to perform the essential tasks of record association. The agencies require the same kind of system capabilities. Beyond this, a number of the programs have a joint interest in the same sorts of file extensions. The new welfare agencies, for example, have a strong joint interest in longitudinal data about the welfare attributes of people that are not currently available. Even where these agencies might have discrepancies in the attributes of specific interest, there is a good possibility that the same collection vehicle could be used in servicing their needs.

It is interesting to note that many of these agencies have had substantial resources given to them by Congress explicitly for the purpose of generating or assessing the information essential to the conduct of program. This constitutes a formal recognition by the administrative-legislative process that the established statistical programs are not meeting these needs. So far, the remedial choice has been to fund programs to meet special requirements rather than system modification. This kind of bypass, however, has proved largely ineffective for several reasons.

1. These agencies have no effective way to apply these resources to system reform that would improve record compatibility.

2. The funds are dissipated because, though significant in total amount and perhaps even adequate to support major improvements, they are fragmented by their attachment to specific and narrowly conceived missions with no appreciation of the overlap or jointness of interest.

Thus, while the new welfare agencies could probably finance a collection vehicle adequate to their joint requirements, no one agency can really accomplish this satisfactorily alone and there exists no coordinating authority that can identify and exploit their joint interest.

Further fragmentation occurs even within agency programs. The Corps of Engineers, for example, has for years spent enormous sums of money on information to serve water resource planning requirements. Much of this expenditure has been duplicative and wasteful because the money for this purpose has always been funded on a river basin project basis so that it was virtually impossible to take advantage of the scale economies for building the servicing capability for the entire set of projects. As a consequence, each river system has tended to be planned in functional isolation without the opportunity to define the linkage between projects or to trace economic and social costs and benefits in an appropriately general context.

The stakes in program improvement in the Federal statistical system are high because the amounts of money being ineffectively spent on statistics

341

in these programs is very large. They are also high because the improvement in the utility of the information base could have an unmeasurable but substantial effect upon the quality of public administration. The ability to ask relevant questions and get prompt relevant answers in planning, administering, and evaluating programs is of considerable importance.

All of this is only by way of recognizing the Federal interests involved. The stakes of State and local public officials, and the business and research community are equally large. These are the decision units which, by the nature of their responsibility, require disaggregate data sets that are especially affected by the problems of file compatibility. They have a common interest in extending the capabilities of the Federal statistical system.

This common interest has an especially important new dimension. The major opportunities that exist for extending the scope of the file available for analysis with some reasonable economy of effort in the near future rest in an exploitation of the records that are (or can be) generated by the State and local public agencies. However, their utility, and the utility of the file of the Federal system, will be immeasurably enhanced if these records can be brought into reasonably compatible association.

We are witnessing a burgeoning interest on the part of the State and local groups in developing the mechanisms for setting standards for these files and for maintaining and servicing them over time. This source of information is bound to emerge in importance and size. It is particularly important, therefore, that improvements in the Federal program lay the groundwork that will permit effective integration of the Federal file with other sources as they emerge. Furthermore, these emergent efforts are going to require guidance and leadership in setting standards and designing systems in a way compatible with total requirements. Much of this leadership must be supplied by example and by cooperative effort by a Federal system that is moving in response to modern requirements and opportunities.

The Solutions Are Complex

It seems clear from the foregoing problem characterization that the solutions to this set of problems will have to be multidimensional.

When it made its proposal for a national data center as a solution and developed its justification, the Ruggles Committee revealed an understanding of many of these dimensions. Its proposal was a constructive one and intended to be interpreted with some flexibility. However, the representation of the solution in this way has had some unfortunate consequences not anticipated by the Committee.

In designating the center as a national data center and placing considerable emphasis upon the collection of tapes—growing out of its concern with the archival problem—the proposal became quickly translated in the minds of many as another data bank proposal.

The data bank idea is enjoying a considerable fad at the present. Many people have grasped this as the solution to their information problems. They have been encouraged by the substantial success that some fairly restricted and specialized information systems have had. A number of businesses, for example, have enjoyed some success in pulling their management

342

records into a compatible and useful information system. The impression is widespread that bringing machine records together into some kind of central file will be instrumental in resolving the data problems of the broad class of users who attempt to use the files of the Federal Government.

This notion is supported by a general misunderstanding about the character of the files and their use. Those supporting this view are impressed with the fact that many different users have intersecting requirements for the same sets of data produced by the Federal statistical system. These records are, accordingly, viewed as general-purpose files. The convenience and economies of scale of bringing these records together into a common repository seem obvious. The obstacles to effective use under the present system are interpreted as technical and bureaucratic limitation amenable to this kind of technical solution.

What is not often adequately appreciated is the fact that general-purpose data are always used to fill special-purpose needs. This means that, while there are many intersecting interests in the same files, the impact on the file of each use may be quite different in terms of the organization, the levels of disaggregation required, and, most importantly, in the way the file needs to be associated with other records. It is this need for record association that is paramount and the source of most of the difficulty as was represented above. What makes a record a general-purpose record is not the fact that many users have an interest in its dimensions. It rests upon the file being constructed on the basis of standards, maintained in effective condition, and serviced by institutional arrangements and a technical system capability that will allow it to be reprocessed and combined successfully with other records in a wide variety of ways that will meet the special requirements of a wide range of users.

Thus, the key to solving these problems does not reside in the assembly of the records in a center but in the capacity to provide certain forms of file management and utilization services to the user. The effective provision of these services may require the assembly of some of these records into an integrated file, but this is defined by technical system requirements and is not the central issue it is made to be by many representations. It is important to characterize such a program as a data service center. The proposal is too important and fundamental to be burdened with its association with the naive data bank concept.

The Ruggles Committee explicitly formulated at least a part of this rationale in their Report and, hence, were putting forward a constructive proposal worth serious consideration. However, the Committee never made explicit the way in which the problems of file compatibility rest upon the collecting and tabulating procedures of the agencies. It needs to be emphasized that these are important dimensions of the problem. Extending the mission of the Federal statistical system to provide user servicing capabilities based upon the new technology can do a great deal to extend the utility of existing records. However, the logic of a flexible service capability rests upon the ability to manipulate statistical building blocks. The development of these building blocks is a production task not contemplated in the suggestions for a data center. Some modification of current production practice will be essential for success. Indeed, if this problem is not tackled on a broad front, the generation of the servicing capability will fail to provide the kind of service intended and aggravate the sources of friction and dissatisfaction vis-à-vis the producing agencies.

RECOMMENDATIONS

The concept of a national data center is an appropriate vehicle for program reform if the concept is broadened to emphasize the role of the servicing capability and if it can be given an important role in assisting the Bureau of the Budget establish standards and monitor compliance. Accordingly, the basic recommendation is for the establishment of a National Data Service Center whose primary mission would be to provide service to users of Federal statistical data both inside and outside of the Government.

This Service Center would have to be designed from the outset to incorporate certain basic functions:

1. Direct the file storage and management for significant archival records in machine readable form for all participating agencies.
2. Provide a central referral and reference source for the users of Federal statistics. This would include the development and maintenance of a formal reference index and the development of statistical reference specialists.
3. Provide explicit facilitating services for the users of Federal data. This capability would consist of the following kinds of services:

   a. File rearrangement and cross tabulation to meet special needs and provide an extended range of output options in the form of maps, graphs, charts, and other media in addition to traditional tabular forms;
   b. Tape translation and other forms of file modification to bypass some of the inconsistencies and deficiencies in file management;
   c. Record matching where file compatibility exists or can be developed by file rearrangement;
   d. Disclosure bypassing where requirements violate legislative or administrative regulations;
   e. Perform standard statistical routines that form an essential part of the strategy of record matching and disclosure bypassing and which join routine computation with retrieval in a manner that makes a whole set of computationally derived numbers a latent part of the file of the Federal statistical system.

The National Data Service Center would be prepared to perform these services for:

   a. Archival records under direct management control of the Service Center;
   b. The current and accumulated records of administrative and regulatory agencies; and
   c. As a system resource or facility available to be used in connec-

344

tion with the current records of any agency where the need cannot be adequately met by the agency.

4. Develop the computer hardware and software systems essential to the file management and servicing functions.
5. Provide the staff support to work in conjunction with the Bureau of the Budget to develop and establish standards essential to the system capability.

There are a number of areas in which new or revised standards will be essential:

a. Standards that define the records to be preserved in archival form;
b. Standards for documentation and file maintenance, and
c. Standards for the classification and coding of statistical data with special attention to respondent units and other forms of statistical building blocks.

(The sooner some of the standards related to the establishment and maintenance of archival records can be established the better. The review of the program [in Appendix B and in the next section] indicates that the most useful archives and the most economical are those that are developed under proper control and coordination from the present forward. The necessary procedures can then be built into the routine processing of data. This suggests some urgency for making as much headway with these issues as possible. The OSS should begin right away to work on establishing these standards without waiting on any formal actions on proposals for a data service center.)

6. A research-analytic capability will be essential to the success of these functions. This does not mean developing the capability for conducting research and analysis directed toward issues of policy and management. Such analytic functions should be centered in the Executive Office and the operating departments. Policy research and analysis should be kept separate from the supporting function of supplying and servicing information.

A research capacity directed to an analytical evaluation of user requirements for the purpose of designing and developing the system components essential to perform these services is the essential capability. The construction of the reference file, the definition of standards in every category and the design of software routines and other system techniques that perform the facilitating services would all be controlled by what could be learned through research and analysis about the systemic elements of user requirements.

Some indication of the direction this analysis will have to take can be gathered from the National Bureau of Standards report in Appendix C. A modest effort made to think through the kind of knowledge about user requirements that will be essential to system design and development is described there. In sum, it will be important to identify major classes of users, to learn the extent to which

345

their requirements intersect the same sets of data, to learn the ways in which they require record matching from similar or different sources and the acceptable levels of aggregation. Only a systematic understanding of the joint and disjoint characteristics of the major requirements can serve to design an effective reference index, design relevant standards, and guide system design.

Resource Requirements

Many of the elements of this kind of program appeared in the Ruggles Committee Report and in the preliminary review. The task that has occupied recent months has been the attempt to document the needs more fully and develop some notion of preliminary specifications and costs.

The problem was broken into three parts for study and discussion and assistance sought with each. First, the essential ingredients for a reference and referral service were considered. A committee of knowledgeable people was assembled on an informal basis to discuss these issues (identified with the report in Appendix A). Second, a more intensive study was undertaken based upon the survey of machine readable records conducted by the Office of Statistical Standards and contained in the appendix of the Ruggles Committee Report. In this way, an attempt was made to specify more clearly some of the costs of the archival function. The Bureau of Labor Statistics made part of the time of Mr. Mendelssohn available to carry this out (report in Appendix B). Third, an attempt was made to specify more clearly the essential elements of the system that would provide the facilitating services and what it would take to provide such services. For this purpose the National Bureau of Standards was used as a vehicle to assemble several people with a considerable range of knowledge of both the uses of Federal data and the production processes that generate them (report in Appendix C). In addition to these organized efforts I have discussed substantive issues with a number of knowledgeable people in the Federal agencies (both statistical agencies and program agencies) and in the universities (including an interview with the professionals involved in Project MAC at MIT).

This effort has yielded a better understanding of the nature of the problem and the system requirements. However, it has been somewhat less successful in specifying in detail the components of the system and the resource requirements. Let me review first the results and then evaluate the shortfall.

THE REFERENCE FUNCTION

In reviewing the requirements for the reference function the committee made a rough judgment that it might take as much as 5 years and an average of $2 million a year to provide a meaningful reference and referral service for the Federal statistical system. This appraisal is limited in two ways, however. It is not the product of the kind of staff work in program planning that would be essential to a refined estimate and, therefore, represents only an informed speculation. More important, this estimate was generated with a view of the reference function as a discrete service unit or capability. It is recognized that a reference service would be more effective as an integrated part of a total service center program because the reference problem forms only a part of the larger problem set. If the provision for reference services is combined with other user services, the professional staff (particularly in its analytical and system development capacity), the computer facilities and other components of the service system could perform many joint functions. It is believed that because of the joint product character of these services, the incremental costs of providing a reference capability as part of a larger service system would be somewhat less.

THE ARCHIVAL FUNCTION

A review of the tape file inventory was undertaken which attempted to identify the important archival records and determine the costs of bringing these files to an acceptable level of file maintenance and documentation to be incorporated into an archive. The question of which records constitute significant archives rests, of course, upon an interpretation of requirements and development of standards not yet undertaken. In the interest of getting some feel for the dimensions of the problems this question was begged by arbitrarily preparing a list of the records considered to be vital general purpose series on a judgment basis to represent a sample archive.

On the basis of the data included in this sample archive it was estimated that a more complete archive would represent about 20,000 reels of magnetic tape and require an estimated $3 to $3.5 million and 3–5 years to develop. Of this amount about $800,000 would be needed to bring data not now machine accessible into usable form, about $500,000 would be needed to transfer punched card data to magnetic tape. In addition, between $500,000 and $1 million would be essential for blank reels and tape copying.

One of the interesting aspects of this report is the fact that almost half of this file (9,000 reels) could be brought into a data center for about $260,000 within a year. This indicates that the files vary widely in the quality of their maintenance and documentation. The incremental costs of the second half is about $300 a reel as compared with $37 a reel for the first 9,000 reels.

Obviously, the costs of bringing existing files into archives are substantial and some review and justification will be needed. This can only be done within the context of a more comprehensive review of the user requirements that must guide planning in this area. A related sidelight of the report is that the files that are best maintained and can most easily be brought into an archive are not necessarily those that are most important in a usage sense. This is largely a function of the size of the files and the frequency with which it is produced. This suggests that an archive based upon considerations of cost and convenience in assembling existing records does not assure the most useful file.

At the same time, a large part of these records can be preserved at such a small cost that there seems little question that the investment in this resource is essential and justifiable. There is another important observation. About half of the total costs estimated are for system development and will have to be incurred even if the archival objective is addressed to current and future records only. These must be thought of as a capital cost of archival development as distinct from the costs of "dusting off" existing records.

It is true that these records will still contain all of the elements of file incompatibility that are the product of the production methods and standards that governed their generation. However, they appear sufficiently vital to current and future analysis that a total program should make a serious provision for trying to salvage some of the loss in data resources that has taken place in the absence of a policy and procedure for file preservation. In addition, every step needs to be taken to place future accumulations on a sound and economical basis.

The costs of bringing these records into an archival file do not represent all archival costs, of course. There are storage costs also (less than $10,000 annually for 20,000 reels in prime air conditioned space), but these are inconsequential when compared to the need for facilitating services resting upon hardware and software systems to allow their effective use. These latter costs, however, cannot be fairly estimated at this point because, again, these services can be provided jointly by a facility which has a broader user service mission. As in the case of a reference service, an archive that is set up as a discrete service function will cost more than one incorporated in the total service complex.

A SYSTEMS CAPABILITY FOR FACILITATING SERVICES

It was through the agency of the Bureau of Standards that we attempted to assemble the intellectual resources to establish the scope of the program and the costs that would be required in establishing a system capability for providing the kind of facilitating services outlined in the recommendation. It is obvious from the foregoing discussion that this is the key to the program concept and to the evaluation of costs.

This turned out to be a difficult assignment. In our early attempts we found it exceedingly difficult to estimate program dimensions and costs without a clearer specification of the requirements the system will be designed to serve. Accordingly, a 3-day study session at Camp Ritchie was planned to see if we could break the back of this problem as the report in the Appendix reveals.

This session made some progress in visualizing the requirements as well as assisted in clarifying some elements of the problem to be solved. In particular, we began to formulate some notion of how an analysis of user requirements might be structured and carried out. We could not, in the time spent, get to a more precise specification of the system elements. I feel that this work has laid the groundwork so that a series of additional work sessions of the same type might lead to a formulation of more specific program options. This task was found to be large enough that it did not seem advisable to undertake this kind of intensive staff work without a more specific decision on the part of the Director of the BOB concerning the kind of effort that is going to be devoted to this problem set and under what auspices.

At the same time some informed speculative judgments about the order of magnitude of costs developed out of the discussion. A total program of the type outlined under the recommendations would probably start out with an expenditure of $1 or $2 million annually in the first years and grow to the neighborhood of at least $10 million a year. In the early years the size of the program will be controlled more by the practical limitations of assembling and training the kind of staff and acquiring the kind of equipment necessary. The fund could not be spent at a rate commensurate with the need and the objectives. A more detailed specification of program objectives, their phasing and the allocation of costs will have to rest upon additional staff work and should be preceded by some tentative policy decisions that will guide the work.

STAFF REQUIREMENTS

Just as it is not possible to detail costs, it is not possible to detail personnel requirements. However, all of the reports or the discussions leading to them emphasized one point. The kind of statistical reference specialist, user service specialist and statistical systems analyst that is required to make this kind of program work either does not exist or is in extremely short supply. This implies (1) that program development will be constrained at the outset by intellectual resources and not financial resources, and (2) a successful program in this field will have to make explicit provision for professional development and training both in its program and in its budget.

TECHNICAL REQUIREMENTS

This is also the place to point out that there has been nothing in the entire review to suggest that an effort of the kind outlined in this report would be technically constrained. There has been some indication that existing computer hardware has been designed with greatest concern for computational capacity and is not as economical or as flexible as possible for the management and servicing of very large scale numerical files. However, the existing state of the art contains the essential elements of a more appropriate hardware system.

Similarly, the software routines for file management and servicing will need to be developed, but there is nothing to indicate that these problems of system development are not tractable. What is indicated is that considerable work must be expended over time to create these capabilities. There is every assurance, however, that the state of the art is adequate to support fully this kind of effort.

Issues of Organization

My views on the organization issue have been strengthened by the months of study since the preliminary memorandum. First, I cannot visualize a meaningful program addressed to the interrelated set of problems discussed above without a considerable degree of centralization of function. Some form of interagency service center will be essential. Second, if such a center is developed with existing agency structure essentially unmodified, it cannot perform its mission without agency cooperation and without explicit accompanying modification of agency missions.

This suggests that an effort of this scope could not be implemented without seeking new legislative authority. Legislation will have to be worked out and sought that will permit the service center to receive file custody, that will relieve the agencies of their disclosure restrictions as they pertain to the release of data to the center, and, at the same time, transfer the agency's disclosure obligations to the center. No workable independent

349

center could be developed without meeting this issue head on at the outset. Further, the kind of program coordination and control of standards that will be essential may require legislation giving some interagency program authority to the new center. In addition, a single budgetary instrument for implementing the new program would be essential.

This kind of formulation inevitably leads to speculation about the organizational forms that might serve this end. I would like to react to some of the speculation proposals known to me:

1. A new independent agency; this is certainly the cleanest solution. It could be accomplished with a minimum of "ad-hoc-ery" and would provide maximum flexibility for planning and innovation. It would be unencumbered by many existing agency jealousies and provide the freest opportunity for developing new leadership. At the same time, it might foster a coalition of agency opposition. Given the attitudes both in the Bureau of the Budget and on the Hill about new independent agencies, it might be difficult to manage. Barring this, some existing agency would have to form the vehicle for the program. Several have been mentioned in this context.

2. GSA-Archives. The General Services Administration and, specifically, Archives, has been pointed to as an agency with already existing interagency authority and concerned with a part of this function. I am extremely dubious about the viability of such a solution. In the first place, this is not primarily an archival problem. It is primarily a complex problem of file management and coordination and rests upon a base of production practice that must be involved in the solution. It must develop a mixed professional staff of reference specialists, statistical specialists, subject matter specialists, system design specialists and programers and technical services staffs. These resources do not exist even in embryo in these agencies. They would be handicapped by their image in building up the quality intellectual resources the program would need to succeed. Furthermore, these functions would not represent a primary mission from the point of view of the management of these agencies. An even more compelling objection is the fact that it would take the first tentative steps toward some integration of the user services of the Nation's statistical system down an organizational path that might make more difficult the achievement of desirable emergent forms.

3. One of the existing statistical agencies: I do not believe that any of the existing agencies offer a desirable home for this function. It is true that they have already accumulated some of the expertise and equipment and management services and experiences that a new venture of this type requires. However, their mission concepts are conservative and inhibited in this area. The leadership is lacking. Perhaps more important, old interagency jealousies, etc., would make it more difficult to develop an atmosphere of cooperation.

4. Compromise between the existing agency and independent agency solution: Of the existing agencies Census is certainly the most logical candidate by virtue of both its mission and the caliber of its professional staff. Many of the disadvantages of assigning this function to a new agency

would be offset if Census were made an independent agency itself. If this were done and the user service functions set up parallel and with equal organizational status to the Census function we might have something of the best of both worlds. Something of this type might also have the advantage of being a constructive first step toward some degree of reorganization of the Federal statistical system.

5. The National Bureau of Standards: It has been pointed out that the Bureau of Standards performs an interagency mission and has an unusual combination of existing legislative authorities to receive funds from and distribute funds to agencies, to set up special institutes, to use visiting scholars, etc. It already has an interagency service tradition and has been explicitly given the responsibility for assisting Federal agencies in planning computer systems. They also have in existence an emerging computer utility that might serve some of the needs.

6. National Resources Evaluation Center: This agency has been suggested because it is an independent agency in the Executive Office of the President with existing interagency authority and responsibilities that extend beyond the mission of the Office of Emergency Planning where it is housed. It already contains a very large file of integrated Federal data from the various statistical agencies and has built up a staff with more experience in integrating interagency records than any other agency. It has a large computer installation organized for large-scale file management. It has an already existing interagency committee with the major statistical agencies represented and each of the agencies has one or several professional employees assigned full time to the activity. It is a conceivable vehicle if its authorities and functions were extended and removed from OEP.

If an effort to implement such a program goes forward, a great deal of thought and discussion will have to go into reviewing the kinds of options represented here. I would like to offer the following related observations: First, there is a major threshold that must be negotiated if we deal meaningfully with the problem and program set at issue here. The kinds of services recommended cannot be subdivided without imposing upon a more limited function, serious functional handicaps, unnecessary expense and, possibly, seriously threatening its chances of success. I am concerned that partial measures may, in the end, do more harm than good. Since such an effort cannot spring into being "full-blown," it will have to be time-phased over a considerable period. However, the program should be considered as a whole.

Second, from an organizational point of view it seems inescapable that whatever initial action is taken, the end result will be a substantial reorganization of the Federal statistical system. It is very important that the organizational vehicle used at the outset does not predetermine the future evolution of the system in a way that limits its ability to implement essential subsequent phases.

Third, it seems to me that in discussing this problem set and proposed program, we are really engaged in a discussion of what kind of Federal statistical system we want to develop in the next generation. I am much less sanguine now about whether it is possible, or even desirable, to keep these issues in the background. I am sufficiently concerned about the abortive potential of solutions that fall short of a critical threshold and organizational arrangements that might inhibit essential lines of development that I feel it important to consider the issues of organization in a straightforward way. I would go further and suggest that every one of the six interim solutions outlined above has serious limitations, although some have a more open-ended character than others. My own preference would be to handle the organizational problem at the outset as a reorganization of the Federal statistical system. There are a number of indications that this might be a favorable time to do so.

Fourth, this predilection is reinforced when I reflect upon the great importance production practice plays in the whole configuration of problems and solutions. I am also inclined to believe that a fundamental improvement in the integration of production practice can offer a constructive solution to the paperwork problem of respondents without jeopardizing important components of a general purpose information system. Another factor reinforcing this inclination is the conviction that some form of integrated leadership can go far in dealing in a creative way with the joint interest of existing Federal programs and agencies whose current large expenditures for data now constitute a large resource waste.

Priorities

The comprehensive scope of the issues presented here plus the fact that preliminary staff work cannot specify and cost explicit program options suggests certain priorities. First, a continuous focus of leadership needs to be generated. The proposal has already been put forward that an interagency committee be established to provide this focus.

Second, wherever the leadership function is vested, it seems to me that the highest priority is to provide this focus with the staff support essential to identify requirements and specify the elements of the system that must be provided for. The earliest requirement is to engage the research-analytic capability identified under item 6 of the recommendations. The development of specific program options, the definition of their specifications, costing these elements, and identifying the essential order of a time-phased program will require early intensive staff support of a very special kind.

Third, a beginning can be made under existing authority upon some of these problems before new programs and organizations can be developed and funded. At least two kinds of effort could be begun right away.

a. The standards that shape the content of archival records and determine the essential forms of file maintenance and documentation need to be worked out and made a part of ongoing programs. A beginning can also be made in formulating the kinds of standards that will produce statistical building blocks essential to file compatibility.

b. The 9,000 tape file record identified in the Mendelssohn Report constitutes a nuclear archive that can be generated quickly at a very modest cost. Funds should be made available to the agencies to begin the creation of this basic archival record.

The Bureau of the Budget should seek funds to carry out these preliminary measures under its own authority. The staff work and the extended effort applied to statistical standards should be centered in the Office of Statistical Standards. The funds to develop the basic archive could be transferred to other agencies as a part of a controlled plan.

Several hundred thousand dollars might profitably be requested in the fiscal 1967 budget for this purpose.

Appendix A

Appendix Memorandum

Subject: Report of informal committee on the reference problem.

The Committee

An informal ad hoc committee was assembled by Edgar Dunn, acting as chairman, to discuss the problem of developing an adequate reference service for the Federal statistical system. The committee was composed of Joe Daly and Edwin Goldfield of the Bureau of the Census, Rudolph Mendelssohn and Robert Steffes of the Bureau of Labor Statistics, Ezra Glaser of the Patent Office and Edgar Dunn, consultant to the Office of Statistical Standards. These individuals participated with the knowledge and consent of their agencies but served as individuals and informed professionals. No attempt was made to get agency clearance or establish agency points of view. It was merely an informal attempt to formulate some judgments about the nature of the problem and its solutions. The committee met on several occasions on an irregular schedule during the summer of 1965.

The Problem

It was agreed that one of the serious obstacles to the fullest utilization of the information resources of the Federal statistical system is the absence of any clearly defined reference function. The inadequate nature of these services is traceable to the production orientation of the agencies stemming from their primary missions as data publishers. The reference function has generally been thought of as the responsibility of the documentary centers. To the extent that the agencies attempt to provide occasional reference assistance, the task falls to an individual whose mission is defined as a production responsibility. The inadequate nature of this kind of service is also traceable to the fragmented nature of the numerical records of the Federal statistical system growing out of the divided agency responsibility for their generation and maintenance. Because of the decentralized nature of the Federal statistical program the referencing problem is made especially complex and no agency has been in a position to perform a generalized service with reference to the total file.

The problem is becoming increasingly important in recent years as important uses of the numerical files are more frequently taking the forms of records in machine readable form rather than the traditional documentary form. The problem is also fed by changes in information usage that are leading to more complicated information requirements. Records are needed more often in disaggregate or special form not met by traditional documentary formats and they are often used in combination in ways that require extensive intelligence about the compatibility of records in several dimensions.

Desired Reference Capability

Ideally the Federal statistical system should be able to develop a reference system that has the capacity to deal with inquiries in an efficient and creative way that would facilitiate access to the records and extend their utility. The clientele is conceived to cover a wide range of sophistication and types of need. However, the requirements for a reference capability stem primarily from a large and growing core of intermediate information processors that service the research aims of academia and the decision and administrative requirements of business and government at all levels.

Such a service should be able to:

1. Help the client refine his inquiry and frame it in a way acceptable to the system and, in the process, give some preliminary information about the scope and nature of materials implied in his request as an aid to further defining, sharpening, and limiting the inquiry. (Experience of the Science Information Exchange and the National Science Referral Center have pointed up the great importance of this function even in dealing with highly trained professionals.);

2. Provide, by drawing upon a reference index and other reference tools, a fairly complete documentation of formal intelligence concerning—

   a. the number and size of relevant file sets,
   b. their taxonomic descriptors,
   c. their mode of preparation (census, survey, etc., questionnaire forms, etc.),
   d. their quality characteristics including (1) quality of the data (sampling and response errors, etc.), and (2) quality of the files (state of documentation and file maintenance),
   e. the extent to which the taxonomic and qualitative characteristics of the data will support merging and collating series for various purposes,
   f. where the data are located and how they may be assessed including such information as the form of the file (published, machine readable, machine language and format, etc.) and access costs in both time and money;

3. To perform a switching service so that the user can assess the needed records efficiently. (The uninitiated user needing to access several

354

data sets in different divisions of several agencies can be faced with a complex switching problem difficult to handle efficiently unaided.);

4. To provide a "semiautomatic Joe finder" to facilitate access to informal and specialized intelligence concerning the records and their characteristics.

This would need to be a person-oriented service that would revolve around the role of the professional reference specialist who would deal with the client by person, by mail, and by phone.

Important Considerations in Implementation

A general consensus emerged from the committee discussion about the principal issues or problems to be resolved in the process of implementing such a goal. There was also agreement about the general form of the solutions. The most important issues revolve around three points:

THE REFERENCE FILE

In order to perform his role effectively the reference specialist would have to have access to a set of formal reference aids that would constitute the elements of an emerging reference system. The principal aid is visualized as a formal reference index that would probably be machine oriented. This index would attempt to bring into a reference file the kind of reference intelligence implied in the previous sections (2 a through f) that could be gathered and formulated in a formal system. Such a file would be designed to facilitate an iterative search procedure and to generate documentation to service each inquiry. After some initial period of development this file might have the capacity to generate, periodically, one or more condensed summary index documents that could serve as visual reference aids not only in the reference center itself but in documentary and service centers throughout the United States.

The construction of such an index would be a professional task of considerable magnitude and complexity. It would take time and resources to develop and maintain on a current basis. Indeed, the development of such a file would represent an ongoing task that, by its very nature, would never be completed.

The order in which the components of this reference intelligence are selected for development and the form of their organization into a file should not be random but governed by systematic priorities. Furthermore, it should be only marginally controlled by the ease with which such reference material can be organized out of existing materials. The development of the file should be controlled by a research-analytic effort on the part of the staff that would provide guides to the emergent usage. Accumulating knowledge about request incidence will be only partially helpful. Maximum effectiveness of the file will rest upon an explicit effort to identify the principal classes of users (in terms of their analytical requirements and problem orientations), the way in which their requirements are common or disjoint, the way in which they generally intersect different statistical records, and, therefore, the nature of the reference intelligence

355

necessary to serve each class of user. Some idea of the systematic character of the requirements is essential in order to do an effective job of designing a responsive reference system.

THE REFERENCE SPECIALIST

The reference file is only a tool. The key to successful data referencing is the reference specialist.

In the context we are discussing here he has three recognizable functions. First, the professional reference specialist is the essential human link in dealing with the reference client. He must often assist the client in refining his inquiry to a form that will facilitate response. He will provide the interface with the formal reference tools such as the reference index and the "semiautomatic Joe finder." He will supplement these sources with his own fund of informal intelligence gleaned from experience.

Second, the reference specialist must provide the professional analytical capability to undertake system-oriented research of user requirements and develop on a time phased basis the operating characteristics of the reference system.

Third, the reference specialist must undertake the task of constructing the reference system and its component formal reference index. This will require bringing together and systematizing large amounts of technical intelligence and incorporating it into an operating system.

One of the biggest problems in developing a reference capability is that the kind of professional reference specialist that is characterized here does not exist. It is a new kind of professional capability of emerging importance. There are a few men in established agencies whose work experience fits them with attributes that come close to the functional requirements outlined above. They are very limited in number, however, and, characteristically, are key men in fulfilling agency missions.

The success of the attempt to develop a reference system will rise or fall on the strength of the kind of professional talent that will guide its development. Since the kind of experience that is necessary in this function is rare, an essential part of any program effort will be an explicit recognition of this fact and an explicit procedure for the training and development of statistical reference specialists.

Ways will have to be worked out so that new professionals could have rotating assignments that would carry them into the primary statistical agencies where they could (1) work on specific components of reference information for the purpose of implementing the reference file, (2) come under the supervision of and receive training from those people who represent the greatest fund of accumulated knowledge, and (3) receive a total system orientation that could be gained in no other way. Project financing would have to incorporate explicitly the resources that would support staff training and development.

The task is made somewhat less formidable by the fact that the three categories of reference functions outlined above are susceptible to some degree of specialization. During developmental phases the intellectual resources of the staff could also be supplemented through consulting arrangements. It would be useful, for example, for the operating agencies to assign

356

some of their specialists to work with the reference service on a temporary or part-time basis. The analytic or system design component might be especially amenable to supplementation during the early phases.

THE ORGANIZATIONAL FORM

The feeling was strong that a successful effort to develop a Statistical Reference Service would require some degree of centralization of function. An important part of the reference function is interagency or total set in character and cannot be handled within the context of an agency orientation. At the same time, the reference agency can perform its function without involving the primary agencies directly. In the previous section we already outlined some of the ways in which agency participation would be indispensable. The agencies will need to play a role as a breeding ground for research specialist, and, of course, will be the source of most of the reference intelligence that must be used to construct and maintain an index. It may also be necessary and desirable to establish within at least some of the larger agencies a companion reference function that would be linked with the total reference capability.

The committee did not discuss the specific institutional form of such a service center within the framework of the existing institutions.

Costs

The committee devoted some time to a consideration of the resources that would be required to establish such a reference service. It came to the conclusion that nothing very precise could be said about costs at this stage for several reasons.

First, the kind of evaluation that can be given by a group of this type at an early speculative state is suspect. A more refined notion would require the application of more staff resources to planning and evaluation than are currently available.

Second, the question of costs is confused by the possible existence of joint costs in this program area. The general problem set of which the reference problem forms a part has several other dimensions that extend beyond the restricted problem this committee has taken for discussion. The costs of establishing a reference service of the kind discussed here would be quite different if it were established as a discrete function of, if it were developed as one component of, a more generalized user service capability. If the provision of reference services were combined with other statistical services addressed to establishing and maintaining archives, servicing administrative records, or providing tape translation, disclosure bypasses and other file management services, the professional staff and program facilities including computer facilities could perform many joint functions. The increment costs of providing a reference capability as a part of a more extensive user service capability could possibly be a great deal smaller than would be required for a separate and independent function.

Despite these obstacles to cost estimation, the committee noted that the operating budgets for two agencies performing related (though in many ways basically different) functions ranged from $400,000 a year for the National Science Referral Center in the Library of Congress to $2 million a year currently for the Science Information Exchange of the Smithsonian Institute. The committee speculated that it probably would take as much as $2 million a year on the average over a 5-year period to develop a meaningful reference service capability including enough resources to involve agency programs in the way necessary.

The committee also discussed the question of the demand for reference services and whether anticipated needs were appropriate to justify such levels of expenditure. The need for the service was judged to be sufficiently great to justify a serious effort.

There is no way, at this preliminary stage, that anything more than a judgment can be offered. In the first place, nothing in present agency experience can serve as a guide to demand levels for a service that has never existed in anything like the form indicated in this prospectus. The judgment rested on several considerations. First, there is considerable evidence of frustration and inefficiency because of the absence of such a service. Second, there already exist other programs, such as the ones referred to, that have been judged essential and for which expenditures substantially exceeding the sums of money mentioned here have been undertaken. Most of these have been undertaken in the interest of improving the efficiency of documentation in the physical sciences. In the circles where public and business policy are made, and social science, management and marketing research undertaken, the most compelling need is not for a way to handle better the traditional documentary materials generated, but for a way to acquire efficient access to relevant numerical files that constitute the main bodies of evidence and of research inputs. The need for expanding the services in this area seems equally as compelling as those in the field of physical science documentation that are already receiving extensive attention.

Appendix B

OCTOBER 1, 1965.

From: RUDOLPH C. MENDELSSOHN.
To: MR. EDGAR DUNN.
Subject: Report on data inventory.

Data Bank Requirements

An estimated $3 to $3.5 million and 3 to 5 years are needed to stock the proposed data center with Federal statistics now in existence. These data would probably comprise about 20,000 reels of magnetic tape. However, a Federal center could be stocked with a respectable volume and variety of data relatively quickly for about $260,000. At the rate of about $27 per reel, a bank of 9,000 tape files could be established in about a year. Such a course would provide a fairly representative selection of significant data including, for example, 750 reels of the census housing data; census current population data on 375 reels; the BLS Consumer Expenditure Survey on 43 reels; the BLS industry hours, earnings, and labor turnover data on 36 reels; the OBE national income accounts on 2 reels; as well as IRS tax data on 5,300 reels and BOASI social security data on 1,900 reels. An insight into the volume of data readily available is gained by the rough calculation that the equivalent of nearly 1 billion punched cards would be included. . . .

Of the $3 to $3.5 million needed to supply the data center over the 5-year period, about $700,000 would be needed to bring data not now machine accessible into usable form. About $500,000 would be needed to transfer punched card data to magnetic tape. And about $1.5 million would be needed to reprocess data now on magnetic tape. Looked at another way, about 100 man-years of professional aid will be required to review and correct the records, develop computer systems and programs to process the data, and provide reference documents to show file contents to the serious scholar from both the substantive and machine processing points of view. Also, about 100 man-years of keypunching and a very rough estimate of 10,000 computer hours are indicated. . . . In contrast, about 13 man-years of professional work and 1,200 hours of machine time would stock the center with half the total in a year.

The major resource requirement of the 5-year effort is for the Census Bureau where $1¼ million is requested. Over half the amount reported for that Bureau, about $700,000, is needed to bring the 25- and 5-per cent population samples for 1960 to acceptable levels. On the other hand, the Internal Revenue Service and the Bureau of Old Age and Survivors Insurance, both among the giants of data processing, have requested relatively limited amounts $17,400 and $14,300, respectively.

In considering the course of stocking the center several key factors should be kept in mind. First, the cost of additional historical reels after the initial storage of 9,000 is quite high—about $300 per reel, compared with about $27. The cost per reel is considerably higher for some of the files. For example, the SEC Quarterly Financial data and the FRB Report of Condition of Insured Banks would cost $20,000 and $8,000 per reel, respectively. Obviously, a careful review and justification for high-cost files is needed before their improvement can be supported. Second, the costs indicated in this report refer only to those needed to make data accessible within the responsible agency. I am assuming that the proposed data center would defray the costs of tape copying and would supply its own blank reels. Such costs are not inconsiderable. The 9,000 reels which could be made ready in about a year would cost the center over a half million dollars for blank reels and for copying.

General Comments

I have the general impression that the larger the volume of data and the higher the frequency of processing the greater is the tendency for the files to be in acceptable order. That is to say, large files like those of the IRS and BOAST and the high-frequency operations in the BLS manpower field and in the FRB are in good shape while some decennial and annual operations at the Census Bureau and the relatively small files at SEC, FTC, OBE, and the Office of Education are either not well maintained with the computer or are not well mechanized at all. In other words, the degree of accommodation to the computer seems to be a function of the work pressures to use it.

The vast majority of available information is already in machine form. The small amounts of significant data not machinable are found in OBE, the Office of Education, and in the Department of Agriculture. The files in OBE and OE are not large, would total about 200 reels, in my estimation, and are not in machine form in appreciable amounts. As you know, efforts are underway to correct this in both agencies. About 25 per cent of the Agriculture data are now machinable, according to Department representatives. It was asserted that the remaining 75 per cent are significant and useful data and should be available to a data bank for research in agricultural economics.

Agency Comments

Three general comments tended to be made by agency representatives. First, and least frequent, assertions that the Budget Bureau survey and the Ruggles Committee Report have brought an increased awareness of the need for more effective file maintenance and that efforts to achieve this end would be incorporated in ongoing operations where feasible. These good intentions should be supported with funds where appropriate and the dilemma in which the Census Bureau finds itself with respect to the 1960 population samples should not be allowed to be repeated. I have no doubt that the $700,000 now required would have been far less if the job had been done as a part of the 1960 census work.

Once the records have been brought to acceptable levels through new financial support, I doubt that programs operated at high frequencies will require more than trifling amounts to maintain this level in current operations. On the other hand, many of the recurring annual and decennial operations need explicit support for the improvement of file management practices. The 1960 population samples are examples of the latter situation. An assessment of these costs is outside the scope of this survey and, in fact, should be considered a part of the cost of the survey without regard to a proposed Federal data center.

Then, there was the comment by the larger agencies, heavily stressed by the Census Bureau, that funds to improve the files would not necessarily generate the desired results. The argument was that only present staff members had the background and professional experience needed to do the job. Since these people were already fully occupied, could not be diverted, and new staff could not do the job, it would not be done even if money is supplied it was asserted. I do not concur with this view. The work can be done if it is properly phased; that is, if sufficient time is allowed, new workers under the supervision of experienced personnel can do the job in the long run (the 5-year span I have suggested). I believe the reaction cited above assumes a crash effort to organize the files on a high-priority basis. I agree that it cannot be done this way and advise against such an approach.

Agency representatives seemed excessively concerned with the confidentiality question. Turning data over to a Federal center would be a breach of contract with respondents who have been assured that none but agency personnel would view their reports, it was said. I tried to convey the assurance that, if a data center were established, it would assume the obligation of protecting both the agency and the respondent. Since feelings on this matter run quite deep, some steps should be taken at the outset to vitiate them or discussions beyond this narrow consideration could founder.

One constructive suggestion was made in regard to confidentiality. Mr. Robert Menke of the Securities and Exchange Commission expressed the view that corporate concern dealt mainly with current affairs. It was his feeling that, after a period of 5 to 10 years, back data could be exposed to public view without serious objection by respondents. There would be difficulty perhaps in applying such a rule retroactively but a notice to this effect on future collections of data might serve to make the problem less troublesome in the years ahead.

Conclusion

I have a final comment. I found the evident loss of data because of the failure to support good file management distressing. Immediate steps ought to be taken to stop this erosion of a national resource. The costs indicated above measure the deficiency of not doing it before, and they will grow as time passes. It is difficult to argue that these losses have immediate meaning. The tools, techniques, and intellectual attitudes needed for their useful exploitation are not yet reflected in our institutions. But, as you know, changes are already underway. And even though we are unable now to predict how the store of data might be used, I am convinced that actions to preserve this national resource will be appreciated by those who follow.

Appendix C

The Design of a Federal Statistical Data Center
(A report to the Bureau of the Budget, prepared by E. Glaser, D. Rosenblatt, M. K. Wood, National Bureau of Standards)

Summary and Conclusions

This report was prepared in response to a letter from R. T. Bowman, Assistant Director for Statistical Standards, Bureau of the Budget, to A. V. Astin, Director of the National Bureau of Standards. The original request was focused principally upon "the possibilities for developing new capabilities in computer hardware systems that will improve their flexibility and economy in specialized file storage, management and retrieval functions" in connection with a national data service center. It directly became evident that any such study would be substantially conditioned by the characteristics of the information system to be mechanized: the scope and content of the economic and demographic data to be included; the degree of detail for each kind of information; the ability to use (a) data of more than one kind in a single analysis or mathematical model, (b) data derived from different reporting systems, (c) data collected by different agencies, (d) data referring to different time periods; the kinds of access to the files and the formats of acceptable queries; the nature and extent of computational and manipulative services to be provided; and other system specifications. Since there was no definite specification with regard to these characteristics, it was decided that a preliminary description of such a system was prerequisite to the requested analysis of hardware characteristics.

Mr. Edgar S. Dunn, consultant to the Office of Statistical Standards, Bureau of the Budget, worked with the staff of the National Bureau of Standards in reinterpreting the original request. As a result, the group's efforts were directed toward the issues that would govern the design of an effective Federal Statistical Data Center. The original intent to explore the potentialities of modern large-scale computers is constantly in evidence in the present formulation.

In preparing the report, the problem of describing the customer population was considered first. Something is known of the kinds of specialists who use data originating in the Federal Government to solve problems in economic policy, public administration, business economics, business administration, and a great range of social science subjects. But it is also apparent that this present user population reflects the capabilities and logistics of present ways of organizing and purveying data. At least equal importance attaches to those needs which are not met by present practices. How can these unmet needs be characterized?

An adequately specified information system would have to be based upon a broad review of the types of analyses that a wide spectrum of social scientists propose and upon the quantitative models that they build. For the present purposes and the limited scale of effort, it was decided to restrict the review to several classes of economic models directed at problems of national economic policy. Even this limited review revealed a variety of possible requirements for socioeconomic information which are not now being met, although many of the basic data are collected and compiled in some form by some Federal agency.

The review of economic models and their needs for statistical information was conducted at a 4-day conference at Fort Ritchie, Md., on August 26–29, 1965. Participants were M. K. Wood, D. Rosenblatt, and E. Glaser of the National Bureau of Standards and E. S. Dunn and P. F. Krueger of the Bureau of the Budget

Subsequent conferences and staff work built upon the Fort Ritchie conference by developing (a) an enumeration of the services to be rendered, and (b) a description of the Federal Statistical Data Center in terms of its functions and principal characteristics. A summary of these is given below.

A. NATURE OF THE SERVICES TO BE RENDERED

An integrated Federal Statistical Data Center appears necessary to perform the following functions:

1. To provide data in cases where the primary agency in possession of the data is not capable of making it available in the required format, detail, flexibility, or quality.

2. To provide data where the information originates in two or more reporting systems or agencies, in order to make available information about interrelationships in maximum feasible detail, without restrictions resulting from screening for improper disclosures at the time of transfer into the

Center and through association of information from multiple sources relating to the same individual reporting unit or analytical unit.

3. To maintain an archive of statistical data, complete in the sense described in (2) above, with all corrections and adjustments carried through in a consistent manner, and with a collection of the accompanying codebooks and manuals.

4. To provide information outputs (responses to queries) in a variety of forms at the customer's option: printed tabulations, machine readable tapes, graphs, diagrams, etc., either locally or through telecommunications.

5. To establish, maintain currently, and operate a reference and referral service for the Federal statistical system.

The creation of such a Federal Statistical Data Center also should provide the following additional services and corollary benefits at minimum cost:

6. ADP equipment would be available for computation and data reduction in response to queries of customers: cross tabulations, averages, distribution statistics, smoothed curves, trend fittings, seasonal adjustments, periodic analyses, correlations, regressions, and more advanced analyses in order to give access to the full range of information computable from the collection.

7. Confidentiality audits would be performed by machine upon the information intended for release to customers.

8. ADP equipment would also support a battery of services to the statistical system of the Federal Government: computations essential to the conduct of test adjustments on statistical series and collections, computations for test reconciliations of data from two or more sources or for two or more time periods, detection of errors in primary collections or derived statistics through consistency tests and anomaly detection routines, computations necessary for the study of error propagation through the Federal statistical system, combinations of the above computations in support of validation studies for Federal statistics and in support of procedures for certification of the accuracy and consistency of Federal statistics.

9. ADP equipment would also be used to provide service agencies with large-scale adjustment and reconciliation tasks (which is already being done by some agencies) in the production of standard series and to assist in the creation of new series through the reconciliation, adjustment and transformation of standard series.

B. CHARACTER AND ORGANIZATION OF THE DATA IN A FEDERAL STATISTICAL
   DATA CENTER

1. Principles must be developed for the initial selection and future accession of data to be included in the Center's collection; they should reflect a broad range of uses and full utilization of basic information rather than a codification of present uses, present practices, and present compromises.

2. Methodology and principles must be developed for the conversion of present files and production data to suitable archive form and quality, and their maintenance in proper form and quality, supported by codebooks, manuals, etc.

a. The principles established for archives must presume that data will be transferred from the collecting agency to the Center in full available detail.

b. The principles established for archives must provide for the systematic completion of all corrections and adjustments to all data affected and all levels of detail, resulting in a fully reconciled and consistent body of data.

c. The principles established for archives must provide for data to be transferred to the Center without screening for confidentiality; all confidentiality audits and checks would be applied to the formats and information content of the output of the Center.

d. The principles established for archives must provide for the preservation of the identity of the reporting unit and the association of all information about the unit without regard to the agency or manner of the collection of the information; the rules and the economics of matching of existing records will be very different from those intended for future production of data.

3. Standards must be developed for definition, coding, classification and aggregation with the intent of maximizing the ability to use different kinds of data in the same analysis and of minimizing the loss of information.

4. Standards must be developed for formats in order to facilitate the management, housekeeping and retrieval of records and to avoid the loss of information.

5. Standards must be developed for quality of data (consistency of definition, error rates, etc.) and for means of assuring maintenance of quality.

6. Automatic data processing (ADP) equipment and systems must be available to the Center to provide economy, timeliness, and flexibility of access to the information in the records.

    a. ADP must be available

       1. to compute statistics that are inherently computable from the records,

       2. To provide answers in the required form, and

       3. To avoid unnecessary withholding of information as a result of using inefficient and redundant disclosure criteria.

    b. ADP must be available for the conduct of confidentiality and other disclosure audits, such rules and procedures to be applied to the data in the form and content intended for release from the Center.

7. Criteria must be developed for assuring that the Center is established, and is maintained, in a manner that is responsive to a broad base of potential users, rather than in a manner which seems to suit the present habitual users at any time.

8. Criteria must be devised for periodic review of the value of the data contained in the archive followed by a selective purging of the data whose retention is no longer justified.

Description of a Federal Statistical Data Center

INTRODUCTION—FEDERAL STATISTICS AND THE COMPUTER

The statistical services of the Federal Government were initially created in response to a variety of unrelated needs. The census of population, in its early simple form, arose in response to a specific constitutional provision. The first census of manufacturers was a purposeful study of the existing status and likely potential economic development of the young Nation. Other collections of data were directed at a continuing study of the operation of the economy: prices, employment, sales and inventories, production of specific minerals, etc. A large number of statistical collections arose in connection with specific Federal programs, the statistics themselves being largely byproducts: activities and finances of regulated industries, internal revenue statistics, health and educational defects among selective service registrants, grants to scientific researchers, veterans' benefits, etc.

Two major influences have been at work to give improved quality and cohesiveness to this initially piecemeal collection of information about all aspects of the Nation and its people. One was primarily organizational and the other technical.

The Federal Reports Act of 1942, building upon such earlier programs as that of the Central Statistical Board of the National Recovery Administration, created a coordinating mechanism for the improvement and rationalization of the Federal statistical system. The Director of the Bureau of the Budget was given staff and responsibility for the development and introduction of standards for the collection, processing, and dissemination of data through much of the Government's activities. The standard industrial classification, the standard metropolitan statistical areas, the standard sample week for monthly surveys, and the standard base periods for economic time series are examples of this standards-setting function. The financial reporting program and the current population and labor force program are examples of the coordination of the work of several agencies to produce data useful for a variety of purposes. The Bureau of the Budget had become an instrument for promoting systematic cooperative efforts among the many Federal, State, and private collectors and processors of information.

The technical base for improved quality of information also has roots in the past. The development of improved techniques for acquiring information, analyzing it, preparing it for publications, and using it for economic, social, and political studies has been active for over a century. With the growth of applied social sciences and the progressive elaboration of the Government's statistical activities, the pace of research in technical methods was greatly accelerated. Trained statisticians brought improved techniques to many aspects of their work: sampling, the design of experiments, seasonal adjustment of time series, the construction of national and regional accounting models, the study of nonsampling errors in surveys and censuses, the development of quality control and other sequential methods, and the interpretation of data in complex situations. The consequences of these technical improvements have been far-reaching.

During and directly after World War II, the design and construction of the first electronic computers foretold a potential for vast improvements in many aspects of statistical technology: the recording and editing of field survey data; the compiling, tabulating, and publication of data; the analysis of data and their use in problem solving. The Federal Government pioneered in exploiting these new capabilities. However, much more can be done, particularly in the design of better ways of organizing economic and social data, more thorough integration of information from the many separate statistical programs, and the reduced loss of information in utilizing data for analytical purposes and purveying it to various classes of customers.

The very general logical powers, the great storage capacity, the high speed of manipulation, and the low unit cost of modern ADP systems combine to promise great potential improvement in information resources and problem-solving capabilities. A number of Federal agencies have learned the advantages of mechanizing their routines. Indeed, the Bureau of the Census contracted for the development of the UNIVAC, the first commercial internally programed computer, and it acquired the first and fourth units produced. Many of the frequently cited Federal statistics are more promptly and more satisfactorily produced than would be possible without computers, whether the statistics arise from a primary function of the agency or as a byproduct.

Yet, the improvements were typically made within the context of a single agency—usually a single reporting system—and without the possibility of raising broad questions about the fundamental organization of the Federal statistical system as a potentially unified and cohesive collection of intelligence. Nor was there any practical way of applying the explosively growing power of computers to general questions of preventing loss of information once it had been brought into the system by one or another Federal agency. Finally, there has been no serious attempt to assess the consequences of the computer for improved access to Federal data or for meeting the need for providing information in the form, degree of summarization, format, and physical output desired by various classes of customers.

The present report is addressed to these questions.

GENERAL PRINCIPLES FOR THE ORGANIZATION OF DATA FOR A FEDERAL STATISTICAL DATA CENTER

The consequent reconsideration of the organization of socio-economic data in the Federal Government is based upon two general guides. The first is to review the implicit informational requirements of the whole range of analyses and formal models proposed by social scientists, rather than to restrict the statement of information requirements to those needs which have been given principal attention in the past. The second is to consider the whole range of relevant tasks that the computer can assist, even if the manner of proceeding is radically different from current practice.

From this reconsideration four general principles emerge for constructing specifications for a Federal Statistical Data Center:

1. Maximum ability to exhibit the interrelations among various kinds of data;
2. The unification of all information about the individual reporting unit or analytical unit;
3. The preservation of detail in the basic records and the avoidance of loss of information in the storage, manipulation, and retrieval of information; and
4. The ability to produce the full measure of inherent information which is computable from the basic records.

366

These four principles will now be developed as groundwork for specifications for the information organization and the services of a Federal Statistical Data Center.

One of the greatest deficiencies of the existing Federal statistical system is its failure to provide access to data in a way which permits identification and measurement of functional interrelationships among interdependent activities. Identification and measurement of such interrelationships are essential to a wide range of economic and social analyses. It is also the chief problem in the design of mathematical models of economic and social processes suitable for appraising the impact of alternative policies and programs as well as possible changes in environmental factors.

Such appraisal is, in turn, prerequisite to effective benefit-cost analysis of proposed and ongoing programs. The essence of rational benefit-cost analysis is the tracing of indirect as well as direct effects of programs and the evaluation and summing of these effects. Typically, the methodology for tracing all but the most obvious linkages is entirely lacking or fails to use the relevant information.

Until recently, economic model builders have been restricted to relatively aggregative economic and resource flow models, and to inferring interrelationships among very few aggregative variables. Such relationships often have considerable predictive value where other conditions remain relatively stable or continue to change at a constant rate. But the essential relationships are correlative or associative rather than structural. Hence, they generally fail to give acceptable prediction when other conditions change markedly, as a result of changes in major program, policy, or environmental factors.

Acceptable prediction under changing circumstances requires analytical models which give much more detailed and explicit recognition to interrelationships among the criteria and variables which will be affected by the changed conditions. Such analytical models generally describe the mechanisms in greater detail than the associative models; they use more information, and they often rely less heavily on trends or the postulation of only slow changes among the variables in the model. The present and prospective accelerated pace of technological and statistical change now requires the development and use of more detailed and complex models than can be created or supported by the present Federal statistical system.

The rapidly developing tools of automatic data processing and systems analysis now make possible—and necessary—both the development of more advanced models and the elaboration of the Federal statistical system which is needed to support them.

Many of the data needed for establishing causal interrelationships among related economic variables are contained in the existing Federal statistical system. But present collection methods, tabulation procedures, and disclosure rules combine to make it difficult and often impossible to extract such data. Where samples are largely enough, it may be possible to cross-tabulate in a way which permits determining the interrelationships between two variables or, rarely, among three. But generally when more than a two-way relationship is involved, it is impossible to tabulate necessary totals in a way which will define the desired relationship without disclosure of proprietary data. Such relationships among many variables can be extended, however, at a much greater level of detail, if it is possible to apply standard statistical analysis techniques to the observations for individual respondent units over the whole range of the relevant variables. It is possible in this way to extract much more useful structural information and still insure that no disclosure of individual respondent data is contained in the results of such analyses.

In many cases, the data necessary to such an analysis require the matching of items from two or more statistical sources. One important class of analyses involves the matching or reports by the same respondent for different time periods. Some data files are so organized as to make this possible, but many are not. An even more complex problem arises when it is necessary to match data from the same respondent collected as parts of different statistical programs, by different agencies. This can be extremely difficult or impossible, though substantial progress has been made in some areas, as, for example among Census, Bureau of Old Age and Survivors Insurance (BOASI), and the Internal Revenue Service. Problems of disclosure are most difficult in this context.

There are several fundamental problems dealing with the coding and classification of original source data. Most serious is the need for uniform identification, definition, and coding of the respondent unit. Unless this is done, matching of data from diverse sources is generally impracticable if not impossible. A uniform system of classification and coding for geographic area is another major deficiency.

In general, the classification and grouping of data are dictated by the problem environment, the basic logic of the analytical model, and the kind and degree of detail in which the results must be expressed and interpreted. In practice, there is frequently need to compromise the ideal classifications and aggregations of data for several reasons; the basis and criteria of classification in the collection agency being inconsistent with the ideal requirements of the model; the lack of sufficient detail (industry, process, product, geographic location, etc.); the withholding of detail under proprietary confidentiality or security restrictions; the noncompatibility of the definitions of the respondent units in the several collection systems which could otherwise provide the information specified by the model, which can be reconciled only by coarse aggregation but with accompanying loss of information and structural detail; the noncompatibility of classification of the data by several collection agencies and information systems also capable of specious resolution by aggregation; the difficulty and cost of identifying and matching the reporting units from two or more reporting systems, so that the information about the reporting unit can be pooled; the absence of technique, staff, funds, and machine time to use large-scale data processing equipment to recode, recompile, reconcile, reclassify, and aggregate data and to perform all manner of statistical procedures upon the data.

Since there are very large numbers of ways in which most economic variables might reasonably be classified and aggregated, it is not practical to prepare the data in all of these formats in anticipation of possible requests. Nor is this necessary. The same results can be achieved with favorable logistics and great flexibility by providing for the basic records to be maintained in machine receivable form and in as fine detail of classification as is practical. The low unit cost and high speed of modern computers can then be exploited to meet requests for data with little loss of the available information inherent in the combined resources of the participating agencies.

The availability of modern computers can meet two important requirements in this context. The first is discussed above: the conversion from finely disaggregated classes to all manner of special purpose classifications and aggregations (and, indeed, conversion to publishable forms). The second requirement is to avoid unnecessary loss of information because of proprietary and confidentiality restrictions. The fundamental rule in this case is to perform all edits and checks relating to unwanted disclosure upon the fully processed data (aggregations, summaries, averages, correlation coefficients, regressions, fitted curves, etc.) rather than upon the detailed raw data. This will assure full use of information consistent with disclosure rules. The logical capability of the computer also provides the key for the necessarily elaborate systems of rules essential to the prescribed protection.

Another major class of problems arises from the fact that errors and inconsistencies in the data as reported, transcribed, and coded are always discovered in the process of editing tabulations for publication. These errors are generally corrected at the levels of aggregation at which data are published, but often are not carried back to the basic records for the individual respondent unit, in machine sensible form. Carrying back such corrections to the basic files is prerequisite to the kind of analysis of interrelationships which is here proposed. Some method of insuring that this is done, and that the basic records meet appropriate standards as archives, is essential. Such tasks generally receive a low priority in the statistical agency whose primary task is production and publication, rather than analysis, of data.

As a technical device, the use of master samples can achieve a high degree of unification of information about the individual reporting unit. Moreover, proper experimental designs provide for the straightforward estimation of sampling variances; differences among subpopulations can be measured with specified precision if this requirement is stated in advance; variance due to differences among samples can often be eliminated; costly matching of units at the later stages can be avoided. Inconsistencies arising from many kinds of differences between surveys can also be avoided.

The use of the current population survey for special questions (veteran status, duration of unemployment, preferred number of hours, work, etc.) permits a number of useful comparisons with standard information about labor force status. Similarly, it may often be practical to use master samples to obtain information about subjects vital to some of the newer Federal welfare programs. Hence, an integrated system of master samples of households could be used to collect information about income, education, health, crime, employment, social services, housing, demography, voting registration, and the effects of opening or closing industrial plants. Not only could

369

information be compiled about each of these subjects, but analyses could be performed which interrelated several of the subjects: education-income-crime rates, health-housing-education, etc., without loss of information or the introduction of uncertainty arising from variances between samples or from different survey practices. Indeed, the judicious use of master samples can lead economically to conformity with the general principles stated above.

The fourth principle is ability to produce any information computable from the basic records. The principle acquires new power when combined with the other three principles, because a great deal more becomes computable. The concept of "inherently computable" is taken literally, and includes kinds of statistical operations not now widely used. The paucity of current use derives from unfavorable economics, unsuitable organization of data, insufficient available detail, failure to use known techniques, obstacles growing out of confidentiality restrictions on data intended for input to the analysis, and current habits and practices deriving from all of the other obstacles. In short, the current ways of doing business fall far short of the potentiality of advanced statistical techniques applied to a well-organized body of Federal data. The present report suggests the means for mitigation or elimination of the shortcomings of the statistical system built before modern computers became available.

In these terms, the notion of "inherently computable" takes on new meaning. Obviously included are the routine computation of averages, cross tabulations, correlations, curve fittings, time series analyses, seasonal adjustments, distribution statistics, and the application of other techniques of mathematical statistics. But it would also now be possible to test the reconciliation of one series of data against others. Test adjustments of all sorts, even very detailed and burdensome adjustments involving manipulation of very large matrices, could be countenanced. Errors could be studied, including those for whose estimation there is little theoretical foundation—the myriad kinds of inconsistencies of definition, practice, error rate, personnel, etc.—when data from two or more sources are used. Propagation of errors through the system, especially in the major synthetic series (national income and product accounts, Federal Reserve Board production indexes, price indexes) could also be studied and estimated. One set of objectives would be error detection and measurement in the primary collections. Another would be consistency testing and anomaly detection in two or more collections from different agencies, geographic regions, time periods, etc.

Computations of this sort could also be used to assist in the setting of quality standards for Federal data and for validation or certification of particular bodies of data.

There is already a praiseworthy trend toward the use of computers in the production of standard series of data by several agencies. The notion of "inherently computable" includes the generation of new series for special purposes through the adjustment of standard series, limited only by the techniques and imagination of social scientists.

This section discusses the services which a Federal Statistical Data Center could render. The characteristics are enumerated as they are in the summary of this report. An information system capable of providing these services is described in the next section.

The services which are proposed for this suggested system are discussed below:

1. The Federal Statistical Data Center would provide data in cases where the primary agency in possession of the data is not capable of making it available in the required format, detail, flexibility, or quality. Primary agencies would continue to provide data which they can furnish in the needed form, even though they had previously delivered the relevant basic data to the Center. For example, an agency might produce statistics as a byproduct of its principal mission, having no resources to organize the information for flexible or rapid access. Or the data might require adjustment or reconciliation which the collecting agency cannot perform as well as the Center.

2. The Center would provide data where the information originates in two or more reporting systems or agencies, in order to make available information about interrelationships in maximum feasible detail, without restrictions resulting from screening for improper disclosures at the time of transfer into the Center and through association of information from multiple sources relating to the same individual reporting unit or analytical unit. The intent of this specification and its improvement over present characteristics of the Federal statistical systems are discussed in an earlier section.

3. The Center would maintain an archive of statistical data, complete in the sense described in (2) above, with all corrections and adjustments carried through in a consistent manner, and with a collection of the accompanying codebooks and manuals. The intent of this item is discussed in an earlier section.

4. Outputs (responses to queries) would be provided in a variety of forms at the customer's option: printed tabulations, machine readable tapes, graphs, diagrams, etc., either locally or through telecommunications.

5. The Federal Statistical Data Center would establish, maintain currently, and operate a reference and referral service for the Federal statistical system. This service is not concerned with the actual provision of data. It deals more with those matters that a user might need before he can formulate a proper query. The reference and referral center would give information about various concepts that lie behind the statistics: general imports in contrast with imports for consumption; total employment and employees in establishment; value of product and value added; industry and product statistics, etc. Questions that could not be answered at the Center would be referred to specialists in the various agencies; the Center would identify and locate the specialists. It would also protect the experts from inquiries that could satisfactorily be managed at the Center. Personnel at the Center would be equipped with reference documents to show

371

dates for which each kind of data is available, changes in coverage, changes in definition, changes in quality, schedules for availability of future statistics; materials available in book or report form both for data and information about their definition, method of collection, adjustment, etc. Reference services would also be provided for information not in the Federal collection: statistics from trade associations, industrial institutes, State and local governments, international organizations and foreign governments. Statistical data that can be obtained directly from the primary collection agency would be known to the Center, which would act as a referral agent for the agency.

6. ADP equipment would be available for computation and data reduction in response to queries of customers: cross tabulations, averages, distribution statistics, smoothed curves, trend fittings, seasonal adjustments, periodic analyses, correlations, regressions, and more advanced analyses in order to give access to the full range of information computable from the collection.

7. Confidential audits would be performed by machine upon the information intended for release to customers. It is recognized that this raises complex and difficult issues which require intensive study. However, there are strong reasons to believe that these issues can be resolved with the aid of modern tools of the mathematical and computer sciences.

8. ADP equipment would also support a battery of services to the statistical system of the Federal Government: computations essential to the conduct of test adjustments on statistical series and collections, computations for test reconciliations of data for two or more sources or for two or more time periods, detection of errors in primary collections or derived statistics through consistency tests and anomaly detections routines, computations necessary for the study of error propagation through the Federal statistical system, combinations of the above computations in support of validation studies for Federal statistics and in support of procedures for certification of the accuracy and consistency of Federal statistics. Much of the work referred to here is not done at present. Ordinarily, the larger synthetic statistical series are prepared by gathering data from many sources and adjusting them in various ways including their reconciliation to benchmarks of higher quality. In many cases, the source series themselves are compounded from smaller elements, sometimes in several stages before reaching down to the point of primary collection from the respondents. Computers are used for convenience and economy to speed up the processing in most of the more elaborate systems. However, in this statistical production network, there is practically no feedback of information from this process to the primary collection agencies. The adjustments required to maintain the larger synthetic series are sufficiently burdensome and closely scheduled that there is neither time nor staff for research on adjustments or the conduct of test adjustments no matter how desirable this might be in the view of the interested agencies. The combination of the comprehensive unified data system and adequate ADP equipment would create a favorable climate for this work. In addition, all manner of test comparisons across different statistical series, and many kinds of consistency

372

tests, could readily be performed. With much of the synthesis of major statistical series on compatible computers, the effects of errors in all stages of collection, estimation, and adjustment could be studied. Hence, studies of the quality of Federal Statistics could add such techniques to existing appraisals which are based on information about the collection (completeness, sampling variance, quality checks), size of adjustments to benchmarks, and a very limited kind and number of consistency checks.

9. ADP equipment would also be used to service agencies with large-scale adjustment and reconciliation burdens (which is already being done by some agencies) in the production of standard series, and to service the creation of new series through the reconciliation and adjustment of standard series. Specialized users could define new synthetic series based upon adjustment of the standard series. However, at present, such adjustments could be applied only to highly aggregated forms of the statistics because of the cost and cumbersomeness of the process. What is contemplated here is a much more complete reprocessing designed to retain a large measure of the detail available for the standard series. For example, the input-output transactions matrices (which are now embedded in the national income and product accounts) could be transformed from the present industry-based sectoral definitions to an activity basis (in which there are no secondary products).

CHARACTER AND ORGANIZATION OF THE DATA IN A
FEDERAL DATA CENTER

This section presents and discusses principles governing a well-integrated body of statistics arising from the work of the Federal agencies. The items discussed below are numbered as they are in the summary of this paper. While there are intimations of services that the Center might perform, there is no attempt to describe the services as such in this section; the preceding section is devoted entirely to that end. This section relates to the internal structure and operation of the Center—in matters of information—and the preceding section views the same Center from the outside, as a series of capabilities to assist the customer to obtain data.

The principles are discussed in numerical order below. While it is convenient to set forth the seven separate items for exposition and reference, the entire characterization is conceived as a single entity: no item is to be read out of its context with the other items. It is the interaction of the points taken two, three, or more at a time that characterizes this report, in contrast with possible studies of the distinct issues one at a time.

1. Principles must be developed for the initial selection and future accession of data to be included in the Center's collection; they should reflect a broad range of uses and full utilization of basic information rather than a codification of present uses, present practices, and present compromises.

The selection should recognize the importance of data acquired in the administration of regulatory programs and welfare or benefit programs. A primary purpose of the Federal Statistical Data Center is the organization of information in such way as to permit the use of data from various sources in the same analysis. The byproduct information from many agencies must now be reconsidered to determine how these data can best be combined with those of other reporting systems to contribute to socioeconomic analysis. Both program data (amount of grant, number of grantees, geographic location of program elements, etc.) and information about applicants can enrich the existing store of socioeconomic statistics from major statistical agencies.

The above paragraph is addressed to only one of the general principles discussed in an earlier section. Issues of inclusion or exclusion of various classes of data must be reviewed with all four general principles in mind and also with appreciation of the remaining items on this list itself.

2. Methodology and principles must be developed for the conversion of present files and production data to suitable archive form and quality, and their maintenance in proper form and quality, supported by codebooks, manuals, etc. It is not to be presumed that complete and consistent records will arise routinely from the collection, adjustment, analysis, and publication of data. Resources must be made available and priorities assigned. Above all, standards of form and quality must be prescribed and checked in some regular manner. Procedures must also be prescribed for work with the archive collection to prevent loss or contamination of the master records by tape erasure, statistical adjustment, aggregation or reclassification.

  a. The principles established for archives must presume that data will be transferred from the collecting agency to the Center in full available detail. The decisions about the lowest level of detail—other than the separate record for each respondent or analytical unit—will often be arbitrary. They will reflect notions of the finest detail that analytical purposes are likely to demand. In principle, there is no such ultimate disaggregation for many reporting units. For example, the use of the establishment as the reporting unit in many standard statistical systems is frequently dictated by the inability to define or obtain information for subestablishment entities; the choice is not based upon satisfaction with the level of detail obtained. The term "full available detail" must be read with a rule of reason.

  b. The principles established for archives must provide for the systematic completion of all corrections and adjustments to all data affected and all levels of detail, resulting in a fully reconciled and consistent body of data.

  c. The principles established for archives must provide for data to be transferred to the Center without screening for confidentiality; all confidentiality audits and checks would be applied to the formats and information content of the output of the Center.

  d. The principles established for archives must provide for the preservation of the identity of the reporting unit and the association of all information about the unit without regard to the agency or manner of the information; the rules and the economics of matching of existing records will be very different from those intended for future production of data.

3. Standards must be developed for definition, coding, classification, and aggregation with the intent of maximizing the ability to use different

kinds of data in the same analysis, and of minimizing the loss of information. The reasons for this requirement are set forth in an earlier section of this report. A large number of standards would have to be developed, beginning with such seemingly elementary concepts as a household, a structure (a building), a business organization, an establishment (industrial), a populated place, a county; and proceeding to a school pupil, a hospital day, a recipient of (some particular) welfare service, etc. Some such standards now exist, although they are neither wholly satisfactory not uniformly observed. These existing standards should be reexamined and many new standards developed. All standards need to be more rigorously defined and more effectively enforced. Ideally, a close matching in many dimensions of classifications, hierarchical aggregation, timing, and spatial extent should apply to all information in the basic record; but a system of practical compromises would unquestionably have to be accepted.

4. Standards must be developed for formats in order to facilitate the management, housekeeping, and retrieval of records and to avoid the loss of information. This item presumes that the characteristics of the information have, in principle, been defined. In practice, formats greatly influence the effectiveness, economy, and error rates of the whole operation.

5. Standards must be developed for quality of data (consistency of definition, error rates, etc.) and for means of assuring maintenance of quality. It is essential to know—and to issue with the statistical data—information on the quality of the data. After standards have been agreed upon, appropriate quality-control procedures would have to be instituted.

6. Automatic data processing (ADP) equipment and systems must be available to the Center to provide economy, timeliness, and flexibility of access to the information in the records. This report does not deal with configuration of computing equipment. It may be noted in passing, however, that various units might be geographically scattered. This would allow inquiries to be made from points distant from the basic record stores and the replies or outputs to be received in these same remote locations. Probably more importantly, computer laboratories in universities, research institutes, business organizations and governmental agencies could be used to transmit requests for information over long-distance lines and to receive and store information. This would provide a convenient location for trial manipulations by those making the inquiries without disturbing the rest of the communication network. Such an arrangement would give increased service and analytical power to the participating analyst.

    a. ADP must be available—

      (1) to compute statistics that are inherently computable from the records,

      (2) to provide answers in the required form, and

      (3) to avoid unnecessary withholding of information as a result of using inefficient and redundant disclosure criteria.

  Note that, for the item immediately above, the confidentiality audit would have to apply before the information was transferred to an off-line computer under the control of the user. This discussion implies that disclosure rules would retain their essentially logical

375

character without taking into account the possibility of introducing elements of probabilistic inference in determining whether or not an undesirable disclosure might be made.

b. ADP must be available for the conduct of confidentiality and other disclosure audits; such rules and procedures to be applied to the data in the form and content intended for release from the Center. The comment on item 6 (a) applies here as well.

7. Criteria must be developed for assuring that the Center is established—and is maintained—in a manner that is responsive to a broad base of potential users, rather than in a manner which seems to suit the present habitual users at any time.

8. Criteria must be devised for periodic review of the value of the data contained in the archive followed by a selected purging of the data whose retention is no longer justified.

In sum, the main purpose of a Federal Statistical Data Center is to create a better integrated information network, for use by Government, industry, and the research community, which will provide better understanding of interdependencies within our pluralistic society, leading to better informed choices among alternative policies and programs, and more effective program implementation.

Statement of Senator Edward Kennedy

August 10, 1966

on a Bill to Authorize a Computerized Information System to Provide State and Local Governments with Information on Federal Programs

Mr. President: I introduce for appropriate reference a joint resolution authorizing the Advisory Commission on Intergovernmental Relations to study and investigate the feasibility and design of an information system which would enable States and localities to participate more effectively in federally assisted programs and to provide Congress and the President with a better measure of State and local needs and performance under these programs.

The relationship between the Federal Government and State and local governments is an increasing paradox: As more and more Federal programs become available, State and local governments become less and less able to sort them out and decide which ones could help them most. The Federal programs are beneficial; the State and local governments want to benefit from them. But the very proliferation of Federal programs is bewildering to the local communities for which they are designed, and this bewilderment is working against the creative federalism which President Johnson spoke of two years ago in an historic speech at Ann Arbor, Michigan: A federalism based on local initiative, Federal support, and close cooperation between Washington and City Hall.

No one in this chamber knows more about the problems of making creative federalism work than the distinguished Junior Senator from Maine. As Chairman of the Senate Subcommittee on Intergovernmental Relations, Senator Muskie has dedicated his energies to finding ways by which we can strengthen the cooperative basis of our Federal system.

The three-year study recently completed by his Subcommittee makes clear the benefits of creative federalism, and it also makes clear the problems which are raised by confusion and a lack of coordination between levels of government. Senator Muskie has introduced a host of extremely constructive legislative proposals to overcome these problems.

The legislation I introduce today supplements his efforts and the efforts of others to build efficiency into government. It is directed at one very important part of the overall problem—the need to build an effective

377

communications system between local, State and Federal levels of government.

We are all aware of the dramatic rise in the demands on State and local governments. This rise reflects increased public needs and responsibilities which have been shouldered by local officials. And there is every indication that these needs will grow because of the innumerable problems associated with urbanization, economic expansion and population growth.

In the face of growing public needs which could not be met completely through local funding, the Federal Government has increased its programs of assistance. In little more than a decade, total Federal aid to State and local governments has quadrupled, rising from $3.1 billion in 1955 to an estimated $14.6 billion in 1967. As Senator Muskie has pointed out, almost twice as much Federal aid has been appropriated during the past five sessions of Congress as the total appropriated by all previous Congresses going back to 1789.

I support these Federal programs. They are designed to help individuals and communities meet their goals for social and economic development. They are intended to build a better and stronger society.

These programs are not predicated on some master plan or grand design of the Federal Government. They depend primarily on the initiative and resource of people at the local level, who get them started and keep them going.

But if our Federal programs of assistance are to be most effective, every State official, every mayor, every city and town administrator, when faced with a community problem, should have complete information on the full range of Federal programs available, so that he can choose the programs that his community needs and shape them so that they will be most effective.

What these local administrators need most is information. Without information to help them make their decisions, many communities miss out completely on programs of Federal assistance for which they are eligible, others are extremely slow in getting programs started, and still others choose to pursue programs poorly suited to meet highest priority needs even though better programs are available.

Government action based upon inadequate information is wasteful and costly. It is costly to the American taxpayer whose money is not wisely or effectively spent; it is costly to the communities who are denied benefits or delayed in getting them; and it is costly to the Nation as a whole when haphazard and ill-informed decisions result in a misallocation of resources.

There is no question that we need a more effective communications system between the various levels of government. Yet it will not be easy to achieve one, because the increase in the number and scope of Federal programs is staggering to contemplate. For instance:

The Federal Government has set up almost 300 programs which deal with education, environment, poverty or community development. They are administered by more than 100 departmental subdivisions at varying organization levels in 18 different departments and agencies.

More than forty different federal programs provide aid for urban development, though there is little evidence of a unified urban development policy.

Four different agencies handle similar grant or loan programs in the area of local waste disposal facilities, and handle them in dissimilar ways.

Five Federal agencies are involved in community planning—the Office of Economic Opportunity, the Economic Development Administration, the Department of Housing and Urban Development, the Department of Agriculture and the Appalachian Regional Commission.

The Senate Subcommittee on Intergovernmental Relations after three years of study observed that there is "substantial competing and overlapping of Federal programs . . . sometimes as a direct result of legislation and sometimes as a result of bureaucratic 'empire building.' "

The conditions precedent to obtaining funds, furthermore, vary considerably from program to program, agency to agency, project to project, and also within agencies and programs over time. And these variances are aggravated by the sheer size and complexity of these Federal agencies and their missions.

Our nation's governors at their Annual Conference in Los Angeles last month described this proliferation of programs as "an administrative jungle" —"lacking in coordination and so complex that state officials are at a loss to keep up with what is going on." What has happened is that Federal programs of assistance have provided community executives with so many alternatives that they cannot keep track of all of them or distinguish between them. The problem has been aptly described by Patrick Healy, the Executive Director of the National League of Cities, and John Gunther, the Executive Director of the U.S. Conference of Mayors:

> The rapid expansion in the number, size and interrelationship of urban oriented Federal programs has resulted in growing concern within many city administrations that they may not be aware of all of the opportunities to effectively utilize Federal programs.

And at the same time, there has been no concerted effort to develop a communications system to keep up with the expansion of activity.

Thus, local participation in these programs has been essentially haphazard. Local officials, lacking large staffs, are often bewildered by the mass of Federal programs which confront them, uninformed about the Federal funds and projects they might obtain, and ill-equipped to determine which available Federal programs best meet their community needs.

In short, we are faced with a crisis in communication. This conclusion is confirmed by the three-year study made by the Senate Subcommittee on Intergovernmental Relations and by a comprehensive survey of Federal programs administration conducted by two private business organizations, Basic Systems, Inc., and University Microfilms, Inc., two subsidiaries of Xerox Corporation. It is the conclusion I arrived at after numerous conferences and conversations with State and local officials in Massachusetts, and with other Congressmen who have observed the same problem in their own States. And it is demonstrated by the great variety of actions already taken by both public and private organizations to relieve this communication bottleneck.

For example, State and local governments on their own have been deploying representatives to Washington to set up a clearinghouse for information

379

on Federal programs. A system designed to provide interested groups with a single, continuing source of intelligible data on Federal programs has been established here by Basic Systems, Inc., and University Microfilms, Inc. And the National League of Cities and the U.S. Conference of Mayors have joined together through the Joint Council on Urban Development to provide such a service to cities on a contractual basis.

Federal agencies have begun to compile catalogs and handbooks on aid programs. Last year the catalog of Federal programs for individual and community improvement published by the Office of Economic Opportunity required 414 pages just to give the briefest description of each program. Similar catalogs have been developed by Senator Muskie's Subcommittee and by the Economic Development Administration, and a Mayor's Handbook of Federal Assistance Programs is currently being prepared by the Bureau of the Budget. In addition each agency charged with the administration of a Federal grant-in-aid program has a vast amount of literature available concerning all aspects of its particular programs.

Indeed, there has been such a proliferation of catalogs to cope with the proliferation of Federal programs that the Advisory Commission for Intergovernmental Relations has recently published an index of them—a "catalog of catalogs."

President Johnson's personal interest in solving these communications problems is reflected in the Federal Inquiry Center recently established in Atlanta, Georgia, as a pilot project of the General Services Administration to supply information about all the functions and programs of the Federal Government.

But none of the initiatives I have mentioned attempts to deal with the problem in comprehensive terms.

The problem will not be solved by an increase in indexes of catalogs. We don't need more books, we need handier information. And we need to coordinate what is becoming a massive effort in duplication of activity, each bit helpful, but not sufficient. We need a single source of detailed information, bringing together the piecemeal information projects presently going on, available through a modern information retrieval system, operated on a decentralized basis, to which officials can turn to identify their options and to select the best of available Federal programs.

The resolution I propose authorizes the Advisory Commission on Intergovernmental Relations to conduct a thorough investigation into the feasibility of developing a comprehensive information service system that would make use of automatic data processing equipment and other forms of advanced information technology to serve our States and localities.

I have no special experience in the area of automatic data processing, but I have long been impressed by the scientific advances which have been made in computer and information retrieval technology, and their possible application to the development of a national intergovernmental information system.

What I have in mind is a computer-based information system, using satellite centers, which would provide each State and local government with detailed information on which programs were available to it and which

380

would be most appropriate for it. With a profile of each community, a satellite computer could be programed to inform the community of what new programs are available, what programs have filled their quotas, what programs have changed, and what programs have been discontinued. In every case, the information provided would be based on the needs of the State or community in question.

Such a system has been used with great success by the National Aeronautics and Space Administration in their Technology Utilization program to provide private industry with detailed information on technological advances that may be of benefit to particular industries. The Post Office Department, the Internal Revenue Service, the Department of Defense, the Bureau of the Census, and other major government agencies are all using data processing equipment to bring greater efficiency to their operations. Given this background, I think it would be a disservice to State and local governments if we failed to investigate the possibilities of using advance information system technology to provide the information which local executives so desperately need.

In recent months I have spent considerable time exploring the feasibility of such a system. I have spoken with representatives of a number of large industrial firms involved in this field, such as Diebold Associates and International Business Machines, and explored this question with knowledgeable people in the Administration and in the universities. My conclusion is that we have every reason to expect that such a system could be constructed. But it is also apparent to me that a comprehensive study of the problem is necessary to determine whether this kind of system should be contructed, and if so, what form that construction should take.

IBM, at my request, did a preliminary examination of the feasibility and appropriate design of such a system. From their conclusions many of the specific questions which must be answered in this study became clear.

To begin with, the appropriate inputs of the systems must be determined. State and local officials must be surveyed and State and local government program-planning and decision-making studied, in order to ascertain exactly what the informational needs and problems are. On the basis of such a study, it would then be possible to determine the extent and form of input data required for the system, the most desirable form in which to receive this information and the degree and kind of interpretation of information needed. For example, IBM concluded that at least four kinds of input data would be required:

1. Socio-economic data involving income distribution, education, law enforcement, health and welfare, etc.
2. Community Resource Data involving labor force and employment, industry and trade, transportation, housing and community facilities, financial, etc.
3. Programs Reference Data concerning the nature and purpose of assistance programs, conditions of eligibility, information contact, authorizing legislation, and the administering agency.
4. Programs Status Data involving the nature and extent of usage of

various aid programs, the status of obligated funds, the names and numbers of communities involved, etc.

In addition, as I pointed out earlier, there are a number of information sources already developed or developing. The study I propose will survey this growing field, determine what action must be taken to merge or otherwise synthesize these other information sources so that duplication of effort is avoided, identify what gaps exist in existing information sources and provide for the collection and indexing of whatever necessary additional information is needed to fill those gaps.

Once the input design is determined and data collected, it should be possible to construct an information system, capable of up-to-date data storage, retrieval and sorting of relevant information, manned by skilled personnel to interpret and evaluate the information, which will enable State and community officials to most intelligently select those programs of Federal assistance which best serve their interests.

Even though feasible, whether such a system should be constructed is another question. The answer will depend on whether the costs of constructing it are less than the social costs involved in continuing as we do now. Thus the study would consider the designs of alternative information systems varying in complexity, provide cost estimates for each, and compare the costs to the benefits accruing from the introduction of such systems.

The system I visualize would be decentralized in nature. But careful study would be needed to determine how many satellite stations should be established, where they should be located and whether the overall system would best be operated under the direction of the Department of Housing and Urban Development, the Bureau of the Budget, the Census, the General Services Administration, the Legislative Reference Service, or some other government agency.

An information system of the type I propose need not be limited solely to offering data on Federal programs. By keeping a record of the projects and programs carried out in the various communities, it should be possible for communities to learn from the system what programs other communities are developing and profit from their experiences.

Moreover, as experience is gained in dealing with communities, it might eventually be possible to assign to the system certain tasks of analysis and evaluation, such as the projection of socio-economic trends, analyses of cost-benefit ratios, and preparation of financial justification of projects.

Furthermore, through data phones and other link-ups, the system might be capable of providing Congress and the Administration with a better measure of the needs and performances of the cities, States and regions operating under these programs.

This could facilitate legislative oversight, as well as make possible speedy and more accurate adjustment of aid programs to meet existing needs.

Constructing such a system would involve certain risks to established political procedures, even though the system is intended solely as an aid to decision-making and not a replacement of the decision-maker. For that reason, I think it important that the study also consider the political problems which may arise, and how we can preserve the existing desirable relationships between city and State officials, members of Congress and Administration officials.

Finally, the study of systems design must carefully consider the fact that the system and the information required by the system will not remain static.

Specific attention must be given to the incremental development of the system. As program requirements change and new ones are added, the store of information must be reviewed and kept up-to-date, and provision must be made for standardizing the structure and collection of data.

In short, Mr. President, though, in my judgment, the basic idea is sound, and the need apparent, a thorough study of the entire question is a prerequisite to effective action.

The Advisory Commission on Intergovernmental Relations seems to me the ideal body to conduct such a study. The Commission was established in 1959 for the specific purpose of studying how our Federal system could be strengthened through greater cooperation, understanding and coordination at all levels of government. Its statutory mandate specifically provides that the Commission should study and provide a forum for discussing administration and coordination of Federal programs as well as encouraging study of emerging problems requiring intergovernmental cooperation.

Furthermore, since its inception the staff of the Commission has concentrated its activities on the problems of Federal-State-local relations, thereby building a base of expertise which should be of great help in performing the study. And their work has been of a uniformly high quality. In addition, the composition of the Commission is uniquely suited to perform this kind of study with insight and understanding.

The Commission is unique among organizations involved in intergovernmental operations because it is both a continuing agency and is also broadly representative of all levels of government. It is not a Federal agency in the usual sense. Its members include representatives of the executive and legislative branches of all levels of government. As Patrick Healy of the National League of Cities put it:

> We believe that the heterogenous nature of the Commission, . . . it consists of both executives and legislators representing all levels of government, . . . is one of the features which allows it to make important contributions to the field of intergovernmental relations.
>
> When this hybrid group of people sit down to consider the research activities of the Commission, the full interplay of opinions and interests creates a new understanding of the problem under discussion. This is governmental interaction at its best, because it maximizes the opportunities the Commission presents for reasonable men to arrive at desirable and practical solutions to the problems of intergovernmental relations in our Federal system.

Finally, it was contemplated at the time the Commission was established that special studies of a long-term nature such as this one would be conducted. Several proposals have already been made to have the Commission conduct a comprehensive study of the Nation's intergovernmental tax and revenue structure.

Congress has recognized that if such studies were authorized, separate appropriations would be provided for that purpose; the legislation establishing the Commission, P.L. 86–388, already provides authority for the Commission to employ the technical consultants necessary to accomplish this study, and the study itself would dovetail with many of the other studies and reports that the Commission is currently engaged in.

Mr. President: I am hopeful that as a result of this study it will be possible to place into operation quickly thereafter an advanced information system providing State and local executives with the kind of information they need to make informed decisions leading to maximum satisfaction of community needs through the fullest utilization of Federal programs of assistance. Such a system could make a tremendous contribution to our goal of a better society.

INDEX

Name Index

Subject Index

The letter "f" after a page number indicates material to be found in footnote.

American Society of Planning Officials, 126f

American Stock Exchange, 9, 10

American Telephone and Telegraph Company, 13, 105. See also *Bell Telephone Company.*

American Way of Death, 158f

America's Industrial and Occupational Manpower Requirements, 225f

Amquote System, 9, 10, 11

Analysis, statistical, new types of, due to computers, 306

Anna M. Rosenberg Associates, 208

Annual Survey of Manufacturers, 310

Appalachia, 251
    computer system service for, 109–110
    economic problems of, due to coal industry, 251
        technological changes and, 247
    rehabilitation of, 246
    unemployment in, 211

Appalachian Regional Commission, 109, 251, 379

Appalachian Regional Development Act, 109

Area Redevelopment Act of 1961, 38

Area Redevelopment Administration, 109, 248

Armed Services Board of Contract Appeals, 170

Arms Control and Disarmament Agency, 139, 208

Army Ordnance Department, 87

Atomic Energy Commission, 209, 288f, 291f

A.T.&T., 13, 105. See also *Bell Telephone Company.*

Automatic data processing. See *Computer(s)* and *Computer system(s).*

Automation. See also *Cybernation* and *Technological change.*
    aftereffects of, 71–187
    as slave labor, 44
    as socioeconomic controversy, 35–45
    disrepute of word, 54f
    effects of, expansion of demand versus, 38
        on middle management, 52
    office, 24
    proposals for coping with, 46–70
    views of, 19–34

Automation Commission, 108, 109

Automation: Impact and Implications, Focus on Developments in the Communications Industry, 222f

Automation in the Fabricating Industry, 225f

Automobiles, safety standards in, 289

Background, Guidelines, and Recommendations for Use in Assessing Effective Means of Channeling New Technologies in Promising Directions, 289f

Ballistics, computers in, 88

Bank of New York, 78

Bank of St. Louis, 12

Bankers Data Processing, Inc., 12

Banking
    Federal data available, on punchcards and computer tape, 324
    need for information in, 163–164
    real-time computer systems in, 12–13, 77

Banking computer system, nationwide, 81

Basic Economic Security, 51–53

Basic Systems, Inc., 170, 379, 380

Batch processing, definition of, 8

Baylor University, 268f

Bell Telephone Company, 13, 23
    national computer system compared to, 105

Bell Telephone Research Laboratories, 20, 22

Big Brother computer surveillance, 100

BOASI, 358, 359, 368

BOB. See *Bureau of the Budget.*

"Boundless Age of the Computer," 28, 31

Brandeis University, 206

Brave New World, 153

Brookings Institution, 300, 324

Building codes, modernization of, 276–277

Bunker Ramo Corporation, 31

Bureau of the Budget, 108, 110, 111, 177, 287, 300, 301, 302, 303, 308, 312, 313, 316, 319, 325, 348, 350, 353, 360, 361, 362, 365, 380, 382
    in coordination of intergovernmental relations, 106–107

Bureau of the Census, 23, 88, 111, 112, 177, 303, 304, 310, 315, 318, 319, 320, 321, 322, 323, 325, 326, 350, 353, 359, 360, 366, 381, 382

Bureau of Employment Security, 321

Bureau of Labor Statistics, 23, 49f, 59, 60f, 111, 112, 213f, 220f, 225f, 226, 243, 303, 316, 320, 321, 322, 335, 346, 353, 358, 359

Bureau of Old Age and Survivors Insurance, 112, 359

391

394

395

Employment— (*Continued*)
  prediction of, gaming and, 64
  public service, 230–232
  social barriers to, elimination of, 247
  standardization of requirements for,
    national computer system and,
    123
  technological change and, in next ten
    years, 225–228
Employment Act of 1946, 38, 53, 193,
  203, 230, 232
*Employment, Output, and Policy Re-
  quirements for Full Employment,*
  229f
Employment Service, 38, 243, 244, 245,
  261
Employment system, computerized, 64
Engineering data, scanners for reading,
  25
ENIAC, 87, 88
Environment
  computer system and, 4
  urban. See *Urban environment.*
  work. See *Work environment.*
Export and import, Federal data available, on punchcards and computer tape, 324–325

Factor *c*, 17
Farm management, Federal data available, on punchcards and computer tape, 323
FBI, 120
Federal agency (ies)
  administrative records problems in, 336
  aid programs from, catalogs of, 380
  archival problems of, 334
  coordination of local agencies with,
    106
  disclosure problems in, 336
  file maintenance problems in, 334–335
  generation of data in, procedural
    problems in, 336–338
  overlap of statistics in, 340
  reference problem of, 335–336
  storage and use of statistical informa-
    tion by, 112
Federal Aviation Agency, 83
Federal Bureau of Investigation, 120
Federal Council for Science and Technology, 291f
Federal Data Center. See *National Data
  Service (Center).*
Federal Department of Transportation,
  182f
Federal Deposit Insurance Corporation,
  163, 256, 320

Federal Government
  access of data from, for private re-
    search, 315
  as experimenter in new technological
    adjustment techniques, 263–264
  as model employer, 262–263
  computer system controlled by. See
    National Computer System.
  economic data of, usefulness of, 317
  funds for technological research
    from, 289
  information control by, 144–146
  intervention in economy by, reduc-
    tion of, 53
  intervention in market mechanism
    by, 52
  licensing power of, in regulating
    cybernation, 202
  programs of. See *Federal programs.*
  promotion of research and experi-
    mentation in technology by, 287–
    289
  statistics of. See *Statistics, Federal*
  statistical system of. See also *National
    Data Service (Center).*
    administrative records in, 336
    data generation in, 336–338
    decentralization of, 303
    desired reference capability of, 354–
      355
    file maintainance in, 334–335
    interagency overlap in, 340
    lack of reference function in, 353–
      354
    problem of, 328–329
      current, 307–310
      of disclosure, 336
      reference, 335–336
      solution of, complexity of, 342–
        344
      importance of, 329, 341–342
  underwriting of local computer sys-
    tems by, 116
Federal Home Loan Bank Board, 163,
  320
Federal Housing Administration, 81,
  320
Federal housing policies, economic
  problems from, 248
Federal Inquiry Center, 380
Federal programs, lack of statistics for,
  338–340
  overlapping of, 379
Federal Regional Coordinator, need
  for, 107
Federal Reports Act of 1942, 365
Federal Reserve Bank of New York, 12,
  81

Railroad equipment, technological changes in, economic changes due to, 248
Rand Corporation, 91, 119, 170, 287
Rapid-transit systems, need for, 201
R. & D. See *Research and Development*.
Readers. See *Scanner(s)*.
Real-time, definition of, 8
Real-time computer systems, 88
Recognition Equipment, Inc., 25
Reference index, for research, from National Data Service, 355–356
Reference specialists, need for, 356–357
Regional Industrial Development Corporation of Southwest Pennsylvania, 208
Rehabilitation, economic, of distressed areas, 245–246
Relationship of Increasing Automation to Skill Requirements, The, 222f
Relief payments, to unemployables, 58
Report of the Committee on the Preservation and Use of Economic Data. See *Ruggles Report*.
Report of Condition of Insured Banks, 359
Report of a Survey of the State of the Art: Social, Political, and Economic Models and Simulations, 286f
Report on the Solid Waste Problem, 274f
Research
  economic, use of data in, 313–314
  institutions in, role of, in preservation and use of economic data, 313–319
  specific, computer tapes for, 316–317
  use of national computer system for, 125
Research and development, expenditures in, 289
  Federal support of, 289–290
Research projects, in economics, 314
  need for coordination in, 315–316
Reservation system(s) airline, automated, 10–12, 13
Resources, management of, systems approach to, 287
Resources for the Future, Inc., 325
Retail Clerks International Association, 205
Retirement, flexible, 279
Retraining. See also *Education* and *Training*.
  layoffs used for, 278
  need for, due to computers, 21, 22

Retraining—(*Continued*)
  programs in, 241
Revenue Act of 1964, 229
Revolution
  Agricultural, 194
  Cybernation. See *Cybernation Revolution*.
  Human Rights. See *Human Rights Revolution*.
  Triple. See *Triple Revolution*.
  Weaponry. See *Weaponry Revolution*.
Rockefeller Panel Report, 66
Rockland County, N.Y., computer system for, 91–93
Rockland County Board of Cooperative Educational Services, 90
Role of the Federal Government in Technological Forecasting, The, 225f
Role of Technological Change in Transportation Policy, The, 272f
Rubel Effect, 114, 115, 120
Ruggles Committee (Report), 111, 162, 300–376
  activities of, from 1962 to 1964, 302
  background and history of, 301–302
  summary of, 300–301
Rural Redevelopment, 161

SABRE system, 10, 11, 83
Safety standards, in automobiles, 289
SAGE system, 88, 104–105
Saturday Review, The, 120
Savings and Loan Associations, real-time computer systems in, 12–13
Scanistor, 25, 26
Scanners, for reading typewritten material, 25, 26
  to replace key-punch operators, 25
School(s), technical. See *Technical schools*.
School Construction Systems Development Program, 276
Schooling, applicants for, screened by national computer system, 123
Science. See also *Technology*.
  benefits of computer to, 29
Science Information Exchange, 291f, 354, 358
Scientific American, 205
SDC Magazine, 109
SEC, 9, 112, 135, 145, 303, 324, 359, 361
Secondary Education Act, 62, 238
Second-level capabilities, of computer systems, 83
Securities and Exchange Commission, 9, 112, 135, 145, 303, 324, 359, 361

403

404

ROBERT MACBRIDE

Robert MacBride has worked for ten years as a specialist in corporate communications in the aerospace and weapons system industries. He became interested in the future of computer systems as a result of working for the Auerbach Corporation, one of the foremost "think factories" devoted to the development of information systems for industry and government. MacBride is the author of *Civil War Ironclads*, published by Chilton, a study of the beginnings of weapons system design, procurement, and development. He is presently a free-lance writer and communications consultant.

• • •